Library of Shakespearean Biography and Criticism

𝕷𝖎𝖇𝖗𝖆𝖗𝖞 𝖔𝖋 𝕾𝖍𝖆𝖐𝖊𝖘𝖕𝖊𝖆𝖗𝖊𝖆𝖓 𝕭𝖎𝖔𝖌𝖗𝖆𝖕𝖍𝖞 𝖆𝖓𝖉 𝕮𝖗𝖎𝖙𝖎𝖈𝖎𝖘𝖒

Series III, Part C

THE COMPOSITION OF SHAKESPEARE'S PLAYS

Library of Shakespearean Biography and Criticism

The COMPOSITION of

SHAKESPEARE'S PLAYS

Authorship · Chronology

BY ALBERT FEUILLERAT

BOOKS FOR LIBRARIES PRESS
FREEPORT, NEW YORK

Copyright © 1953 by Yale University Press

Reprinted 1970 by arrangement in an
unaltered and unabridged edition

INTERNATIONAL STANDARD BOOK NUMBER:
0-8369-5505-6

LIBRARY OF CONGRESS CATALOG CARD NUMBER:
76-128885

PRINTED IN THE UNITED STATES OF AMERICA

EDITOR'S NOTE

$\mathcal{A}$ number of friends, colleagues, and students have assisted in the preparation of this book for the press. As M. Feuillerat points out in his preface Mrs. Charles Prouty and Dr. William Woglom worked with great care and devotion in translating the first draft of the English manuscript from the original French before the author made his final revision.

Professor Feuillerat died just after completing the manuscript. It was intended, as will be seen from several allusions in the text, as the first of three volumes on the vexed questions of Shakespeare's authorship, but the succeeding books were not finished although M. Feuillerat was well launched on the second volume at the time of his death. The proofs of the present book have been read by Professor Andrew Morehouse of the French Department and Charles Prouty, Professor of English, at Yale University. Mr. Prouty with the assistance of his wife has read and compared the text with the manuscript, checked references, remedied errors, and done many of the onerous chores of proofreading that ordinarily fall to the author. In addition a group of Professor Prouty's graduate students checked the texts and citations of the plays quoted in these pages. Their names should be recorded: Miss J. R. Buchert, A. B. Kernan, E. A. Langhans, L. J. Lanich, R. P. Patterson, A. D. Richardson.

PREFACE

*T*he reader will not find here any of the brilliant controversies that have recently transformed some provinces of Shakespearean criticism into eloquent debating societies. The present volume is simply an unimaginative, minute analysis, verse by verse, line by line, of the text of Shakespeare's plays, a steadfast search of facts, facts turned into percentages leading to inevitable deductions which are still facts and which I believe have some importance for a true understanding of Shakespeare's genius.

This work has been maturing for more than thirty years. I think that during that time I have read everything of value written on the subject, and many things, alas, upon which I have wasted my time. It would have been convenient to supplement each chapter with a complete bibliography. This has not been possible for lack of space. And there are excellent bibliographies in which books I mention without description will be easily identified. But I can say that I have cited the more recent publications and that I have never borrowed an idea without acknowledging it.

In a study in which I have had to give so many references to Shakespeare's text I cannot hope that I have made no mistake; first, because the reproductions of the old editions I have used do not have the same method of numbering the lines; above all, because I know how treacherous a typewriter can be when one has to deal with numerals. I apologize in advance for such errors.

This book was hard to write. Such as it is, it has given me one of the joys of my life in affording a proof that the words "human kindness" are not an empty phrase. At a moment when my time was doubly precious, Mrs. Charles T. Prouty and Dr. William H. Woglom helped me in the preparation of what has become the final text of this volume. Professor Andrew R. Morehouse and Professor Theodore Andersson read my typescript and suggested valuable corrections. I have also consulted Professor Helge Kökeritz, whose knowledge of Shakespeare's language and pronunciation is unparalleled. Lastly I shall never forget the unfailing sympathy with which, from the first, the Yale University Press followed the progress of my book; in the person of the editor, Eugene Davidson, I found a sure and ever-ready guide. To all of these I address my very grateful thanks.

A. F.

CONTENTS

INTRODUCTION

Modern scholarship has greatly increased our knowledge of the dramatic companies in Shakespeare's time. Diligent research into public records has resulted in the discovery of valuable documents, so that we are now reasonably well informed regarding the organization of such companies, the way in which they functioned, the theaters where they performed, and the audience whose tastes they sought to satisfy. Out of the mass of conclusions reached on the subject and admirably summarized by Sir Edmund Chambers in his four-volume *The Elizabethan Stage* (1923) and his two-volume *William Shakespeare* (1930) I should like to recall and comment upon certain facts concerning the administration of the troupes of players and the way in which they acquired and preserved their repertoire, for a familiarity with those facts is indispensable for the understanding of the present study.

One cannot, indeed, speak of an Elizabethan dramatist without bearing in mind the customs which prevailed in the theatrical world of his day. First of all, the principal troupes of actors were under the patronage of some noble lord by whose name they were known and whose livery they wore. This dependency upon patronage was beneficial in several ways: it protected them from the rigor of the law against vagabonds with whom the strolling players were classed; it gave them certain privileges and provided a support when their effrontery embroiled them with the City authorities. Thus there were companies known as the Queen's men, Leicester's men, Pembroke's men, Strange's men, Derby's men, the Lord Chamberlain's men, the Lord Admiral's men, Sussex' men, and Worcester's men, to mention only the most important.[1]

The actors belonged to the household of their patrons and as

1. There existed also companies of children—Children of the Chapel, Children of Paul's, Children of Blackfriars, Children of the King's Revels, Children of the Queen's Revels—which had their own special administration, different from that of the adult troupes with which they often competed.

1

such were expected to render service whenever called upon—on the occasion of a marriage within the noble lord's family or to help in entertaining a distinguished visitor by giving a performance after dinner. But here their obligations stopped. For their livelihood they could count only on cash receipts when they performed in town or on royal rewards when they played at Court. In this sense the dramatic companies were actual corporations, drawing their strength from the solid union of their members. They were established in much the manner of what we call today "cooperative societies." Their labor or production consisted in giving performances for the recreation of their fellow citizens; their capital consisted of costumes, properties, and, last but not least, manuscripts of plays. Once their expenses—the furnishing of the wardrobe and properties, the wages of the minor personnel, etc.—were paid, the balance of the sums that had been collected at the entrance of the theater was divided between the principal actors, or sharers, according to previously agreed terms, for there were whole shares and half shares (cf. *Hamlet* III.ii.286).

The actor-sharers were bound by a contract, or "composition," according to which they consented not to leave the company for a number of years, and when the association was dissolved they received their share of the capital. This arrangement afforded the company a certain stability, which was strengthened by the way they were bound to the owner of the theater where they performed. Instead of paying rent the company in general gave over a part of the takings. For example, the elder Burbage, builder of the first theater, received the money collected at the entrance to the galleries. His sons Cuthbert and Richard, proprietors of the Globe, reserved for themselves half of the gallery takings and half of the receipts at the entrance of the tiring house through which the noblemen passed on their way to the seats on the stage. Henslowe, proprietor of the Rose, had complicated arrangements with the Lord Admiral's men, but he too seems to have collected part of the gallery receipts in lieu of rent. After building the Globe theater the Burbage brothers inaugurated a system which linked them even more closely with the principal actors. Their scheme was to divide in half a sum representing the rent for the building. One half they kept for themselves as owners, the other half was given to five actors who thereafter became known as "house-keepers" and who thus received a premium in addition to their income as sharers. This plan proved so successful that it was later adopted by the Queen's men and the Prince's men, two other companies of the time of James I.

The actor-sharers designated one of their number to represent their financial interests. It was the duty of this treasurer to collect the receipts, to accept the rewards or gratuities for Court performances, to settle the accounts, to keep the contracts, and in general to watch over the interests of the organization. But in all matters relating to the actual management the actors remained the absolute masters, sharing with each other the responsibility of the enterprise just as they divided the profits. They did not know that autocrat of the modern theater, the producer; the decisions were the expression of the collective voice of this small but all-powerful partnership.

One of the advantages (possibly some may think of the inconveniences) of such an organization was that the actors themselves chose the plays for their repertoire, and this fact had an enormous influence over the dramatic conceptions of the time. Today the fate of the dramatic development lies largely in the hands of the authors and of the producers. Aloof from the players, often ignorant of the exigencies of the stage, modern authors are above all animated by the desire to achieve a notable literary work, for the theater has definitely become a province of literature, which it was not originally. Certainly no author is so high minded that he can overlook entirely the possibility of a public or box-office success, but I do not think it an exaggeration to say that an author (and it is to his credit) is guided in his choice of a subject, and in his treatment of it, by the sort of literary standard which can apply as well to a novel or to a poem. Of like mind is the producer who, when he comes to choose a new play he feels sure will attract large audiences, is apt to be impressed by the originality of the formula or by the brilliant manner in which the subject is handled. In the face of such an accord between author and producer the actors have no recourse but to hope that at least the parts will be distributed to their satisfaction.

In Shakespeare's time the situation was exactly the reverse. It

was the actors who made up their repertoire, and as their livelihood depended on success they had a candid respect for the public taste which alone was responsible for lucrative returns. They
did not endeavor to influence those tastes but merely to satisfy
them. They knew well enough that people do not go to the theater
in order to exercise their critical sense, but to be moved or amused.
They were not hypnotized by the literary excellence of the parts
which they had to play; new formulas with their attendant uncertainties held no attraction for them; they preferred to rely on
the lessons of the past. Not that they were incapable of adapting
themselves to the fluctuations and changes going on around them,
for never were people more prompt to follow the fashion of the
moment when assured that it pleased the public taste. What they
insisted upon above all was that their plays be adapted to the
special atmosphere of the stage, which they knew well because
they themselves lived in it. They were aware that in such an
atmosphere the most common experience of real life may appear
unreal, while the most unlikely situations can assume the look
of truth itself. And they saw to it that the laws of the theater were
observed in every case.

Nor did the authors think differently. First of all, many among
them—Anthony Munday, Thomas Heywood, Nathan Field, William Birde, Samuel Rowley, Ben Jonson, and, one forgets but too
often, Shakespeare—were themselves actors and they shared that
same conception of the theater. As for those who made it a profession to write plays (with a few exceptions, Chapman, perhaps,
and Ben Jonson, certainly, who was sure he wrote for posterity)
they were needy fellows who considered their dramatic productions as a means to supplement the slender resources which they
drew from the sale of a manuscript to a publisher or such gratuities
as they received from the noblemen to whom they addressed their
dedications. Playwriting was a profession, as was that of the actors,
subject to the same commercial fluctuations, and they offered
without shame whatever the actors demanded. Furthermore they
considered that their work was so ephemeral it would lose its
vitality as soon as it had attained the dozen performances which
marked a reasonable success. It certainly never occurred to them

that they might achieve any lasting reputation as writers of the spoken word.

This was so true that several authors often joined together to write one play. Dramatic collaboration dates from the very beginnings of the Renaissance. *Gorboduc* (1562) and *Jocasta* (1566) were each written by two authors, while *Tancred and Gismund* was the work of four. The University Wits, who were as pretentious as any, were not above calling in the aid of other dramatists: Greene and Lodge wrote together *The Looking Glass for London and England* (1590), and Marlowe had Nash as co-author in *Dido, Queen of Carthage*. By the end of the sixteenth century the custom was so widespread that one might say it had become the rule. Henslowe's *Diary* [2] offers us proofs of this on almost every page. Of all the writers who were regular contributors to the Lord Admiral's company and that of the earl of Worcester, Chapman alone assumed complete responsibility for his plays; all the rest —Chettle, Dekker, Hathway, Haughton, Heywood, Middleton, Munday, Porter, Rankins, Robinson, Rowley, Smith, Webster, Wilson—operated in combinations comparable to those of the actors. The leaders of these groups, whose composition apparently varied according to the nature of the plays, were Chettle and Dekker, the most frequent associations being Chettle-Dekker-Drayton-Wilson, Dekker-Hathway, Drayton-Munday, and Chettle-Dekker-Heywood-Smith-Webster. Ben Jonson succumbed to the practice and allied himself with Chettle and Porter in writing *Hot Anger Soon Cold* (1598), with Dekker in his *Page of Plymouth* (1599), and with Chettle, Dekker, and an unknown author in *Robert the Second, King of Scots* (1599). In the "Epistle to Readers" of his *Sejanus* Ben Jonson acknowledged replacing the text of a collabo-

2. Henslowe's *Diary* is the most important document we possess for the history of the English stage at the end of the sixteenth century and the beginning of the seventeenth. It is the account book of Philip Henslowe, the owner of the Rose and Fortune theaters, in which he recorded not only his personal affairs but all sorts of data relating to theatrical business—receipts at the entrance of the theater, advances made to the companies for the purchase or the revision of plays, itemized accounts for costuming and properties, payments to the Master of the Revels, loans to actors, etc.—and for the period of 1592–97 there is a list of performances given by the companies playing at his theaters. This precious document has been scrupulously and admirably edited by Walter W. Greg (2 vols., London, 1904–08).

rator by passages written by himself, not wishing to pass off as his own what was another's.[3]

This honest act, tinged with a touch of indubitable pride, marks the beginning of a change in the social position of dramatic authors by making the theater, up to then commercial, an admittedly literary genre. But during Queen Elizabeth's reign most dramatists were uninterested in their works in the sense of writing for future literary fame rather than present monetary reward, and the majority of plays, including the first ones of Shakespeare, appeared without an author's name on the title page.[4]

As for the actors, when they had bought a play they considered it their exclusive property. The price of a manuscript, if one takes into account the value of money at that time, was relatively high. In the sixteenth century it varied from £4–10 and it continued to increase afterward. In the seventeenth century an author like Robert Daborne, practically unknown today, boasted that he received as much as £25 from the King's men. Thus the repertoire formed the most precious capital of the company, which had the right to dispose of it as it thought fit. The actors could lend the manuscript to another company, they could sell it to a printer in time of stress, and so long as it was in their library they could alter it to suit their needs.[5]

The possession by a dramatist of his own productions, today

3. "I would informe you that this Booke, in all numbers, is not the same with that which was acted on the public Stage, wherein a second pen had a good share; in place of which I have rather chosen, to put weaker (and no doubt less pleasing) of mine own, then to defraud so happy a genius of his right by my lothed usurpation." *Sejanus* was played by the Lord Chamberlain's company in 1603, and Jonson's use of the phrase "so happy a genius" suggests that this mysterious collaborator was no other than Shakespeare.

4. The only authors who cared to put their names on title pages were writers in Latin, translators of Greek, Latin, Italian, or French, and some later practitioners of interludes and moralities, probably because those books were of an educational nature and for that reason could be regarded as recognized literature. It should be added, however, that Greene, Lodge, Peele, Wilson, and Porter published some plays under their names.

5. An actor who had received some manuscript as his share when the company was dissolved considered the play his own property and could transfer it as his portion to any other company he might join. We know, for example, that in 1589 Edward Alleyn acquired from the Lord Admiral's first company a certain number of manuscripts which he subsequently sold to the new Admiral's company when it was formed.

well established and protected by law, was another idea which never entered the mind of an Elizabethan. Plays were in a continual state of transformation. A certain amount of reworking came naturally enough during the rehearsals, but far more important revisions of an author's text were frequent and often went so far as to change the very nature of the play. This sort of thing inevitably happened in refurbishing an old play the success of which had begun to lag. Today in the case of a revival it is possible to omit out-of-date passages or add contemporary allusions, but on the whole the play is presented almost exactly as it was first conceived. In Shakespeare's day, and even for a long time afterward, the revival of a play was often an attempt to pass it off as a new play. When William Cartwright, the actor, brought before the Master of the Revels an old play which was to be produced at the Fortune, he asked for authorization to add scenes for the express purpose, as Sir Henry Herbert noted in his account book, "to give it out for a new one," a reason which seemed natural to the Master of the Revels for he gave the permission (*The Dramatic Records of Sir Henry Herbert*, ed. Joseph Quincy Adams, 1917, p. 37). And it was natural at that time. With a public eager for change the theater developed with prodigious rapidity. To realize this growth one has only to remember that it began about 1585 with crude historical dramas which were simple dramatizations of the chroniclers' texts, or psychologically primitive melodramas such as *The Spanish Tragedy*, and that by the end of the century the drama could boast tragedies like *Hamlet*. To have bought new manuscripts for each change in the repertoire would have been too costly; it was more economical to disguise an old play in a new garb. And that was what the stationer William Aspley thought when on February 20, 1600, he registered a manuscript with the Stationers' Company under the title of A *comedy called old Fortunatus in his newe lyuerie.*

$$\int \quad \int \quad \int$$

HENSLOWE's *Diary* is filled with illuminating information on the art of making old plays look like new ones. The owner of the Rose and of the Fortune minutely recorded all the sums he advanced to the companies performing in his theaters for the renovation of their repertoire, and to follow with the help of his notes the metamorphoses of certain plays is to gain an extraordinary insight into the theatrical practices of the time.

To distinguish the different types of revision Henslowe makes use of three terms with a remarkable regularity: "mending," "additions," "altering."

Mending, to judge by the modest sums granted—10s. as a rule— had to do with unimportant changes, simple alterations of detail no doubt, deletion of dated passages, adaptations necessary to meet particular occasions such as a performance at Court. In this category may be classed the two parts of *Robin Hood* known to us under the titles of *The Downfall of Robert Earle of Huntington, afterward called Robin Hood of merrie Sherwood* (1590) and *The Death of Robert Earle of Huntington, otherwise called Robin Hood of merrie Sherwood* (1601). The first part was bought from Munday on February 15, 1597/8, for the sum of £5 (Henslowe, fol. 44); an order for the second part was placed with Munday and Chettle on February 25 for the same sum (fol. 44v). The two parts were licensed by the Master of the Revels on March 28 (fol. 45) and probably were played soon after. In the month of November the play was accepted for performance at Court and this was no doubt what made some changes necessary, for there were things which could be said on the public stage but which the queen should not hear. Some compliment was also indispensable. Chettle was entrusted with the modifications and on November 18 he received 10s. "for the mendynge of the first part of Robart hoode" (fol. 52), and 10s. more on the 25th of the same month, probably for the second part. Since two weeks had been sufficient to finish the work, it must not have been very considerable.

Friar Rush and the Proud Woman of Antwerp is another of the plays having received modifications of the same kind. The commission to write it was given to John Day and to William Haughton on July 4, 1601, and the two collaborators worked on the subject for more than five months, until November 29, when Haughton received 20s. in full payment of a total sum of £5 (foll. 91, 91v, 94, 94v, 95). *Friar Rush* must have been one of the new plays for the winter season and had had only a few performances when

Chettle was asked to modify it. On January 21, 1601/2, he received the usual sum of 10s. (fol. 104). The reason for that revision may have been the hope entertained by the Lord Admiral's men to play at Court. If so they were disappointed, for that year the Lord Chamberlain's company was the only one that performed before the queen. The fact that Day and Haughton were not requested to make the changes is a good example of the off-hand manner in which the actors often treated the authors.

The modifications made on a play called *Vayvode* may be said to fall in the category of simple improvements. This play was one of those belonging to the actor Edward Alleyn, as is shown by the fact that on January 21, 1598/9, the Lord Admiral's company bought it from him for £2 (fol. 53). In August 1598 preparations were made to present it, and from the 21st to the 25th £17 5s. were paid out for costumes and accessories (fol. 49v). Since Alleyn, as we have seen, had sold it, and since Chettle received only 5s. on August 29 "ffor his playe of vayvode" (fol. 49v) the supposition is that Chettle was not really the author but was merely responsible for a reworking. Nothing is known of this play with its mysterious title, and further conjecture would be futile.[6]

Additions were an easy way to modify a play without upsetting its subject matter. As already said, the actor William Cartwright considered this kind of revision perfectly acceptable to mask the age of a play. And as greater demands were laid upon the reviser's powers of invention there was a higher monetary reward than for simple emendations.

Concerning three of the plays which Henslowe mentioned as having received additions we have little information and we can dismiss them briefly. Together they formed a unit in the sense that all three belonged to the period when the Earl of Worcester's men, who had first played in the provinces during the last decade of the sixteenth century, associated themselves with the Earl of Oxford's men and occupied the Rose theater, which had been vacant since the Lord Admiral's company left it for the Fortune.

6. Hazlitt believed that the play was based on incidents in the war between Transylvania and Austria, since the word "vaivode" was a title used in the Balkans to denote the chiefs of the army or the state. This is indeed an ingenious proof of an equally ingenious hypothesis.

One of these plays, *Sir John Oldcastle*, appeared originally in two parts in the repertoire of the Lord Admiral's men. On October 16, 1599, it had been bought (foll. 65, 66v) from Munday, Drayton, Wilson, and Hathway in order (rather maliciously) to compete with the Lord Chamberlain's production of *Henry IV*. Apparently the two parts had exhausted their success by August 1600, for on the 11th of that month the manuscript was registered with the Stationers' Company and was published that same year. But on the very day, August 17, 1602, when it was decided that the Earl of Worcester's men would take over the Rose, Henslowe advanced 40s. to Thomas Dekker "for new adysions in owldcastelle" (fol. 115), and on September 7, 10s. more (fol. 116). If this means that the Lord Admiral's men ceded their rights in the play to the new company, it was a cheap enough gift as the play had already been printed. Since the only extant edition is that of the first part, dated 1600 (prior to the transfer), it is impossible to say what modifications the play received; what is certain, however, is that judged by the fee paid the revision must have been reasonably extensive.

The second play, *Cutting Dick* (the name of a bandit who had acquired considerable notoriety in robbing travelers),[7] belonged to the old repertoire of the Earl of Worcester's company. Although the play delighted its provincial audiences it must have been in need of some refurbishing, for on September 20, 1602, Henslowe paid to Thomas Heywood 20s. "for the new adycions of cutting dicke" (fol. 116). Neither the old play nor the revision are extant: we shall never know just how Heywood succeeded in embellishing the terrible career of that famous highwayman.

The third play, *The Black Dog of Newgate*, was one of the new acquisitions made when the company reorganized. The first part had been commissioned November 24 from Hathway, Day, Smith, and another dramatist who has remained anonymous; that was completed December 20 (fol. 118, 118v). A second part was required from the same authors on January 29, 1602/3, and was delivered February 3 (fol. 119v). The source of this play was a

7. Some idea of the effect which the robber's exploits produced on the popular imagination may be gleaned from William Kemp's *Nine Days Wonder*, 1600, and George Wither's *Stript and Whipt*, 1613, Bk. II, satire ii.

chapbook entitled *The Black Dog of Newgate, both pithye and profitable for all readers,* dedicated to Lord Justice Popham. The author is believed to have been Luke Hutton, a young man of good family who had gone to the dogs and become noted for his audacious robberies; in 1598 he was arrested and executed. Thus like *Cutting Dick* the play was one of the melodramas depicting the contemporary underworld. Hutton seems to have repented and his last moments must have constituted an edifying denouement.[8] Material for the costumes in the play was purchased on January 10, 16, and February 16, 1602/3 (foll. 119, 120), and it was ready for performance when the actors evidently noticed that the second part was too short; on February 21 they asked the authors to furnish additions. The additions completed on February 26 (fol. 120) must have been considerable, for the company was obliged to add £2 to the 13 which the manuscript had cost.

With *The Spanish Tragedy* we are on firmer ground. Kyd's play which about 1585 gave the formula for revenge tragedies was extraordinarily successful during the last years of the sixteenth century; under the title of *Hieronimo* it still held the stage in 1592/3. Played by Strange's men, it was performed sixteen times between March 14, 1591/2, and January 22, 1592/3 (foll. 7–8). It was revived again by the Lord Admiral's men in January 1596/7, and since on that occasion Henslowe marked it "ne"[9] it is reasonable to suppose that it had been revised. After a single performance by the Lord Admiral's men and Pembroke's men, which brought the number of performances in 1597 to thirteen, it must have been laid aside and was not heard of again until 1601. That year Henslowe noted in his *Diary:* "Lent vnto m^r alleyn the 25 of september 1601 to lend vnto Bengemen Johnson vpon his writting of his adicions in geronymo of xxxx^s" (fol. 94), and again in 1602 he noted: "Lent vnto bengemy Johnsone at the apoyntment of E. Alleyn & wm birde the 22 of June 1602 in earneste of a Boocke called Richard crockbacke & for new adycions for Jeronimo the some of x^{ll}" (fol. 106v).

Two different texts of the play exist and these enable us to see

8. A ballad entitled *Luke Hutton's Lamentation,* which he wrote the day before his death, appeared in 1598.

9. Cf. Greg's note in Henslowe's *Diary,* 1, 25v, 31, 223.

how the play was transformed. The earlier version consists of three quartos, one undated, the other two dated 1594 and 1599. A quarto, reprinted many times up until 1633, gives a text which according to the title contains additions, one of which is specified: *The Spanish tragedie: Containing the lamentable end of Don Horatio, and Bel-imperia: with the pittifull death of olde Hieronimo. Newly corrected, amended, and enlarged with new additions of the Painters part, and others, as it hath of late been diuers times acted.*[1]

A comparison of the two texts shows that certain passages totaling some 350 lines were not in the first version and thus constitute the important additions announced in the title. The pertinent passages are: II.v.977–1068, Hieronimo discovers the body of his son; III.ii.1272–81, Hieronimo ironically refuses to divulge why he wishes to see Bel-imperia; III.xi.1866–910, Hieronimo, meeting with two Portuguese who think he is mad, dilates on the virtues of his lost son; III.xii.2063–247, the painter Bazardo, whose son also has been assassinated, comes to sue for justice, and Hieronimo in another fit of madness gives the painter instructions for a portrait which he orders of his son's assassination; IV.iv.3126–71, Hieronimo, at the denouement, triumphs in his revenge.[2]

It is reasonable to suppose that these additions are those that the Lord Admiral's company ordered from Ben Jonson. Certain critics, however, have claimed not to find Jonson's "style" in the new passages and have argued that these additions belong to the revival of 1597 when Henslowe marked *Hieronimo* as new. This opinion has prevailed to the present day, but I am not sure that such doubts are well founded. Was Ben Jonson incapable of adapting his style to the general tone of the play which he undertook to enlarge? In fact certain speeches of Hieronimo's—for example, III.ii.1272–81—have something of that caustic irony characteristic of *Volpone*'s author. And these additions are certainly those of a great dramatist, so much so that some have even wished to attribute them to Shakespeare.

1. For the history and description of these different quartos see the edition of 1602 in the Malone Society Reprints, 1925, introduction by W. W. Greg. See also Greg's *A Bibliography of the English Printed Drama*, 1939, Vol. 1, No. 10.

2. This passage is rewritten from one in the first form, a few lines of which have been preserved.

However that may be, the reason for this reworking is clear enough. At a time when Shakespeare, by his own example, had shown that the portrayal of character was of prime importance, *The Spanish Tragedy* in its original form must have appeared particularly deficient in this respect. It was what one might call a tragedy of intrigue, its interest lying more in the complications of the plot than in the moral sufferings of the protagonists. There were dramatic possibilities in Hieronimo which Kyd had not exploited. The purpose of the additional material was manifestly to increase the pathos of this role by developing Hieronimo's eccentricities to the point where it became credible that overwhelming sorrow had caused him to go mad. The scene with the painter, especially, offered a great actor many opportunities for touching effects. And it is not difficult to guess who was the instigator of the additions. That Edward Alleyn, the chief actor of the Lord Admiral's company, twice took part in the negotiations with Ben Jonson is tantamount to saying that he was thinking of himself when he sought, and perhaps inspired, those changes which were to make the part of Hieronimo equal to some of the celebrated roles of Burbage.

The Tragicall History of Doctor Faustus offers a more complicated example of revision by means of additions. Written by Marlowe about 1590, this play was still successful in 1594. On October 2 of that year it was revived at the Rose theater by the Lord Admiral's company and held the boards until January 5, 1596/7, having been performed twenty-four times during that period (foll. 10–25v). A twenty-fifth performance was given in October 1597 by the combined companies of the Lord Admiral and Lord Pembroke (fol. 27v). In November 1602 the company of the Lord Admiral—or rather that of the Earl of Nottingham, the name borne by the company after October 22, 1597, when its patron Lord Howard was made an earl—decided to give the play again, but this time in a revised version, and on the 22d of that month paid to William Birde and Samuel Rowley, two of its actors, the significant sum of £4 "for the adycions in Doctor fostes" (fol. 108v).

The first extant quarto of *Doctor Faustus* was printed by V[alentine] S[immes] for Thomas Bushell in 1604. Though this edition

bears a date later than that of the commissioned revision as noted
by Henslowe, it does not contain the additions of Birde and
Rowley. Probably the text came from the "Book called the play
of Doctor Faustus" which the bookseller Bushell had registered
with the Stationers' Company on January 7, 1600/1, and which
for some unknown reason had not been printed immediately after
its registration. It is only in the edition published in 1616 by John
Wright (to whom Bushell sold his rights in 1610) that we find
these additions.

The text of the 1604 quarto, however, already contained modifications. In an article entitled "The 1604 Text of Marlowe's *Doctor Faustus*" (*Essays and Studies by Members of the English Association*, 1921, Vol. 7) Percy Simpson has shown that Marlowe's
play had been tampered with, and he pointed out as proofs several
passages that make no sense and some evidence of cutting. Furthermore, two allusions which could not have been written until
after Marlowe's death (May 30, 1593) confirm the fact of revision.
In sc.ix a reference is made to Dr. Lopez, the Jewish physician who
was executed in June 1594, and there is a joke about the depreciation of French money in England which is certainly later than
1595.

Marlowe's style is so personal that it is not very difficult to dis-
engage it from parasitical excrescences. Scenes i, iii, v, and the
beginning of sc.vi [3] show Faustus deciding to devote himself to
magic (sc.i), turning a deaf ear to his Good Angel and succumb-
ing to his Bad Angel's inducement (sc.i), making his first attempt
to invoke spirits when Mephostophilis appears (sc.iii), signing
the pact by which he abandons his soul to Lucifer (sc.v), for a
moment having misgivings, but being reassured through conversations with Mephostophilis, who reveals to him the existence
and motion of the different spheres, and finally submitting completely after a personal intervention by Lucifer and Belzebub

3. I have adopted the division into scenes and the numbering of the lines of
Hermann Breymann's edition (Marlowe's *Werke*, Heilbronn, 1889, Vol. 2), which
has the advantage of reproducing the two texts on opposite pages.

This note was written after the appearance of a new edition of the two texts by
W. W. Greg, who with his usual admirable minuteness and also by ingenious typographical devices in the text and signs and references in the margins has greatly
facilitated the comparison of the two quartos.

(sc.vi). A (shortened) prologue to sc.vii, tells us that Faustus went to Rome in a chariot "burning bright," drawn by "yoky dragons neckes." The scene then begins with Faustus enumerating the countries over which he flew, and after a description by Mephostophilis of the beauties of Rome the two travelers decide to attend, unseen, the feast of St. Peter and particularly the banquet which the pope is going to give for the cardinal of Lorraine. Here Marlowe's style suddenly disappears and reappears only toward the end of sc.x, where there is a fragment in which Charles V asks Faustus to evoke Alexander and his mistress (ll. 1050–73). After two other fragments of six verses each in which Faustus dreams of returning to Wittenberg (ll. 1134–9), he is driven to despair at the approach of death (ll. 1176–81). It is only in sc.xiii that one picks up again portions of the play as written by Marlowe: at the request of several disciples Faustus evokes the immortal Helen, seems to give way momentarily to the remonstrance of an old man who urges him to renounce his sins, but finally obeys Mephostophilis who gives him Helen for his mistress (ll. 1273–80, 1290–391). This is his last earthly pleasure, and at the end of sc.xiv (ll. 1460–518) we witness his anguish as he sees the minutes slip away at the inexorable approach of eternal damnation.

In the gaps left by the incisions made into Marlowe's text several scenes in prose have been interpolated, mostly comic in tone. Two scenes (ii and iv) have been introduced, no doubt to fatten the part of Wagner, Faustus' servant.[4] At the end of sc.vi there has been added a show of the seven deadly sins, a pastime offered to Faustus by Lucifer. Three scenes which must have existed in verse in the original play have been rewritten in prose and probably enlarged: the seventh, showing Faustus playing sleight-of-hand tricks at the banquet given for the cardinal of Lorraine, snatching away the dishes, and slapping the pope; the tenth, in which Faustus evokes Alexander and his mistress before the emperor and takes revenge on the knight, who had offended him, by planting horns on his forehead; and the beginning of the fourteenth, where Faustus admits to his disciples that he has sold his

4. In these scenes Wagner is Faustus' page and is, in fact, presented as one of those saucy and disputatious pages whom John Lyly had made fashionable. In the rest of the play the character is different and has a minor role.

soul to the devil. These incidents are drawn from the German Faust-Buch,[5] and the same source is the basis for the scenes in which Faustus mystifies the horse-courser (sc.xi) and produces grapes in midwinter for the pregnant duchess of Vanholt who has expressed a desire for some (sc.xii). Finally, two other scenes (viii and ix) are devoted to the antics of two clowns and are entirely irrelevant. All this is written in a flat prose which lapses at times into coarse indecency and which was meant to appeal to the most crude among the spectators.

These undesirable additions to Marlowe's text must have been successful, for Birde and Rowley, in their turn, in 1602 supplied material of a similar nature. They provided the principle character with further proofs of his magical powers: Faustus, disguised as a cardinal, releases from prison Bruno,[6] a candidate for the papacy with the German emperor's support (III.i); he thwarts the attempted revenge of the knight on whose forehead he had caused horns to grow, inflicts severe and humiliating punishment on him, transforms a forest into soldiers, and puts to flight the mercenaries posted to bar his way (IV.iii.1361–496); he diverts himself by eating a cartload of hay for the sum of three farthings which the carter has imprudently fixed, and as the horse-courser and carter, somewhat the worse for drink, pursue him to the duke of Vanholt's, he orders that they be served the beer they ask for but strikes them dumb when they attempt to upbraid him for the tricks he has played on them.

Birde and Rowley also added several scenes, these in verse: Lucifer and Belzebub appear to see how Faustus demeans himself during his last moments (sc.xiii.1861–80); Mephostophilis, triumphing, comes to urge him to give up hope and think only of hell (sc.xiv.1955–66); finally the Good and the Bad Angels contribute to make his torments more poignant, the former by recalling the celestial happiness which he has sacrificed, the latter by describing the tortures of hell (sc.xiv). A last scene shows two of Faustus' disciples, terrified by the cries which they have heard

5. *Historia von D. Johann Fausten, dem weit-beschreyten Zauberer und Schwartz-künstler*, Frankfort, 1587. An English translation appeared in 1592; a modern reprint was issued in 1925.

6. This episode is pure invention, Bruno having no historical existence.

during the night, setting out to search for their master and finding his limbs "all torn asunder" by devils.

Birde and Rowley were not content merely to furnish the additions asked of them; they also modified several passages introduced by the first revision.[7] They shortened the end of sc.xi; they deleted the references to the depreciation of French money (sc.iv.393–6) and to Dr. Lopez (sc.xi.1183), two allusions which would not have been understood in 1602; they suppressed some indecent jokes (sc.v.427–31 and sc.viii.941–4, 968–74); they rewrote sc.ix in a prose not much better than the original, and part of sc.x they put into verse which has nothing of Marlowe's touch.

To judge by quantity alone, Birde and Rowley really earned the £4 they were paid for their work. But after all these revisions the original play had lost its significance. The pathetic adventure of a man who sold his soul for a few transitory pleasures had been submerged under an afflux of a comic, even farcical element, and Marlowe's colossal tragedy now appeared more like a torso by Michelangelo covered with the scurrilous scribblings of irreverent passers-by.[8] The play had been in fact completely transformed and I might just as well have listed it under the third category of revision which Henslowe designated by the word "altering." The sums paid out in such cases—sometimes equaling the cost of a whole new play—prove that the term applied to a profound and meticulous revision.

The Pleasant Comedie of Old Fortunatus is an example of this type of alteration. According to Henslowe's *Diary* it was played by the Lord Admiral's men from February 3, 1595/6, until May 26, 1596 (foll. 14v–15v). It was already an old play and the fact that it was described as "the first parte of fortunatus" implies that there must have been a second part. But the *Diary* does not men-

7. Even Marlovian passages contain interpolations (some in prose) and modifications; some have been expanded or rewritten. It has not been possible to enter into all those details for lack of space, and it would be irrelevant. But I may perhaps say that my interpretation of the facts, in spite of its brevity, is the result of a long, minute, independent comparison of the two texts and a careful scrutiny of all that has been written on this question.

8. For Birde's and Rowley's respective contributions, see H. D. Sykes, *The Authorship of "The Taming of the Shrew," "The Famous Victories of Henry V" and the additions to Marlowe's "Faustus,"* Shakespeare Association, 1920; and Boas' edition of the play.

tion any performance of a second part, and one is led to suppose
that this was a project that was never carried out for the simple
reason, probably, that the play had not had a great success: in
fact after a good start the receipts fell off rapidly.

In November 1599 the company decided to revive the play
but in a new form, and the renovation was entrusted to Dekker.
On November 9 the sum of 40*s*. (fol. 65v) was paid to him in earnest of a "booke cald the hole history of fortunatus," and £3 more
on the 24th of the same month (fol. 65v). Dekker must have turned
in his manuscript on November 30 for he was then given 20*s*.
(fol. 66) "in full payment of his booke of fortunatus," which
raised the total to £6, nearly the usual price for a new play.

And it was, in large measure, a new play. There was no question of uniting two plays into one since, as we have seen, in all
likelihood the second part had never been written. By the words
"the hole history" Henslowe meant that Dekker would dramatize
Fortunatus' life in its entirety, just as it was related in the German
Volksbuch,⁹ the source of the legend.

This Volksbuch falls naturally into two parts. The first part
treats of Fortunatus' life: his youth, his travels after Fortune presented him with an inexhaustible purse which assured him of sensational success wherever he went, his return to his native Cyprus,
his marriage, his departure in search of new adventures, his stay
with the sultan of Turkey from whom he stole the magic cap which
enabled its possessor to obtain all he wished, his final return to
Cyprus, and his death. The second part was devoted to the adventures of Andolosia, one of Fortunatus' sons: his intrigue with
an English princess, the loss of the purse and of the magic cap, his
stratagem to recover them, and finally the assassination of Andolosia and of his brother Ampedo. The 1596 play must have contained only the life of Fortunatus; thus Dekker's task was to abbre-
viate this subject and in the space thus gained to introduce the
lives of Andolosia and of his brother Ampedo. This is no doubt
what Dekker had done when he submitted his manuscript to the
company on November 30.

9. The history of Fortunatus was published for the first time in Augsburg in 1509
and was reprinted in *Neudrucke deutscher Litteraturwerke der XVI und XVII Jahr-
hunderts*, ed. W. Braune, Halle, 1914, Vols. 240–1.

On perusal the manuscript must not have satisfied the actors, for the very next day, December 1, they paid Dekker 20s. "for the altrenge of the boocke of the wholl history of fortewnatus" (fol. 66), and on December 12, 40s. "for the eande of fortewnatus for the corte" (fol. 66v)—a total of £3, half of what the first revision had cost; the second alteration called for must have been extensive.

What had happened? The terms of the last payment furnish us with the explanation. The company had been ordered to be in readiness to take part in the Christmas and New Year's revels [1] and expected to offer a recently remodeled play which they evidently hoped would be a great success, for they spent £10 for the costumes and properties (fol. 66). But if Dekker had followed the Volksbuch closely the play could not be presented at Court: in that version one saw an English princess behave more like a courtesan than a king's daughter. Exploiting Andolosia's passion, she feigned to respond to his ardent love-making by giving him a love potion, and then during his sleep stole his magic purse. And the king of England not only encouraged his daughter to trade on her beauty but rejoiced when she compassed her ends. Such a situation might pass before the general public but at Court it would have been scandalous. It certainly was going too far to present such characters, even fictitiously, as predecessors of the All-High Spectatrix Queen Elizabeth, who was to be present at the performance. Of this the actors must have been conscious; they knew besides that the Master of the Revels, always uneasy when royal personages were to be presented on the stage, would scarcely allow such an act of lese majesty. Furthermore, the total effect of the "pleasant" comedy, like the German legend from which it was taken, was completely amoral: most of the characters thought only of the pursuit of happiness, and the ways in which they achieved their pleasures were unscrupulous, robbery being common and even admirable. It was by all means necessary to eliminate the crudity of such situations.

This was not easy: to omit them was equivalent to doing away

1. According to the accounts of the treasurer of the Chamber, the Earl of Nottingham's men played at Court on December 27, 1599, and on January 1, 1599/1600. On January 1 they gave *The Shoemaker's Holiday;* December 27 must have been the day on which *Fortunatus* was performed. The title page of the 1600 edition says "as it was plaied before the Queen's Majestie this Christmas."

with the play. And time pressed. Dekker, however, was a resource-
ful man. He knew that on the stage the effect produced by dramatic action often depends on the general atmosphere. Some
incidents, shown, as in the Volksbuch, in the unconventional
simplicity of their realism, would be impossible; placed against
another background they would lose their unsavory character. So,
disregarding the incidents, he simply changed the tone and meaning of the play.

Charles H. Hertford in his study of *Fortunatus* (*Studies in the
Literary Relations of England and Germany in the XVIth Century*,
pp. 211–16) has convincingly shown the changes which Dekker
made on the first version. He points out that the end of the play,
where Virtue triumphs over Vice and Fortune, has no analogue
in the Volksbuch, and that in the play the final unraveling of the
plot is brought about by two additional scenes which have no
precedent in the German legend: that in which Virtue and Vice
plant the trees of Good and Evil and that in which Vice and Virtue try to win Andolosia (I.147–51).[2] These three scenes form a
secondary, independent plot, and it is not difficult to see that
their addition was the means by which Dekker solved his problem.
The fact that they are an interpolation is shown by the inconsistencies which their introduction brought in its wake. One of
these is particularly striking. In an old passage (p. 170) Fortune
believes that one cannot make use of her gifts without following
the precepts of old-fashioned Virtue, which she considered an
indispensable adjunct. She affirms to King Athelstane, whom she
has just reproached for his avarice, that

> England shall ne'er be poore, if England striue
> Rather by virtue than by wealth to thrive.

Immediately following (p. 171), Dekker added the final scene
showing Virtue's triumph, and to make the triumph more impressive he thought it a good idea to precede it with a scene showing
Fortune furious at discovering a rival in the person of Virtue, who
appears crowned with olive and laurel branches and escorted by
a respectful train of kings. Fortune spitefully greets this intrusion:

2. References are to Pearson's edition, Vol. 1.

> How dar'st thou come
> Thus trickt in gawdy feathers, and thus guarded,
> With crowned kings and Muses, when thy foe
> Hath thus trod on thee, and now triumphs so?
> Wher's virtuous Ampedo? see, hees her slaue,
> For following thee this recompense they haue.

Dekker forgot to cancel the two verses of the old version and Fortune contradicts herself with scarcely time to recover her breath.

It is rare, in fact, that similar modifications, often done rapidly as in this case, do not cause some trouble in the smooth development of the plot. But at this high price Dekker had skillfully transformed the character of the play. In its original form Fortune was a sovereign power making or breaking the mighty at will, now she was obliged to renounce her supremacy in favor of Virtue. In the moral atmosphere which was made to envelop the action the pursuit of pleasure was no longer a desirable end; the wicked characters lost their attractiveness and even all reality: they became salutary examples of the evil which the abuse of wealth brings in its train, of the punishment awaiting those who prefer earthly pleasures to the more solid satisfactions of goodness. And Virtue's modesty offered, in addition, an occasion for a somewhat clumsy piece of flattery: bowing before the Royal Spectatrix of the evening, she admitted that she was an imperfect image of the queen of England, to whom she offered this homage:

> Virtue alone liues still, and liues in you,
> I am a counterfeit, you are the true,
> I am a shadow, at your feete I fall,
> Begging for these, and these, myself and all (p. 173).

By a wave of his magic rod the author had substituted for a realistic picture of human greed an allegory in the true tradition of the old moralities. To such metamorphoses the revision of a play could sometimes lead under the pressure of intentions that had no literary character about them!

Phaeton, a play of the same period, underwent a similar transformation. It had been bought from Dekker on January 15, 1597/8, for £4, possibly 5 if the 20s. paid out on January 8 for an un-

named manuscript refer to the same order (Henslowe, fol. 44).
In December 1600 the company was invited to perform at Court
and Dekker was asked to revise his play. The actors no doubt
thought that a simple freshening up would be sufficient since
they offered the reviser, "for his paynes in fayeton," only 6s., the
usual price for this type of work (fol. 70v). But Dekker must have
found that the play needed more serious changes, for on December 22 he was paid 30s. more, this time "for alteringe of fayton for
the corte" (fol. 71). Neither the 1598 *Phaeton* nor the 1600 revision
have survived, so it is impossible to say just what changes Dekker
judged necessary to make.

But we do possess an entirely new transformation of the subject
in *The Sun's Darling*. This "moral masque" was licensed by the
Master of the Revels on March 3, 1623/4, performed at the Cock-
pit by Lady Elizabeth's men, and published in 1656 as being written by John Ford and Thomas Dekker. There can scarcely be any
doubt that *The Sun's Darling* and *Phaeton* are fundamentally the
same play.[3] To be sure, the Sun's "darling" is not called Phaeton,
but as Raybright he still recalls the well-known legend when he
says:

> I in your sphere seem a star more divine
> Than in my father's chariot should I ride
> One year about the world in all his pride.

The character has simply acquired a new name just as the play
has changed its title.

Resemblances in technique and in detail show not only that
Dekker is co-author of *The Sun's Darling*, as the title page proclaims, but that this play must have been conceived at the time
when he was revising *Fortunatus*, as Henslowe's accounts show
to have been the case with the 1600 *Phaeton*. Like *Fortunatus*,
The Sun's Darling is a sort of allegory: Raybright's adventures
through the seasons, leaving spring for summer, summer for
autumn, and autumn for winter, symbolize the different ages of
man's life. And like Fortunatus and Andolosia, Raybright is constantly drawn toward new adventures in his pursuit of pleasure

3. The majority of the critics, Gifford, Dyce, Fleay, Collier, Swinburne, Ward,
Greg, admit the fact.

until he finds himself again at his starting point. In this circuitous search Fortune plays a role analogous to the one she plays in *Fortunatus:* she is the all-powerful dispenser of wealth, honor, and glory (IV.i). In order to dupe Longaville, Montrosse, and Agripina, Summer offers Raybright apples (III.iii), the same no doubt that Andolosia used when disguised as a costermonger; and the author certainly had this scene in mind when he had Folly declare: "Upon my life, he means to turn costermonger and is projecting now to forestall the market; I shall cry pipping rarely" (IV.i).[4]

The versification and style of Dekker and Ford are so different that it is relatively easy to distinguish the hand of each.[5] Strictly speaking there was no collaboration, as one might think from the title page, but revision or more exactly transformation by Ford of a play by Dekker. Dekker's *Phaeton* served as a basis, and Dekker's style is recognizable throughout the play, especially in the first three acts. Ford simply touched up the first and fourth acts, but rewrote the fifth act almost entirely to adapt it to a purpose of the Lady Elizabeth's men—a fact revealed by a flagrant inconsistency in the portrayal of the principal character. Raybright, who in the first four acts is shown as a somewhat frivolous youth principally entangled in his mythical existence, is abruptly transformed into a virtuous prince wholly occupied with the welfare of his subjects. He arrives at the Court of Winter accompanied by a brilliant retinue of courtiers. Immediately the "clowns" of the country object to his coming. They are afraid the virtue of their wives and daughters will suffer from the presence of these idlers; above all they are fearful that new rites will be introduced into the temples of their gods. Winter rebukes the impertinent fellows for their opposition to a prince who is wisdom and goodness incarnate:

> Whose laws are so impartial, they must
> Be counted heavenly, because they're truly just,
> Who does with princely moderation give
> His subjects an example to live.

4. In *Fortunatus* (p. 152) Andolosia, disguised as a costermonger, seeks to attract customers by crying: "Buy any apples, feene apples, feene apples of Tamasco, feene Tamasco peepins: peeps feene, buy Tamasco peepins."

5. Cf. F. E. Pierce, "The Collaboration of Dekker and Ford," *Anglia*, 1902, Vol. *36.*

And in this lies the explanation for this change of personality. The play has offered an opportunity for the defense of Prince Charles, son of James I (who finds himself transformed into a star) and heir to the throne, whose marriage to a Catholic princess was dreaded by the clowns (that is to say the Puritans). Prince Charles had, in fact, recently returned from Spain where he had gone to negotiate his marriage with the Spanish infanta, and one condition of the marriage was that the laws against the Catholics should be mitigated if not repealed. When the clowns stubbornly persist in their opposition, Winter predicts that in spite of them the Prince will come "armed with the justice that accompanies his cause"; to the cold climate of this country of the north he will bring a temperate warmth which will change night into perpetual day, abundance and happiness will increase, and peace will dance as a nymph in his kingdom. The actors' patroness, Princess Elizabeth, sister of Prince Charles, was not forgotten in this glorification of the ruling family. The "queen of hearts," as she was called, under the name of Bounty welcomes this charming prince who in his turn assures her of his fidelity.

> All-conquering Bounty, queen of hearts, life's glory,
> Nature's perfection: whom all love, all serve;
> To whom Fortune even in extreme's a slave;
> When I fail of my duty to thy goodness,
> Let me be rank'd as nothing.[6]

After a masque of the four elements and four complexions brought together by Harmony to celebrate the arrival of the Sun's darling, all those fine political schemes disappear with the same abruptness with which they had been brought in. The Sun's son, following Humour's advice, leaves the country of Winter, where long and tedious nights are not propitious to noble deeds, and goes back to Spring to begin again his journey from season to season. The play ends with a ponderous explanation of the moral and allegorical significance to be found in Raybright's adventures —a remnant, no doubt, of Dekker's *Phaeton*.

6. There must have been a close connection between the actors of Prince Charles and those of Princess Elizabeth, which was favored by the family ties of the two patrons. This explains the part played by Lady Elizabeth's company in this political propaganda in favor of Prince Charles.

Concerning *Tasso's Melancholy* nothing is known except that it was performed twelve times by the Lord Admiral's company from August 11, 1594, when it was new, to May 14, 1595. On July 21, 1601/2 the company paid to Dekker £1 "toward the alterynge of Tasso" (fol. 96). The change made cannot have been very great, but it must not have been sufficient for in November 1602 Dekker was again called upon "for the mendinge of the play of tasso," and the company on November 3 and December 4 paid him diverse sums totaling £3 (foll. 108, 108v). This time there must have been a complete revision.

It is difficult to reconstruct the history of the alterations to which a play on the subject of Cardinal Wolsey was submitted. Henslowe's *Diary*, however, supplies enough details to enable one to follow the attempt at least in its principal steps.

On June 5, 1601, the Lord Admiral's company paid Henry Chettle 20s. "for writtinge the Boocke of carnalle wolsey" (fol. 87v). That the play was to be a life of this famous cardinal is attested by the very word "life" inserted between the lines. But something must have been disliked in the manuscript submitted by Chettle for on June 28 Henslowe paid 20s. "for the alterynge of the booke of carnowll wollsey" (fol. 91). The correction did not take long and on July 4 Chettle received 40s. more "for the Booke of carnowlle wollsey in fulle payment" (fol. 91). But at this date Chettle had not yet delivered his manuscript and on July 17 the company was obliged to give Chettle 20s. "for the Boock of the carnawlle wollsey to paye vnto Mr. Bromffelld" (fol. 91v). As W. W. Greg has suggested, Chettle, in need of money, had pawned his manuscript to Bromfeld. That this seems to have been a custom with Chettle is indicated by another payment of the same sort noted on fol. 109v.[7] The company had not yet come to the end of its worries concerning this manuscript, and on August 18 they were obliged to spend another 20s. on this elusive book of "carnowlle wollsey," no doubt for more corrections.

In the meantime, on August 7 the company had started to get ready for performances, and for two weeks scarcely a day passed without Henslowe advancing money for the necessary purchases.

7. "Pd at the appyntment of the companye the 7th of marche 1602 vnto mʳ brom-flde for the playe wᶜʰ harey chettell layd vnto him to pane [pawn] for."

Evidently the production was to be sumptuous, for no less than
£38 12s. 2d. were spent for satin, taffetas, silk gauze, and velvet
to go into costumes and other accessories (foll. 92v, 93).

The preparations were hardly completed—on August 21 they
were still settling a bill for a doctor's gown—when the actors suddenly changed their minds. On August 24 they paid Chettle 20s.
"in earnest of a play called the j part of carnall wollsey" (fol. 93);
in other words they gave up the idea of performing the play as it
had been written and wished to replace it with another play on
the same subject but which was to be only part of the life of the
cardinal.

What could have been the reason for this change, coming as it
did at the very moment when everything seemed ready for a performance? It certainly was not out of a mere whim that the company abandoned a project on which they had already spent more
than £40. It is not difficult to imagine the reason. The subject of
the play was so delicate that, in the first place, one wonders at
Chettle and the actors ever daring to deal with it. No life of
Wolsey could be presented without showing at the denouement—
assuredly a pathetic denouement—the sensational disgrace which
brought that brilliant career to an end. Now in England it was
well known that this disgrace had been inspired by Anne Boleyn,
who could not forgive the domineering cardinal for opposing the
dissolution of the king's marriage with Catherine of Aragon and
thus blocking the way for her own marriage plans. Now Anne
Boleyn was the mother of Queen Elizabeth; was it possible to
present on the public stage, even with the greatest tact, events
awakening unflattering memories of the queen's mother? Edmund
Tilney, the Master of the Revels, evidently could not admit that
it was. He must have prescribed extensive curtailments, so extensive that they would have deprived the play of all dramatic
value. It was certainly better to have the play rewritten entirely.[8]

8. Probably the Master of the Revels examined the play by sections as they were
submitted to him. This is apparent in one of Henslowe's notations dated September
3, 1601: "To pay vnto the M^r of the Revelles for licensynge of the thirde part of
Thome strowde & the Remaynder of carnowlle wollsey x^s" (fol. 93v). Since the fee
for licensing was 7s., 3s. out of the 10 must have applied to the remainder of
Cardinal Wolsey. The company must have paid 4s. while waiting for the end of the
play to be completed. And this explains why the Master of the Revels did not see

Chettle did not set about his new task with any great enthusiasm: for more than six weeks there is no reference in Henslowe's *Diary* to any payment for the play which was supposed to be written. Not until October 10 is *Cardinal Wolsey* mentioned again, and from this notation it turns out that Chettle had so far produced no manuscript in return for the pound he had received as earnest-money; Henslowe, using the phrase customary for plays proposed but not yet begun, noted that the company had advanced 40s. to Chettle, "in earneste of a Boocke called the Rissenge of carnowlle wolsey" (fol. 94). And this time Chettle was no longer the sole author; he had chosen or had assigned to him as collaborators Anthony Munday and Michael Drayton. Later Wentworth Smith was added as a fourth author.

This last notation indicates also that the actors and Chettle had agreed as to what ought to be the subject of the "first part" of the play: the title *The Rising of Cardinal Wolsey* makes this clear. The play was to show only the extraordinary rise of that son of a simple commoner, who cleared at a bound all the steps of the ecclesiastical hierarchy up to that of cardinal, to become lord chancellor of England, the highest post next to that of king. For a month the four collaborators worked on this subject, and on November 12 Henslowe noted that the company paid to Anthony Munday, Harry Chettle, Michael Drayton, and Wentworth Smith "in fulle paymente of the first part of carnowlle wollsey the sum of iij^{ll}" (fol. 94v). The total payment reached £7.

The Rising, of Cardinal Wolsey was still to undergo more changes. Six months later, May 15, 1602, Henslowe advanced 20s. to "harey chettell for the mendynge of the fyrste parte of carnowlle wollsey" (fol. 105v). These changes were probably necessary to adjust the first part to the second, which had finally been written and which they started on May 18 to prepare for presentation.[9] The production must have been as luxurious as that prepared for *The Life of Cardinal Wolsey,* and though the same accessories must have been usable they bought additional goods

the denouement until the last moment, at which time he must have refused his permission.

9. There is no trace in Henslowe's *Diary* of payments for this second part; no doubt the actors did not have recourse to Henslowe but themselves paid the author or authors when the manuscript was turned over to them.

until June 2. A masque of "anticks" alone cost £3 5s.; there was
an exceptional expense of lace and leather (£2 5s.); a coat for
the actor playing the part of William Sommers, Henry VIII's
jester, cost £3.

From a letter written by William Hardsor to Robert Cecil in
July 1602 we learn that the play was being performed at that
time. Hardsor, intervening in behalf of the earl of Kildare, recalls
that this gentleman's grandfather had been accused "by the policy
of Cardinal Wolsey as it is set forth now vpon the stage in London"
(Chatfield MSS, *12, 248*). Several cabals had, in fact, been formed
against Gerald Fitzgerald, ninth earl of Kildare, between 1518
and 1525, and it was well known that Wolsey supported them with
all his power. A rumor was even circulated that the cardinal had
attempted to have that high functionary of the Irish administration assassinated. These cabals against the earl of Kildare thus
constituted one of the notable incidents in the play, indicating
that Wolsey was being presented in an unfavorable light; this
way of treating the character was the means adopted to lull the
susceptibilities of the government.

It is unfortunate that we do not possess the text of this play. It
would have been very interesting to see what relation existed between Chettle's *Cardinal Wolsey* and Samuel Rowley's *When
You See Me, You Know Me,* a play performed and published in
1605. The action took place in Henry VIII's time, and Cardinal
Wolsey of course figured in it. He was presented as an ambitious
man, dreaming of becoming more powerful than the king, taking
the side of France, and accusing the queen—at that moment
Catherine Parr—of heresy, an act which cost him the king's favor
and was the cause of his disgrace.[1] There was another character
common to both plays: William Sommers. In *When You See Me*
the role of that buffoon is almost as important as that of the king,
and in *Cardinal Wolsey* the part must also have been played by
one of the best actors, else why should such a high sum have been
paid for his costume? It is indeed difficult to resist the idea that

1. It is significant that only by twisting historical facts was Rowley able to attribute
the cardinal's disgrace to the intrigues of one of Henry VIII's wives: Wolsey had
been dead thirteen years when the king married Catherine Parr. The real culprit,
Anne Boleyn, was not even mentioned.

Rowley's play was a metamorphosis of Chettle's play. Good reasons can be advanced in favor of such a hypothesis. *When You See Me* was performed by Prince Henry's company, which had been formed by the Lord Admiral's men and had inherited the manuscripts of the old company. Its author was one of the Lord Admiral's men and one of the most important by reason of the services he rendered in his capacity as playwright. He helped with the difficulties attendant upon the composition of *Cardinal Wolsey*, perhaps played in it. At any rate he knew it. What was more natural then that, wishing to write a play on the reign of Henry VIII, he should take over a repertoire play of his older company with the intention of salvaging all that was usable?

However that may be, the history of the composition and revisions of *Cardinal Wolsey* furnishes an excellent example of the unquestioned authority of the actors not only to choose their plays but also to intervene in the composition. From the day when they accepted or commissioned a play they supervised, modified, and sometimes quite upset the original treatment of the subject. In so doing they were moved by reasons which had only a distant connection with the pursuit of artistic perfection, and the authors had to satisfy as well as they could the requirements placed upon them.

Such were the customs that affected the composition of dramatic writing in Shakespeare's time. The dozen plays which I have cited in this short history of dramatic revision at the end of the sixteenth and the beginning of the seventeenth centuries all appeared within the short space of six years at most. They give some idea of the number of examples which could be assembled if we had the account books of all the other companies playing in London. For this practical means of artificially prolonging the life of a play was general. It was so general that a word existed to designate those who made their living by rejuvenating old plays. Dekker speaks in his *News from Hell* (1606) of a "cobbler of Poetrie called a play-patcher" (*Non-Dramatic Works*, ed. A. B. Grosart, 2, 146); and Ben Jonson, caricaturing Dekker himself under the name of Demetrius Fannius, calls him a "dresser of plaies about the towne" (*Poetaster*, III.iv.367).

Shakespeare's company was no exception. We know that the

Chamberlain's company also practiced this easy way of econo-
mizing in the purchase of plays. The custom is openly acknowledged on the title pages of many of its repertoire plays, including
three of Shakespeare's. And it is notable that the company uses the
same terms Henslowe customarily used:

> *Love's Labor's Lost.* As it was presented before her Highnes this last
> Christmas. Newly corrected and augmented by W. Shakespeare
> [Q₁1598].

> *Romeo and Juliet.* Newly corrected, augmented and amended [Q₂1599].

> *The Malcontent.* Augmented by Marston. With the Additions played by
> the King's maiesties seruants. Written by Iohn Webster. 1604.

> *Hamlet, Prince of Denmark* . . . Newly imprinted and enlarged to al-
> most as much againe as it was [Q₂1604].

> A *Most pleasant Comedie of Mucedorus* . . . Amplified with new addi-
> tions, as it was acted before the King's Maiestie at White-hall on
> Shroue-sunday night. By His Highnes Seruanes vsually playing at
> the Globe. 1610.

> *The Maides Tragedy* . . . Newly perused, augmented and enlarged.
> The second impression. 1622.

> *The Maides Tragedy* . . . The third impression. Revised and Refined.
> 1630.

> *Phylaster, Or Loue Lyes a Bleeding* . . . The second Impression cor-
> rected and amended.

> *The Faithfull Sheperdesse* . . . Newly corrected.

If we had this company account book, as we have Henslowe's
Diary, we should probably see that the Chamberlain's men practiced this method of prolonging the usefulness of their repertoire
more than any other company, for the simple reason that they
need not rely on the costly help of the "play-patchers." Always
available among their actors was an incomparable poet, the personification of dramatic genius, capable of transforming any
"book," tragedy, or comedy with that marvelous facility which
Heming and Condell have praised in the preface of the First Folio.
Shakespeare was of his own time, living fully the life of his fellow
actors, and as we shall see there is no doubt that he did "amend,"
enrich with "additions," or even transform not only his own plays

but those of other authors whenever the interest of his company demanded it.

During the first years of the seventeenth century this habit of dramatic revision continued to spread. In 1615 Chamberlain could write (cf. Thomas Birch, *The Court and Times of James I*, p. 290): "Our poets' brains and inventions are grown very dry, insomuch that of five new plays there is not one that pleases, and therefore they are driven to furbish over their old, which stand them in best staid and bring them most profit"; and in his *London and the Countrey Carbonadoed and Quartered* (1632) D. Lupton expressed the same idea in a more picturesque image: "The players are as crafty with an old play, as bauds with old faces, the one puts on a new fresh colour, the other a new face and name." In the prologue of *The False One* (c. 1620) Beaumont and Fletcher chimed in, affirming that "New Titles warrant not a Play for new."

∫ ∫ ∫

KNOWLEDGE of the conditions under which the dramatic companies operated and, in a general way, of the manner in which plays were written has opened many perspectives, not all of which, unfortunately, lead to the discovery of the truth. The first effect has been to give new impetus to study of the authenticity of the Shakespearean canon. This question has been raised with more or less insistence ever since the eighteenth century. Patient editors of Shakespeare's text have noted that side by side with passages of incomparable beauty are others which are unworthy of a great dramatist. And some of these editors expressed their suspicion that perhaps not everything in the text is Shakespeare's. Pope conjectured that in *Love's Labor's Lost, The Winter's Tale, The Comedy of Errors,* and *Titus Andronicus* there was nothing authentic except a few scenes and some characters; he was convinced that in *Richard II* certain lines were too bad to be Shakespeare's, and he ruthlessly suppressed those passages which appeared to him inferior (1725). Similar doubts were expressed by Theobald regarding *Henry V* (1734), by Hanmer regarding *The Two Gentlemen of Verona* (1744), by Samuel Johnson regarding *Richard II* (1765), and by Farmer regarding *The Taming of the Shrew*

(1767). Ritson found some disparities so evident that in *The Two Gentlemen, Love's Labor's Lost,* and *Richard II* he claimed he could distinguish Shakespeare's hand as easily as one could recognize the brilliant brush strokes with which a Titian might have sought to touch up a mere daub. Malone in 1790, in his often quoted dissertation on *Henry VI* (Vol. *18* of his edition of Shakespeare, revised by Boswell), did not recognize Shakespeare's hand except in some passages of the second and third parts and thought that the first part came entirely from one of Shakespeare's predecessors. Among the critics of the eighteenth century we might include E. H. Seymour, although his *Remarks Critical, Conjectural and Explanatory upon the Plays of Shakespeare* was not published until 1805. It was his belief that the texts of all Shakespeare's plays (with the exception of *A Midsummer Night's Dream*) were corrupt; he disclosed traces of other dramatists in Shakespeare's plays and, in certain cases, suggested that Shakespeare revised a play of some earlier writer.

But these pronouncements were often made with no other reason than the dictates of an instinctive discernment considered as infallible. Except in the case of Malone no method justified the attacks made on the integrity of the plays. And differences of style were vaguely attributed to unintelligent interpolations made by mediocre writers who had taken the liberty to alter works the beauty of which they did not understand. The revelations of Henslowe's *Diary* on the role played by collaborators in the composition of dramatic works in Shakespeare's time gave a basis and a priori proof to the conviction that many passages which had passed as being Shakespeare's were attributable to other dramatists. And through the nineteenth century there were a number of critics who attacked the Shakespearean canon with more or less irreverence.[2]

The most active and the most audacious of those whom Sir Edmund Chambers has termed "disintegrators" is certainly Fred-

2. Malone had had Henslowe's *Diary* at his disposal and had quoted important extracts from it in his "Historical Account of the Stage" (printed at the beginning of his 1780 edition of Shakespeare). But it was especially J. P. Collier's publication (Shakespeare Society, 1845) of this document concerning the administration of the Rose and the Fortune that influenced subsequent critics.

erick G. Fleay. He was one of the first to realize the necessity, in any study of Elizabethan dramatic literature, of taking into account the conditions under which dramatic works were written. First in his *Shakespeare Manual* (published in 1876, reprinted in 1878, and revised under the title of *A Chronicle History of the Life and Work of Shakespeare,* 1886), next in his *Chronicle History of the London Stage* (1890), complemented by *A Biographical Chronicle of the English Drama* (1891), Fleay inaugurated a system of research which might have entirely altered the history of the Elizabethan drama. Endowed with insatiable curiosity, ingenious, knowing at first hand all the literature of the period, having examined with care a mass of documentation and absorbed the information furnished by Henslowe's *Diary* (his researches are, in fact, based on the conviction that collaboration and revision explain the greater part of the anomalies in dramatic texts), he is the author of the first serious attempt to follow the history of the various actors' companies between 1583 and 1642. By a direct study of the plays he brought together a mass of details on the composition and chronology of Shakespeare's plays, raising many problems which have often irritated the critics but which even more often have served as stimulants for their own studies.

Unfortunately Fleay never realized that erudition is not a game but a science which exacts from those who embrace it a severe discipline and the rigorous application of a method with certain well-defined principles. Without the observation of these principles one is apt to accumulate errors infinitely more harmful than ignorance. Fleay was never able to master a chaotic imagination; with him impressions took the place of proofs and were set forth in the form of assertions which he never took the trouble to prove but which presently became facts. His lack of exactitude, his changes of opinion from one book to the next are proverbial. The result is that this admirable intellectual activity has created more disorder than useful additions to our knowledge.

Fleay's books, in spite of the justified suspicion in which they have been held, have had, nevertheless, more indirectly than directly, considerable influence on the scholars following him. At the end of the last century the idea that the Shakespearean canon was not entirely authentic was so firmly established that it was generally admitted that *Titus Andronicus* and the three parts of *Henry VI* contained traces of Shakespeare's hand, that in *Henry VIII* one must acknowledge Fletcher's collaboration, and that in *Richard III, Hamlet, The Two Gentlemen of Verona, The Taming of the Shrew*, and others there appear some remnants of older plays which served as models.

It remained, however, for the twentieth century to launch the most vehement attack on the integrity of Shakespeare's works. In books richly documented, bolstered by an enveloping and subtle argumentation—*Did Shakespeare Write Titus Andronicus?* (1905) reprinted under the title *An Introduction to the Study of the Shakespeare Canon* (1924), *Shakespeare and Chapman* (1917), *The Problem of Hamlet* (1919), *The Shakespeare Canon* (4 vols., 1922–32)—J. M. Robertson undertook to demonstrate that much foreign matter must be withdrawn from many of Shakespeare's plays. He believed he saw the style (or more particularly the vocabulary) and the manner of Marlowe, Greene, Peele, Chapman, Kyd, and even Ben Jonson in the early plays and in some also which are generally assigned to a later period.

It must be recognized that Robertson too had qualities which started him on the track of incontestable truths and which should have led to a successful conclusion the task he had taken upon himself. Like Fleay he possessed an extensive knowledge of Elizabethan literature; he loved Shakespeare to the point of idolatry; he had read and reread the plays and had developed an instinct which frequently served him to uncover those passages which lacked the usual Shakespearean ring. I know nothing more just or more penetrating than Chapter 10 of *An Introduction to the Study of the Shakespeare Canon* (pp. 416–56) on versification as a means of investigation. The idea that versification is one of the surest ways of distinguishing Shakespeare's style from that of his contemporaries is excellent, and if Robertson had taken the trouble to separate Shakespeare's text from all foreign matter by this method he would have accomplished an eminently useful work. But from the moment he suspected the presence of another author all his energy was bent on discovering the identity of this author and he lost sight of the object of his search. When by complicated and naïve means he had, as he thought, discovered the

supposed collaborators, it was difficult to see what remained of
Shakespeare, so numerous and all-pervading were the intruders.
The final result is that all this labor is purely negative and looks
like an enormous expenditure of ingenuity to produce ruins instead of a whole edifice.

∫ ∫ ∫

THE QUESTION of authenticity is closely linked with that of the
transmission of the text. We have two kinds of text: quartos published during Shakespeare's lifetime and the collection of the complete works published in one folio volume in 1623. These texts,
play for play, are not always identical. Thus from the moment
when critical editions began to be published the question arose:
which of these different texts is the most authentic and consequently the best?

In the eighteenth century it was decided that the texts furnished
by the quartos were corrupt. Theobald advanced reasons which
gave weight to this opinion. Many of the plays published during
the author's lifetime, he said in the preface of his edition (1773),
were taken down in shorthand during a performance, others were
incorrectly assembled from actors' parts, fraudulently obtained
without the author's knowledge (pp. xxxvii–viii). Theobald was
relying on two pieces of evidence. The first was a passage by
Thomas Heywood who complained that some of his plays "unknown to me and without any of my direction accidentally have
come into the Printers handes, and therefore so corrupt and so
mangled (copied only by the eare) that I have bene as unable to
know them, as ashamed to challenge them" (Epistle to *The Rape
of Lucrece*, 1608), one of the plays being *If You Know Not ME,
You Know Nobody*, printed in 1605, of which he wrote:

> Some by stenography drew
> The plot: put it in print scarce one word true
> (*Pleasant Dialogues and Dramas*, 1637)

The second was a phrase of Heming and Condell (preface to the
First Folio) affirming that the public had been deceived by the
publication of "diverse stolne, and surreptitious copies, maimed,

and deformed by the frauds and stealthes of injurious impostors, that exposed them." Theobald concluded that only the folio could be relied upon.

The belief that the Shakespearean quartos gave a corrupt text persisted, with a few rare exceptions or attenuations, to the end of the nineteenth century. In 1909 a distinguished bibliographer, A. W. Pollard, published a volume entitled *Shakespeare's Folios and Quartos: A Study in the Bibliography of Shakespeare's Plays, 1594–1685,* upsetting this belief. In this book Pollard showed that the passage in which the folio editors complain that Shakespeare's plays had been published without their knowledge had been mis-understood: Heming and Condell had not meant to say that *all* the plays published prior to the folio had been stolen from them; they merely wanted to indicate that *some* of these plays—the word "diverse" which they used implies this—gave a text "maimed and deformed." The truth is that fourteen of these texts, until then considered unauthentic, reproduced, except for several differences in detail and expression, almost word for word the corresponding text in the folio. It was even obvious that several had served as a basis for the folio text, and Pollard went so far as to advance the hypothesis that some of these had been printed from manuscripts of the company which, in certain cases, had found it profitable to facilitate the printed reproduction of its plays. Certainly these quartos deserved the epithet "good" which Pollard used to dis-tinguish them.

Pollard set five quartos in a second category: *Romeo and Juliet* (Q₁), *Henry V, The Merry Wives of Windsor, Hamlet* (Q₁), and *Pericles.*[3] These give a text that differs considerably from the corresponding folio text, not so much in plot, which is largely the same in both, as in details of composition affecting the order of some scenes and, above all, in the style. Compared with those in the folio these texts are inferior, and in opposition to the "good" quartos Pollard termed them "bad" quartos.[4]

3. To this list has since been added *The First Part of the Contention between York and Lancaster,* 1594, and *The True Tragedie of Richard Duke of York,* 1595, as "bad" quartos of 2 and 3 *Henry VI* (cf. Peter Alexander, *Shakespeare's Henry VI and Richard III,* 1929).

4. For the moment I use this derogatory appellation; it will be seen later that this word does not exactly apply to the nature of these quartos.

Actually all this was not entirely new. In 1768, in the introduction to his edition of Shakespeare, Capell had already distinguished two groups among the quartos, one consisting of several plays which he considered "either first draughts or mutilated and perhaps surreptitious impressions," the other of plays that probably "depended" on "the poet's own copies." Malone in 1790, in the preface to his edition of Shakespeare, accused the editors of the folio of wishing to increase the public's interest in their own publication by implying that all previous editions were mutilated and imperfect, although thirteen quartos gave a text preferable to that of the folio. Pollard's study showed these ideas to advantage: it was founded upon a technical analysis of the bibliographical characteristics of each quarto and of the four folios; above all it was pleasant reading; the book was a great success among scholars. It was recognized that the question of the transmission of the text could not be solved solely by means of assumptions based on simple aesthetic "appreciations"; and the result was the birth of a new branch of Shakespearean criticism, namely the bibliographical school.

The aim of this new type of study has been clearly defined by W. W. Greg in *The Editorial Problem in Shakespeare* (1942, pp. 3-4):

> Bibliographers have in fact brought criticism down from the fascinating but too often barren heights of aesthetic and philosophic speculation to the concrete familiarities of the theatre, the scrivener's shop and the printing-house. As soon as the new point of view suggested the formulating of new questions, all sorts of neglected facts took on significance, and in response to new demands whole new fields of evidence were discovered and explored. It soon came to be recognized that the form and fashion of literary and theatrical documents, the operation of agencies of production and transmission, and many other relevant circumstances, raised questions that were to be answered, not out of the critics' inner consciousness, as had been the fashion hitherto, but in accordance with whatever historical evidence lay to hand or could be discovered by properly directed research.

A considerable amount of work has already been accomplished, of which Greg's *The Variants of the First Quarto of King Lear* (1940) is the most perfect and most characteristic example. So many studies have appeared in the form of articles that it is impossible to give any list of them. It will suffice to name the principal representatives of that school: W. W. Greg, P. Simpson, J. D. Wilson, H. T. Price, R. B. McKerrow, R. C. Rhodes, W. J. Lawrence, Madeleine Doran, G. I. Duthie, L. Kirschbaum, and, naturally, the man who inspired these researchers, A. W. Pollard.

In the various investigations of a typographical nature extremely important results have been obtained. I cannot say as much for certain other investigations which have been made on the bad quartos denounced in *Shakespeare's Folios and Quartos*. In 1915, in the Clark Lectures which he delivered at Cambridge University, Pollard again insisted on the necessity of not confusing the bad and the good quartos; he reaffirmed his conviction that some of the good quartos had been printed from the company's manuscripts and that there were many reasons why these were closer to Shakespeare's intentions than later editions which had been corrupted either by the vagaries of ignorant compositors or by the misguided intervention of zealous editors who took upon themselves the task of improving Shakespeare. These lectures were published in 1919 (revised edition, 1920) under the title of *Shakespeare's Fight with the Pirates and the Problems of the Transmission of His Text*. Actually Shakespeare played no part in this fight: Pollard merely wished to suggest the means by which the Lord Chamberlain's company tried on several occasions to protect its repertoire from possible theft, and he thought that he had some idea of the way these thefts were accomplished. He had already admitted in *Shakespeare's Folios and Quartos* (pp. 72, 79) that the pirate was someone sent to the theater by unscrupulous booksellers to take notes and thus procure the texts of successful plays. But if the title *Shakespeare's Fight with the Pirates* was not very exact it was suggestive, all the more so as these thieves were not even vaguely described. Curiosity was aroused, and investigations were begun to discover who these pirates were and what means these bold fellows had used to commit their thefts. Thus a fabulously interesting subject opened up for the enthusiasts of critical bibliography; it was as though the detective story entered a field of research where it had previously never been usual to yield to the attraction of imaginative flights.

Studies of bad quartos multiplied, with the principal object of uncovering the villainous practices of the pirate.

The old theory based on Heywood's statement quoted above (p. 35) had been accepted as a fact during the eighteenth and nineteenth centuries; the pirate was regarded as a necessitous person who, in order to earn some money, took down the text in shorthand at the theater and sold it to a bookseller dishonest enough to pass off this forgery as the very play then being performed.

This theory at first found some old-timers to give it new expression, but it could not satisfy the new critics who were in the habit of scrutinizing the most minute characteristics of printed texts down to the punctuation, and were capable of writing whole volumes on the text of *Henry V, Hamlet,* and *Lear.* As W. Matthews has shown,[5] the only system of shorthand that was in use at the time of the bad Shakespearean quartos was the system Timothy Dwight set out in *The Charactery* (1588), and this was incapable of giving a text that was even approximately correct. A text obtained in this manner could only be bad from beginning to end, "scarce one word true" as Heywood put it when he spoke of his pirated play. But in the so-called bad Shakespearean quartos continual and profound irregularity is the rule: side by side with passages that have only a distant connection with the folio text are to be found others almost identical with the corresponding passage in the folio; in some cases the identity is absolute.

Some other solution became necessary. And thus the pirate appeared in a different incarnation. The culprit was sought among the members of the company: an actor betraying his comrades must have attempted to reconstruct the play around his own part in it; or the members of a company which for some reason or other had mislaid its own manuscript might have united to reproduce it from memory. Instead of to some impossible system of stenography scholars now had recourse to the memory of people familiar with the play; hence the name "memorial reconstruction" which was given to this theory, now spreading fast, drawing recruits from the ranks of the best critical bibliographers.

5. "Shorthand and the Bad Shakespearean Quartos," *Modern Language Review,* 1932, pp. 243–62; "Shakespeare and the Reporters," *The Library,* 1934, *15,* 481–98.

Even this idea is not entirely new. It was in the making when Theobald affirmed, without proof, that some of the Shakespearean quartos were "printed from piece-meal parts surreptitiously obtain'd from the Theatre." In 1857 Tycho Mommsen had helped this idea to grow when, apropos of the first *Hamlet*, he thought he could distinguish an actor who had written down a plot of the play from memory. W. H. Widgery in an essay on the first quarto of *Hamlet* (1880) identified the traitor with the actor who had played the part of Voltemar. And Greg, lending the weight of his name to this theory, gave it more attractive expression and rendered it popular. In the introduction to his edition of the quarto of *The Merry Wives of Windsor* (1910) he pointed out that the host's part was particularly well reproduced, and that every time this character is on the stage the text is much better. He concluded (not without some reservations) that the actor playing that part was probably the reporter of the text printed in the quarto, and that the quarto was a memorial reconstruction.

The case was ingeniously presented. But when one verifies the facts on which this hypothesis is based it soon becomes apparent that to maintain the host's part is uniformly well rendered would be saying a great deal. In Act IV.sc.v the host learns that his horses have been stolen and thus becomes involved in one of those situations designed to produce a comic effect which an actor would hardly forget; but after a fairly good start the scene ends with a passage that no longer follows the folio text except in a few speeches, and the host's speeches are the most imperfect of his role. The same thing occurs in Act IV.sc.vi, which the actor playing the host's part should have known particularly well for he has nothing to do but listen to young Fenton's long tirade; nevertheless only a dozen verses remain out of the forty in the folio. More than that, there are passages where the host is on the stage—for example in the beginning of Act II.sc.i—that are rendered less accurately than others—such as the beginning of II.ii—where he is off the stage. In one of his later books, *The Editorial Problem in Shakespeare* (p. 71), Greg with scrupulous honesty has recognized that his explanation presents "difficulties."

The same difficulties, indeed, are met in all similar attempts to identify the pirate, or the reporter, as this elusive personage is now euphemistically called. The actor-reporter is certainly a curious specimen of human nature, one well calculated to puzzle a psychologist. Though professionally he should have been gifted with a retentive memory and though he belonged to the best dramatic company in London, he has the most capricious of minds: at times he can remember his role with perfect correctness, in a few cases even reproducing the original printed text right down to spelling, capitalization, and punctuation; but at other moments he remembers only a few words of forgotten sentences, he confuses or misplaces speeches, juggles with the vocabulary, paraphrases, invents, and ends, out of mere weariness I suppose, by substituting a text entirely of his own. For it is admitted that this muddle-headed fellow can now and then write verse, not comparable of course to that of Shakespeare, but correct and on the whole respectable. And what is more singular, all the actor-reporters are similarly constituted: they make exactly the same mistakes—which have been listed as a methodical compendium of rules to be applied to all future identifications of bad quartos—they falter in the same places, are pretty good at the beginning of the play, and collapse in the last scenes. Truly this is too improbable; and when we are told besides that these actor-reporters remember fragments of other parts they have assumed in other plays with which they fill in the gaps created by their loss of memory, then it is no longer a question of improbability but of absurdity. The theory of memorial reconstruction proves to be, after all, as disappointing as the theory of stenographic reconstruction—if not more so. It certainly offers no better explanation for the extraordinary inequality of the style in the quartos where accuracy and inaccuracy vie with each other; and yet in this contradiction is to be found the crux of the problem.

Indeed the theory could hardly have been anything else but disappointing. For all the theories on the nature and value of the quartos are based upon a series of misconceptions and fallacious modes of reasoning that confuse the question instead of clarifying it. The first mistake was to take for granted and postulate that the folio text, being longer and better, was the first and only authentic text, and that the quarto text, being shorter and often inferior, was consequently a truncated and corrupted form of the folio text. It is difficult to believe that plays which in certain cases were in the possession of Shakespeare's company, for thirty years remained untouched at a time when the practice was to refurbish the repertoire constantly. My own experience, after a long and minute examination of the different texts—as the present book will I hope show—is that very often the folio text has been tampered with and cannot be relied upon. If one takes the facts for what they are, it is just as reasonable to say, as the old theory did, that the folio text, being longer and better, represents the augmented and improved form of the corresponding quarto. The truth is that both theories posited in that way are equally arbitrary. Such difficult problems cannot be solved by a priori affirmations: affirmations are not proofs; they are even the opposite of a demonstration.

On the other hand, the often quoted sentence (see pp. 35–6) from the preface of the 1623 folio, to which the actor-reporter partly owes his existence, does not substantiate the deductions that have been derived from it. Not only has the word "diverse" been misunderstood, as Pollard has shown, but the whole sentence has been given a meaning which it does not have. What did Heming and Condell really say? They complained that before the publication of the folio there had been circulated without their permission copies which had been stolen (and by stolen they actually meant a theft) and "maimed," i.e., deprived of some member or limb, and thus were "deformed." The folio, they promised, now offered the same copies "cur'd, and perfect of their limbes"; in other words the missing limbs were restored and the copies were therefore complete, for that is the Middle English meaning of the word "perfect," still in use in the seventeenth century. In this sentence of Heming and Condell there is not a word that suggests "piracy" in the very particular sense which the term has been given by modern critics, nor is there any word leading one to suppose that the "injurious imposters" belonged to Shakespeare's company. And we have an excellent proof that this was really what they meant to say. When the company published the second quarto of *Romeo and Juliet* they specified on the title page that the new edition had been "newly corrected, augmented and amended," and when they published the second quarto of *Hamlet* they were still more precise and stated that the play was newly imprinted and "enlarged to almost as much again as it was according to the true and perfect copy," "perfect" here again having the sense of "complete." They could not have said more clearly that the first quartos of *Romeo and Juliet* and of *Hamlet* were incomplete forms of the plays that were performed in their finished versions at the time of the corrective publication. And this, by the way, was implicitly to acknowledge the authenticity of the two Shakespearean quartos which today are considered as particularly deserving the infamous epithet of bad.

The method used to show that a quarto has been reported is what it can be in an inquiry where conjecture and guessing are rampant. It has been noticed that all bad quartos have certain defects or imperfections in common: there are metrical irregularities, transpositions of lines or phrases from one place to another (called anticipations or recollections), verse lines badly divided or printed as prose, prose printed as verse, inferior verbal variants, a vulgarized vocabulary and a generally platitudinous style, omission of passages which are in the folio. Now we are confidently told that modern scholarship considers bad quartos as essentially reports of more authoritative texts. Therefore every time we find such defects or imperfections in a quarto we can be certain that it has been reported, even if we judge that, all things considered, it is remarkably good for a bad quarto. This way of giving as a conclusion the very hypothesis upon which the conclusion has been founded is, I imagine, what a strict logician would call a vicious circle. And when, my suspicion being aroused by this strange mode of reasoning, I examined those condemnatory defects more carefully, it did not take long to realize that there is not one of those proofs of corruption that cannot be taken as well for a proof of correction. Inferior variants, a vulgar vocabulary, a platitudinous style, and irregular verses can be the signs of a mediocre author and make it reasonable to believe that a revision has been considered necessary; what appears to be an omission in the quarto may equally well indicate an addition to the folio; transpositions of a word, a phrase, a passage from one part to another may also be a sign that some rehandling has taken place, for to transfer an idea where it is more relevant is one of the elementary means of stylistic improvement. (Indeed the various manuscript revisions of the present book supply numerous examples of the process. As a matter of fact, the preceding paragraph served first as an introduction to the chapter on the composition of 2 *Henry VI.*) And verses wrongly divided or printed as prose, in the opinion of some experts of the bibliographical school, are indications of marginal corrections in a manuscript.

The confusion of ideas described above has rendered many conscientious studies useless. It is not surprising that equally well-informed critics fail to agree. Excellent Shakespearean scholars have been known first to adopt one interpretation as convincing and subsequently to hold a diametrically opposed opinion as eminently satisfactory. Thus it will always be so long as one makes use of double-edged arguments to prove a preconceived idea. The only method that can give dependable results is the one which will carefully and without bias analyze the quarto and folio texts of a play and will let the facts obtained lead to inevitable conclusions. This, I may as well say now, is the method I have tried to apply in the present book.

∫   ∫   ∫

HAPPILY, critical bibliography has other more valid achievements. Pollard's conviction that the good quartos had for the most part been printed from the company's manuscripts led to the idea of establishing, as far as it was possible, the nature of the manuscript which the compositor had before him when he set his type, for on this identification rested many problems of composition and even of authenticity. In this almost entirely new field of study W. W. Greg, one of the rare Shakespearean critics to possess a practical and extended knowledge of Elizabethan handwriting, took a leading part. In the typographical reproductions of manuscripts published by him or under his direction for the Malone Society collection, in articles, and in some of his books,[6] he brought up to date our knowledge of the different dramatic manu-

6. See in particular "Prompt Copies, Private Transcripts and the Playhouse Scrivener," *The Library*, 4th ser., 1925; also chap. 2 in *The Editorial Problem in Shakespeare.*

scripts which are extant, a knowledge which he himself helped increase through his own research.[7] We are now sufficiently well informed on the different types of manuscripts in use in Elizabethan and Jacobean theaters—author's rough copies (or foul papers), fair copies for the Master of the Revels, promptbooks, copies made for collectors—and the manner in which these manuscripts were prepared that there is little to add concerning the sometimes adventurous journey of a dramatic play from the moment it left the author's hand until it came to rest at the printing house.

Thus the door was opened to the development of a fertile idea which has already produced important results, though their value has not been sufficiently recognized. John Dover Wilson who was the first to exploit it observed that, except in rare cases, dramatic manuscripts of the Elizabethan period do not seem to have received any preparation for publication. They were given to the printer just as they were when used in the theater, with all the visible signs of the changes they might have undergone, the cuttings, additions, and above all the revisions we have been made aware of through Henslowe's *Diary*. Sixteenth-century compositors were not more independent than those of today and they rightly had no ambition but to reproduce faithfully the text supplied to them. If the manuscript contained corrections, additions, or deletions they did not attempt to put things in order; all the imperfections and abnormalities of the manuscript were repeated in the printed text. The dramatic quartos, the good as well as the bad, are full of surprising irregularities: names of actors sometimes slip into the list of dramatis personae; names of characters may vary; passages are given in two different forms, where evidently one was intended to replace the other; verses are badly divided or are printed as prose, and prose is printed in irregular lines which seem to be verses; characters announced in a stage direction do not appear; flagrant contradictions put the plot out of joint, etc. These irregularities disfigure nearly all the dramatic publications

7. Some interesting studies are F. P. Wilson, "Ralph Crane, Scrivener to the King's Players," *The Library*, 4th ser., 1926; W. J. Lawrence, "Early Prompt Books and What They Reveal," *Pre-Restoration Studies*, 1927; C. J. Sisson, "Bibliographical Aspects of Some Stuart Dramatic Manuscripts," *Review of English Studies*, 1925, Vol. *1*, "Shakespeare Quartos as Prompt-Copies," *ibid.*, 1942, Vol. *18*.

of that period, but for the literary historian they provide precious information on the state of the manuscript at the moment when it left the company. Thanks to them it is possible to have an idea of the modifications to which the manuscript has been subjected during its existence.

As early as 1918 J. D. Wilson, bearing in mind the existence of these anomalies, in two articles, "The Copy of Hamlet 1603" and "The Hamlet Transcript 1593" (*The Library*, 1918, Vol. 9), combined that same year in one volume published by the Delamore Press, attempted to reconstruct the composition of the first quarto of *Hamlet*. The following year, in collaboration with Pollard, he contributed to the London *Times Literary Supplement* (January 9, 16, March 13, August 7, 14, 1919) five articles on "The Stolne and Surreptitious Shakespearean Texts" in which he applied the same bibliographical method to the so-called bad quartos. But it was when he was commissioned by the Cambridge University Press to undertake with Sir Arthur Quiller-Couch the editing of the New Cambridge Shakespeare that (in the introductions to each play) Wilson began systematically to point out the scars in the text and to draw from them deductions about the nature of the original manuscript and the revisions that might explain these typographical accidents.

I do not think I exaggerate in saying that this way of studying the text (which met at once with incomprehensible opposition) is one of the most fecund methods that have been applied since work on Shakespeare's plays began. I confess that to me it was a revelation. In my earlier days I accepted as gospel truth the portrait of Shakespeare which, by dint of being repeated, had acquired a permanence that permitted only variations of detail on an unalterable theme. I could not bring myself, however, to reconcile what I knew of dramatic production in the sixteenth century with the established image of a Shakespeare composed of many literary types which existed only after him: a Shakespeare working for posterity, painfully amassing the matter of his subject and then, with that exceptional facility which his theatrical comrades recognized in him, at one stroke creating the works we so admire today, without "a blot in his papers," in so definitive a manner that modifications and improvements were unthinkable. The textual introduction to the edition of *The Tempest* of the New Cambridge Shakespeare (1921), in which Wilson described his method, made me see at once the possibility of a more realistic conception of a Shakespeare belonging to his time, living with and for his company, familiar with its needs and resources. The idea of the present book was born then: I would take up again the composition of the plays, a subject which has never been studied in its entirety; and in applying the principles of critical bibliography, somewhat enlarged and perfected, I felt it would no doubt be possible to establish on a newer and firmer basis what constituted the superiority of those plays, which still retain an eternal freshness. It will be readily apparent that I do not always agree with J. D. Wilson, but I like to acknowledge that it is from him I derived the idea which inspires this book.

$$\int \quad \int \quad \int$$

I SHALL AVOID many tedious repetitions later on if I state now the principles and tests which I have applied in the following studies. After a few words on the publication of a play I shall first try to determine the kind of manuscript which served as copy for the printing of the text. It may be useful to recall that there were two kinds of manuscripts from which all the others stemmed—the original or author's manuscript and the fair copy of the same made after a careful preparation for the use of the prompter, that is to say the man (sometimes called the bookholder) who apparently was charged with the double task of preparing and directing the performances.

When the author had completed his play, if he was conscientious, he would himself make a fair copy. Robert Daborne's correspondence with Henslowe (preserved in the Dulwich Library) shows the dramatist's unhappy efforts to deliver a fair copy of his work to the actors, which ended in his sending instead the rough draft or foul sheets of several scenes. Several manuscripts in the author's hand do exist; but it is doubtful that many dramatists were so careful, to judge from the frequency with which the expression "foul papers" appears in dramatic documents to designate author's manuscripts. It seems, in particular, that Shakespeare

only submitted "foul papers." Had he done otherwise the editors
of the folio would not have expressed their admiration at having
"scarce received from him a blot in his papers."

To obtain the license to perform a play the company had first
of all to submit the text to the Master of the Revels. If the author
had turned in a manuscript well written and in good order it was
possible to use it for this purpose; but if he had sent his foul papers
a copy had to be made by a professional scrivener.[8] Such must have
been the custom in the case of Shakespeare: there are good reasons to believe that his handwriting was not of the best. We have
six of his signatures; from a paleographical point of view they are
all so characteristic that one can easily deduce from them the
imperfections of his writing. Shakespeare used what is commonly
called the English hand. He made an exception in the case of one
letter, the medial s, to which he gave the long form of the cursive
Italian letter, following a tendency which spread toward the end
of the sixteenth century to replace the English hand by the Italian
script. A study of his signatures shows two characteristics that are
constant. 1) In five cases the signature is abbreviated; one is complete, but it it evident that Shakespeare had first left it unfinished,
according to his habit, and added the missing letters later, probably after someone pointed out that since the signature was on his
will it would be prudent to leave no uncertainty as to the name.
2) The same letter is not always formed in the same fashion; the
three signatures on the will are so different that Sir E. Maunde
Thompson has admitted they might at first sight be taken for the
signatures of three different people (*Shakespeare's Handwriting,*
1916, p. 12). From this we can imagine that Shakespeare had a
jerky kind of handwriting, the pen with difficulty following the
rapidity of the thought, and that abbreviations and inconsistencies
must have made his writing hard to decipher.[9]

8. There were scriveners specializing in this kind of work. Cf. F. P. Wilson,
"Ralph Crane, Scrivener to the Kings' Players," *The Library,* 1926, 7, 194.
9. No doubt many readers will be surprised that I take no account of the three
manuscript pages of *Sir Thomas More* (Hand D) which have sometimes been considered as Shakespeare's autograph. Sir E. Maunde Thompson lent the authority of
his name to this identification and thus contributed to the general acceptance of this
belief. In spite of the respect which I entertain for this eminent paleographer I cannot be persuaded that these pages are Shakespeare's. Hand D of the *Sir Thomas More*

When the manuscript returned from the Revels office it might serve as a promptbook after receiving the necessary annotations, but such cases must have been fairly rare. Often the Master of the Revels demanded suppressions or modifications which, after they had been made on the manuscript, did not add to the cleanness of the text. Now the prompter needed a page so arranged that he could at a glance follow the stage directions throughout a performance—for entrances or exits of actors, stage business, sound effects, properties to be held in readiness for the moment when they were needed, etc. To adapt an author's manuscript to this purpose numerous and important notes had to be added. Of course the author had furnished some useful details for the staging, but his point of view was not that of the prompter. In general his notations were few and simple, limited mostly to the entrances and exits of the characters. If he saw the life of his characters vividly—and one can boldly maintain that such was the case with Shakespeare—if he saw them move before him in imagination while he heard their words and reported them rapidly on paper, he may now and then have sought to communicate his vision to the actors; he may have noted their facial expressions, fixed certain details of costumes if these details created an atmosphere. In a word he may have described what was not mentioned in the dialogue, but he did not meddle with matters presupposing a knowledge of the company's resources. Thus he left certain instructions indefinite, such as the number of supernumeraries: "Enter Hostess of the tavern, and an Officer or two" (2 *Henry IV*). This kind of notation is the surest sign that the stage direction is the author's.

The prompter had other preoccupations. The management of the play rested entirely on him and his constant care was to foresee what in theatrical slang are called howlers. Any number of accidents can happen and his promptbook must aid him in preventing

---

manuscript is a specimen of the English hand in use in the sixteenth century (and Shakespeare's signatures belong to this type of writing), but it has characteristics which are just the opposite of those revealed by the signatures: the ends of words are not only perfectly marked but are ornamented with flourishes, curls, and useless horizontal strokes. It is the handwriting of a man who delights in his work, possibly a scrivener, who experiences a real pleasure when his pen caresses the rounded contours of letters such as *h* or *y* which he greatly enlarges.

these. Thus he read over the original and annotated it carefully, with only a moderate respect for the author's directions. Naturally he preserved them if they were necessary, but suggestive descriptions are literary ornaments and he did not care for them. If in his view they were verbose he cut them, for he had need of notes short and easy to read at a glance, which is why they are often written in the imperative mood. On the other hand, he added all the directions the author had not thought of—exits, for example, which were often forgotten. Above all he kept a sharp lookout to see that the entrances were complete, for it is a catastrophe if an actor does not take up his cue. If he was particularly cautious he noted each entry several lines ahead of the actual entrance of the actor and did the same for the properties which would be needed. The prompter who prepared the manuscript of *Believe as You List* took care to have important properties ready long before they were used: "the great booke of Acomptes ready" (this appears at line 962 instead of line 1115): "All the swords ready" (line 2378 instead of line 2717). The prompter had also to decide the most minute details of the stage setting; he noted in the margin the musical and warlike sound effects which were so important in performances: "a song," "a flourish," "alarum and chambers go off," etc. He ordered the military marches with drums, trumpets, and flags. And if by chance the author had vaguely indicated such directions he completed them as he thought fit. In the second quarto of *Hamlet* (V.ii.236) one finds in unaccustomed confusion "A table prepared, Trumpets, Drums, and Officers with cushions, King, Queen and all the state, foils, daggers, and Laertes." This direction is attributable neither to the author nor to the prompter; it is the result of an unpremeditated collaboration between the two. If we had the manuscript we should no doubt see that Shakespeare had simply written "Enter King, Queen and all the state," and that the prompter had added the details of the Court entrance, with the honorary flourishes and the officers bearing the cushions for the king and queen, and that in the remaining blank spaces he had inserted the foils and daggers together with Laertes to remind himself that a duel was to take place in the scene.

This example demonstrates that in a Shakespearean play it is not always easy to determine where the author's work stopped and the prompter's began. Shakespeare was an actor and as such he was familiar with theatrical parlance. Probably he encroached sometimes upon the prompter's duty, and one may wonder if it is really possible to distinguish his original manuscript from that revised by the prompter. Fortunately, as will be seen in the following pages he concerned himself only occasionally with details of staging. He was as irregular in his stage directions as in forming the letters of his signatures. When he began a scene and as long as his mind worked dispassionately he was relatively careful, and it is then that he gave the descriptions necessary for understanding the action of the play. But the moment he became caught up in the acts and words of his imaginary world he forgot everything else. A character might enter—Shakespeare knew it and that was enough; but he omitted to warn us of the entrance and we should never perceive it but for the dialogue. As for the exits, he often forgot to mention them. The prompter could not indulge in such carelessness: his directions had to be precise, minute, and above all complete. And therein lies the difference that will enable us to discern with some certainty whether we are dealing with the author's manuscript or a prompt copy. If the directions are simple, at times vague or incomplete, then we can say the manuscript is original; if no stage direction is missing, if the entries and exits are all noted, if there is an abundance of sound effects and properties, we can be sure that the printed manuscript reproduces the prompt-book of the company.[1]

Sometimes the nature of Shakespeare's handwriting will be manifested in the printed text by the difficulty the compositor (or the copyist) had in deciphering certain passages, and the result will be a number of misreadings. But one must not consider as misreadings all the words which in a quarto differ from those given in the folio. Some may be variants, some errors which can be explained by a similarity of spelling, and these may be the result of the compositor's carelessness. I shall mark as mistakes due to the bad handwriting of the manuscript only those words which make no sense in their context. It sometimes happens that the composi-

1. Or transcripts of those manuscripts. But since a transcript is by definition a faithful reproduction it is of no importance whether the compositor had before him the original or a copy—unless it is possible to believe that the manuscript is in Shakespeare's hand; in that case I shall mention it.

tor, giving up, reproduced only the letters he could recognize, without minding whether the words thus obtained ever existed. In cases like these we can be sure that the passage was indecipherable.

In some quartos one finds that the name of an actor has been substituted for the name of the character represented; for example, William Kemp, the well-known comic actor, appears instead of Peter in a scene in *Romeo and Juliet*. Such substitutions have often been attributed to the prompter, but if the substitution has been made in all the speech headings of the scene it is more natural to suppose that it was Shakespeare who unconsciously wrote the name of the actor for whom he intended the part.[2] For the purpose of the present work it is not necessary to solve this little problem; but the presence of an actor's name in a manuscript is pretty certain proof that the manuscript came from the library of a dramatic company.

$$\int \quad \int \quad \int$$

WHEN IT HAS BEEN determined what kind of manuscript served as copy for printing a given play, there still remains to be seen whether the text retains signs of having been modified. On this point J. D. Wilson has proposed a method of investigation which I adopt in part, limiting the applicability of some of the tests while adding several of my own.

1. The most evident sign that a play has been touched up is the presence of a double redaction of the same idea. A typical example is to be found in *Love's Labor's Lost* IV.iii. In Biron's speech verses 296–301 and 316–21, 302–4 and 350–3 express the same thought in slightly different forms; one of these forms must have been abandoned by Shakespeare and should have been replaced by the other. The author probably forgot to strike out what he was discarding, and the compositor docilely reproduced the two passages which have thus remained as a testimony of cor-

2. Cf. Allison Gaw, "Actors' Names in Basic Shakespearean Texts," *Publ. Mod. Lang. Assoc.* 1925, *40*, 530; and R. B. McKerrow, "The Elizabethan Printer and Dramatic MSS," *The Library*, 1931, *12*, 274.

rection. Were the canceled passages false starts made at the time the scene was originally written, or were the corrections made in rewriting the play? This is a point that study of the versification should be able to clarify.

2. Very often in Shakespearean texts, especially in the quartos, verses are badly divided or not divided at all but printed as prose. A compositor would not have used this arrangement unless he had found it in the manuscript he was setting in type. On the other hand, it is difficult to imagine a poet whimsical enough to spoil his text with such anomalies, which extend sometimes to a whole speech, when in the greater part of the play he conforms to usage. Such an arrangement must have been forced upon him through lack of space. The playbooks of that period were generally composed of folio sheets, about twelve inches long by eight inches wide. It was the custom to divide the sheets lengthwise into four equal parts, the two center parts of about two inches each were reserved for the text, leaving two margins of two inches each. In the left margin were written the names of the characters and some of the annotations of the prompter. An author revising a manuscript had no free space except between the lines and in the right margin, where two inches were not always sufficient for decasyllabic verses. Hence the necessity of splitting up the verses and writing them on two lines or even, to save space, one after the other with no interval between them. Verses incorrectly divided or printed as prose are a sure sign of marginal corrections or additions.[3]

3. Prose passages are sometimes printed in lines of unequal length, giving the impression that they are verse. Here two distinctions should be made:

a. There are lines which, while being unequal and able to pass as verse, do not differ greatly in length. The reason for this is that the author in writing his prose did not utilize all the space at his disposal in the center part of his manuscript, and the compositor,

3. In the folio badly divided verse is not always an indication of a correction: the text was printed in two relatively narrow columns wide enough for a verse of normal length; but when a verse line was particularly long or a speech heading preceded a line, the compositor was obliged to divide the line as best he could. Naturally I shall not take such cases into account.

mistaking those lines for verse, reproduced them just as he found them in the manuscript. Such anomalies of course have no significance.

b. There are prose lines of very unequal length, as in the following passage from the quarto of *Henry V:*

> Now, Kate, you haue a blunt woer here
> Left with you.
> If I could win thee at leapfrog,
> Or with a wawting with my armour on my backe,
> Into a saddle,
> Without brag be it spoken,
> Ide make compare with any.

Here the author wrote his revisions in the uneven space on the right of the page, where a scene originally in verse had been deleted. The short prose lines thus faced the longer verse, the long lines faced the shorter verse; the fourth line probably coincided with the space between two lines and could for that reason be inscribed in its entirety. Prose thus printed is also a sign of marginal correction.

4. Incomplete verse lines can indicate modifications of another sort. Certain critics explain the presence of such lines as the author's device to allow the actor time to make a gesture, as though the actors could not pause in the midst of a verse if they thought fit. Or again, it is said, Shakespeare through the use of those short lines achieves rhythmic effects agreeable to the ear. It may be that my sense of poetry is blunted, for I admit that I have never perceived those admirable effects. The real explanation is, I believe, more prosaic. A truncated verse can be the result of a cut. Since such abridgments often took place during a rehearsal, these cuts are of no interest for the composition of the play. But a short line may also be the sign of an addition. If the interpolated passage does not fit exactly in the passage being revised there will be, either at the beginning or at the end of the addition, an incomplete verse revealing the alteration. In such cases the interpolation is recognizable by a certain awkwardness in the development of the idea or even by a solution of continuity.

This test, it must be admitted, is difficult to apply, for as his versification became more supple Shakespeare more easily ad-

mitted verses lacking the regular number of feet, especially at
the end of a scene or of a speech.

5. Prose passages are frequently found in a scene in verse. This
is fairly surprising, for it was the practice in the pre-Shakespearean
drama to employ prose only in comic scenes. And in the beginning Shakespeare observed that custom. What, then, can be the
reason for this mingling of verse and prose? Here again, critics
who are persuaded that Shakespeare had only intentions inspired
by his genius have a ready explanation for this peculiarity: the
author, with infallible art and a fastidious sense of style, used such
variations to create heights and depths in the dramatic or lyric
tension. This explanation makes no sense to one who has studied
the distribution of prose in all of Shakespeare's plays. The bits of
prose interlaced in a passage in verse rarely change the tone. When
Desdemona asks Iago what he thinks of womankind why does she
speak in verse, as throughout the play; and why does she use prose
in only three speeches (II.i.139–42,144–8,162–5) in the same
conversation with Iago? Is her indignant reaction to Iago's skepticism of such a vulgar nature that she feels obliged to employ prose?
Almost a third of *Hamlet* is written in prose; is this study of a
tortured soul in large part comic? One of the most pathetic passages of Act III.sc.i is in prose. After the soliloquy on suicide the
scene continues with Ophelia speaking first in verse, then suddenly in prose which provokes deep emotional responses in Hamlet. It is evident that originally the scene was entirely in verse
(as soon as Hamlet has left the stage Ophelia, who had replied
in prose, naturally returns to verse to express her sorrow) and
that Shakespeare wanted to enlarge it and wrote the addition in
prose. He had arrived at a moment in his career when he tended
more and more toward a rhythmic form, freed of the strict regularity of verse and approaching the liberty of prose. The two
means of expression had become for him almost equivalent, and
no doubt only the time at his disposal determined his use of one
or the other.[4] Henslowe's *Diary* has shown that authors sometimes

4. It should be added that this mingling of verse and prose passes unnoticed when
the play is performed. An actor does not speak a passage in verse as the poet does;
instead of carefully bringing out the undulations of the rhythm in a sort of monotonous chant, he adapts the lines to the movement of his action or his gestures, breaking

had but a few days to revise a play. When time pressed, Shakespeare adopted the form which came most easily to his pen. It will be seen in the course of the present study that what I have just given in the form of a hypothesis is almost always supported by confirmations, which prove that there has been revision whenever prose appears where it is not expected.

6. Many of Shakespeare's plays contain passages where rhymed verse is mingled with blank verse. It is customary to suppose that a play presenting such a mixture belongs to the early period of his career. But the matter is not so simple as that. Except for *Love's Labor's Lost* and *A Midsummer Night's Dream*, where the quantity of rhymed verse is considerable, rhymed verses are found only in fragments, of varying importance and often of inferior quality. Once more the question of authenticity has to be raised, and if the rhymed verse is not Shakespeare's its combination with the blank verse will indicate that the play has been revised.

But this will not always be the case. Among non-Shakespearean rhymed verses will be found rhymed verses which are Shakespeare's, interpolations which he added while revising the play. Furthermore Shakespeare at first followed the fashion of his age and ended scenes with a couplet; in the Elizabethan drama, which did not use division into acts, this was a means of warning the audience of a coming change of scene. Often, at least in the earlier plays, Shakespeare also ended a long speech in the same manner. Lastly it must be admitted that two blank verses following one another might accidentally have the same final sound. If one adds up end-of-scene couplets, couplets at the end of speeches, and accidental rhymes, it is possible sometimes to reach significant totals. It would be a grave error to consider these examples fragments of an earlier play. Only rhymed passages of a certain length and of a character definitely pre-Shakespearean should be viewed in this way.

7. Occasionally a character is mentioned in a stage direction but nothing in the scene shows that he is present. J. D. Wilson sees in this a proof that the character must have disappeared in the course of a revision. This is sometimes true but not always. In each

---

them with pauses or emitting several verses all in one breath. Verse in the mouth of a good actor is scarcely distinguishable from poetical prose.

play there are characters known as supers whose role consists precisely in being present without speaking. When a king is on the stage courtiers can only keep silent while he talks or acts. Or again, in scenes where two principal characters hold our attention it is natural that the other characters should listen. But there are some cases where it must be admitted that when a character is announced but never appears he must have been eliminated, either to cut down the number of actors or to make room for other characters introduced as an afterthought. In *Much Ado* Leonato is twice accompanied by his wife Innogen, who not only never says a word in the scenes where she is reputed to be on stage but who never appears in the place where she ought especially to be —at the marriage of her daughter. Again, an important character becomes mute at a moment when his intervention is expected. Isabella, in *Measure for Measure*, finding herself face to face with her brother whom she believes to have been executed, does not say a word when she should at least express some surprise. Apparently this final scene was shortened, and Isabella bore the brunt of the cutting.

8. Variations in the names of the characters are frequent. In either the stage directions or the speech headings one and the same character is introduced sometimes by his patronymic, sometimes by a generic name: Capulet or Father, Dogberry or Constable, Holophernes or Pedant, etc. To suggest, as has been done, that Shakespeare forgot the name he had given to the character does not do justice to his intelligence. And could he not have turned back a few pages to refresh his memory? There must have been a more natural cause for this anomaly. And the history of the English drama furnishes us with it. Such duplication is the sign that two kinds of play have been combined: the one going back to a period still close to the moralities, when the characters were exclusively types and designated by their quality or profession—pardoner, pedlar, braggart—the other belonging to Shakespeare's period, when the characters were individualized and had a personal name. The presence of generic names suggests that the Shakespearean play was based upon an earlier one and that Shakespeare, following the old text, sometimes let the original appellations stand in some of the passages which he kept. But there never

was any method or regularity in those borrowings, and to consider that all the passages where generic names are found are pre-Shakespearean would be to engage in extravagant deductions. All they mean is that Shakespeare must have written his own text on the manuscript of the old play he was revising and did not always take the trouble to unify the nomenclature. This test can serve only to indicate that the scenes exhibiting those anomalies had at one time been of pre-Shakespearean conception.

9. Finally, contradictions either in the plot or in the conception of the characters are not rare. An event announced to take place in the morning of the next day later turns out to have taken place in the afternoon; a character tells us that he has made a decision, but the expected action never follows; a character appears in a scene though we know from what precedes that he is supposed to be occupied elsewhere; and so on. These contradictions are an indication of hasty revisions.

ʃ ʃ ʃ

IF THE APPLICATION of these tests has convinced us that a play has been revised it will be necessary to seek the reasons for the revision, its extent, and the period in which it took place: in a study such as this these are essential questions. And here it will be necessary to abandon the bibliographical method, which has only helped us explore the approaches to the work. To penetrate the mystery of its birth and development we must undertake an inquiry of another type; and it is in a critical study of the text, according to the old literary method, that we must seek the answers to the questions we shall raise.

First of all we shall have to decide which kind of revision has been effected, because two types will be found which require different applications of the method.

Shakespeare is reworking a play by one of his predecessors. No one denies today that Shakespeare utilized as sources old plays which he recast. Fragments of the source plays should remain embedded in the new matter, and thus the eternal question of authenticity will reappear. But how are we to discover those fragments? The example of Fleay and Robertson should serve as a lesson: we are not going to trust our impressions alone. No doubt a man who has studied a piece of work with meticulous application and love develops a sense which enables him instinctively to distinguish the style of his author from the style of others; this intuitive guide must not be ignored completely. But we ought to consider it solely as an indication. The most subtle flair offers no guarantee, for it can—and often does—find itself at fault. It is not sufficient to repeat, as is frequently done, "This I feel is Shakespeare's." To reach certainty it is indispensable to have as precise a definition as possible of Shakespeare's style, to which one can refer wherever there is a doubt as to the authenticity of a passage.

Studies of Shakespeare are not lacking, but they all are useless for my purpose. They are based on the plays as a whole, and since there is a presumption that certain parts of those plays may not be Shakespeare's it follows that the definitions thus obtained are valueless because they may have taken foreign elements into account. Only the poems, *Venus and Adonis, The Rape of Lucrece,* and the *Sonnets,* are indisputably Shakespeare's,[5] and these are the only writings—nondramatic, it is true, but where the author's dramatic sense shows forth at each instant—which will enable us to define what properly characterizes Shakespeare's poetic style.

Venus and Adonis was registered with the Stationers' Company on April 18, 1593, and *The Rape of Lucrece* on May 9, 1594. These two poems therefore belong to the earlier period of Shakespeare's career. The *Sonnets* were not published until 1609; they represent, in part at least (see below pp. 70–3), a period considerably later. With these three works we shall have sufficient material, covering the principal part of Shakespeare's development, for analysis.

I shall begin therefore with studying *Venus and Adonis* and *Lucrece* as points of departure in this development. When these poems were written, probably between the time of Shakespeare's arrival in London (c. 1585) and 1593, when they were certainly finished, the Renaissance was beginning to show the efforts made to endow England with a poetic language capable of competing in beauty with those of Italy and France. After a preliminary

5. Even the authenticity of the *Sonnets* has been doubted, but for this there is really no valid reason.

attempt to naturalize the sonnet in 1557 with the publication of
the poems of Sir Thomas Wyat and Henry Howard, earl of Surrey,
poetry did not receive a definitive renovation until 1590 when
there appeared the first three books of Edmund Spenser's *Faerie
Queene* and *The First Sett of Italian Madrigals* by Thomas Watson; to which might also be added, although it is in prose, another
memorable book, Sir Philip Sidney's *The Countess of Pembroke's
Arcadia,* for it contains a considerable number of poems interspersed throughout the narration. From that moment on there was
a sudden blossoming after a long winter. In rapid succession there
followed in 1591 Spenser's *Complaints,* Sidney's *Astrophel and
Stella,* Nicholas Breton's *Bowre of Delights;* in 1592 Samuel
Daniel's *Delia with the Complaint of Rosamond,* Henry Constable's *Diana;* in 1593 Michael Drayton's *Idea,* Giles Fletcher
the Elder's *Licia or Poems of Love,* Thomas Watson's *The Tears
of Fancy,* Thomas Lodge's *Phillis,* Barnabe Barne's *Parthenophil
and Parthenophe;* in 1594 Samuel Daniel's *Delia and Rosamond,*
Michael Drayton's *Idea's Mirrour,* William Percy's *Sonnets to the
Fairest Coelia,* and a second edition of Henry Constable's *Diana.*
This was a beautiful flowering, but too often spoilt by laborious
imitations of foreign literatures. The classics, the Italians, the
French were models incessantly copied not only for ideas but also
for style. It would have been surprising if the young provincial,
arriving from his small town of Stratford, had not been dazzled by
the luxuriance of this new poetry and, above all, by the excesses
which were its least precious part. He who was to take first place
among the poets of his own country became the imitator of the
imitators, and what strikes one in the style of *Venus and Adonis*
and of *Lucrece* is the inordinate number of all the mannerisms
which were then considered the quintessence of the ornate poetic
form.

From those who tried to give distinction to their style by applying the figures of speech recommended by the ancient rhetoricians,
Shakespeare borrowed the practice of dividing a thought into two
symmetrical and balanced parts of more or less equal length, often
constructing each part according to the same grammatical model,
a scheme dear to the Greek orator Isocrates.

> Wreck to the seaman, tempest to the field,
> Sorrow to the shepherds, woe unto the birds
> (Venus and Adonis, 454–5)
> This blur to youth, this sorrow to the sage,
> This dying vertue, this surviving shame (Lucrece, 222–3) [6]

The similarity of the form is sometimes accentuated by the repetition of a word or the same grammatical construction at the beginning of the parallel clauses, according to the figure called *anaphora:*

> Still he is sullen, still he lours and frets (Venus and Adonis, 75)

> Or like a fairy trip upon the green,
> Or like a nymph with long dishevelled hair (ibid., 146–7)

> What could he see but mightily he noted?
> What did he note but strongly he desired?
> What he beheld on that he firmly doted (Lucrece, 414–16) [7]

Shakespeare has a marked preference for the association of two words—nouns, adjectives, or verbs—expressing two aspects of the same idea and connected by a conjunction such as and, or, nor:

> More white and red than doves or roses are (Venus and Adonis, 10)

> Who blushed and pouted in a dull disdain (ibid., 33)

> pure thoughts are dead and still
> While lust and murder wake to stain and kill (Lucrece, 167–8)

This is a form of the figure called *hendiadys.* With Shakespeare its use was in part due to that overflowing facility which Ben Jonson censured in him. It is, in fact, dangerous to use for it leads easily to tautology, and Shakespeare did not always avoid this fault. We find in *Venus and Adonis* "to fan and blow" (52), "nurse and feeder" (446), "reek and smoke" (555), "shake and shudder"

6. Cf. *Venus and Adonis:* 22, 51, 58, 61, 76, 101, 104, 107, 219, 221, 232, 236, 238, 247, 254, 276, 278, 286, 311, 332, 456, 496, 557, 629, 651, 655, 659, 666, 690, 713, 738, 752, 754, 808, 868, 882, 934, 936, 1059, 1079. *Lucrece:* 103, 110, 172, 197, 244, 247, 277, 279, 287, 537, 659, 695, 793, 940, 942, 966, 1005, 1145, 1168, 1239, 1381, 1497, 1792.

7. Cf. *Venus and Adonis:* 140–3, 373–4, 459–60, 651–2, 655–7, 675–6, 705–6, 765–6, 803–4, 837–8, 872–3, 899, 1061–2, 1123–5, 1153–5. *Lucrece:* 290–1, 380–1, 491–3, 521–2, 535–6, 569–72, 660–2, 689–91, 841–2, 849–52, 883–8, 890–4, 918–21, 940–3, 946–51, 953–8, 981–5, 1025–6, 1105–6, 1170–2, 1357–8, 1466–9, 1485–7, 1835–9.

(880); and in *Lucrece* "dread and fear" (117), "spots and stains" (196), "repose and rest" (757), "mute and dumb" (1123), "quake and tremble" (1393).[8]

In many of the preceding examples the parallelism is accompanied by an opposition in the thought. But Shakespeare also cultivated antithesis for itself, the two opposing parts not necessarily being balanced or of equal length:

> Is love so light, sweet boy, and may it be
> That thou shouldst think it heavy unto thee
> *(Venus and Adonis,* 155–6)
>
> Showing love's triumph in the map of death,
> And death's dim look in life's mortality *(Lucrece,* 402–3) [9]

From the admirers of Italian poetry Shakespeare borrowed that kind of *concetto* which consists in repeating a word in a phrase, in either its proper form or under a grammatically derived form, for the simple pleasure the ear takes in the repetition of the same sound (jingle):

> Hunting he loved, but love he laughed to scorn
> *(Venus and Adonis,* 4)
>
> Strong-tempered steel his stronger strength obeyed *(ibid.,* 111)
>
> But king nor peer to such a peerless dame *(Lucrece,* 21)
>
> Beauty itself doth of itself persuade *(ibid.,* 29) [1]

8. Cf. *Venus and Adonis:* 21, 26, 35, 52, 98, 105, 106, 132, 142, 198, 211, 279, 304, 305, 316, 326, 415, 419, 446, 493, 555, 573, 654, 682, 704, 725, 858, 860, 902, 920, 935, 987, 988, 1023, 1081, 1082, 1186. *Lucrece:* 23, 27, 117, 136, 171, 196, 230, 232, 236, 238, 242, 250, 267, 275, 310, 441, 448, 456, 466, 489, 497, 674, 738, 757, 765, 766, 795, 838, 991, 995, 1094, 1120, 1123, 1139, 1199, 1387, 1389, 1393, 1452, 1543, 1569, 1592, 1639, 1656, 1719, 1720, 1741, 1760, 1809.

9. Cf. *Venus and Adonis:* 36, 42, 60, 94, 122, 150–8, 172–3, 214, 246, 292, 338, 364, 401, 402, 413, 414, 481, 544, 545, 594, 600, 658, 671, 802–4, 805, 842, 845–6, 908, 961, 966, 986, 988, 989–90, 1017, 1080, 1138, 1139, 1143, 1145, 1146, 1150, 1150–8. *Lucrece:* 48, 91, 137, 213, 223, 252, 284, 406, 468, 572, 595, 659, 661, 662, 663, 668, 691, 747, 831, 865, 867, 889, 890–3, 923, 924, 959, 995, 1032, 1045, 1051–2, 1055, 1071, 1078, 1092, 1124, 1154–5, 1187, 1188, 1190, 1412, 1434–5, 1483, 1489, 1498, 1530, 1544–6, 1556–7,1571, 1617, 1646, 1647, 1770–1, 1801.

1. Cf. *Venus and Adonis:* 77–8, 93, 159, 161, 168, 202, 215, 226, 270, 300, 357–8, 370, 375–8, 379, 412, 433, 464, 468, 474, 497–8, 511, 520, 525, 610, 636, 763, 768, 789, 805, 832, 864, 907, 911, 912, 944, 952, 962, 962–4, 995, 1007–8, 1019–20, 1129, 1164. *Lucrece:* 29, 43–4, 59, 96, 131, 133, 144, 146, 147, 157, 160, 181–2, 190–1, 194, 201, 260, 308, 316, 346, 401, 414–15, 417, 418, 472, 585, 587–8, 610–11,

These conceits, of an almost mechanical nature, have little to do with imagination; they affect above all the structure of the sentence; they are in truth plays on words, occasionally degenerating into puns. Shakespeare has other more refined conceits, concetti proper in the Italian manner, which require a real concentration of thought. The fancifulness at the source of this other kind of figure is manifested by a laborious development of farfetched comparisons, ingenious sometimes to the point of extravagance, original by their very strangeness. Venus, feeling the hot breath of Adonis on her face,

> feedeth on the steame, as on a prey,
> And calls it heavenly moisture, aire of grace,
> Wishing her cheeks were gardens full of flowers
> So they were dued with such distilling showers
>
> *(Venus and Adonis, 63–6)*

In such a passage, if we forget the affectation of the thought, poetry receives its due by the imaginative effort which transposes a real experience into an unusual image. But other conceits keep no possible contact with reality. Adopting a stylistic device which Sir Philip Sidney employed to excess, Shakespeare lent human sentiments to objects the least susceptible of being moved; for example, the sight of Lucrece, asleep with her hand under her cheek, suggests the wrath of the pillow at being deprived of its pleasure:

> Her lily hand her rosy cheek lies under
> Cozening the pillow of a lawful kiss;
> Who therefore angry, seems to part in sunder,
> Swelling on either side to want its bliss *(Lucrece, 386–9)* [2]

French poetry also exercised its attraction and influence as shown by the numerous compound words which Shakespeare

---

657–8, 659, 660, 664–5, 689, 700, 761, 795, 927, 935, 943, 953–4, 963, 964, 969, 970, 973, 974, 975, 976, 977, 978, 979, 980, 983, 987, 990, 998, 999, 1001, 1004, 1006, 1033, 1044, 1083, 1115, 1117, 1131, 1148, 1186, 1191, 1196, 1203–4, 1205–6, 1208, 1209, 1210, 1211, 1233, 1256, 1303–4, 1311, 1316, 1322, 1327–8, 1336, 1337, 1352, 1354-5, 1419, 1480, 1482, 1531, 1537–9, 1566, 1570, 1602, 1649, 1666, 1673, 1676, 1715, 1754, 1821, 1822, 1827.

2. Cf. *Venus and Adonis*: 241–6, 247–8, 345–8, 355–60, 485–92, 629–30, 721–3, 728–32, 979–84, 1031–2, 1037–44, 1049–56. *Lucrece*: 52–70, 397–401, 426–41, 442–8, 460–2, 1298–9, 1436–42, 1735–41, 1744–50.

liberally distributed throughout the two poems under discussion. Du Bellay in his *Défense et illustration de la langue française* had recommended, in imitation of the Greeks and Latins, the creation of words by combining two terms: "Je veux bien avertir celui qui entreprendra un grand oeuvre," he said, "qu'il ne craigne point d'inventer, adapter et composer à l'imitation des Grecs quelques mots françoys, comme Cicéron se vante d'avoir fait en sa langue" (Bk. II, chap. 6). And Ronsard in 1565 in his *Abrégé de l'art poétique* had gone further: "Tu composeras hardiment des mots à l'imitation des Grecs et des Latins, pourvu qu'ils soient gracieux et plaisants à l'oreille" (*Oeuvres*, ed. Elzevir, 7, 335). These precepts had reached England with the translations of Du Bartas which appeared between 1584 and 1593, and the creation of words in this manner then became so widespread that Sidney was able to say in his *Defense of Poesie* (1595) that English "is particularly happy in compositions of two or three wordes togither, neare the Greeke, farre beyond the Latine, which is one of the greatest bewties in a language" (*Works*, Cambridge English Classics, 3, 44).[3]

Venus and Adonis: angry-chafing (662), bottom-grass (236), butcher-sire (766), cold-pale (892), deep-sore (432), deep-sweet (432), foolish-witty (838), foul-cankering (767), green-dropping (1176), grim-grinning (933), hard-believing (985), marrow-eating (741), raging-mad (1151), red-rose (110), ripe-red (1103), scent-snuffing (692), sick-thoughted (5), silly-mild (1151), true-sweet (1080), wax-red (516), wrinkled-old (133).

Lucrece: all-hiding (801), all-too-timeless (44), birth-hour (537), burden-wise (1133), cave-keeping (1250), close-tongued (770), cloud-eclipsed (1224), cloud-kissing (1370), comfort-killing (764), crest-wounding (828), curious-good (1300), curse-blessed (866), dead-killing (540), death-worthy (635), deep-drenched (1100), ever-during (224), false-creeping (1517), feast-finding (817), feeling-painful (1679), fiery-pointed (372), foul-defiled (1029), foul-reeking (799), heaved-up (111, 638), heavy-hanging (1493), hell-born (1519), hollow-swelling (1122), late-sacked (1740), long-experienced (1820), long-hid (1816), long-living (622), low-declined (1705), lust-breathed (3), night-

3. Cf. A. H. Upham, *The French Influence in English Literature*, 1908, p. 67.

wandering (307), night-working (554), pity-pleading (561), poor-rich (140), rich-built (1524), rough-grown (1249), sad-beholding (1590), salt-waved (1231), silver-shining (786), skill-contending (1018), sober-sad (1542), soft-slow (1220), still-slaughtered (188), strong-besieged (1429), subtle-shining (101), surfeit-taking (698), tear-distained (1586), weake-built (130), weak-made (1260), wracke-threatening (590).

To the French influence must also be attributed a certain taste for words which, though they were in use in the Middle English period, had preserved something of their French consonance:

Venus and Adonis: aidance (330), closure (782), defeature (736), embracement (312, 790), forage (554), moisture (64, 542), semblance (785), verdure (507).

Lucrece: champaign (1247), conduit (1234), continuance (1097), mot (830),[4] parling (100), pillage (428), rigol (1745), semblance (1113, 1246, 1453, 1759).

Because they are to be found in all the poets of the age, these mannerisms cannot be considered a distinctive mark of Shakespeare's style. Were it not that they are found in excessive numbers they would hardly deserve to be mentioned. Besides, they were only a temporary characteristic. Shakespeare was not slow in discovering their superficiality; they soon diminished in quantity and some of them disappeared altogether. In the earlier plays, however, they serve as a test in all questions of authenticity, for the dramatists prior to Shakespeare rarely used that kind of ornamentation.[5] They wrote their plays in verse but were not poets. They tried to reproduce actual speech as closely as possible, no doubt finding in this observance of everyday language the realism needed by the drama. Shakespeare, on the contrary, introduced a lyrical tone into his plays from the first. His mannerisms are a part of that initiative, so that for the earlier plays, where they appear in especially great numbers, they are practically a proof that the passage is Shakespeare's.

But there are other more lasting and above all more personal characteristics upon which a definition of Shakespeare's style can

4. Some commentators think that *mot* is an abbreviation of the Italian *motto*.

5. Marlowe has a few antitheses and even tautological phrases, but they occur rarely and are in no way comparable with Shakespeare's profusion.

be founded. Writers of genius possess from birth qualities which are their own, which can be perfected but not acquired; and every time Shakespeare forgets to imitate and is himself, his liberated originality expresses itself fully, with an innate sense of the richest resources of the English language.

The essential trait of Shakespeare's originality is the extraordinary activity of his imagination. He can hardly conceive an idea without immediately perceiving its similarity to some manifestation of the exterior world and blending the two in a natural and indissoluble association. He possesses an inexhaustible store of such analogies, with which he enriches the most commonplace facts. When he wrote the poems Shakespeare had barely reached thirty, but one might think he had already fathomed all human experience. The images of his poetry derive not only from natural phenomena, the source common to all poets, but also—and it is here that the dramatic author discloses his full power—from everything that concerns man, from the little problems or accidents of social and material life to the adventures of the spirit, its intellectual discoveries and its aspirations.

Even more than for its universal richness Shakespeare's imagination is remarkable for the truth and vividness of the associations it forms. One feels that every detail is the result of a personal observation recorded with the distinctness of a photographic plate, a distinctness, however, that does not prevent a suggestiveness which extends the picture beyond its limits and opens the door to fancy and to imagination. See, for example, this little description of nightfall in *Venus and Adonis:*

> Look, the world's comforter, with weary gait,
> His day's hot task hath ended in the west;
> The owl, night's herald, shrieks, " 'Tis very late;"
> The sheep are gone to fold, birds to their nest,
> And coal-black clouds that shadow heaven's light
> Do summon us to part and bid good night (529–34)

Such precise notations as the sun sinking beyond the horizon, the lugubrious cry of the owl, the bird of the shadows, or the rolling clouds indicate that Shakespeare viewed the enveloping night with the eyes of a painter; but he also caught the mood which accompanies nightfall with the sudden absence of life and the ensuing silence, and this silence in its turn took on a psychological value because for Adonis who had long resisted the vain solicitations of the goddess it brought the moment of liberating separation.

In such passages Shakespeare is inimitable and it is by these above all that he can be distinguished from the dramatists preceding him. They too from time to time used some similes, but they were either banal or bookish. Classical mythology and ancient history were their preferred sources, and when they drew comparisons from nature they turned to the bestiaries or herbals of the Middle Ages—taking from them those fabulous qualities of animals and plants that euphuism was popularizing—or else to the treatises on rural economy which multiplied through the whole sixteenth century, such as *The Booke of Husbandrie* by John Fitzherbert (?) or *Foures Bookes of Husbandrie* by Thomas Tusser, which had numerous reprints. Moreover these comparisons were chosen by the pre-Shakespeareans for their demonstrative value. "A similitude," writes Arthur Wilson in his *Arte of Rhetorike* (1560), "is a likenesse when two thinges or moe then two are so compared and resembled together, that they both in some propertie seeme like. Oftentimes brute Beastes and things that have no life, minister great matter in this behalfe. Therefore, those that delite to proue thinges by similitudes must learne to know the nature of diuers beastes, of mettalles, of stones, and al such as haue any vertue in them and can be applied to man's life." Comparisons of that type are sometimes to be met with in Shakespeare who, like everybody else, has spoken of the cruelty of the tiger (*Venus and Adonis,* 1096; *Lucrece,* 955, 980) and the fox's subtlety (*Venus and Adonis,* 675); one can even cite an example of the use of the "cockatrice' dead-killing eye" (*Lucrece,* 540). But such comparisons are exceptions with him, legacies from an older age: Shakespeare's images are unique and cannot be confused with those of his predecessors or even with those of his contemporaries.

In addition to the style there is in a poet another element which is even more personal—his versification. Style can be imitated, but not the manner in which the composition of verse is conceived. Each poet has his own way of hearing inwardly the verses he feels urged to write, and that way is recorded in the verses when they have been given utterance. Shakespeare adopted the most common type of verse in the English language, the iambic pentameter or five-stress iambic meter, in both the rhymed and unrhymed forms. Normally this verse is composed of five dissyllabic feet, the first syllable being unaccented, the second accented. Verse so constructed is not lacking in possibilities of variation, for there are several kinds of accents—grammatical, secondary, rhythmical, emphatic—and each kind has a different degree of intensity. But in addition to these natural differences a poet has at his disposal other means of introducing variety into his rhythm. The first of these consists in substituting feet of another kind for the normal iambic foot. In Shakespeare's day only two kinds of feet were used for such substitutions: [6] the trochee, composed of an accented syllable followed by an unaccented one, and the spondee, composed of two accented syllables. These modifications of the iambic rhythm produce different effects: the trochee, being the reverse of the iamb, dislocates the normal rhythm so that the ear, expecting the ascending movement of the iamb, is surprised; the spondee,[7] on the other hand, with its two equally accented syllables, simply interrupts the ascending movement and holds it in suspense. If the poet has a preference for one or the other of these substitutions the rhythm will be differently modified. A great number of trochees render the rhythm more agile and on the whole more lively, or even jerky as of a man who staggers; a great number of spondees make the rhythm sonorous, weighty, at times pompous.

Another way to avoid monotony consists in giving flexibility to

6. Toward the end of the sixteenth century English prosody did not admit trisyllabic feet in iambic pentameter. The critics who discover trisyllabic feet in Shakespeare ignore the fact that the pronunciation of the period differed from modern pronunciation. Syncopation was more frequent, and many words which today are dissyllabic or trisyllabic had only one or two syllables: for example, spirit was often pronounced "sprit," cardinal was pronounced "cardnal" (a fact, by the by, which many times enabled the enemies of Roman Catholicism to make a pun with the word "carnal." It cannot be repeated too often that the pentameter was decasyllabic.

7. I shall use these two names of feet; though being borrowed from the classical terminology, they represent in English meters phenomena different from those described in classical prosody. They have been used for such a long time that the English meaning is well understood, and they are, besides, brief and convenient.

the rhythmical construction. A verse is a unit in itself, and a natural tendency is to mark that unity by making the end of a line coincide with the end of a phrase or idea. But a poem composed only of verse units would be as tedious as one composed entirely of regular iambic feet. A poet with a fine ear will attempt to break up that coincidence by making the phrasing of an idea run on from one line to the next, a process generally called enjambment or overflow. Or if the form of the iambic pentameter is unrhymed, an unaccented syllable added to the last foot will prolong the meter sufficiently to destroy the finite character of the line. Lastly, more flexibility can be obtained by the distribution of pauses within the verse. Those pauses can correspond with the grammatical division of the phrasing and in that case are indicated by the punctuation, or they can be imposed by the necessity of drawing in the breath necessary to pronounce a phonetic group of sounds; phonetic pauses, which often are not distinguished typographically, are as real as grammatical ones.

Such are the elements which enter into the structure of verse,[8] and their combination will determine the definition of Shakespeare's versification, a definition which will be all the more precise as it can be formulated in percentages, since the relative importance of the elements depends upon the number of times that each of them is used.

I have analyzed one by one the verses of Venus and Adonis and of Lucrece. In this analysis, for the sake of clarity, I have reduced the number of accents to two: strong (marked 2) and weak (marked 1). I have considered as strongly accented those syllables which normally bear a grammatical or an emphatic accent, as weakly accented those syllables which have a secondary accent or which, being naturally unstressed, have assumed a rhythmical accent because they occur in a place where the metrical scheme requires one. For in practice there is not much difference between a grammatical and an emphatic accent, or between a secondary

---

8. I have omitted two elements—the length and the pitch of the syllables—upon which some metricians insist excessively, though not without some good reasons. They belong more to the style than to the versification; they are elements which contribute to the music of the verse and to the harmony, of which I shall speak later; they do not affect the rhythm proper.

and a rhythmical one. To give an instance, this is how I scan the
following line:

$$\overset{2}{\text{Coura}} \mid \overset{1}{\text{geously}} \mid \overset{2}{\text{to pluck}} \mid \overset{1}{\text{him from}} \mid \overset{2}{\text{his horse}} \mid$$

which gives a sufficiently correct idea of the effect produced by the
rhythmical variations.

The two narrative poems yield the following percentages:

	Venus and Adonis 1194 *lines* = 5970 *feet*	*Lucrece* 1855 *lines* = 9275 *feet*
Weakly accented feet	1429 or 23.9%	2134 or 23.0%
Trochees	239 or 4.1%	278 or 2.9%
Spondees	249 or 4.1%	369 or 3.9%
Internal pauses	731 lines or 61.8%	829 lines or 44.7%
Enjambments	172 lines or 14.3%	260 lines or 14.0%

It is impossible to draw percentages for the total of the 154
poems which make up the collection of *Sonnets*. Published in
1609, they belong to several periods as might be expected. A
lapse of time is suggested by several of them: when sonnets 2,
22, 62, 63, 64 were written the friend bore the "proud livery" of
youth; in sonnet 104, after three years of intimacy, he still appeared
to the poet, in all his freshness; in sonnet 70 he had passed, un-
assailed it seems, the "ambush of young days"; finally, poem 106
shows him "declining" though growing in beauty. Differences of
value and of structure form groups within the whole. Some of the
sonnets are particularly artificial, developing themes overworked
by the Petrarchists of the period and employing subjects in which
ingenuity alone counts and in which one finds the greater part
of the mannerisms listed for the two narrative poems. In addition
the structure sometimes lacks precision because the thought is
developed from the first to the last line without a clear distinction
between the quatrains and the final distich, a fundamental division
in the English sonnet. Shakespeare does not seem yet to have
understood that the value of the sonnet rests in large part in its
strict sculptural construction. To tell the truth, several of the
poems are *quatorzaines* rather than sonnets. Take sonnet 46, for
example:

Mine eye and heart are at a mortall warre,
How to deuide the conquest of thy sight,
Mine eye my heart their pictures sight would barre,
My heart, mine eye the freedome of that right.
My heart doth plead that thou in him doost lye,
(A closet neuer pearst with cristall eyes)
But the defendant doth that plea deni,
And sayes in him their faire appearance lyes.
To side this title is impannelled
A quest of thoughts, all tennants to the heart,
And by their verdict is determined
The cleere eyes moyity, and the deare hearts part.
　　And thus, mine eyes due is their outward part,
　　And my hearts right, thy inward loue of heart.

Other sonnets, on the contrary, express the keenly felt sentiments of the poet's inner life, and their sincerity cannot be
doubted. These are the most beautiful in the collection: their
style is compact and supremely suggestive; the most insipid mannerisms have disappeared; and the structure now has a compact
distinctness which, although very different, equals the rigorous
solidity of the Italian sonnet. The three quatrains, each containing a complete idea, present three aspects of the dominant idea,
and the distich carries either a brusk reversal or a confirmation of
the idea, always with an effect of surprise which accentuates the
epigrammatic form of this ultimate expression. Sonnet 73 is perhaps one of the most characteristic of this second type:

That time of yeeare thou mayst in me behold,
When yellow leaues, or none, or few, doe hange
Vpon those boughes which shake against the could,
Bare ru'ind quiers where late the sweet birds sang.

In me thou seest the twilight of such day,
As after Sun-set fadeth in the West,
Which by and by blacke night doth take away,
Deaths second selfe that seals vp all in rest.

In me thou seest the glowing of such fire,
That on the ashes of his youth doth lye,
As the death bed, whereon it must expire,
Consum'd with that which it was nurrisht by.

　　This thou perceu'st which makes thy loue more strong,
　　To loue that well, which thou must leaue ere long.

Even if we make allowance for the exaggeration which is every poet's right, Shakespeare was not young when he wrote this sonnet. It is overcast by the shadow of death and belongs to a date perhaps not far from 1609.

Sonnet 107 at any rate can be dated with sufficient certitude. There is no reason to doubt that "the mortal moon" which "hath her eclipse endured" is Queen Elizabeth and that an allusion is made to her death. When Shakespeare states that all the predictions of the "sad augurs" have been belied, that all the uncertainties have been succeeded by the assurance of an eternal peace, he is certainly thinking of the anxiety of the English about the succession to the throne and of their relief on seeing the question settled by the acceptance of the king of Scotland, James VI. Since Shakespeare together with his company had become the "servant" of the new king a compliment from the principal member of the company was almost obligatory. The date of the sonnet would therefore be 1603, and we cannot be very wrong in assigning the poems of the final group to the opening years of the seventeenth century.[9]

Sonnets 46 and 73 thus mark two extreme states of the development of Shakespeare's versification, the first representing the period of imitation and artificiality, the second the final period rich in the inner experience of the poet. Between the two are sonnets which have, in varying degrees, characteristics of either the first or the second, corresponding no doubt to the intermediate periods in this progress toward a perfect form. There is thus a certain difficulty in forming completely homogeneous groups. Nevertheless, I have been able to compose two groups having essentially the characteristics of the sonnet-types 46 and 73. If I express the versification of these groups in percentages analogous to those which I have established for *Venus and Adonis* and for *Lucrece,*

9. This date of 1603 has been accepted by a great number of Shakespearean critics (cf. the excellent article of the historian Garrett Mattingly, "The Date of Shakespeare's Sonnet CVII," *Publ. Mod. Lang. Assoc.,* Sept. 1933, pp. 705–21. Recently J. L. Hotson, to whom we owe interesting discoveries, has tried to demonstrate that Shakespeare made an allusion in this sonnet to the defeat of the Spanish Armada in 1588. This would not be possible unless the sonnet was written during the period of joy experienced in England when the news arrived of the defeat of a redoubtable enemy, that is in 1589 at the latest. At that time Shakespeare was incapable of writing so perfect a sonnet.

it will be possible to get an idea of the progress made by Shakespeare during the period when the *Sonnets* were written. I place
in the first group sonnets 18, 20, 24, 28, 46, 51, 68, 75, 83, 113; in the
second group sonnets 26, 38, 55, 56, 57, 71, 72, 73, 78, 107.

	Early group	*Late group*
	140 lines = 700 feet	
Weakly accented feet	166 or 23.7%	202 or 28.8%
Trochees	21 or 3.0%	16 or 2.2%
Spondees	27 or 3.8%	24 or 3.4%
Internal pauses	52 lines or 37.1%	72 lines or 51.4%
Enjambments	18 lines or 12.8%	44 lines or 31.4%

If we compare these percentages with those for *Venus and
Adonis* and *Lucrece,* the first thing noticeable is the remarkably
small number of rhythmical variations. Weakly accented feet do
not much exceed one foot to a line (about 23 in 20 lines of *Venus
and Adonis, Lucrece,* and the early group of *Sonnets;* about 28 in
20 lines of the late group of the *Sonnets*). The substitutions of
trochees and spondees together vary between 6 and 8 in 20 lines,
which is extremely moderate, or even exceptional, for the poets
of the time seem to have considered a generous number of such
substitutions a true distinction of their poetry. What is more
significant, as Shakespeare advanced in his career he diminished
rather than augmented these proportions in his plays. If I may
anticipate, his most frequent proportions in his plays will be
roughly around 3% for the trochees and 4% for the spondees.

Among the elements that contribute to the flexibility of the
rhythm, on the contrary, the enjambments never ceased to grow
in number, passing from 9.1% in *Venus and Adonis* to 12.8% in
the early sonnets, to 14.0% in *Lucrece,* and to 31.1% in the late
sonnets. It is impossible on the other hand to find any regularity
in the use of internal pauses. The average number of breaks in the
rhythm of the verse is smaller in the last sonnets than in *Venus
and Adonis.* Evidently this characteristic depends largely upon
the material of thought, a lively story or an animated dialogue
lending themselves to a broken rhythm more readily than a
sumptuous description or a meditative monologue.

Such then are the chief characteristics of Shakespeare's versification. The verse is delicately organized to avoid monotony without destroying the specific quality of the iambic scheme. It is resonant without being strident, supple without being invertebrate. In a sense Shakespeare's versification in its avoidance of all excesses may seem banal, but it has an advantage, which the dramatic author in Shakespeare instinctively discovered, of not differing essentially from the natural cadence of spoken English, which is unmistakably iambic. This restraint upon the rhythm is compensated by the ever increasing audacity with which the shackles of the verse are broken to allow the meaning to range freely from line to line and adapt itself to all the curves that the dramatic action may take. Shakespeare thus resolved the difficult problem posed by the use of verse in the drama. The theater seeks to give an exact image of life, but the question is how to reconcile the truth of this image with a means of expression that is admittedly artificial, for when man laughs or suffers he does not express himself in verse. Shakespeare's verse has a flexibility which can vie with the liberty of periodic prose but which, at the same time, sufficiently retains the pattern of the poetical form to record the vibrations of the most lyrical inspiration.

There is another characteristic of Shakespeare's verse which I have not yet mentioned, for it is difficult to classify. By the choice of the words it belongs to style, by the sound of those words it has a part in the modulation of the rhythm. I mean the art with which Shakespeare combines vowels and consonants so that an ineffable impression of harmony results. This is a quality precious above all others in dramatic writing: it permits an actor to speak his lines without effort, leaving him complete liberty for the stage action. It is also the most constant of Shakespeare's qualities, for it appears in *Venus and Adonis* as well as in the plays of the better period. Such an art cannot be expressed in terms of statistics; only the laws of phonetics can explain it.[1] But it is easily perceived by someone with an ear for music, and it will suffice to give a few examples, this one taken from *Venus and Adonis:*

1. A verse is harmonious when its component sounds do not compel the organs of speech to make an exaggerated effort, as for example in passing abruptly from sounds articulated in the throat to sounds produced on the lips or on the teeth. The most harmonious effects are obtained when the consonants and vowels of a sentence are produced in neighboring parts of the palate.

> Lo here the gentle lark wearie of rest,
> From his moyst cabinet mounts up on hie,
> And wakes the morning, from whose silver brest
> The sunne ariseth in his maiesty,
> > Who does the world so gloriously behold
> > That Ceader tops and hills seem burnisht gold (853–8)

or this one from *Lucrece:*

> By this lamenting Philomele had ended
> The well-tuned warble of her nightly sorrow,
> And solemn night with low sad gait descended
> To ugly hell, when loe the blushing morrow
> Lends light to all faire eyes that light will borrow,
> > But cloudie Lucrece shames herself to see,
> > And therefore still in night would cloistred be (1079–85)

Sonnet 73 quoted above may serve as an example for the sonnets.

In passages such as these it can be truly said that poetry and music are united, and it is perhaps in this happy mingling of harmony of style and fluidity of rhythm that we must look for the key to that Shakespearean sweetness—so different from the Marlovian vigor—which his contemporaries noticed and tried to describe by such words as "sugared," "honey-tongued," and "mellifluous."

Some of these elements that enter into a definition of Shakespeare's style and versification are so unusual that by observing their occurrence it will, I hope, be possible to separate what is Shakespearean from what is un-Shakespearean in a play and thus solve the problems of authorship that may arise. But it will not be necessary to make use of all those elements, particularly of all the metrical characteristics, in the demonstrations I shall have to undertake in the following chapters. Some of them are not peculiar enough to Shakespeare; no poet for example can exceed two weakly accented feet to a verse without weakening his metrical scheme. The proportions of internal pauses, as I have shown, are so variable that nothing certain can be founded upon them. Critics have often concluded from the presence of a considerable number of feminine endings in a passage that it must certainly be Shakespearean; the truth is that in his initial use of blank verse Shakespeare followed the pattern of rhymed verse and admitted

practically no hypermetrical syllables at the end of his verses.[2]
If by chance the sense required that a verse end with a word having a syllable after its last accent, he submitted to that necessity,
considering it poetic license; before him other poets took this
liberty more easily. The enjambments, like the internal pauses,
depend too much upon the subject for use in our analysis: a dialogue in alternate lines, modeled after the Greeks' *stichomythia*,
offers no opportunity for enjambments, while a rhetorical speech
lends itself to a periodic development of ideas. The same thing
can be said of certain characteristics of Shakespeare's style. The
presence of mannerisms which we shall find swarming in some
of the plays will be significant only in the early plays, and their
absence at any rate can never be considered as an un-Shakespearean indication. To introduce such elements into the discussions would serve only to complicate or rather to confuse the
issue.

In questions of authenticity I shall therefore use only those characteristics that are constant and essentially peculiar to Shakespeare: the percentages of trochees and spondees, which are as
good as a signature of Shakespeare; the mannerisms when they
appear in combined and excessive variety; and, throughout, the
images of the kind I have described above (pp. 66–7). When
all these are intimately mingled they will afford what is tantamount
to a proof that the texture examined is truly Shakespearean. On
the other hand, if we find in a passage a mechanical and monotonous rhythm or one displaying an abnormal number of trochees
and spondees, and if, to boot, the style is flat with bookish comparisons, we shall be able to affirm that the passage is not Shakespeare's. These incongruous pieces will have no importance in
themselves, but their presence will indicate that Shakespeare
used an earlier play as a source, and in certain cases they will
furnish valuable indications as to the nature of that source.

It will be more difficult to resolve the question of the authenticity of prose passages. The dedications of *Venus and Adonis* and
Lucrece are the only examples of prose which we can consider

2. Shakespeare's rhymed pentameter has some feminine rhymes (morrow, sorrow)
which are the nearest thing to a feminine ending. But the effect produced is quite
different, and their use is limited by the fact that such rhymes are rare.

unquestionably Shakespeare's; and these show only that in 1593 and 1594 Shakespeare was under the influence of John Lyly: they are written in pure euphuism. The chief characteristics of Lyly's style are to be found here—isochronous balance, synonymous or antithetical, and use of alliteration to accentuate the parallelism of the sentences.

> I know not how I shall offend in dedicating my unpolished lines to your lordship nor how the world will censure me for choosing so strong a prop to support so weak a burden: only if your honour seem but pleased, I account myself highly praised, and vow to take advantage of all idle hours, till I have honoured you with some graver labour. But if the first heir of my invention prove deformed, I shall be sorry it had so noble a godfather, and never after ear so barren a land, for fear it yield me still so bad a harvest. I leave it to your honourable survey, and your honour to your heart's content; which I wish may always answer your own wish and the world's hopeful expectation. (*Venus and Adonis*)

But this is the sort of language used at the time in all dedications to noble patrons, and dramatic characters speaking in that way would be insufferably tedious; it cannot therefore be of any assistance as a test in our investigation. Fortunately the question of the authenticity of prose fragments will occur rarely, since Shakespeare's predecessors employed this mode of expression only in comic scenes and these formed a very small part of their serious plays.[3]

∫   ∫   ∫

BUT SHAKESPEARE may also have wished to "amend, augment and alter" one of his own plays: then the problem will be a question of chronology. In a given play one is often confronted with passages in rhymed verse, in blank verse, in prose, all intermingled without apparent reason, and in such cases there is room for the conjecture that perhaps these passages are not all of the same period. A study

3. A theory which had a momentary success gave the spelling and punctuation of the original editions as a means of recognizing Shakespeare's style, for these editions were believed to reproduce his manuscript. If we take into consideration the unsystematic nature of sixteenth-century spelling and punctuation this can have but little value as a test, especially if the manuscript sent to the printer was only a copy of the author's manuscript, which would have been subjected to the combined whims of the scrivener and the compositor. I have therefore taken no account of this theory.

of the versification and style will be the means of solving the problem here, too. But the characteristics which help in deciding questions of authenticity cannot be used this time. The presence of mannerisms will indicate only that a passage was written in an early period, but it will not determine the precise date. The essential qualities of the style, such as the images, will not prove anything since they are found in the earliest plays as well as the later; and their beauty, which is difficult to evaluate, is not always a sign of development. As for the versification, the characteristics of the rhythm, which is so important a part of Shakespeare's poetic individuality, tell us nothing since of all the prosodic elements in his verse the rhythm changed least.

Only the elements productive of flexibility will be of use but with the reservation that they are not all significant. The internal pauses, as we have seen, depend too much upon the subject; and the same thing can be said of the enjambments. In fact the enjambments will be an indication only when they are very numerous or completely absent from passages where there is every reason to expect them. In such cases I may quote them to corroborate some statement. All things considered, only the feminine endings will give sure results; like the distribution of trochees and spondees they are the effect of the poet's instinctive yearning and they crop up independent of the meaning or the kind of dramatic action. On the percentages of feminine endings alone I shall base the probable date of a passage or scene.

This test is not new. Toward the end of the nineteenth century several studies appeared on the evolution of Shakespeare's blank verse, and what was then called the feminine ending was subjected to statistical investigation on which rests, in large measure, the chronology of Shakespeare's plays.[4] But these statistics cannot serve my purpose. The scholars who established them believed not only that most of Shakespeare's plays were entirely authentic but also that each was the result of a single effort. They did, indeed, point out that the feminine endings were not uniformly distributed in all the scenes, that there were at times great

4. Another characteristic that has also been examined statistically is the "light" and "weak" endings of verses. But there are so few in most cases that one wonders why they were ever counted. All they show is that they meant nothing to Shakespeare.

inequalities from one scene to another and even within a single scene, and to get around this difficulty they hit upon the procedure of drawing up percentages for entire plays. The troublesome variations thus disappeared magically and there remained only accommodating numbers. But if one admits a priori that a play may contain portions belonging to different periods it is nonsensical to establish the averages for the whole play. A scene without feminine endings and one having 50% feminine endings are not the equivalent of two scenes with a proportion of 25% each. In the inquiries we shall undertake it will be necessary, on the contrary, to note those inequalities carefully, for when they are important they will be a sure sign of different states in the evolution of Shakespeare's blank verse.

In practice, however, things will not always be simple. In renouncing the convenient expedient of percentages for whole plays we shall have to solve a problem which the authors of the old statistics succeeded in evading. Let us suppose that we are dealing with a play written when Shakespeare was not familiar with the feminine ending and that it was reworked at a period when an average of 30% of his lines had feminine endings. If Shakespeare was satisfied with adding several long passages, these new bits will be easily distinguished by their percentages. But he almost always touched up the play here and there and more or less, and as a result there may be a series of percentages varying between 0 and 30% according to the extent of the modifications. In such cases there will be a way of solving this problem. We will put the passages which have a minimum of feminine endings on one side and on the other those which have a maximum. This will give two extreme averages which will yield the percentage of the original form and that of the revision.

I have chosen as an example a simple case and in fact the one that will turn up most often. But it can happen that some of the percentages between the two extremes correspond to an intermediate revision. It must be recognized that it will not always be possible to isolate such a revision, and this fact must be acknowledged as one of the insurmountable difficulties which are met in all historical research.

In questions of chronology it will be wise not to give absolute and definitive value to the percentages: matters of the intellect are not regulated by mathematical laws. The proportions which will be considered should be a little elastic, and to be significant the differences should be rather marked. One of the ludicrous aspects of the application of percentages to establish the chronology of Shakespeare's plays is that sometimes some tenths of one unit have sufficed to justify the dating of one play after another. Variations of even several units may mean nothing. To anticipate the results of the chapters which are to follow, this is how I see the evolution of Shakespearean verse. In his early works a percentage between 0 and 5% and even more is not distinguishing, for to produce any effect a phenomenon of this kind must be repeated at fairly close intervals. Shakespeare at this period had not yet discovered the advantage of the hypermetrical syllable. Little by little, however, he noticed the service that those light prolongations of sound at the end of a line rendered to the end of the verse by freeing it from too definite a termination, thus creating a modulation pleasing to the ear; and moderately at first, possibly with the restraining idea that he was doing something irregular, he began to employ consciously what he had previously considered as license. In this period of discovery the percentages can fluctuate around 10–15%. A third period followed rapidly when Shakespeare went so far as to use the feminine ending every three or four lines; that is to say the percentages range between 25 and 33%. After that, the use of a hypermetrical syllable at the end of a verse developed further and in the late plays could reach 60% and even more. These divisions are certainly arbitrary, but to attempt greater precision would be counter to common sense. And this rough outline of a somewhat widespread chronology may not be too far from the truth.

For the prose passages the task of establishing their date will be particularly difficult. As I have already said, the only information we possess is that in 1593–94 Shakespeare seems to have been under the influence of John Lyly. We shall not, however, be without some external evidence furnishing milestones in Shakespeare's dramatic career. Certain dramatic fashions will in themselves be dates. Ben Jonson, with his insistence on the eccentricities of his characters and his picture of London life, created a type of comedy which will have as a signpost the word "humour." A change in the personnel of the Lord Chamberlain's company resulted in a change in the character of the "clown." Shakespeare originally accepted the type which the pre-Shakespearean drama bequeathed to him—the dull-witted fellow whose nonsense and *quid pro quo*'s sufficed to amuse the spectators—though he soon gave life to that type by doubling the fool with a braggart. After Will Kemp, who portrayed the two types, left the Lord Chamberlain's company in 1599, he was replaced by the elegant and literary Robert Armin, and the clown was transformed into a Court fool, witty and insolent but wise under his apparent lightness.

At the end of this research on the authenticity and the chronology of the plays we shall have gathered valuable information upon Shakespeare's development as a dramatist but we shall not have exhausted all possibilities of investigation. The most important and most exciting task of critical construction will remain to be done: namely, to try to find out the reason for the changes which will have been indicated. Henslowe's *Diary* has given us an insight into some of these reasons, the principal one being to rejuvenate a play and sometimes the desire to adapt it to new dramatic fashions or a performance at Court; sometimes it was necessary to satisfy a noted actor by lengthening his part. At the end of the seventeenth century a tradition was current to the effect that Shakespeare had put "several words, and expressions into the part of Iago (perhaps not so agreeable to his Character) to make the Audience laugh." [5] During the "war of the theaters" actors and authors made use of plays as weapons of combat, and it will be seen that in *Troilus and Cressida* a classical figure was transformed into a caricature of Ben Jonson. Finally, and above all, there is the possibility that when Shakespeare revised one of his own plays he wished to utilize the experience he had acquired both as a man and as an actor-author. The development of his versification and style is but the shadow of the perfection which was being achieved in his mind. From imitation to mastery the journey for a man like Shakespeare must have been rich in adventures, and traces of them must be preserved in his works, where they may

5. Charles Gildon, "Reflections on Rymer's Short View of Tragedy," in *Miscellaneous Letters and Essays on Several Subjects,* 1684, p. 88.

be discovered. We shall be penetrating into the secret recesses of Shakespeare's intentions, and each play will no doubt give the evidence of its documentation and thus lay the foundations of an intellectual biography somewhat different perhaps from those which have appeared till now. But this will be the subject of another book when this one is finished.

CHAPTER ONE. 2 AND 3 HENRY VI

𝒞here exist two quartos—*The First Part of the Contention betwixt the two famous Houses of Yorke and Lancaster* (1594) and *The True Tragedie of Richard Duke of Yorke, and the death of good King Henrie the Sixt with the whole contention betweene the two Houses of Lancaster and Yorke* (1595)—which are parts of the same play. Their subject matter is, scene for scene, that of the second and third parts of *Henry VI* in the 1623 folio, which are attributed to Shakespeare; and a close relationship undoubtedly exists. But the text of the quartos in many places differs greatly from that of the folio. Two theories have been advanced to explain this. According to the older theory, *The Contention* and *The True Tragedie* are a first draft, held by some to be partly by Shakespeare, while 2 and 3 *Henry VI* are Shakespeare's revisions of those quartos. According to the second theory the folio text is Shakespeare's original and authentic text, and the quartos are spurious and imperfect versions, procured by a "pirate" or—a last variant of this theory—by an actor-reporter of fallible memory.[1]

In conformity with the method which I have adopted I shall study each text separately, without any preconceived opinion. I begin with the earlier edition.

THE SECOND PART OF HENRY VI

The Quarto of 1594 or "The Contention"

ON MARCH 12, 1593/4, Thomas Millington registered with the Stationers' Company a manuscript entitled "The first parte of the Contention of the twoo famous houses of York and Lancaster with the deathe of the good Duke Humfrey and the banishment

---

1. The principal supporters of the more recent theory are Peter Alexander, *Shakespeare's Henry VI and Richard III*, 1929; Madeleine Doran, *Henry VI, Parts II and III; Their Relation to the "Contention" and the "True Tragedie,"* Humanistic Studies (University of Iowa, 1928), Vol. 4, No. 4; John E. Jordan, "The Reporter of *Henry VI*, Part 2," *Publ. Mod. Lang. Assoc.*, Dec. 1949.

and Deathe of the Duke of Suffolk and the tragicall ende of the prowd Cardinall of Winchester, with the notable Rebellion of Jack Cade and the Duke of Yorkes ffirste clayme vnto the Crowne." A quarto bearing this title, printed by Thomas Creede, appeared the same year.[2]

The manuscript furnished to the printer does not seem to have given much trouble to the compositor. All passages, however, were not easily legible, for the quarto contains a few misreadings: "then the" for "twenty" (sc.i.8), "place" for "presence" (sc.iii.80), "Standbags" for "sand-bags" (sc.iii.127), "erre" for "teare" (sc.x. 119), "leaue fast" for "lean faced" (sc.x.151), "Irish" for "Iris" (sc. x.173); "penny-inckhorne" for "pen and inkhorne" (sc.xiii.68), "age" for "badge" (sc.xxi.116), "eternest" for "eternized" (sc.xxiii. 28). The classical and foreign geographical names are all mangled: Towres for Tours (sc.i.5), Cyssels for Sicily (sc.i.44), Anioy for Anjou (sc.i.78), Sosetus for Cocytus, Dytas for Ditis, Stykes for Styx (sc.iv.16,34). And the French "baise mon cul" must certainly have been very badly written to have been rendered "bus mine cue" (sc.xviii.26).

The stage directions are the author's, as is shown by the tendency to let the company fix the number of supers:

Enter one or two (sc.iii.30)

Enter the Lord Skayles vpon the Tower walles walking. Enter three or foure Citizens below (sc.xvi.1)

Enter the Duke of Yorke, and the Duke of Buckingham, and others (sc.iv.38) [3]

The entrances are centered between two lines and precede the first words of the actor; the exits are also printed interlinearly but closer to the right-hand margin.

2. A facsimile of this quarto was published by Praetorius in the collection of the Shakespere Quarto Facsimiles, 1889, No. 37. It is to this reproduction that I turn for references and citations. A second quarto, printed by Valentine Simmes for Thomas Millington, appeared in 1600 and is a reimpression of the first. Finally a third edition appeared conjointly with *The True Tragedie* under the general title of *The Whole Contention betweene the two famous houses of York and Lancaster . . . Divided into two parts; And newly corrected and enlarged*, Praetorius Facsimiles, 1919, Nos. 23 and 24. This edition does in fact contain some additions but these are of no value for the present purpose.

3. Cf. sc.xii.1; sc.xxii.61.

QUEENE. Go then good Vawse and certifie the King.

Exet Vawse.

Oh what is worldly pompe, all men must die (sc.x.191–2)

The entrances are exceptionally detailed, sometimes occupying several lines:

> Enter Dame *Elnor Cobham* bare-foote, and a white sheete about her, with a waxe candle in her hand, and verses written on her backe and pind on, and accompanied with the Sheriffes of London, and Sir *Iohn Standly,* and Officers, with billes and holbards (sc.viii.10–11)

They specify the rank and relationships of the characters, the noblemen's names being preceded by their titles:

> Enter at one doore, King Henry the sixt, and Humphrey Duke of Gloster, the Duke of Sommerset, the Duke of Buckingham, Cardinall Bewford, and others.

> Enter at the other doore, the Duke of Yorke, and the Marquesse of Suffolke, and Queene Margaret, and the Earle of Salisbury and Warwicke (sc.i.1)

> Enter Duke Humfrey, and dame Ellanor, Cobham his wife (sc.ii.1)

They sometimes point out details which are not indicated in the dialogue:

> Enter the Duke of Suffolke with the Queene, and they take him for Duke Humphrey, and giues him their writings (sc.iii.7–8)

> The Queene lets fall her gloue, and hits the Duches of Gloster, a boxe on the eare (sc.iii.132–3)

They often fix the movements and gestures of the actors:

> Enter King Henry, and the Duke of Yorke and the Duke of Somerset on both sides of the King, whispering with him (sc.iii.69–70)

Some peculiarities in the phrasing of the entrances should be pointed out; we shall find them in other manuscripts. One is the habit of preceding each name with the conjunction "and" when enumerating the entrants or of separating groups of people by the words "and then":

> Enter to the Parlament.
> Enter two Heralds before, then the Duke of Buckingham, and the Duke of Suffolke, and then the Duke of Yorke, and the Cardinall of Winchester, and then the King and the Queene, and then the Earle of Salisbury, and the Earle of Warwicke (sc.ix.1)

Another consists in using the words "and the rest" to sum up supers too numerous to be designated in detail:

> Exet King, Queene, and Suffolke, and Duke
> Humphrey staies all the rest (sc.i.66)

> Enter Iacke Cade, Dicke Butcher, Robin, Will Tom, Harry and the
> rest, with long staues (sc.xiii.20–1)

The use of this phrase is another indication that the stage directions were written by the author of the play, for it is also found in the dialogue:

> QUEENE. Had the noble Duke of Suffolke bene alive,
> The Rebell Cade had bene supprest ere this,
> And all the rest that do take part with him (sc.xix.6–8)

In spite of the care with which the author mentioned these details of staging, he was not always thorough enough; notably he forgot sixteen exits and the prompter had to add the necessary indications in the blank space after the exiting actor's last speech.

> SUFFOLKE. You must either fight sirra or else be hangde:
> Go take them hence againe to prison. *Exet* with them (sc.iii.131–2) [4]

It was probably the prompter too who had the idea of showing the repentant rebels entering with ropes about their necks:

> Enter the Duke of Buckingham and Clifford, with the Rebels, with
> halters about their necks (sc.xix.8–9)

for Clifford in engaging the rebels to accept the king's offer of pardon had put no condition on their surrender. Furthermore, the second "with" of the stage direction looks very much as though it introduced an afterthought.

The manuscript bore marks of fairly numerous revisions. In sc. viii there is a passage in two redactions. Elinor Cobham, condemned to cross London in penitent's garb, tells her husband, Duke Humphrey, how cruel the thought is to her that she, the wife of the most powerful lord of the realm, should be the object of the crowd's jeerings; and as the duke advises her to bear her grief patiently she exclaims:

---

4. Cf. sc.iii.168; sc.v.127; sc.vii.33,108; sc.x.11,49,219,220; sc.xii.78; sc.xiii.69; sc.xvii.15; sc.xviii.122.

Ah Gloster teach me to forget my selfe,   25
For whilst I thinke I am thy wedded wife,
Then thought of this, doth kill my wofull heart.
The ruthlesse flints do cut my tender feete,
And when I start the cruell people laugh,
And bids me be aduised how I tread,
And thus with burning Tapor in my hand,
Malde vp in shame with papers on my backe,   32
Ah, Gloster, can I endure this and liue.
Sometime Ile say I am Duke Humphreys wife,
And he a Prince, Protector of the land,
But so he rulde, and such a Prince he was,
As he stood by, whilst I his forelorne Duches
Was led with shame, and made a laughing stocke,
To euery idle rascald follower (sc.viii.25–39)

It is clear that lines 25–32 and 33–39 express the same idea and
even have some words in common; one of these drafts should
have replaced the other. Was the sign indicating the cut passage
forgotten, or was it overlooked by the compositor? It is impossible
to tell.

Among the other signs of revision are:

a. Verses badly divided: sc.vi.7–15; sc.vii.32–3; sc.ix.29–30;
sc.x.197–9; sc.xi.1–11; sc.xii.46–8; sc.xix.1–5; sc.xx.12–13; sc.xxii.1–
7,28–30.

b. Verses printed as prose: sc.i.57–61,133–7; sc.ii.39–41,53–8;
sc.iii.70–1; sc.iv.28–9; sc.v.27–9,44–6.

c. Lines of prose printed as verse: sc.iii.29–35; sc.vii.50–5; sc.
xiii.31–5,58–9,61–5,89–91,97–102; sc.xvi.1–6; sc.xvii.1–7,12–15; sc.
xviii.3–8,75–84,113–17.

The correction that occupies the major part of sc.vi is particularly interesting. The scene opens with six lines correctly printed,
which must have been in the manuscript from the beginning:

YORKE. My Lords our simple supper ended, thus,
Let me reueale vnto your honours here,
The right and title of the house of Yorke,
To Englands Crowne by liniall desent.
WAR. Then Yorke begin, and if thy claime be good,
The Neuils are thy subiects to command

York then begins to trace the genealogy of his family from Edward III, his royal ancestor, on. It was not an easy task; Edward

had had seven sons, and for following his line of descent in all its ramifications the author had at his disposal only the fragmentary information which the chroniclers had furnished by chance in reporting events. This information was often erroneous; where historians were led astray it is not surprising that a dramatic writer erred. None of the genealogies presented in the different texts of the play is exact. The Third Quarto corrected some of the most egregious errors of the First Quarto but in so doing introduced new ones. The folio text avoided some of the quarto's errors but in turn confused characters of the same name belonging to different generations: Edmund Mortimer, fifth earl of March, for example, with his uncle, Sir Edmund Mortimer.[5] *The Contention* itself presents one of those unfortunate attempts to reach exactitude. The first five lines of the pedigree made out by York are an obvious marginal correction intended to replace a defective version. The corrector began by writing the new text opposite the old draft, in the blank space at the right side of the page. This space was far from sufficient since four of the five original lines were alexandrines. This explains the irregularity of the new lines: the shorter ones correspond to the long verses, the longer ones to the short verses of the suppressed passage:

> YORKE. Then thus my Lords.
> Edward the third had seuen sonnes,
> The first was Edward the blacke Prince,
> Prince of Wales.
> The second was Edmund of Langly,
> Duke of Yorke.
> The third was Lyonell Duke of Clarence.
> The fourth was Iohn of Gaunt,
> The Duke of Lancaster (7–15)

At lines 16, 17, and 18 the verses are correctly printed, no doubt as they appeared in the first copy. But with line 19 a long passage begins which looks like a solid block of prose, although it is really verse printed without separating the lines except to designate new speakers. There can be only one explanation of this phenomenon: the corrector had reached the bottom of the page on which he could continue his addition without being hindered by the old

5. Already noticed by P. Alexander, *Henry VI and Richard III*, pp. 61–2.

text; he therefore wrote the new text across the width of the page without taking the trouble to mark the necessary divisions, and as the correction was a long one he very likely made similar use of the top of the following page.[6] It is one of the most curious examples I have found in the course of my research, and one of the most evident, for looking at the printed page we may have the illusion that we are catching a glimpse of the manuscript itself.

To summarize the facts brought out in the preceding pages: the manuscript which served as copy for printing *The Contention* was an author's manuscript (or a copy of it), worked over and completed by a prompter; it belonged to a company and had already been the object of an important revision. The only thing which is still problematical is who made the modifications. Was it the author who at one time wished to improve his play, or a second author who intervened to revise it? A study of the versification and of the style will provide the answer to that question.

ſ   ſ   ſ

A CAREFUL ANALYSIS of the versification, line by line, shows distinctly that two authors worked upon *The Contention*. The first, whom I shall call author A,[7] has a versification recognizable among many others. He adopted the five-stress iambic blank verse which from the time of *Gorboduc* was considered the best mode of dramatic expression; the greater part of the play is written in that form. But author A is far from holding to his choice. One finds in the play verses of almost every length from two syllables to sixteen. Lines of one to three feet (a score) can be the result of a cut or an interpolation or they can come at the end of a scene

6. It is amusing to note that the correction has a double redaction of its own. At lines 22–3 the corrector had written at first: "Edmund of Langly Duke of Yorke died, and left behind him two daughters, Anne and Elinor"; he stopped, perceiving he had made a mistake, and beginning again wrote: "Lyonell Duke of Clarence died, and left behinde Alice, Anne, and Elinor," which is another error for Lionel had only one daughter who was named Philippa. The compositor printed the two redactions one after the other.

7. In this book I shall not try to identify the anonymous authors we may meet along the way; that will be possible only when we are better informed on the versification and style of Shakespeare's predecessors.

or a long speech, and in such cases they may not constitute an anomaly. Nor is the presence of alexandrines extraordinary, except for their number (about fifty), for they are found mingled with pentameters in almost all the dramatic writers of the period. But lines of eight to sixteen syllables cannot be considered accidents or examples of allowable license, for they are too numerous and are too closely fitted into the dialogue: they are conscious or unconscious deviations from the chosen norm.

Author A's versification is not merely heterogeneous; it has another characteristic which renders it exceptional for its period. A great number of lines of four, five, six, or seven feet contain a trisyllabic foot which, as I have already said (p. 68), was not in general use at the end of the sixteenth century.

Trisyllabic feet in four-stress lines:

> Cosin Yorke, | the victories thou hast wonne (sc.i.120)
>
> There goes | our Protec | tor in a rage (sc.i.93)
>
> All in this place | are thy bet | ters farre (sc.iii.80)
>
> Is ouercome my Lord, | all is lost | (sc.ix.31) [8]

Trisyllabic feet in five-stress lines:

> Proud Protec | tor, enuy in thine eyes I see (sc.i.85)
>
> Then what | shouldst thou lacke | that might content thy minde (sc.ii.7)
>
> Stood readie to set it | on my Prince | ly head (sc.ii.28)
>
> Till when, drinke that | for my sake, | And so farwell (sc.ii.67)
>
> And had I not bene cited thus | by their meanes | (sc.x.133) [9]

Trisyllabic feet in six-stress lines:

> | Come sirrha, | thy life shall be the ransome I will haue (sc.xii.26)

8. Cf. sc.i.121; sc.iii.56,94,124; sc.iv.42,47,48; sc.v.108; sc.ix.82,148,155,157,178, 179; sc.x.2,4,70; sc.xi.9; sc.xii.4,16; sc.xiii.82,88; sc.xv.2,13,15,16; sc.xix.24; sc.xxi.44, 87,95.

9. Cf. sc.i.73,88,99,125; sc.ii.36,38,51; sc.iii.54,65,70,81,128,131,134,150; sc.iv.39, 44; sc.v.3, 12, 17, 23, 45, 129; sc.viii.60,83; sc.ix.42,62,64,71,79,92,96,158,163,187; sc.x.7,31,32,123,132,135,142,188; sc.xi.7; sc.xii.33,46–7,53,63; sc.xiii.93,98; sc.xv.11, 17; sc.xvi.9; sc.xviii.99; sc.xix.11; sc.xx.18,20; sc.xxi.8,20,21,30,31,34,58,60,93,94,96; sc.xxii.27.

In the five-stress verses the tendency is to have the trisyllabic foot at the beginning of the line.

My lord, | I pray you | let me go post vnto the King (sc.iv.46)

And I am go | ing to cer | tifie vnto his grace (sc.x.189)

And good my Lords proceed no fur | ther against | our vnkle (sc.x.12)

Away with him Water, | I say, and off | with his hed | (sc.xii.62) [1]

Trisyllabic feet in seven-stress lines:

| Oh Henry, | reuerse the doome of gentle Suffolkes banishment (sc.x.137) [2]

Another characteristic of author A is an excessive use of trochaic feet. The proportion of this kind of rhythmic variation rarely goes below 5% of the total number of feet, generally varies around 6%, and sometimes reaches 10% and even more.[3] Trochees are found not only at the beginning of the verse line or after a strong pause, where they produce their effect more naturally, but also in the middle of a phonetic group [4] or at the end of the line, where they are most disturbing. These trochees produce a jerky modulation; and when they appear in excessive numbers in one verse, which happens fairly often, the fundamental rhythm is destroyed. This is illustrated in the following lines (the trochaic feet are italicized):

And that is the *mightie Duke of Suffolke* (sc.ii.75)

Gloster is no *little man in England* (sc.ix.13)

Yet let not that *make thee bloudie minded* (sc.xii.13)

Brutus bastard-hand stabde *Iulius Caesar* (sc.xii.73)

Go bid *Bucking*ham and *Clifford, gather* (sc.xv.18)

Humphrey Duke of Buckingham, pardon me (sc.xxi.19)

1. Cf. sc.x.47; sc.xiii.81,97; sc.xv.6,25–6; sc.xviii.115; sc.xxi.9.
2. Cf. sc.xix.13; sc.xx.12.
3. Cf. sc.i.105–16; sc.ii.1–7; sc.ix.9–13,112–26,133–50; sc.x.9–17,39–48,66–79, 180–91; sc.xii.1–24,62–75; sc.xv.1–21; sc.xvi.1–13; sc.xxii.9–23.
4. By a "phonetic group" phoneticians mean that part of a sentence which can be pronounced in a single breath. These groups are not determined by the punctuation; only the ear perceives them when the speaker stops, however briefly, to draw breath. These stops are of prime importance in the theater for they give life to the dialogue, and actors observe them very carefully in their delivery.

The result is a rather high number of lines which are rhythmically poor, and author A's versification often gives the impression of being not only irregular but also without principle.

These peculiarities have a common cause. The author adopted the fashionable instrument of dramatic expression while he was still not completely free from the influence of the old versification. When the decasyllabic principle of the iambic pentameter had already been established and was even undergoing a crisis of purism, it was still possible to find examples of old verses in the work of those who had contributed to the radical transformation of the prosodic system—in poets such as Wyat, Andrew Borde, Udall, Tusser, Spenser. Author A's numerous four-stress verses make one think of Chaucer's octosyllabic verse; there are also some examples of decasyllabic verse, the first foot of which is monosyllabic, again as in Chaucer:

> Faith | my Lord, it is but a base mind (sc.v.11)
>
> Go | take hence that Traitor from our sight (sc.vii.74)
>
> Ah | Gloster, now thou doest penance too (sc.viii.17)
>
> Yorke, | if thou meane well, I greete thee so (sc.xxi.6)
>
> Nay, | do not affright vs with thy lookes (sc.xxi.92)

The Contention must have been written during that period when the newly favored form had not yet completely ousted the old versification, that is to say around 1570–80.

The vocabulary, like the versification, retains several elements of another age: "sith," "I trow," "maugré"; "that" used as a conjunctional affix, "if that" (sc.ix.124; x.30), "before that" (sc.ix. 145–6); "for" in the sense of "because" (sc.v.163); "for to" before an infinitive (sc.i.70; sc.iv.7,13; sc.vi.58); the third person plural of the indicative present ending in *s* as in "strangers in the Court *takes* her for the Queene" (sc.iii.54), "Bewfords firie eyes *showes* his enuious minde" (sc.ix.78), "The Commons *cries*" (sc.x.130); a redundant pronoun after the subject of the verb, "Gloster *he* is none" (sc.ix.111).

The style is without distinction. Author A uses the language of everyday life, which when spoken by persons of high rank is rendered even vulgar by the use at every turn of exclamations and interjections—look you, come, but soft, why, what, how now, ay, nay, well, oh, ah, loe, tush, marry, forsooth, faith, etc.[5]

There are, it is true, a few similes, but they are limited to such notions of animal life as had been made popular by the bestiaries —of wolves (sc.ix.102), fox (sc.ix.122), lamb (sc.x.14), bees (sc. x.42), kite (sc.x.78), partridge, puttock (sc.x.74); and to knowl-edge derived from books of husbandry—wheat drooping when it is too ripe (sc.ii.1), planting and harvesting (sc.ix.182). Not one is introduced into the dialogue to give a picturesque or poetic tone; they are all employed for their explanatory or demonstra-tive value.

Author A's versification and style are thus as different as pos-sible from Shakespeare's. But this does not mean that they lack all dramatic fitness. The versification is incorrect according to the prosodic rules of the sixteenth century, but it does not lack supple-ness. When we read a scene aloud without thinking of the prosodic correctness, it is surprising to find how easy and natural the dif-ferent speeches are. Author A was not tormented by a desire to give his verse poetic qualities, but he had a good understanding of the theater. Having to resolve the problem which comes up every time verse is used as a means of expression in a comedy or tragedy, he sacrificed prosodic regularity to dramatic necessity. Through indifference to the rules of his own time he obtained what Shakespeare accomplished more brilliantly in exploiting the possibility of improving the generally accepted prosody. Nothing is more counter to the truth than to say that *The Contention* is a shapeless mass of adulterated verse. On the contrary, it is the play of a man who knew very well the needs of dramatic diction. Al-

5. Cf. sc.i.65,79,82,138; sc.ii.20,29,34,37,43,48,50,53,68; sc.iii.1,8,9,16,20,24,26, 29,31,34,38,104,134,165; sc.iv.6,21,38,45,52; sc.v.11,14,19,21,25,32,43,44,47,51,71, 72,73,77,80,82,91,107,113,115,119,120,121,130,167,170; sc.vi.27,61; sc.vii.15,56,58, 59,60,72,73,74,79; sc.viii.1,17,20,23,25,33,56,70,75,78,80; sc.ix.26,37,40,58,63,71, 92,99,112,127,132,145,154,164,169,170,180;   sc.x.1,7,16,17,20,33,50,52,60,68,113, 137,166,176,182,192,210,211; sc.xi.1,3,8,9,10,11,12,15,16,21; sc.xii.8,26,31,33,54,69, 78; sc.xiii.4,5,6,8,10,12,13,53,59,66,74,79,83,85,86,88,89,90,92,95,96,100,106,115, 119,122,128; sc.xv.7,8,12,20,26; sc.xvi.1; sc.xvii.1,9,12,15; sc.xviii.1,11,19,40,56,66, 73,75,82,85,87,99,122; sc.xix.10,23; sc.xx.6,18,21,23,33; sc.xxi.5,15,24,30,33,35,45,50, 55,68,88,92,94,95,96,116,125,127; sc.xxii.1,2,6,20,27,32,40,45,47,64,65; sc.xxiii.1,26.

though it cannot be compared in any manner with the most
juvenile of Shakespeare's productions, it is an honorable specimen
of the skill of a pre-Shakespearean author in the technique of
dialogue.

The passage below will give a fair idea of this type of versification and the effect it produces. It contains five four-stress lines
(143, 148, 149, 150, 155), one alexandrine (147), a pentameter
with the first foot truncated (157), five trisyllabic feet (143, 146,
148, 155, 163), and thirteen trochees, i.e., a proportion of 10.1%
in 128 feet. One can get an idea of the suppleness of the rhythm if
I add that of these 26 lines 23 or 84.4% contain internal pauses and
26.9% have enjambments; that is to say, this versification is more
supple than Shakespeare's in the final period of the *Sonnets*.
(Trochees are italicized and trisyllabic feet are indicated by vertical
lines in the following quotation.)

> QUEENE. What re*dresse shal* we haue for this my Lords?
> YORKE. Twere very good that my *Lord of Somerset*
> That fortunate *Champion* were sent *ouer*,   140
> And burnes and spoiles the Country as they goe.
> To keepe in awe the stubborne Irishmen,
> He did so much *good when* he was in France.
> SOMER. Had Yorke bene there with all | his far fetcht |
> *Pollices*, he might haue lost as much as I.   144
> YORKE. *I, for Yorke would* haue lost his life before
> That France should haue | reuolted | from Englands rule.
> SOMER. I so thou might'st, and yet haue gouernd worse then I.
> YORKE. What worse then nought, | then a shame | take all. 148
> SOMER. *Shame on* thy selfe, that wisheth shame.
> QUEENE. *Somerset* forbeare, good Yorke be patient.
> And do thou take in hand to crosse the seas,
> With troupes of Armed men to quell the pride   152
> Of those ambitious Irish that rebell.
> YORKE. Well Madame sith your grace is so content,
> | Let me haue | some bands of chosen soldiers,
> And Yorke shall trie his fortune against those kernes.   156
> QUEENE. | York | thou shalt. My Lord of Buckingham,
> Let it be your charge to muster vp such souldiers
> As shall suffise him in these needfull warres.
> BUCK. *Madame* I will, and leauie such a band
> As soone shall ouercome those Irish Rebels,
> But Yorke, where shall those soldiers staie for thee?

YORKE. | At Bristow, | I wil expect them ten daies hence (sc. ix.138–63) [6]

Another passage, written in an entirely different versification, is given below:

> YORKE. Anioy and Maine, both giuen vnto the French,
> Cold newes for me, for I had hope of France,
> Euen as I haue of fertill Eng[e]land.   145
> A day will come when Yorke shall claime his owne,
> And therefore I will take the Neuels parts,
> And make a show of loue to proud Duke Humphrey:
> And when I spie aduantage, claime the Crowne,
> For thats the golden marke I seeke to hit: 150
> Nor shall proud Lancaster vsurpe my right,
> Nor hold the scepter in his childish fist,
> Nor weare the Diademe vpon his head,
> Whose church-like humours fits not for a Crowne:
> Then Yorke be still a while till time do serue,   155
> Watch thou, and wake when others be asleepe,
> To prie into the secrets of the state,
> Till Henry surfeiting in ioyes of loue,
> With his new bride, and Englands dear bought queene,
> And Humphrey with the Peeres be falne at iarres,   160
> Then will I raise aloft the milke-white Rose,
> With whose sweete smell the aire shall be perfumde,
> And in my Standard beare the Armes of Yorke,
> To graffle with the House of Lancaster:
> And force perforce, ile make him yeeld the Crowne,   165
> Whose bookish rule hath puld faire England downe (sc.i.143–66)

This second author, whom I shall call B, employs a normal versification, too normal in fact. It is as regular and strongly marked as that of author A is capricious and uncertain. The verse is strictly decasyllabic: in the whole passage there is only one feminine ending, at line 148. The rhythm is vigorous: the accents fall on essential words and the last word of the verse is often monosyllabic and sonorous. There are only two trochaic feet (lines 145 and 156),[7] but on the other hand a substantial number of spondees—

6. In scanning this passage I have followed the pronunciation of the sixteenth century and treated "pollices," "Somerset," "tune against," and "let it be" as the equivalent of two syllables.

7. I have counted "euen as" as a trochee; but in the pronunciation of the sixteenth century it was an iamb as well.

9 in 120 feet, or 7.5%. The flexibility of the rhythm is reduced to a minimum in this ticktack metronomic versification, for the internal pauses are scanty, 6 in 24 lines (143, 144, 149, 156, 163, 165), or 25%; and although the passage is a monologue, favorable to enjambments, there are only two verses (158, 161) where the meaning overflows into the following line. One could not imagine versification more opposed at once to that of author A and to Shakespeare's.

Author B's style is more literary than author A's. Clearly oratorical in tone, it never falls into the familiarity of spoken English. On the other hand, it is without archaisms and makes no exaggerated use of exclamatory words. Although this author can repeat some of the most euphuistic comparisons of the period— the lizard's sting, the snake's hissing, the ill-omened cry of the owl (sc.x.162), the basilisk whose glance was death-dealing (sc.x.27), the mandrake that groans when torn from the earth (sc.x.147)— he has two or three similes which prove that he was capable of appreciating the contribution to dramatic style of the poetized evocation of incidents in real life. He compared the separation of Suffolk and the queen to a jewel locked in a casket and to a boat breaking up on the rocks (sc.vi.216–18), and in hyperbolic language which classes him as an imitator of Marlowe he made Suffolk say:

> Well could I curse away a winters night,
> And standing naked on a mountaine top,
> Where byting cold would neuer let grasse grow,
> And thinke it but a minute spent in sport (sc.x.167–70)

In its lack of verisimilitude, and though based upon knowledge culled from books of husbandry, the speech is undoubtedly imaginative.[8]

The versifications and styles of these two authors are so different that it is not very difficult to distinguish the passages written by one from those written by the other. The greater part of the play is in author A's hand. To author B may be attributed:

8. Such imitations of Marlowe's style have led certain critics to believe that the author of *Edward II* collaborated with the author of *The Contention*. Marlowe's versification is more flexible, however, and his style more poetical.

sc.i.1–16	Suffolk presents Marguerite of Anjou to Henry VI.
132–42	Salisbury and Warwick disapprove of the cession of Anjou and Maine.
143–66	York's soliloquy.
sc.iv.6–19	The sorceress and Bullingbrooke invoke Askalon's spirit.
sc.viii.3–10,23–33	Humphrey bids farewell to his exiled wife.
sc.x.21–8	The king is indignant when Suffolk wishes to comfort him on the death of Duke Humphrey.
50–63	Warwick maintains that Humphrey has been suffocated.
80–112	Warwick and Suffolk quarrel.
147–63	Suffolk curses his enemies.
164–81	The queen insists on Suffolk going to France and promises to have him called back from there.
sc.xxi.45–67	The king looks at Cade's head which Eyden has brought to him.
112–30	Clifford and Warwick quarrel.
sc.xxii.40–61	Young Clifford finds the body of his dead father and swears revenge.
sc.xxiii.1–21	York and his adherents rejoice over the results of the day's battle.[9]

Altogether there are a little more than 600 lines inserted into the scenes written by author A, and they are discernible by their declamatory tone and their anecdotal character, as in the guilty love of Suffolk for the queen.

The fragmentary character of the passages written by author B precludes the possibility of a collaboration between the two authors. We have here an example of those partial reworkings which were frequent at that time and which the study of the manuscript implied. Author B was called in to rejuvenate a play which was beginning to appear old-fashioned at a moment when the English drama was veering toward a more magniloquent conception of great historical events.

In *The Contention* several incidents have been treated comically and for that reason are given in prose.

1. Petitioners wishing to expose their grievances to Duke Humphrey mistakenly submit their requests to Suffolk, one of the nobles of whom they are complaining, and are badly received (sc.iii.8–28).

9. Several passages should probably be added, such as sc.i.32–9; sc.iii.47–50,59–62; sc.iv.32–6; but these are too short to allow the test of versification to be used.

2. An apprentice armorer accuses his master of seditious talk (sc.iii.106–23). Duke Humphrey decides to settle the affair by a judicial combat in which the apprentice kills his master (sc.vii. 41–73).

3. A man who pretends he was once blind and had his sight miraculously restored at the shrine of Saint Albans is unmasked by Duke Humphrey.

4. Jack Cade, instigated by York, revolts and endangers the throne momentarily until he is killed by a simple esquire named Eyden (sc.xiii.1–124; sc.xiv.1–6; sc.xvii.1–15; sc.xviii.1–49,54–66, 119–22; sc.xx.6–9,14–17,23–31).

Such a large proportion of prose in a play of that kind is really astonishing; historical plays did not usually contain so much comic matter. In fact there are good reasons to believe that these semi-historical anecdotes (they had been reported by the chroniclers) [1] were originally treated in verse, as historical events proper. At the beginning of sc.iii the petitioners waiting for Duke Humphrey express themselves in verse (1–9), and the rhythm indicates that those lines are author A's. Similarly, in sc.xviii Cade, who always speaks in prose, unexpectedly begins to discourse in a literary style which hardly recalls the popular and gross language that is habitual with him:

> Why how now, will you forsake your generall,
> And ancient freedome which you haue possest?
> To bend your neckes vnder their seruile yokes,
> Who if you stir, will straightwaies hang you vp,
> But follow me, and you shall pull them downe,
> And make them yeeld their liuings to your hands (sc.xviii.99–104)

The first foot of line 99, with its three syllables and exclamatory words, warns us that this passage must have been written by author A. A natural inference, therefore, is that the episodes were rewritten in prose in order to transform them into comic scenes

1. The incident of the judicial combat between the armorer and his servant, and the episodes of Cade's rebellion had been reported by Holinshed with many details. The incident of the petitioners is the dramatization of a remark of Holinshed on the affection which the good Duke Humphrey had for the "poore commons" and of the veneration in which they held him. Finally, the incident of the invented miracle had been cited as a real fact by Sir Thomas More in his *Dialogue*, chap. 14.

and that they were a part of the reworking undertaken by author B.

But this, after all, is of little importance. What cannot be doubted is that in *The Contention* there is not a line that can be attributed to Shakespeare. This play is a characteristic specimen of pre-Shakespearean "histories," a historical play which had already suffered modifications. It is simply a dramatization of the political events reported by Holinshed, with the more or less exact chronological succession of those events constituting the plot— if such a term can be applied to action lacking both order and artistic intentions, except in the passages written by author B. And even here the psychology of the characters is rudimentary, a simple echo of the judgments incidentally voiced by the chroniclers. The play's interest lies entirely in the great number of intrigues, provocations, murders, and battles, which portray a tempestuous era vividly enough to arouse the passions of the rough public for which it was intended.

The Folio Text of 2 "Henry VI"

The second part of Henry VI with the death of the good Duke Humphrey appeared in the 1623 folio under the heading "Histories" and occupies pages 120–46.

The manuscript furnished to the printer was certainly a company manuscript, for in the beginning of Act IV.sc.ii the stage directions as well as the speech headings give the names of two actors, Bevis and John Holland, instead of the names of the characters represented. There are no misreadings, the foreign geographical names are correct—Toures, Sicilia, Calaber, Alanson, Aniou, Britaigne—and so are the names of the historical personages— Beauford, Stanley, Scales, Iden Vaux. The care with which the entrances and exits are indicated shows that the prompter had revised the manuscript. This is confirmed by several indications given in the imperative mood: "Sound a Sennet" (I.iii.103–4; III. i.1), "Sounds Trumpets" (II.iii.1; III.ii.9–10; IV.ix.1), "Sound a flourish" (II.iii.108).

The sound effects in the folio text are more varied than in the quarto. In this respect the staging of *The Contention* was simple; the prompter had been principally occupied with military signals, the alarms, rolling of drums, and blowing of trumpets that accompanied troop movements; once cannon shots were fired to accompany a naval battle. Musical sounds were rare: the miraculously healed man made his entrance with music and the queen was saluted with a flourish when she was presented for the first time to her husband. But the entrances of the king and the Court on their official duties were made without fanfares. In the folio, in addition to the usual warlike sounds, the king's movements were accompanied with summons varying according to the occasion: a sennet marked the more important moments, for example when the regent of France had to be chosen (I.iii.103–4) or when Parliament convened to judge Duke Humphrey (III.i.1); a flourish announced more intimate or more usual circumstances such as the presentation of the queen to the king (I.i.1), and in this case some "hautboyes" were added. Flourishes also accompanied the exits of the king after the scene of the false miracle and after the combat between the armorer and his apprentice.

It is evident that the folio reproduced the text of the company's promptbook which had received a few marginal corrections at a time impossible to date:

a. Verse lines badly divided: I.iv.28–30; II.i.23–5,51–4,87–94; II.ii.45–51,²64–5; II.iii.22–5.

b. Passages of prose printed in unequal lines, as though they were verse lines: II.i.124–37; IV.vii.138–46; IV.viii.3–5.

The entrances are in general simple; the names of the characters are rid of their titles and are enumerated without the useless conjunctions "and," "and then" which are the peculiar characteristic of *The Contention*. But the stage directions are not always simple; several are practically the same in both texts:

Q. It thunders and lightens, and then the spirit riseth vp (sc.iv.20–1)
F. It thunders and lighten terribly, then the spirit riseth (I.iv.26–7)

Q. Enter the Maior of Saint Albones and his brethren with Musicke, bearing the man that had bene blind, betweene two in a chaire (sc.v.55–6)

2. Passage II.ii.45–51 is an unfortunate attempt to correct an error in York's difficult genealogy.

F. Enter the maior of Saint Albones, and his Brethren, bearing the man betweene two in a Chayre (II.i.67–8)

Q. After the Beadle hath hit him one girke, he leapes ouer the stoole and runnes away, and they run after him, crying, A miracle, a miracle (sc.v.123-4)
F. After the Beadle hath hit him once, he leapes ouer the Stoole, and runnes away: and they follow, and cry, A Miracle (II.i.153–4)

Q. Enter Duke Humphrey and his men, in mourning cloakes (sc.viii.1)
F. Enter Duke Humfrey and his Men in Mourning Cloakes (II.iv.1)

Q. Enter the Lord Skayles vpon the Tower walles walking. Enter three or foure Citizens below (sc.xvi.1)
F. Enter Lord Scales vpon the Tower walking. Then enters two or three Citizens below (IV.v.1)

Q. Alarmes, and then Mathew Goffe is slaine, and all the rest with him. Then enter Iacke Cade again, and his company (sc.xviii.1)
F. Alarums, Mathew Goffe is slain, and all the rest. Then enter Iacke Cade, with his Company (IV.vii.1)

The longest of the stage directions is absolutely identical in the two texts:

Q. Enter at one doore the Armourer and his neighbours, drinking to him so much that he is drunken, and he enters with a drum before him, and his staffe with a sand-bag fastened to it, and at the other doore, his man with a drum and sand-bagge, and Prentises drinking to him (sc.vii.40–1)
F. Enter at one Doore the Armorer and his Neighbors, drinking to him so much, that hee is drunke; and he enters with a Drumme before him, and his Staffe, with a Sand-bagge fastened to it: and at the other Doore his Man, with a Drumme and Sand-bagge, and Prentices drinking to him (II.iii.58–9)

Such similarities are striking; they cannot have come about by chance and they cannot be explained unless we admit that *The Contention* and 2 *Henry VI* are derived from the same manuscript, the author's original one as indicated by the use of that peculiar phrase "all the rest" which, as I have shown (p. 86), belongs to the language of author A.

Some stage directions disclose another interesting fact: the two texts were written for two different theaters. *The Contention* was performed in a theater which had a tower with a stairway leading to it from the stage. This disposition had permitted a picturesque entrance in the conjuring scene (sc.iv). Elinor arrived, carrying the list of questions which she wished to ask the spirit, and after delivering her paper to Bullingbrooke she added:

> And I will stand vpon this Tower here,
> And he[a]re the spirit what it saies to you

Then according to a stage direction "She goes vp to the Tower," where she stood during the ceremony. The same tower probably also served to represent the Tower of London in sc.xvi, when Lord Scales appeared on the walls to listen to three to four citizens below asking for his help.

The theater where *The Contention* was performed also had an inner stage enclosed by curtains where interior scenes could be played. It was thus possible to show the spectators Duke Humphrey's assassination.

> Then the Curtaines being drawne, Duke Humphrey is discouered in his bed, and two men lying on his brest and smothering him in his bed (sc.ix.1)

The inner stage was also used for the scene in which the king came to ascertain that his faithful servant was dead and Warwick pointed out that the Protector had certainly been stifled.

> Warwicke drawes the curtaines and showes Duke Humphrey in his bed (sc.x.49–50)

The inner stage was used on a third occasion for the scene of Cardinal Winchester's last moments:

> Enter King and Salsbury, and then the Curtaines be drawne, and the Cardinall is discouered in his bed, rauing and staring as if he were madde (sc.xi.1)

The theater for which the text of 2 *Henry VI* was written evidently had neither tower nor inner stage, and the scenes had to be conducted differently. In the scene of the evocation of the spirits the witch Mother Jordan, two priests, and Bullingbrooke entered first, and when the invocation began Elinor appeared "aloft," according to the customary phrase. Humphrey was not assassinated before the eyes of the spectators; the murderers were

only seen running across the stage to report the result of their
mission to suffolk (III.ii). When the moment came for the king to
lament the death of Duke Humphrey it was necessary to resort
to an awkward piece of stage business. The bed on which the
cardinal lay was simply "put forth," as the stage direction artlessly
indicates (III.ii.146–7), and then Warwick said to the king, "Come
hither, gracious Soueraigne, view this body" (149). The king
turned round and then saw the corpse of Humphrey. For the
cardinal's death the players must have resorted to some similar
device, for the stage direction simply says,

> Enter the King, Salisbury, and Warwicke, to the Cardinal in bed
> (III.iii.1) [3]

Besides these four scenes where the staging is totally different,
there are many other passages which, in the manner in which
incidents are treated, present variations perhaps less striking but
far more important in that they concern the dramatic possibilities
which the author (or authors) found in the incidents.

In sc.iii of *The Contention* the queen interposes only once, when
the legitimacy of the king's title to the throne is questioned; she
leaves it to the duke of Suffolk to examine the petitions, his reac-
tions supplying the movements of the action. The first complaint,
that against the cardinal's servant who stole the goods and the
wife of the petitioner, leaves the duke indifferent and provokes
only an ironic remark from him. The denunciation of the apprentice, who reports that his master, the armorer, considers the duke
of York the rightful heir to the throne, catches the queen's ear;
but it is Suffolk who orders the apprentice's arrest, intending to
exploit this fact against his enemy. The charge against Suffolk
himself of having enclosed the commons of Long Melford makes
him fly into a rage; he tears up the supplications and sends the
petitioners back to Humphrey with these words:

3. I have not tried to identify the two theaters: it is a difficult question to solve,
for we are not sufficiently well informed upon the construction and history of the first
London playhouses. I can only offer a hypothesis. Judging from the early probable
date of *The Contention* I suppose that the theater where it was originally performed
was not a well-equipped building but an innyard. In the sixteenth century these often
had an exterior staircase leading from the ground to the different stories, and a room
on the ground floor could serve as a spacious backstage behind the platform.

> So now show your petitions to Duke Humphrey.
> Villaines get you gone and come not neare the Court,
> Dare these pesants write against me thus (sc.iii.41–3)

Throughout this scene Suffolk is the chief character, and it is the
intriguing politician that especially stands out.

In the folio (I.iii) Suffolk's only intervention is in the form of
remarks or threats; it is the queen who dominates the scene. She
opens the examination of the complaints, and she closes it with
a violent explosion of wrath. The reason for this is that the order
of the last two petitioners has been reversed: the second petitioner
is the one who complains about the enclosure of the commons,
and the apprentice's denunciation comes at the end, with the result that the queen is beside herself. Pronouncing almost the same
words spoken by Suffolk in *The Contention:*

> And as for you that loue to be protected
> Vnder the Wings of our Protectors Grace,
> Begin your Suites anew, and sue to him (I.iii.40–3)

she tears the petitions and emphasizes this gesture with an insult:
"Away, cullions." Queenly even in her anger, she orders Suffolk to
dismiss the petitioners. In the scene of *The Contention* the queen
is a sort of nobody, entirely under the domination of Suffolk. In
the scene of the folio, by assuming the duties appertaining to her
rank she has been given an opportunity to bring out the resolute,
violent sides of her character.

What follows next in the same scene increases the contrast between the queen of *The Contention* and the queen in 2 *Henry VI.*
In both texts Margaret in a long speech confesses her anger at the
way the affairs of the state are handled. In *The Contention* (sc.
iii.44–62) she begins by pointing out that, as the incident of the
petitioners shows, Humphrey is more powerful than the king, who
is always poring over his books and "nere regards the honour of his
name." No less proud than Humphrey is his wife whose pomp is
such that she is sometimes taken for the queen. This reminds
Margaret that when she saw Suffolk win all female hearts, running
at tilt in France, she had imagined the king would be like this—or
she would never have left France.

In the folio text the complaints are practically the same, only
more detailed (40 lines against 19 in the quarto), but the order

in which they are presented is quite different. The speech is divided into two parts. In the first part (I.iii.45–67,71–4) she makes a bitter criticism of the king's foibles: he allows himself to be protected like a child by Humphrey, a thing which renders dubious her own situation as a queen. Incidentally she owns that on seeing Suffolk steal away the French ladies' hearts when he ran at tilt "in honour" of her love, she had thought that the king would resemble him in chivalric virtues. But all his mind is bent on holiness, his study is his tiltyard, his champions are the prophets and apostles; he might as well be a pope. And it is not only Duke Humphrey against whom she has a grudge: all the great nobles, Somerset, Buckingham, York, Cardinal Beauford, can do more in England than the king.

In the second part (I.iii.78–90) of her speech, she lengthily emphasizes the pride and luxury of Duke Humphrey's wife, which was only suggested in *The Contention*. The duchess "sweeps it through the Court with troops of Ladies more like an Empress," and "strangers do take her for the Queen; she beares a duke's reuenewes on her backe" and scorns the poverty of the legitimate rulers. The queen further recalls an incident which humiliated her deeply:

> Contemptuous base-born Callot as she is,
> She vaunted 'mongst her Minions t'other day,
> The very trayne of her worst wearing Gowne,
> Was better worth than all my Fathers Lands,
> Till Suffolk gaue two Dukedomes for his Daughter

The vulgar acerbity with which she expatiates upon her mortification, the fact especially that she keeps it for the end in an exasperated crescendo of discontent, shows the place it occupies in her mind and makes of Margaret of Anjou an entirely new character. The Margaret of *The Contention* is only an intriguing queen, jealous of her importance; the Margaret of the folio is that too, but she is more than that: female jealousy of the coarsest kind can rankle in her heart; she is a woman sharing with women their petty vanities, and from a dramatic point of view this makes a great difference, for she is a human being.

In the same sc.iii of *The Contention* the king has to choose a regent for France. York and Somerset are possible candidates and each has his partisans. The queen declares herself in favor of Somerset. Duke Humphrey's dry remark that the king is old enough to give his answer without the queen's advice shows, though he does not say so openly, that he is opposed to this solution. Suffolk, in accordance with the plan he has formed to use the affair of the armorer against York, adroitly recalls that a man has been accused of treason and the moment has come to settle that question. The armorer is sent for; Humphrey listens to the accusation of the apprentice and to the defense of the armorer and, at the invitation of the king, answers that the case being dubious only a judicial combat can "trie each others right or wrong." Having given his opinion he exits. A moment later he comes back and the king says to him, "Whom thinks your grace is meetest for to send?" to France. He answers:

> For that these words the Armourer should speake,
> Doth breed suspition on the part of Yorke,
> Let Somerset be Regent ouer the French,
> Till trials made, and Yorke may cleare himselfe.

It is so settled: the armorer and his apprentice are sent to prison, there to wait for the day of the judicial combat, and the scene ends upon that order.

In the folio text the scene begins in the same way: the queen proposes Somerset; Humphrey reminds her that the king is old enough to answer; and as the queen and her partisans accuse the Protector of malversation, the duke leaves the room, choking with anger as he himself acknowledges afterward. When he comes back, his "Choller being ouer-blowne," he announces that he is ready "to talke of Common-wealth Affayres," and he takes up the matter which the king had in hand and says that in his opinion York is the meetest man. It is only then that Suffolk to ward off this blow broaches the question of the armorer's treason. The interrogation of the armorer and of his apprentice is about the same as in *The Contention*, only a little longer. At the end, as the king wants to hear the Protector's legal opinion, Humphrey retracts the opinion he has expressed a few moments before and, for the same reasons as in *The Contention*, declares that Somerset should be sent to France.

On the whole the result seems to be the same in the two texts, with this difference, however, that it is hard for a man like Humphrey to have to retract his opinion openly and so rapidly as he does in the folio. In *The Contention* he can do so without losing face since he has not yet acknowledged with whom he sides, but now he has to support the choice of his enemies at the very moment when they are vilifying him. There is more in this retraction than obedience to a strict sense of political opportunism; he is giving proof of the real greatness of his character. And yet, before settling into this courageous attitude, he had a moment of weakness: he lost his temper like an ordinary man, which, to be sure, is a welcome attenuation of the good duke's monotonous perfection. Like Queen Margaret, Humphrey has gained a good deal in the human complexity of his nature.

That this improvement is an addition to the text of the folio is pretty certain, as is shown by the awkwardness that the change of place of the armorer's incident has introduced into the even development of the scene. In *The Contention* the events succeed each other most naturally. The thought that the words attributed to the armorer might be true troubles Humphrey, and after settling this affair provisionally he goes out to collect his ideas; when he comes back his decision is taken: to the king asking for his opinion on the question of the regency he proposes Somerset as a safer choice. The king approves and names Somerset regent. Somerset thanks the king and takes leave to post to France. And so ends sc.iii. All this is perfectly clear and logical.

In the folio the question of the treason of the armorer being transferred to the end of the scene leaves the question of the regency in suspense with no reason to resume it. But Humphrey's retraction was evidently the aim of the author and must be made, and so it had to be slipped into the first place left free. That is why Humphrey, instead of answering directly the king's question on the affair of treason, first gives his opinion on the regency, which nobody asked of him. After this irrelevance the whole end of the scene is a confused medley of the two incidents. Somerset, without knowing whether the king agrees with Humphrey, humbly thanks his Royal Majesty, the armorer accepts the combat, the apprentice whimpers that he cannot fight, and the king, in the same breath, sends the armorer and his man to prison and, though he has never named Somerset regent, promises to "see him away."

It would be difficult to find a more desultory, erratic ending.

On the other hand it should be noted that a certain number of incidents in the quarto have no analogue in the folio: [4]

sc.ii.59–67 Elinor arranges with John Hum for the evocation of the spirits to take place in the back part of her orchard while the king and all the Court are at Saint Albans.

sc.iii.145–7 The king blames the queen, who has slapped the duchess of Gloucester on the face.

sc.iv.31–6 Bullingbrooke sends the spirit back to Pluto's infernal kingdom.

sc.xiii.119–24 Cade demands of Stafford, who has just ordered him to surrender, that the king come first to be pardoned.

sc.xviii.71–84 When a sergeant complains that Dick has stolen his wife, Cade orders that the sergeant's tongue be cut off.

sc.xxii.57–61 Young Clifford puts Richard to flight.

After such a long list of differences between the two texts it is difficult to accept without restriction the opinion constantly repeated—and which I myself have repeated at the beginning of this chapter—that *The Contention* and the second part of *Henry VI* are one and the same play. It is true that the two texts exploit the same period of English history, beginning with the marriage of King Henry VI to Marguerite d'Anjou and ending with the victory of Saint Albans, the first important success for the Yorkist faction. But there are events or incidents in the folio which are not in the quarto, and events or incidents in the quarto which are not in the folio. And a critical examination of some of those differences has shown that behind them there was a systematic intention as to what a dramatic character can be and should be. We have caught a glimpse of an author different from author A and from author B, one who is more interested in the human side of historic personages than in their acts or their intrigues. It now remains to identify this third dramatist, and this will be possible only through an analysis of the style in the folio text.

ʃ ʃ ʃ

Such an analysis gives the following results.

In the first place, 337 verse lines are identical in the two texts.

4. A few short speeches do not occupy the same places in the quarto and the folio, but that does not affect the structure of the play.

They appear from time to time throughout the play, often alone, sometimes in small groups of two to seven verses, in one instance forming a long passage of 24 lines (I.i.233–56, York's soliloquy quoted at page 95).[5]

Mingled with these verses in which there is an absolute identity of expression are about 800 lines that may be called mixed; they contain fragments of the quarto embedded in a different text but expressing the same idea. The size of these fragments varies; sometimes most of the mixed line is identical in the quarto and the folio (in the following examples the words common to both texts are in italics):

Q. *To you Duke Humphrey must* vnfold *his griefe* (sc.i.69)
F. *To you Duke Humfrey must* vnload *his greefe* (I.i.76)

Q. Reuersing *Monuments of conquered France* (sc.i.80)
F. Defacing *Monuments of Conquer'd France* (I.i.102)

Sometimes only a few words are identical:

Q. *For griefe that* all is lost that Warwick won (sc.i.131)
F. *For griefe that* they are past recouerie (I.i.113)

Q. Nay my Lord *tis not my* words *that* troubles *you* (sc.i.88)
F. *'Tis not my* speeches *that you* do mislike (I.i.140)

It may even happen that only parts of a word are in both texts:

Q. By *wich*crafts, sorceries, and *coniu*rings (sc.v.138)
F. Dealing with *Witch*es and with *Coniu*rers (II.i.172)

Q. Who by such meanes did *raise* a *spirit* vp (sc.v.139)
F. *Rays*ing vp wicked *Spirit*s from vnder ground (II.i.174)

Finally, 1482 verses (out of 2611 in the whole play) are independent in the folio, that is, they do not contain a single word in

5. I give the complete list in order to show their distribution in the play: I.i.2,4,6– 7,12–15,20,24,37–9,41,44–5,61–5,71–4,75,147,162,206,209–10,233–56;   I.ii.1–2,33, 77; I.iii.113,121,150,180,209,216; I.iv.33–4,36,38; II.i.17,22,30,32,36–7,114; II.ii.8, 11,41,66; II.iii.36,38,102–8; II.iv.10–14,19,27,31,42,45,54,84; III.i.14,39,44,56–7,83, 87,95–7,108,121,125,171,183,197,257,292,356–7,359,382; III.ii.15,42,48,56,74–5,82, 158,160,161,190–1,193–4,196,199,203–5,211,213–19,224–7,229–37,240–1,245,248, 272–3,275–6,290,299,303,309,313,315–17,321,323,325,327–9,333,335,337–8,357, 368–9,375,399,402,408–9,412; III.iii.10; IV.i.35,45,51,69–70,76,126,136–7; IV.iv.20– 1,24–5; IV.v.7–8,10–13; IV.ix.22; V.i.136,192–3,198–201,203–8; V.ii.1–7,69; V.iii. 27–33.

common with the quarto. This is by far the most important part of the play, and this time the verses appear not only singly or in little groups but also in fairly long passages varying from 10 to 44 lines, sometimes expanding an idea from the quarto, sometimes constituting an entirely new development.[6]

It is not necessary to be gifted with exceptional acuteness to see that the versification and style of this independent element are not the same as the versifications and styles of *The Contention*, and that if Shakespeare had anything to do with the second part of *Henry VI*—which no one doubts—his hand will be found here. A critical examination of the rhythm of the verse leaves no uncertainty on that point. Disregarding the smaller portions, too short to yield normal percentages, I have analyzed the longer passages, namely: I.i.212–32 (21 lines); III.i.199–221 (23 lines), 223–56 (34 lines), 258–81 (24 lines); III.ii.87–121 (35 lines), 136–52 (17 lines), 250–70 (21 lines); IV.i.1–28 (28 lines), 77–105 (29 lines); IV.viii.36–50 (15 lines); IV.ix.23–49 (27 lines); V.i.149–92 (44 lines); V.ii.31–56 (26 lines), totaling 344 lines or 1720 feet. The percentages of rhythmic variations are as follows:

6. The following complete list will, I think, be of interest to those who study it carefully. I.i.23–31,33–5,77,79–81,89–91,93–4,96–8,100–1,104–8,112–14,131–9,144, 149–57,163–6,170–3,175–7,179,182–4,187,189,193,195,197–8,200–7,210,212–32; I. ii.3–6,8–10,13–16,18–21,27,31,35,41–2,45–6,48–9,56,62–7,69,82,84–7,90–2,94,96–7, 100–7; I.iii.40–4,46–52,57–67,71–81,83–6,90,92–103,108–9,116–18,128–40,149,151– 67,170–7; I.iv.19,21–30,42–3,47–58,64–6,73–5,77–80,82; II.i.1–2,6,8,18,23–7,42, 47–8,50,53,56–9,61–5,67–74,84–9,92–4,100–1,103–4,155–8,166–8,170,173,175–9, 184–96,199,202–5; II.ii.3,6,22,25,28–39,42,50,61,67–78,80; II.iii.2–10,15–18,21–2, 28–31,39–46,50–8,95–6; II.iv.1–4,7–9,15–16,22,33,38–41,56–63,65,67–9,75,80,88– 90,92–102,106–10; III.i.2–3,5,7–8,10–12,15–19,21–7,31–5,41,54,58–70,72–82,100– 2,109,113,117–20,126–7,130,135,139,143–50,153–60,163–7,169,172–7,181,193–4, 199–221,223–56,258–81,284–9,291,295–6,298–303,305,308,311–17,319–27,329–30, 332,344,346–7,349–55,360–73,376–7,379,383; III.ii.1–5,8–13,17,22–6,30–2,34–7,41, 45–7,51,54–5,58–71,76–81,87–122,128–9,133,136–52,163–8,169–74,176,178–80, 182–4,186–7,230–6,238–9,242,246–7,250–70,282–4,286,291–2,296–7,301–2,304–6, 312,330–2,339,342,344–8,351–6,360–6,370–2,374,376,379,381–5,403–4; III.iii.1,5–8, 11–14,16,19–23,24–5,32–3;   IV.i.1–28,31,39–43,59–62,65–7,72,74,77–105,109–10, 115–16,118,123,127–34,139–47;   IV.ii.130–5,138–9,141,150,152–3,159–60,183–4, 188–98; IV.iv.1–12,15–18,26,28–9,32–8,40,45–60; IV.vii.62,66–8,71–5,77–83,86–7, 90,93–4,103–10,121–4; IV.viii.6–10,13–18,36–50,52–4,71–2; IV.ix.1–9,11–21,23–49; IV.x.18–19,22–5,36,50–7,74–6,82–7,90;   V.i.2,6–11,13,20–31,35,37,40,45,48–53,55, 58–60,63–5,68–9,71–3,76–7,80–1,88–93,95–105, 108–10,112–13,115–23,127–8,130, 135,141–3,145–7,149–92,194–5; V.ii.10–11,13,31–56,58–61,70–1,73–82,84–90; V.iii. 1–14,16–17,19–23,26.

Weakly accented feet	463 or 26.9%
Trochees	54 or 3.1%
Spondees	64 or 3.7%
Internal pauses	162 lines or 47.0%
Enjambments	62 lines or 18.0%

And when we examine the style of these passages we find the same mannerisms that abound in *Venus and Adonis* and *Lucrece:*

1. Division of the thought into symmetrical and balanced parts of more or less equal length:

> Great King of England, & my gracious Lord (I.i.24)
>
> Shall Henries Conquest, Bedfords vigilance (I.i.96) [7]

2. Repetition of a word or grammatical form to accentuate the symmetrical construction:

> Is this the Fashions in the Court of England?
> Is this the Gouernment of Britaines Ile? (I.iii.46–7)
>
> Blotting your names from Bookes of memory,
> Racing the Charracters of your Renowne (I.i.100–1) [8]

3. Marked preference for the association of two words expressing two aspects of the same idea and connected by a conjunction:

> France should haue torne and rent my very hart (I.i.126)
>
> Bewitch your hearts, be wise and circumspect (I.i.157) [9]

4. Antitheses:

> By day, by night; waking, and in my dreames (I.i.26)
>
> In Winters cold, and Summers parching heate (I.i.81) [1]

5. Concetti appear less frequently than in the *Poems,* that kind of mawkishness being hardly suitable to the violence of the incidents in the play. A few, however, can be found.

7. Cf. I.i.81,136; I.ii.42; I.iii.133; I.iv.22; II.i.205; II.ii.71; II.iii.14,21; II.iv.33; III.i.73,174,268; III.ii.60,62,119,171,257,282,301,385; IV.i.122; IV.viii.14; V.i.24,37.

8. Cf. I.i.159–60; I.ii.3–6; II.iii.14,45–6; III.i.7–8,75–8,143–6; IV.ii.191–2; IV.vii.108–9; V.i.166,185–8.

9. Cf. I.i.91,134,187,198,200,230; I.ii.20,46,62; I.iii.60,129,132,138,161; I.iv.28; II.i.168,170,175,183,191,195,198; III.i.9,263,275,303,350,376; III.ii.147,167,250,267,354,371; IV.i.5,19,42,101,121,144; IV.ii.130,135,152; IV.iv.2,33,35,50,60; IV.vii.73,93,104; IV.viii.39; IV.ix.6,12,14,16,20,25,33; V.i.9,27,50,58,100,101,107,152,194; V.ii.11,22,26,31,42,74.

1. Cf. I.i.27,91; I.ii.49; II.i.175; II.ii.30; II.iv.4,40; III.i.263; III.ii.55,71,152,234; IV.ix.5–6,12; IV.x.54–5; V.i.31,97–8.

a. Concetti which consist in a repetition of the sound of a word or jingle:

> And with my fingers feele his hand, unfeeling (III.ii.145)

> For in the shade of death, I shall finde ioy;
> In life, but double death, now Gloster's dead (III.ii.54–5) [2]

b. Concetti proper, in the Italian manner: The queen's speech (III.ii.88–113) is composed of a series of conceits of the most far-fetched variety: during her journey to England Aeolus would not be a murderer, so he left that task to King Henry; the "pretty-vaulting Sea refus'd to drowne" her, knowing that on land the king would do so "With tears as salt as Sea . . . The splitting Rockes cower'd in the sinking sands,/And would not dash" her "with their ragged sides," etc.

6. Compound words after the Greek and Latin manner: tender-feeling (II.iv.9), teare-stayn'd (II.iv.16), mad-bred (III.i.354), sharpe-quill'd (III.i.363), shag-hayr'd (III.i.367), heart-offending (III.ii.60), blood-consuming (III.ii.61), blood-drinking (III.ii.63), pretty vaulting (III.ii.94), earnest-gaping (III.ii.105), loud houl-ing (IV.i.3), bloodshedding (IV.vii.108), stedfast gazing (IV.x.48), long imprisoned (V.i.88), false-heart (V.i.143), fell-lurking (V.i.146).

7. Words of French consonance: Taincture (II.i.188), affiance (III.i.74), aydance (III.ii.165).[3]

And in the midst of these mannerisms Shakespeare's active imagination is busy exploiting the impressions of an existence already rich in recollections; here and there the dialogue is adorned "like rich hangings in a homely house"—the simile is Shake-speare's own (2 Henry VI V.iii.12). These are not images which search the mysteries of life, for the author is still marveling at the beauty of the universe, and some are perhaps a little too familiar, such as the succession of seasons:

> Thus sometimes hath the brightest day a Cloud:
> And after Summer, euermore succeedes
> Barren Winter, with his wrathfull nipping Cold;
> So Cares and Ioyes abound, as Seasons fleet (II.iv.1–4)

2. Cf. I.i.219; II.iv.96–7; III.i.209; III.ii.257,356,365–6; IV.iv.52; IV.vii.87–8; IV. ix.5–6; V.i.29,129–30; V.ii.32,38,77.
3. Aidance is in *Venus and Adonis*, 330.

snow melting in the sun:

> Cold Snow melts with the Sonnes hot Beames:
> Henry, my Lord, is cold in great Affaires (III.i.223–4)

nightfall:

> The gaudy blabbing and remorsefull day,
> Is crept into the bosome of the Sea:
> And now loud houling Wolues arouse the Iades
> That dragge the Tragicke melancholy night;
> Who with their drowsie, slow, and flagging wings
> Cleape dead-mens graues, and from their misty Iawes,
> Breath foule contagious darkness in the ayre (IV.i.1–7)

But there may also be found some images that already have that rare quality which is one of the marks of great poetry, like the simile lent to York:

> And this fell Tempest shall not cease to rage,
> Vntill the Golden Circuit on my Head,
> Like the glorious Sunnes transparant Beames,
> Doe calme the furie of this mad-bred Flawe (III.i.351–4) [4]

As for the parts of the play written in prose, they present exactly the same differences. A portion is identical in the two texts (sc.iii. 116–21 = I.iii.200–6; sc.v.92–123 = II.i.119–53; sc.vii.41–67,74–9 = II.iii.59–70,74–88,104–8; sc.xvi.1–6 = IV.v.1–6; sc.xvii.1–7,13–18 = IV.vi.1–7,13–18; sc.xviii.1–8,62–7 = IV.vii.1–8,127–33); most of the rest is of a mixed kind, fragments of *The Contention* more or less modified; a third part has no analogue in *The Contention*, for instance IV.viii.20–34 and IV.x.1–17, two speeches in which Cade shows that he is surprisingly familiar with the courtly euphuistic style—which permits one to say that they are Shakespeare's.

To conclude, it now appears clearly that the second part of *Henry VI* is a hybrid play, composed of a small portion reproducing word for word the text of *The Contention*, which therefore is not Shakespeare's; of a much larger portion, important since it amounts to more than half the lines of the whole play, which has

---

4. A certain number of these images are to be found in *Venus and Adonis* in almost the same form. Cf. 2 *HVI* III.i.223 and *V & A*, 750; 2 *HVI* 228–30 and *V & A*, 878–9; 2 *HVI* III.i.248–9 and *V & A*, 55; 2 *HVI* III.ii.106–9 and *V & A*, 823–4; 2 *HVI* V.i.151–4 and *V & A*, 923–4.

the character of an accession to the text of *The Contention* and which the versification and the style prove to be Shakespeare's; and of a third portion which is the text of *The Contention* more or less modified, evidently by the same author who wrote the accessions. The lines of *The Contention,* whether identical or in a mixed form, are distributed throughout the whole play and provide a complete outline of the action into which the modifications and accessions are dovetailed. In other words, the second part of *Henry VI* is a perfect specimen of the plays which Henslowe called "altered." It is, in fact, comparable to the *Doctor Faustus* of William Birde and Samuel Rowley—an old play first partly revised with the introduction of a comic element, then thoroughly transformed a second time—with this difference, however, that a good play by Marlowe had been altered by third-rate dramatists, while in 2 *Henry VI* an inferior play had been finally revised by a play-patcher of genius.

∫ ∫ ∫

THE FORTUITOUS CIRCUMSTANCE that has preserved the text of *The Contention* will enable us to see with absolute precision of what the labor of revision in the second part of *Henry VI* consisted. Shakespeare accepted as a matter of course the development of the action as it had been conceived by his predecessors, since it dealt with historical events that could not be changed in their broad outline; and he made only a few modifications of details, the chief of which I have enumerated above (cf. pp. 103 ff.). His work consisted largely in amending a style which he had no difficulty in recognizing as inferior to the one he felt himself capable of. He read over *The Contention* from beginning to end and modified it according to the inspiration of his nascent genius.

First of all he cleared the text of its many prosodic irregularities. With a remarkable respect for the rules observed in his own time, he turned lines either too short or too long into correct decasyllables.

Q. We thanke thee Clifford (sc.xxi.91)
F. I thanke thee Clifford: say, what newes with thee (V.i.125)

Q. A poore Esquire of Kent (sc.xxi.59)
F. A poore Esquire of Kent, that loves his King (V.i.75)

Q. Yet do not goe. Come Basaliske (sc.x.27)
F. Yet doe not goe away: come Basiliske (III.ii.52)

Q. As by your high imperiall Maiesties command (sc.i.1)
F. As by your high Imperiall Maiesty (I.i.1)

Lines rhythmically poor were either simply deleted or by light adjustments given the fluidity they lacked. Thus a somewhat halting line is redressed by a small change at the beginning:

Q. Gloster is no litle man in England (sc.ix,13)
F. And Humfrey is no little Man in England (III.i.20)

The trisyllabic feet of author A have disappeared in the same way:

Q. There goes | our Protec | tor in a rage (sc.i.93)
F. So, there goes our Protector in a rage (I.i.147)

Q. And haue not I and mine | vnckle Bew | ford here (sc.i.73)
F. Or hath mine Vnkle Beauford, and my selfe (I.i.89) [5]

Q. | Crying Ie | sus blesse your royall exellence (sc.i.99)
F. Iesu maintaine your Royall Excellence (I.i.161)

This weeding out of the versification has been carried out with a care whose extent will be appreciated if I add that almost all the prosodic abnormalities I have noted have been corrected. Only a few irregular lines have been retained,[6] but they are in passages that have been reproduced word for word, which explains why they escaped Shakespeare's attention. One trisyllabic foot [7] has not been touched, but it too is in one of the lines identical in the two texts.

Shakespeare does not seem to have been disturbed by the numerous trochaic feet (after all they were not irregularities); they have remained or disappeared according as the pattern of the sentence in which they occurred was adopted or changed. But he did correct trochees in the last foot of a verse.

5. Shakespeare's purism in this case is all the more remarkable as the word "uncle" could be syncopated and the verse scanned: "And haue | not I | and mine | unckl' Bew | ford here | "
6. Sc.ix.176=III.i.357; sc.i.100=I.i.162; sc.iv.25=I.iv.35; sc.x.46=III.ii.131; sc. xix.22=IV.ix.22; sc.vii.74=II.iii.102; sc.xxi.4=V.i.5.
7. Sc.xv.ii=IV.iv.25.

It was primarily style that engaged Shakespeare's attention. When a phrase was commonplace, which often happened, he modified it, and hence comes the great number of mixed lines. He gave substance to a shadowy meaning, and then one or two words were sometimes sufficient to instill life into a dull sentence. The authors of *The Contention* were chiefly interested in the action of the play and said what they had to say with conciseness; Shakespeare, while reading the unpolished text, perceived everywhere a world of possible additions. He developed ideas that were too succinctly worded:

> What did my brother Henry toyle himselfe,
> And waste his subiects for to conquere France?

says Duke Humphrey in *The Contention* (sc.i.69–70). Shakespeare expanded the word "toil" into:

> What? did my brother Henry spend his youth,
> His valour, coine, and people in the warres?
> Did he so often lodge in open field;
> In Winters cold, and Summers parching heate,
> To conquer France, his true inheritance? (I.i.78–82)

The poet is continually on the alert. His predecessor had often come close to a poetical sensation without realizing it; Shakespeare seizes upon it and inserts some of his own visions between the lines of the inert text. Suffolk, in order to calm the wrath of the queen, who was jealous of the duke and duchess of Gloucester, promises her that she will have her vengeance: "I have set," he says in the quarto, "lime-twigs that will intangle them." Shakespeare extends this banal metaphor, transforms the lime-twigs into a bush, and imagines a little picture of the duchess riding her horse and dismounting when lured by birds in the bush.

> Madame, myself haue lym'd a Bush for her,
> And plac't a Quier of such enticing Birds,
> That she will light to listen to the Layes,
> And neuer mount to trouble you again (I.iii.91–4)

In the conjuring scene (iv) Bullingbrooke begins his invocation with the words:

> Darke Night, dread Night, the silence of the Night (l.14)

but this suggestive line leaves no echo; for Shakespeare it is an
occasion to evoke the mysterious life which night brings with it:

> Deepe Night, darke Night, the silent of the Night,
> The time of Night when Troy was set on fire,
> The Time when Screech-owles cry, and Bandogs howle,
> And Spirits walke, and Ghosts breake vp their Graues (I.iv.21–3)

These poetical ornaments do not always contribute to dramatic
truth. It can happen that Shakespeare develops an idea to the
point where it becomes pure padding. An example of those excessive amplifications is furnished by the passage in which the king,
saddened by the hostility of the lords and the queen toward Duke
Humphrey, wishes to retire, leaving Parliament to decide what
is best to do. And as the queen asks him if he really intends to retire, in the quarto he replies:

> I Margaret. My heart is kild with griefe,
> Where I may sit and sigh in endlesse mone,
> For who's a Traitor, Gloster he is none (sc.ix.109–11)

The style of these three lines is mediocre, but the short answer
did not interfere with the action; the queen and the lords started
at once to plot the duke's assassination. In place of the second
verse line, between the first and the third lines which he preserved
almost exactly, Shakespeare inserted 22 lines of lamentations (III.
i.199–220), 7 of which compare the Protector to a calf led to the
slaughterhouse while the lowing dam searches for her young one
(III.i.210–16), an image in doubtful taste and one which, at any
rate, would have been better suited to a poem like *Venus and
Adonis* than to a historical play. "Sometimes it was necessary he
should be stop'd," Ben Jonson once said of Shakespeare.

While the poet in Shakespeare thus "turned to shape the forms
of things unknown" the dramatist did not remain idle, and many
additions had no other purpose than to give relief to the characters.[8] It was not an easy task. Because they were engaged in the
intrigues and maneuvers which made up the subject matter, the
dramatis personae were indistinguishable from each other except
by their part in the action, and their individuality rarely had an

8. See the article by Clayton Alvis Greer, "The York and Lancaster Quarto-Folio
Sequence," *Publ. Mod. Lang. Assoc.*, Sept. 1933, *48*, No. 3, 655–704.

opportunity to influence their acts. Shakespeare overcame this difficulty by applying a technique which he was to perfect later and which in the better plays contributes something to the extraordinary life they possess. He made the characters reveal the opinion they have of each other, thus bringing out aspects of their personalities which otherwise would have remained ignored. Suffolk would not have been so familiar to us if the queen had not let it be known that she admired his "Courage, Courtship, and proportion" (I.iii.57); she is astonished that his murderers were not moved by his "louely face" (IV.iv.15–18). York speaks of his insolence (II.ii.70) and accuses him of having dimmed "the Honor of . . . warlike" England in giving Anjou and Maine to France (I.i.125). Finally the captain of the boat on which Suffolk had been taken prisoner recalls in detail the bad influence the queen's lover exercised over England's political affairs (IV.i.80–103). It is from York that we learn that Beauford, cardinal of Winchester, was a proud man (II.ii.71), and Salisbury is more explicit in adding that this man of the church behaved in a fashion unworthy of a ruler, "As stout and proud as he were Lord of all" (I.i.187,189); this opinion is confirmed by the queen who applies to him the epithet "imperious" (I.iii.72). The cardinal in turn terms Warwick "Ambitious" (I.iii.112), and Salisbury informs us that this same Warwick is just as popular as Duke Humphrey (I.i.192–3) and that York who is criticized by the queen for his grumbling (I.iii.73) is feared and honored for his exploits (I.i.196–8). Shakespeare has thus provided a number of informative passages through which the spectators are acquainted with certain hidden aspects of the minor characters' individuality.

The principal characters were more clearly drawn in *The Contention*, though all their traits were seen as manifestations of their political parts. But much remained to be done in order to individualize them. Here Shakespeare's work has been direct and far-reaching. By their acts, their attitudes, their thoughts, he has succeeded in disclosing much of their inner life. The scheming nature of the queen has been rendered striking by the ingenious way in which she brings accusations against Duke Humphrey that will discredit him in the king's eyes (I.iii.138–40; III.i.5–12,21–8). I have already pointed out how a clever change in the construction of a speech has shown her tendency to jealousy; and the falsely pious tone with which she expresses the hope that God will acquit the duke of suspicion (III.ii.25) denotes her shameless hypocrisy. And thus the masculine queen of *The Contention* has been provided with some of the weaknesses of human nature.

Humphrey's case was more difficult. As history shows him, the duke was really good, loyal, disinterested, respectful of the law even when it was enforced against him. Shakespeare could only intensify those qualities, which he has done by little touches (I.i. 132–5; I.ii.42–9; I.iii.160–1; II.iii.15–16); but he has also added some attitudes or incidents which certainly render the character more complex. I have shown on pages 106–7 that the duke had moments of anger which he could not restrain; the way in which he speaks of the uncertainty of human joys (II.iv.1–4) proves that he was capable of accepting misfortune with the patience that knowledge of life gives, and the manner in which he lets his sorrow burst forth after his wife's banishment also shows that power had not stifled all sensibility in him (II.iii.17–19).

King Henry has naturally received the greatest number of those revealing additions. His language, crammed with devout sentences (a characteristic also present in *The Contention*), has been retained and accentuated (II.i.70–1,84–6,186–7; III.ii.139–40; IV. iv.55; IV.ix.13–14); his exclamation "the treasury of everlasting joy," with which he punctuates the word "heaven" pronounced by Gloucester, not only shows how automatic this language has become with him but also produces that effect of simultaneous surprise and verisimilitude which the most profound phrases of Shakespeare sometimes have. When the king hears of the so-called miracle of the blind man he says that the man in recovering his sight has multiplied the occasions to sin, a remark that speaks eloquently of the little faith he has in human morality (II.i.71). Shakespeare also quotes the opinion others have formed of him; the most impressive portrait is made by the queen when she depicts his bigotry, his lack of courtly qualities, his childish submission to the control of ambitious subjects (I.iii.58–67), his susceptibility to being taken in by appearances, which makes him incapable of handling affairs of state (III.i.224–30). Elsewhere Henry himself recognizes that his tastes are more those of a sub-

ject than of a king (IV.ix.1–6); he even has a presentiment that
one day his reign may be found to have been calamitous to his
country (IV.ix.48–9). Henry VI is not one of those Shakespearean
characters whose psychological portrayal is so rich and true that
they remain profoundly engraved in our memory, but neither is he
the slightly ridiculous puppet of *The Contention*.

$$\int \quad \int \quad \int$$

MOST OF THE longer passages among those that are entirely in
Shakespeare's hand (see above, p. 110 n.) have a small number of
feminine endings.

	Feminine endings	Verse lines	Percentages
I.i.212–32	3	21	14.2
III.i.199–221	0	23	0
223–56	4	34	11.7
258–81	3	24	12.5
III.ii.87–121	2	35	5.7
IV.i.1–28	0	28	0.0
77–105	3	29	10.3
V.i.149–92	4	44	9.9
V.ii.31–56	3	26	11.5

The average proportion is 8.4%

These passages must have been written at a period when Shakespeare was just beginning to understand how the feminine ending
could give flexibility to the verse.

In four passages the proportions are higher:

	Feminine endings	Verse lines	Percentages
III.ii.136–52	5	17	29.4
250–70	4	21	19.0
IV.viii.36–50	3	15	20.0
IV.ix.23–49	7	27	25.9

A total of 19 feminine endings on 80 verse lines or an average of 23.7%

These four passages must belong to a later period. It is to be noted
that they all seem to have been added with the intention of rendering King Henry sympathetic, possibly on the occasion of a performance at Court where, in the presence of Queen Elizabeth, one
of her ancestors had to be presented in a favorable light.

The Third Part of Henry VI

The Quarto of 1595 or "The True Tragedie"

THE PROBLEM POSED in the case of the third part of *Henry VI* is exactly the same as for the second part, and the comparison of the quarto and the folio texts leads to the same solution.

The quarto entitled *The true Tragedie of Richard Duke of Yorke, and the death of good King Henrie the Sixt, with the whole contention betweene the two Houses Lancaster and Yorke,* printed by P[eter] S[hort], appeared in 1595. Its publisher was Thomas Millington, who the preceding year published *The Contention.* This quarto was not registered with the Stationers' Company, doubtless because the publisher thought that since *The True Tragedie* was a continuation of *The Contention* the permission to print the first part covered the second. The title page made it clear that "it was sundrie times acted by the Right Honourable the Earle of Pembrooke his seruants." [9]

The manuscript reproduced by this quarto presented most of the characteristic peculiarities of the manuscript of *The Contention.* In places the handwriting was difficult to decipher for I have noted a number of misreadings, some of them surprising—"death" for "deaf" (sc.iv.41), "Arcadia" for "Hyrcania" (sc.iv.140), "captaines" for "captiues" (sc.v.94), "whose" for "who" (sc.vi.14), "fainting" for "stinging" (sc.vi.135), "famous" for "foeman's" (sc. ix.27), "stormes" for "taunts" (sc.x.59), "busie" for "buzz" (sc.x. 88), "godsforbot man" for "god forbid that" (sc.xii.38), "shrimpe" for "shrub" (sc.xii.122), "loue" for "leaue" (sc.xiii.24), "Summerfield" for "Somerville" (sc.xxi.7), "yer night" for "yet ere night" (sc.xxiv.37), "Ranard" for "Regnier" (sc.xxvi.38).

Entrances and exits are neatly inscribed interlinearly, the entrances in the center, the exits toward the right.

The entrances are not so fully detailed as in *The Contention.* They generally enumerate only the names of the dramatis personae, most of the time without their ranks or functions. Two of

---

9. A new edition of this quarto appeared in 1600, and a third edition together with *The Contention* under the title of *The Whole Contention . . .* came out in 1619.
References in this chapter are to the Praetorius Facsimile, 1891, No. 38.

them, however, are of the same descriptive kind as in the quarto
of *The Contention:*

> Sound a Parlie, and Richard and Clarence whispers togither, and then
> Clarence takes his red Rose out of his hat, and throwes it at Warwicke
> (sc.xxi.55)

> Alarmes to the battell, Yorke flies, then the chambers be discharged. Then
> enter the king, Cla & Glo, & the rest, & make a great shout and crie,
> for Yorke, for Yorke, and then the Queene is taken, & the prince, &
> Oxf. & Sum. and then sound and enter all againe (sc.xxiv.46)

The use of the conjunctions "and" and "then" in the enumeration
of the characters, the phrase "and the rest" as a synonym of et
cetera, the verb form of the third person plural of the indicative
present ending in *s* ("Richard and Clarence whispers") show that
they were written by author A.

Again as in *The Contention* the author occasionally encroaches
upon the task of the prompter by indicating the properties, the
gestures, and movements of the actors:

> Enter one with a letter to Warwike (sc.xix.22–3)

> The Maire opens the dore, and brings the keies in his hand (sc.xviii.18–
> 19)

> Enter Richard running (sc.vii.14–15)

> Enter two keepers with bow and arrows (sc.xi.1)

The task of fixing the number of supers is left to the prompter:

> Enter king Lewis and the ladie Bona and Queene Margaret, Prince
> Edward, and Oxford and others (sc.xiii.1)

The work of the prompter is recognizable by the addition at the
end of a line of one entrance, and twenty-one exits forgotten by
the author.[1] Numerous badly divided lines show the existence of
marginal corrections.[2]

1. Sc.i.174,177,179,196,197,198,222,224; sc.ii.55; sc.iii.10,49; sc.x.101; sc.xii.102;
sc.xiii.169; sc.xvii.23; sc.xix.47; sc.xxi.39,44,47; sc.xxii.44; sc.xxiii.21.
2. Sc.i.137–8,149–50,187–8; sc.ii.39–43; sc.iii.23–4; sc.iv.51–2; sc.v.12–13,63–4;
sc.vi.86–8,90–2,105–9,139–40; sc.x.46–7,93–6; sc.xi.10–11,32–3,40–1; sc.xii.19–21,
33–6,79–80,95–6,101–2; sc.xiii.56–9,63–8,74–5,125–6; sc.xiv.12–14,27–30,37–40,45–
6,50–3,71–5,86–8,91–5; sc.xv.23–4,29–31; sc.xvi.11–13,16–19; sc.xviii.29–30,38–40;
sc.xix.2–7,10–11,17–22; sc.xxi.9–10,50–1,72–4; sc.xxiii.18–21; sc.xxiv.23–7,40–3,99,
103,116–17; sc.xxv.46–7; sc.xxix.23–7,33–4,61–3,100–3,110–12; sc.xxv.12–14.

The manuscript of *The True Tragedie* was clearly an author's manuscript, heavily corrected, revised by the prompter, and of the same origin as the manuscript of *The Contention*.

∫ ∫ ∫

The True Tragedie was, as a matter of fact, written by the same authors as *The Contention*. And all the characteristics of author A's versification and style are to be found again in this text:

a. Verse lines of every length from two to seven feet.[3]

b. Trisyllabic feet:

in four-stress lines:

Proue it Henrie | and thou shalt | be king (sc.i.127) [4]

in five-stress lines:

And thine Clifford: | and you both | haue vow'd reuenge (sc.i.50) [5]

in six-stress lines:

And whilst I liue to honour me | as thy king | and Soueraigne (sc.i.198) [6]

3. Two feet: sc.i.200; sc.v.109; sc.vi.40,58,168; sc.vii.47; sc.viii.13; sc.xiii.10; sc.xiv.73,106; sc.xv.5; sc.xxiv.88. Three feet: sc.i.164; sc.ii.22; sc.iii.10; sc.iv.15,81; sc.v.44,66,159; sc.vi.161; sc.x.1; sc.xi.33; sc.xii.11,25; sc.xiii.85,144; sc.xiv.42; sc.xvi.20,23. Four feet: sc.i.126,127,172,198,201; sc.iv.82,87,117; sc.v.110,143,158; sc.vi.76; sc.x.44,93; sc.xi.16,17,24; sc.xii.32,48,52,72,109,110; sc.xiii.45,50,52,89,109,110; sc.xiv.17,26,31,46,58,101,103; sc.xv.24,33,39; sc.xvi.1,5,7,10; sc.xviii.12,31,41,54,57; sc.xix.45; sc.xx.5; sc.xxi.6; sc.xxiii.5; sc.xxiv.3,10,60,84,87,89,93,102; sc.xxv.28,64. Six feet: sc.i.101,102,108,119,149–50,180,185,187,188,214,225,227; sc.ii.1,12,47; sc.iii.15,45; sc.iv.105; sc.v.23,43,53,54,61,69; sc.vi.39,78,104,123,143; sc.ix.47,48,61,64; sc.x.34,58,61,71,88; sc.xi.3,10,11,28,37,39; sc.xii.18,27,38,49,87–8,90–1,112,113; sc.xiii.74–5,93,96,109,125–6,134; sc.xiv.2,7–8,21,32,43,57,60,69,71,90,91–2; sc.xv.28,30–1,55; sc.xvi.16; sc.xvii.7; sc.xviii.29–30,32–3,37; sc.xix.12,13; sc.xx.4; sc.xxi.12,26,40; sc.xxii.25,34; sc.xxiii.9; sc.xxiv.72,79; sc.xxv.19,21,23,66; sc.xxvi.26,29,43. Seven feet: sc.ii.9; sc.iii.1–2; sc.ix.48; sc.x.94,96; sc.xi.36; sc.xii.45,46,58; sc.xvii.1–2.

4. Sc.ii.43; sc.iv.82,87,117; sc.v.110,143; sc.xi.24; sc.xii.48,52,109,110; sc.xiii.50,52,104,108,146; sc.xiv.17,26,31,58; sc.xv.39; sc.xvi.5; sc.xviii.31,41,54; sc.xxi.6; sc.xxiv.3,84,89,93,102,110.

5. Sc.i.16,78,83,128,137,189,213,218,220; sc.ii.4,23,26,27,32,34,35,40–1,45,53; sc.iii.35,36; sc.iv.58,80,88,95,104; sc.v.39,63–4,95,113; sc.vi.86–7,95,101,103,110,130,139; sc.x.39,52,60,67; sc.xi.22,38,40; sc.xii.3,4,15,16,28,78,88–9,93,97; sc.xiii.22; sc.xiv.35,44,49,59,63,87–8; sc.xv.23–4,25,46; sc.xvi.15; sc.xvii.6,8,12,16; sc.xviii.18; sc.xx.4; sc.xxi.9–10,16,17,41,65; sc.xxiii.3,10,17; sc.xxiv.21,34,40–1,45,53,91,106,122; sc.xxv.24,29,30,31,61,80,81.

6. Sc.xiii.73; sc.xv.43.

in seven-stress lines:

We here create thee Duke of Clarence, | and girt thee | with the sword (sc.x.94) [7]

c. Excessive proportion of trochaic feet, often reaching more than 10% [8] and in all positions in the verse:

Chargde our maine battels front, and therewith him (sc.i.6)

Like men *borne to* renowne by life or death (sc.iv.8)

Whereat the great *Lord of* Northum[ber]land (sc.i.4)

The armie of the Queene *meanes to* besiedge vs (sc.ii.46)

Can but amount to 48 *thousand* (sc.v.147)

d. Five-stress lines with the first foot truncated:

Come, | lets take our stands vpon this hill (sc.xi.1)

Naie | I feare her not vnlesse she fall (sc.xii.37)

No, | if thou saie no to my demand (sc.xii.60)

Well, | least on brothers, I can tell you (sc.xii.95)

What, | are you provided to depart (sc.xvi.13)

Truth | my Lord, we know you for no lesse (sc.xviii.11)

Yes | Warwike he dares, and leades the waie (sc.xxi.78)

What | is pompe, rule, raigne, but earth and dust (sc.xxii.35)

Which | by Gods assistance and your prowesse (sc.xxiv.36)

Well, | discharge the common souldiers with paie (sc.xxiv.119)

e. Conversational language, overloaded with exclamations and interjections such as come, look, what, how now, I (ay), nay, well, oh, ha, tush, marry, loe, God.[9]

7. Sc.x.96; sc.xii.45,58; sc.xvii.1–2.

8. Cf., for instance, sc.i.45–60; sc.iv.117–29; sc.x.61–78; sc.xiii.95–108; sc.xiv.58–109; sc.xvi.1–23; sc.xviii.1–23; sc.xxiv.87–122.

9. Sc.i.16,45,54,149,157,201,218,222,228; sc.ii.2,4,17,23,36,42,48,54; sc.iii.1,3,7,8, 11,16,33,35,42; sc.iv.1,13,20,33,49,55,75,81,91,122,140,157; sc.v.9,14,62,63,68,69, 154,172; sc.vi.53,64,79,111; sc.vii.10,14,40; sc.ix.1,7,19,23,28,29,46,59,64; sc.x.11,57, 70,78,99; sc.xi.1,10,11; sc.xii.11,19,24,33,37,38,42,51,91,93,95,103,117,126,132; sc. xiii.10,50,106; sc.xiv.35,58,81; sc.xv.21,39,51; sc.xvi.7,12,13,14,15,21; sc.xvii.5,6; sc. xviii.9,15,21,23,36,41; sc.xxi.13,16,18,25,26,37,50,54,71,72,75; sc.xxii.5,14,18,23,39; sc.xxiii.19; sc.xxiv.23,24,47,67,69,81,87,100,116,119; sc.xxv.11,21,48,49,51,65.

f. Colloquial and obsolescent expressions: "be" for "are" (sc.vi. 70; sc.xiii.140; sc.xiv.74; sc.xxiv.75), sith (sc.iii.40), for to (sc.viii.6; sc.xiii.155; sc.xxiv.20), manie flies to him (sc.vi.69), whither flies the Gnats (sc.x.9), no humble suters sues (sc.xi.8), such as subjects owes and the lawes commands (sc.xii.47), Sommerset and Clarence comes (sc.xv.3), Gloster and Hastings flies (sc.xv.27, stage direction), the huntsman and he doth come (sc.xvi.9), But God he wots (sc.iv.114), well I wot (sc.vi.131), My father he came (sc.ix.21), if that (sc.xiii.148), moe (sc.v.32,138; sc.xxii.25).

Here is a passage characteristic enough to compare with the one quoted from *The Contention,* on pages 94–5.

> QUEEN. Good Clarence doe, sweet Clarence kill me too.　　105
> CLA. Didst thou not heare me sweare | I would not | do it?
> QUEEN. *I, but* thou vsest to forsweare thy selfe,
> Twas sinne before, but now tis charitie.
> Whears the *Diuels butcher, hardfa*uored Richard
> *Richard* where art thou? He is not heere,　　110
> *Murder* is his almes deed, petitioners
> For bloud he nere put backe.
> EDW. Awaie I saie, and take her hence perforce.
> QUEEN. So come to you and yours, as to this prince. Ex.
> EDW. *Clarence, withers* Gloster gone?　　115
> CLA. *Marrie* my Lord to London, and as I gesse,
> To make a bloudie supper in the Tower.
> EDW. He is sudden if a thing come in his head.
> Well, | discharge the common souldiers with paie
> And thankes, and now let vs towards London,　　120
> To see our gentle Queene how she doth fare,
> | For by this | I hope shee hath a sonne for vs (sc.xxiv.105–22)

It contains 9 trochees out of 88 feet, or a proportion of 10.2%, 2 trisyllabic feet (106,122), 2 four-stress lines (110,115), 1 three-stress line (112), 1 truncated five-stress line (119).

There is not a scene in which this versification cannot be found: *The True Tragedie,* like *The Contention,* was first conceived by author A. But author B has also had his share in the play. His regular lines, heavily accented, anchored at the end with a sonorous word, frequently a monosyllable, with few trochees and rather numerous spondees, oratorical in tone, easily rising to hyperbolism, can also be discerned, mixed with the variable, spasmodic versification of author A—in the following passage for instance:

YORK. That face of his the hungrie Cannibals
Could not haue tucht, would not haue staind with bloud
But you are more inhumaine, more inexorable,
O ten times more then Tygers of Arcadia.
See ruthless Queene a haplesse fathers teares.
This cloth thou dipts in bloud of my sweet boy,
And loe with teares I wash the bloud awaie.
Keepe thou the napkin and go boast of that,
And if thou tell the heauie storie well,
Vpon my soule the hearers will sheed teares,
I, euen my foes will sheed fast falling teares,
And saie alas, it was a pitteous deed.
Here, take the crowne, and with the crowne my curse,
And in thy need such comfort come to thee,
As now I reape at thy two cruell hands,
Hard-harted Clifford, take me from the world,
My soule to heauen, my bloud vpon your heads (sc.iv.137–53)

In passages like the above the style is not only more vigorous but also more literary. Author B, like author A, has probative comparisons with animals; but he can also observe a "woodcocke strive with the gin" or a "cunnie struggle with the net" (sc.iv.49–50), note that the owl has a "lasie flight" (sc.v.97), and he may even have, in an exceptional flash of poetry, a striking simile applied to the last words of dying Montague:

And more he would haue spoke and more he said.
Which sounded like a clamor in a vault,
That could not be distinguished for the sound (sc.xxii.31–2)

an image which, in spite of its precarious validity, shows at least that, as already suggested in *The Contention*, this imitator of Marlowe was not entirely indifferent to stylistic effects.

The share of author B in *The True Tragedie* is infinitely more important than his share in *The Contention*. There are few scenes retaining indubitable traces of author A's versification or style which do not also contain some passages that have the ring of author B's versification, the two being so intimately intermixed that only an analysis of the rhythm of the verse permits distinguishing them. The interpolations or modifications vary from a few lines to fairly long passages, the chief of these—I do not give this list as absolutely complete—being as follows:

sc.i.16–44	York and his supporters occupy the king's palace.
52–92	King Henry and his supporters want to reoccupy the palace.
149–79	King Henry accepts York as his successor to the throne.
sc.iii.1–49	Clifford kills the young earl of Rutland.
sc.iv.10–79	Queen Margaret and her supporters surprise York flying and insult him.
96–165	York, dying, reproaches the queen for her cruelty and curses his enemies, who, by order of the queen, later set his head on York gates.
sc.v.1–108	Richard and Edward see three suns in the sky and take them for the symbol of a necessary union. A messenger brings the news of York's death, and Warwick adds the news of a defeat.
sc.vi.8–78	Clifford and the queen blame the king's lenity.
120–70	Edward and Richard stigmatize the queen for her origin and challenge Henry's party.
sc.vii.1–48	Richard brings the news that Salisbury has died and swears to avenge him, in which vow he is joined by Edward and George.
sc.ix.14–55	A soldier discovers that he has killed his father, and another soldier that he has killed his son.
sc.x.1–29	Monologue of Clifford wounded.
78–91	Warwick offers to go to France and negotiate the marriage of King Edward with Lady Bona.
sc.xi.10–19	King Henry thinks of Warwick's mission in France.
24–37	King Henry is recognized by a keeper.
sc.xii.112–82	Richard, now duke of Gloucester, thinks he is better fitted for political dissimulation and intrigues than for love.
sc.xiii.110–37	Warwick, infuriated by Edward's marriage with Lady Gray, promises "to replant Henry in his former state."
146–67	Warwick proposes to give his eldest daughter in marriage to Prince Edward.
sc.xxii.1–44	Death of Warwick and of Montague.
sc.xxiii.1–13	Edward rejoices at his success but is made anxious by the thought that the queen has landed with French forces.
sc.xxiv.1–30	The queen and the prince encourage their troops.
55–75	Edward kills the young prince.
sc.xxv.1–16	Henry asks Gloucester what "scene of death" he is going to act.
33–45	Henry recalls the prophetic signs which accompanied Richard's birth.
66–79	Richard himself thinks of those presages and plans to conquer the throne.
sc.xxvi.1–25	Edward rejoices at his victory.
30–6	Richard hypocritically promises to love Edward's son.

From the number of these passages and from their distribution in the whole play it is evident that author B was not satisfied this time with scattering here and there some instances of the dramatic style which he admired; his aim was more ambitious. The historical material was of a more dramatic quality, and one of the characters, Richard, was entering a career of ambition and crime that had something of the unquenchable thirst for power of a Tamburlaine. Here was a possibility of transforming a simple "historie" into one of those impressive plays which Marlowe liked to call "tragedies" or to qualify by the word "tragical." [1] Hence the change of what must have been the original title, *The second part of the contention between the Houses of York and Lancaster* (or perhaps the subtitle of *The True Tragedie*, preserved on the same title page: *The whole Contention betweene the two Houses Lancaster and Yorke*), into *The true Tragedie of Richard Duke of Yorke*. This title, it should be noted, discloses the aim of the reviser rather than describes the result of the revision. For although Richard is quite active in the play, he is nevertheless a character of secondary importance, and there is nothing tragical in his fate; on the contrary, in the end the assassination of King Henry opens the way to his final success. This is by no means a tragedy in the proper sense of the word; in spite of the modifications it has received it remains like *The Contention* a "history" of the struggle between supporters of the house of York and those of the house of Lancaster, and, again as in *The Contention*, there is not one line that can be attributed to Shakespeare.

The Folio Text or 3 "Henry VI"

IN TWO SCENES the folio text gives the names of three actors instead of those of the persons represented: "Enter Gabriel" (probably Gabriel Spencer) instead of a messenger (I.ii.47–8), "Enter Sinklo and Humfrey" (probably Humphrey Jesse) instead of two keepers (III.i.1). The manuscript sent to the printer was therefore a book of the company, the prompter's own book, for the work of that use-

1. *Tamburlaine the Great.* Divided into two Tragicall Discourses; *The Tragedie of Dido Queene of Carthage; The Tragicall History of Doctor Faustus; The Famous Tragedy of the Rich Jew of Malta.*

ful member of the company is visible in the addition of twenty
"exits" or "exeunts" and six mentions of stage business (III.iii.16,
46–7,59,131; V.vi.56,61), and the manuscript was certainly a read-
able one that gave no trouble to the compositor.

Most of the stage directions are simple, even simpler than those
in the 1595 quarto. They give only the names of the entrants without mentioning their ranks or titles: "Enter Plantagenet, Edward,
Richard, Norfolke, Mountague, Warwicke and Souldiers" (I.i.1).
In one case, however, the detail of a direction recalls the elabora-
tion of the stage directions in *The Contention:*

> Warwicke and the rest cry all, Warwicke, Warwicke, and set vpon the
> Guard, who flye, crying Arme, Arme, Warwick and the rest following
> them.

> The Drumme playing, and Trumpet sounding.
> Enter Warwicke, Somerset, and the rest, bringing the King out in his
> Gowne, sitting in a Chaire: Richard and Hastings flyes ouer the Stage
> (IV.iii.27–8)

The use of the phrase "and the rest" and of the form "Richard and
Hastings flyes" are a certain sign that this indication was written
by author A. In several other places the gestures and movements
of the actors are indicated with unusual care: They goe vp (I.i.
32–3), He stampes with his foot (I.i.169–70), Here they come
downe (I.i.205–6), Clifford grones (II.vi.41–2), Seats her by him
(III.iii.16–17), Hee descends. Shee ariseth (III.iii.46–7), Speaking to Bona (III.iii.59), Speaks to War. (III.iii.131), They all
reade their Letters (III.iii.166–7), He giues his hand to Warw.
(III.iii.255–6), Takes off his Crowne (IV.iii.48–9), They leade
him out forcibly (IV.iii.57–8), Layes his Hand on his Head (IV.
vi.67–8), He descends (IV.vii.29–30), Takes his Keyes (IV.vii.37–
8), Throwes downe his Gauntlet (IV.vii.74–5), Here they beare
away his body (V.ii.51), Stabs him (V.v.38–9), Rich. stabs him
(V.v.39–40), Clar. stabs him (V.v.40–1), Offers to kill her (V.v.
41), Stabbes him (V.vi.56), Dyes (V.vi.61), Stabs him againe (V.
vi.67–8).[2]

Now all these directions are in passages which reproduce the

2. In sc.x of the quarto a detail of the same kind is given which is not in the folio
(II.vi): "Enter Clifford wounded, with an arrow in his necke."

text of the 1595 quarto word for word, and none of them (except II.vi.41–2; V.vi.67–8) is found in that quarto. It cannot be supposed that they are additions made by the editor of the 1623 folio in order to facilitate the reading of the printed text, for if such were the case they would be scattered throughout the play instead of being concentrated in eight scenes. They must have come from a text of *The True Tragedie*, with the passages to which they are attached. It is therefore certain that the text of the folio derives from a manuscript nearer to the author's manuscript than the one reproduced by the quarto,[3] possibly from the foul papers of the author.

This implies a close connection between the manuscript of the quarto text and the manuscript of the folio text. Such a connection is corroborated by some typographical similarities and several incomplete verse lines which appear in both texts, inserted in identical passages.[4]

A few badly divided verse lines indicate that this promptbook preserved marks of marginal corrections.[5] Above all, like the promptbook of 2 *Henry VI*, it received a considerable number of sound effects: I have counted 14 flourishes, 12 alarms, 9 marches, 2 retreats, and 1 sennet. Variety not being the chief quality of the play, no doubt it had been thought necessary to add these diversions to lessen the monotony of battles incessantly won or lost.

$$\int \quad \int \quad \int$$

IF WE NOW COMPARE the two texts, we find again that mixture of differences and likenesses which the comparison of *The Contention* with 2 *Henry VI* revealed. The conduct of the play is about the same in both. The only addition proper is a little bit of scene showing the watchmen who guard Edward's tent idly talking at the very moment when Warwick is preparing to seize the king.

3. Those indications may have been cut in the manuscript sent to the printer of the quarto, for reasons that it would be idle to guess.

4. II.ii.60,174=sc.vi.58,168; II.iv.11=sc.viii.13; III.iii.108=sc.xiii.63; IV.ii.5=sc. xv.5.

5. I.iii.21–2; III.iii.15–18, 169–70; IV.i.22–3,89–90; IV.vi.68–9. Many other single lines are variably divided into two lines, but these can be explained by the insufficient width of the folio columns.

Aside from this the only important change is in Act IV where
some scenes are not given in the same order. In *The True Tragedie*
the chain of events is as follows: 1) Gloucester, Hastings, and Stanley in a sudden attack remove Edward from the bishop of York's
custody (sc.xvi). 2) The queen, having heard that her husband,
Edward, has been taken prisoner, tells her anxiety to Lord Rivers
and asks him to help her reach sanctuary where she may safely
give birth to her child (sc.xvii). 3) Edward, who has recruited
soldiers in Holland, forces the gates of the city of York and is again
proclaimed king by Sir John Montgomery (sc.xviii). 4) King
Henry, having recovered his liberty, is reinstalled on the throne
but learns that Edward has returned. Warwick makes arrangements to resist (sc.xix).

In the folio the scene between the queen and Lord Rivers takes
place first (II.iv = sc.xvii), and Edward's deliverance comes next
(II.v = sc.xvi). Henry VI in turn is delivered and reinstalled on
the throne (IV.vi = sc.xix). Finally Edward seizes the city of York
and is again proclaimed king (IV.vii = sc.xviii). It is difficult to
say which of these sequences is the better. The first has the advantage of suggesting how ignorant we sometimes are of those events
which touch us most closely, and from the dramatic point of view
this is not valueless; the second, presenting the events in their
strictly chronological order, is more natural. But I must own that
I am not sure the sense I see in *The True Tragedie* was really intended by the author.

Some lines have been transferred from one place to another in
the same scene, in III.ii (sc.xii), for instance, or from one scene
to another, but without changing either the sense or the movement
of the scenes.

Passing now to a comparison of the dialogue in the two texts we
find that the folio text is composed of:

1. 840 verse lines which reproduce word for word as many lines
in the quarto.[6]

6. As I did for 2 *Henry VI,* I give here the complete list of those lines, showing
their distribution in the play. I.i.1,3,5–7,12–16,18,21–4,27–8,31,33,39–40,42,44,47,
49,51–6,58,61–6,68–9,71–2,74–5,77,79–83,85,87,89,91–4,96–7,99,100,102,104–6,
108–9,111–20,125–6,128–32,134–7,139–40,143,146–8,151–2,155–6,158–61,164–8,
172–3,176,178,180–1,185,187,191–4,202,204–5,207,251–2,257,260–1,264; I.ii.3,41,
62,64–5,67; I.iii.5,17,19–26,29–31,35–7,39–42,44–7,49–52; I.iv.7,26,33–4,38,42–3,

2. 1100 mixed verse lines, in which fragments of lines in the quarto are blended with a new element, the parts common to both texts varying from one word to nearly a whole line.

3. 941 verse lines which have not a single word in common with the text of *The True Tragedie*.[7]

As is the case with 2 *Henry VI*, the lines in 3 *Henry VI* which have nothing in common with *The True Tragedie* are the only ones which are in Shakespeare's versification and style. An analysis of the longest passages—II.v.20–54 (35 lines), III.i.70–92 (23 lines),

---

47,49–51,53–8,61,63,66–7,69–70,72–4,76–7,80,82–3,85–7,88,92–4,98–9,101–2,104–8,111,113–14,116–18,121–4,126–7,131,133–40,146–7,152,154,156–7,161,163,165,167–8,172–3,179–80; II.i.9–10,22,25,29,31,34–5,40,45–6,61,62,68,74,89,91–3,95,97–9,101,107–8,111–12,115–17,120–2,124,126,130,134,137–41,143,148,151,153–7,159–60,162–5,167,173,178,179,183,185–7,189,191–2,195,198–9,206,208; II.ii.1,7–8,10–11,16–17,19–23,25–6,32,34,36–40,43–4,46,48,50–1,54,61,63–7,69,73–4,77,84,88,91,95–6,98,103–4,106,110–11,115–16,118–20,123–4,128,130,134–7,139,141,144,152–5,161–2,165,169–74; II.iii.2–3,6,13,43,48,51; II.iv.5–7,9–11; II.v.55,91,94,97–8,101,104–5,121–2;   II.vi.5,8,10–12,21,23,28–9,33,38–40,44,52–3,55–6,62–4,69–71,75–6,86–7,90–1,93,106–7,109–10; III.i.13,18,29,43,45,58,97; III.ii.13,28–9,43,53–4,56–7,73,75–6,81,87–8,90–2,95–6,98–9,101–4,106–8,111,113,117,125,133,150,158,163,191; III.iii.46,50–7,59,61–3,65,78–81,91–4,98–100,102–4,107–9,122–8,130,132,152–3,155,164,167,173,180–9,196,198,202–7,223–5,227–8,230–3,240–3,256–65; IV.i.37–9,59,68,93–100,105,107,111,117,123,144; IV.ii.2–18,28–9; IV.iii.26,29,35,38,40,48,54, 62–3; IV.iv.4; IV.v.28–9; IV.vi.1–29,43–4,75–6; IV.vii.40,44,67,71,76; IV.viii.1–2,9–10,16–17,22–4,32,53; V.i.1–2,5,10–11,19,27–8,35,37,41,46,59,72–4,76,80–4,104,107–8,113; V.ii.5–7,9–12,14,19–26,29,44,28,48–9; V.iii.5,17–19,21; V.iv.51,53,73; V.v.2–3,5,17–21,24–6,28–30,32–5,41–2,44,46,53,66,69–70,74–6,80,82,85; V.vi.3,10,16–19,30–1,35,44,47,49–50,52–4,59–61,63,67–8,70,75,77,79,80–93; V.vi.1–17,19–20,22–8,30,33,35–42,44–6.

7. I.i.6,17,35–7,75,121–3,149–50,174–5,183–4,189,199–200,210,217–29,234–8,241–2,246,254,256,263,267–71,273;   I.ii.5,7,11–14,18–21,24,26–32,39,42–7,52–61,70–2; I.iii.1,6,9,13,18,48; I.iv.1–5,14–21,24,46,70,89–90; II.i.1–8,12,15–18,23–4,33,37,41–2,47,50–2,54–7,64,71–3,76,81–6,201–5; II.ii.79,82–3,143,146–9; II.iii.9–13,15–18,20–1,25–8,30–2,35–6,38–41,44–5,49–50,52–4,56; II.iv.4; II.v.2–4,6,8–15,20–54,59–60,71–2,77–8,81,84–8,95–6,99–100,112,114–20,123,126–7,129–32,138–9; II.vi.32,34–6,47–50,58,100–2; III.i.1,4–10,16–17,20,24–7,35–42,47–54,63,70–92,94–6,100–1; III.ii.5,11,15,20,22,36–41,59–60,63,65–8,85–6,110,128–9,134–46,152,160–2,165–81,184–90; III.iii.4–44,47–8,67–77,112,135–7,141–50,156–61,177,179,191–4,208–18,221,226,234–8,244,247–50,254; IV.i.3–10,27,30–1,39,41–6,50–4,61,71–4,80–3,98,114,119–22,124–6,128–30,132–3,138,140–2,147–8; IV.ii.19–27; IV.iii.1–22,27,37,39,41–2,44,46–7,50–1,58–61; IV.iv.6–8,10,12,16–23,25–30,32–5; IV.v.2–3,6–7,10–13,17–18,22,24; IV.vi.1–37,39–40,43,46–64,73–4,78–102; IV.vii.1–4,6–7,9,11–16,24,31–4,39,59–66,70,78,83–8; IV.viii.6,8,20–1,26–31,33–52,55–7,60,62–4; V.i.12–16,22,31–3,39,48–57,60,62,64–6,69–71,78–9,87,89–97; V.ii.1–4,8,15–18,30,32,34–9,46–7; V.iii.2,9–14,20,24; V.iv.1–2,4–18,21–43,45,47,58–9,64–5,70–2,78–9,82; V.v.7–13,16,37,39–40,54–5,59–62; V.vi.5–9,26,29,38.

III.ii.165–81 (17 lines), III.iii.4–44 (41 lines), IV.iii.1–22 (22 lines), IV.vi.1–37 (37 lines), 46–64 (19 lines), 77–102 (26 lines), IV.viii.33–52 (20 lines), V.iv.4–18 (15 lines), 21–43 (23 lines), that is 278 lines or 1390 feet—gives the following percentages:

Weekly accented feet	380 or 27.3%
Trochees	37 or 2.6%
Spondees	44 or 3.1%
Internal pauses	146 lines or 52.5%
Enjambments	35 lines or 12.5%

These percentages are nearly the same as in *Lucrece*.

The style is full of the mannerisms which abound in Shakespeare's poems:

Division of the thought into symmetrical and balanced parts of more or less equal lengths:

> Pardon me Margaret, pardon me sweet Sonne (I.i.228)

> Teares then for Babes; Blowes, and Reuenge for mee (II.i.86) [8]

Repetition of a word or grammatical form to accentuate the symmetrical construction:

> O pitteous spectacle! O bloody Times! (II.v.73)

> Had he been ta'ne, we should haue heard the newes;
> Had he been slaine, we should haue heard the newes (II.i.4–5) [9]

Marked preference for the association of two words expressing two aspects of the same idea and connected by a conjunction:

> By words or blowes here let vs winne our right (I.i.37)

> And be you silent and attentiue too (I.i.122) [1]

Antitheses:

> And cry'de, A Crowne, or else a glorious Tombe (I.iv.16)

8. Cf. I.i.200; I.iv.16; II.i.42,203; II.v.73,78,112,138; III.i.54; III.ii.63; III.iii.36, 77, 150, 157; IV.vi.4,18; IV.vii.85; V.i.22; V.iv.12,58,79; V.v.61.

9. Cf. II.iii.9–10; II.v.5–8,26–29,31–8,48–9; III.i.37–8; III.ii.186–8; III.iii.36,40–1, 217–18; IV.viii.41–3; V.iv.12,25–7,78–9; V.vi.7–8.

1. Cf. I.i.183,199,210; I.ii.11,27,31; I.iii.9; I.iv.4; II.i.55,69; II.v.4,20,50,77,87; II.vi.102; III.i.41,52; III.ii.145; III.iii.42,48,74,75,156,158,211; IV.ii.20; IV.iii.16, 59; IV.iv.23,33; IV.v.12,18; IV.vi.1,27,28,35,55; IV.vii.14; V.i.53,71; V.iv.1,11,18,21,23, 36,38; V.v.61.

> The one, his purple Blood right well resembles,
> The other his pale Cheekes (me thinkes) presenteth (II.v.99–100) [2]

Concetti: There are no concetti of the Italian type, the subject not lending itself to that kind of figure, but there are a good number of concetti-jingles:

> And if what pleases him, shall pleasure you (III.ii.22)

> And I, who at his hands receiu'd my life,
> Haue by my hands, of Life bereaued him (II.v.67–8) [3]

Compound words in the Greek and Latin manner: heart-blood (I.i.223), hunger-starued (I.iv.5), ouer-matching (I.iv.21), hardest-tymber'd (II.i.55), base-borne (II.ii.143), sad-hearted (II.v. 123), Beare-whelpe (III.ii.161), mis-shap'd (III.ii.170), tongue-ty'd (III.iii.22), Night-foes (IV.iii.22), blood-sucking (IV.iv.22), water-flowing (IV.viii.43), great-growne (IV.viii.63), coale-black (V.i.54), bright-shining (V.iii.3).

And characteristically Shakespearean images are also present, drawn directly from the impressions stored by memory in the course of the poet's experience. Some are remembrances of the Stratford countryside,[4] such as the two greyhounds in pursuit of a frightened hare:

> Edward and Richard like a brace of Grey-hounds,
> Having the fearfull flying Hare in sight,
> With fiery eyes, sparkling for very wrath,
> And bloody steele graspt in theyr yrefull hands (II.v.129–32)

the famished eagle tearing at its prey:

> Whose haughtie spirit, winged with desire,
> Will cost my Crowne, and like an emptie Eagle
> Tyre on the flesh of me, and of my Sonne (I.i.267–9)

the man who has lost his dog in the woods:

> That rents the Thornes, and is rent with the Thornes,
> Seeking a way, and straying from the way,

2. Cf. I.ii.11; I.iv.17; II.v.4,138; III.i.42; III.ii.39,63; III.iii.157,199; V.ii.16–17; V.iv.24.

3. Cf. I.iv.23–4; III.i.84–6; III.ii.68,175–8,179–80; III.iii.34,191–3; IV.i.42; IV.iv. 34; IV.vi.39; IV.viii.46; V.i.57; V.ii.1–2.

4. Several have also been used in *Venus and Adonis;* cf. 679, 825–8.

> Not knowing how to finde the open Ayre,
> And toyling desperately to finde it out (III.ii.175–8)

the swan vainly trying to swim against the stream:

> We bodg'd againe, as I haue seene a Swan
> With bootlesse labour swimme against the Tyde,
> And spend her strength with ouer-matching Waues (I.iv.19–21)

The following is borrowed from the pastimes of London:

> Or as a Beare encompass'd round with Dogges:
> Who hauing pincht a few, and made them cry,
> The rest stand all aloofe, and barke at him (II.i.15–17) [5]

And this one may be a reminiscence of the performance of Pyramus and Thisbe in *Midsummer Night's Dream:*

> And looke vpon, as if the Tragedie
> Were plaid in iest, by counterfetting Actors (II.iii.27–8)

Other images, without losing contact with life, are inspired by a curiosity which is no longer satisfied solely by the spectacles of the world and submits the real to the fantasies of invention. Henry VI, thanking the lieutenant of the Tower for his kindness, assures him that in captivity he has found a pleasure which, in a moment of imaginative flight, he compares to what

> incaged Birds
> Conceiue, when after many moody Thoughts,
> At last, by Notes of Household harmonie,
> They quite forget their losse of Libertie (IV.vi.12–15)

And it is through a similar sally of the imagination that Shakespeare has lent to Richard a wish that he himself must have had one day: [6]

> Why then I doe but dreame on Soueraigntie,
> Like one that stands vpon a Promontorie,

5. Almost the same image was used in 2 *Henry VI* V.i.149–54. Cf. also *Venus and Adonis*, 884–7.
6. In fact, in sonnet 56 Shakespeare felt similarly when he wrote:
> Let this sad interim like the Ocean be
> Which parts the shore, where the contracted new
> Come daily to the banks that when they see
> Return of love, more blest may be the new (9–12).

> And spyes a farre-off shore, where hee would tread,
> Wishing his foot were equall with his eye,
> And chides the Sea, that sunders him from thence,
> Saying, hee'le lade it dry, to haue his way (III.ii.135–9)

I note also a refinement of the vision which allows the poet to discover in customary things a hidden, mysterious world such as the one wherein the midday sun, in its brilliance, seems to search out hidden actions:

> These eyes, that now are dim'd with Deaths black Veyle,
> Haue bene as piercing as the Mid-day Sunne,
> To search the secret Treasons of the World (V.ii.16–18) [7]

An image such as this one heralds the great period of Shakespearean poetry.

Thus 3 *Henry VI* is composed of a large portion of a pre-Shakespearean play, of another, still larger portion fundamentally pre-Shakespearean but more or less modified in the expression, and of a third portion entirely by Shakespeare. The pre-Shakespearean element, both in its identical and mixed forms, constitutes about two-thirds of the whole play and provides the entire structure of the action; the Shakespearean element is inserted by fragments of sometimes only one or two lines and indisputably has the character of amplifications or accessions. 3 *Henry VI*, exactly like 2 *Henry VI*, is an old play, written by author A, first amended by author B, and finally revised and partly rewritten by Shakespeare.

The only difference is that this revision has not been so important as the revision of *The Contention*. I have already pointed out that the structure of the play received only a few changes, if the simple modification in the order of four scenes can be called a change. Whether he was pressed for time, or whether he was less interested in a subject full only of political complications, Shakespeare kept as much of the original play as possible; and this was rendered easy by the fact that the regular versification and oratorical manner of author B were more to the taste of the day. The number of lines identical in the two texts is here more than double

7. To the images cited above may be added I.iv.3–5; II.i.15–17,82–4; II.v.85–7, 115–20,126; II.vi.35–6,47–50; III.iii.47–8;V.vi.7–9.

those in 2 *Henry VI* (840 opposed to 337). And in these identical parts Shakespeare did not even take the trouble to do away with irregular lines or trisyllabic feet.

This restriction being made, it can be said that the reworking of *The True Tragedie* was of the same nature as that of *The Contention*. First of all, in the mixed portion it consisted in freeing the versification of its abnormalities. Lines either too long or too short were, with a few rare exceptions, transformed into decasyllables; trisyllabic feet were eliminated. Numerous improvements were made on the dialogue. For a banal expression there was substituted a more precise or more suggestive synonym. Ideas too curtly or too simply expressed were expanded and often enriched with poetical embellishments, sometimes extended to the point of exhaustion—for instance, Queen Margaret's comparison of the Lancastrian's situation to that of a ship foundering on the rocks (V.iv.1–38). These stylistic improvements were the part of the revision that was the most carefully done.

Some of the additions proper were intended to give life to the characters. But here again it seems that Shakespeare's part was less extensive than in 2 *Henry VI*. Several characters, such as Warwick and Edward, who were somewhat overshadowed in *The Contention*, gained in importance in *The True Tragedie*, but they belonged exclusively to the category of ambitious men; they acted, they had political opinions, but their sentimental life was rarely expressed. To reveal certain traits of their nature Shakespeare made use of the opinions their friends or their enemies held of them. Henry and Margaret dread Warwick's eloquence (III.i.48–52; III.iii.112); Margaret attributes to his machinations her ill success in her suit to the king of France and accuses him of being a "setter vp and puller downe of Kings" [8] (III.iii.141–3,156–61); Edward, for his part, calls him "wind-changing Warwicke" (V.i. 57). As for Edward, Richard and Clarence agree in pointing out his debauched life (II.i.41–2; III.ii.129; III.iii.208–11).

In *The True Tragedie* the role of Richard had acquired considerable development. He it was who had incited first his father

8. This expression has been borrowed by Shakespeare from *The True Tragedie*, where it is given to Edward (sc.vii.33), and repeated in 3 *Henry VI* (II.iii.37).

(sc.i.103–14), then his brother Edward (sc.v.58–61) to claim the throne; his lack of scruples, his hypocrisy had been emphasized up to the denouement when he assassinated King Henry. To this Shakespeare added only a few passages amplifying the same thoughts or situations (I.ii.11–14,25–8; I.iii.25–8; II.i.81–6; IV.i. 83, 124–6; IV.vii.62–4). He simply made Richard's desire for power more insatiable by greatly expanding the soliloquy in which this outcast of nature examines the means of attaining the power from which he is separated by the existence of his brothers (III.ii.134–46,165–91,184–90), and finally by having him finish killing young Prince Edward whom the king had just stabbed (V.v.39).

In 2 *Henry VI* Queen Margaret had been portrayed with some complexity, and Shakespeare did not add much to this portrait. He only endowed Margaret with two new bursts of anger, one against King Henry (I.215–26), the other against Warwick (III.iii.141–50,156–61), and he gave another example of her feminine suppleness. On her arrival at the court of France she appears humble and resigned in order to awaken pity in the king whose help she is about to beg (III.iii.4–43). She defends the rights of her husband and of her son skillfully (III.iii.67–77), thus confirming the exactness of King Henry's remark on the power of her sighs and tears (III.i.37–41); and at a moment when all seems lost she rallies her partisans and makes a show of courage that draws a cry of admiration from Prince Edward (V.iv.1–38).

King Henry seems to have been the only personage whose character Shakespeare took delight in enhancing. Several additions bring out his horror of political dissensions (IV.vi.39–40), his pity for the sufferings of the people (II.v.111–12), his taste for a simpler life and particularly for pastoral pursuits (II.v.21–54), his dream of retiring to a place where no one would be able to harm him and where he himself could not harm anyone (IV.vi.19–22), his respect for the plighted word (III.i.72–92), his admiration for the qualities of his wife (III.i.35–43), his affection for her and for his son (IV.vi.59–63), his courtesy extended so far as to thank the lieutenant of the Tower for his attentions (IV.vi.1–22), and finally—a detail which does not lack originality—his naïveté in believing that his virtues and his goodness must have earned him

the love of his people (IV.viii.38–48). Henry VI is certainly the
most human of all the characters in the play.

∫ ∫ ∫

Two PERIODS can be distinguished in the Shakespearean additions
to the third part of *Henry VI*. Most of the passages which I have
analyzed for their rhythmic variations (cf. pp. 132–3) have an insignificant number of feminine endings, varying between 5 and 9%.
They must have been written a little earlier than the first revision
of the second part, though this is not absolutely certain: the difference between the proportions of the variations in each play is
so small that they may very well belong to the same period.

	Feminine endings	*Lines*	*Percentages*
II.v.20–54	2	35	5.7
III.ii.165–81	0	17	0.
III.iii.4–44	2	41	4.8
IV.iii.1–22	2	22	9.0
IV.viii.33–52	1	20	5.0
V.iv.4–18	1	15	6.6
21–43	2	23	8.6

A total of 10 feminine endings in 173 lines or an average of 5.7%

A few passages have a distinctly higher proportion of feminine
endings:

	Feminine endings	*Lines*	*Percentages*
III.i.70–92	4	23	17.3
IV.vi.1–37	5	37	13.5
46–64	5	19	26.3
77–102	5	26	19.2

A total of 19 feminine endings in 105 lines or an average of 18.0%

These passages must belong to a later revision, and this second
revision must have been made at the same period and for the same
reason as the second revision of 2 *Henry VI*, not only because
three of those passages have pretty much the same percentages as
the passages with the higher percentages in 2 *Henry VI*, but also
because they have the same aim—to make King Henry a sympathetic figure.

It is possible to give an approximate date for Shakespeare's first revision of *The True Tragedie*, thanks to the well-known attack that Greene made on the actors in his *Groatsworth of Wit with a Million of Repentance* (Stationers' Register, September 20, 1592). This attack has been given various interpretations,[9] which I shall not discuss. I shall retain only what information may be gathered from the explosion of anger of a sick and destitute writer. Greene did not accuse Shakespeare of plagiarism; this is a modern idea which would never have occurred to an Elizabethan, since the revision of other people's dramatic works was at that time considered normal. He was only complaining that a newcomer, "with his Tygers hart in a player's hide," believing himself the only "shake-scene" of his country (this pun clearly indicates the identity of the man alluded to), meddled in writing plays instead of being content to perform in the plays of others. The quotation with which he lashed the "upstart" was a parody of a line in *The True Tragedie*, preserved word for word in 3 *Henry VI* (I.iv.137). But Greene, unless he was author B, in which case he was quoting himself, was certainly unaware of this fact, and for him the only play which could pass as being Shakespeare's was what we call now the third part of *Henry VI*. Thus Shakespeare's revision of *The True Tragedie* existed before September 3, 1592, the date at which the *Groatsworth of Wit* was registered for publication. Besides, it should not be forgotten that on June 23, 1592, the London theaters were closed and that there were no public plays until December 29. It is therefore somewhat earlier, probably during the winter of 1591–92 (the bitterness of Greene's invective suggests that his discovery of the actors' ingratitude was recent), that Greene saw the play performed, the only way he could have known it.

Now on March 3, 1591/2, Lord Strange's men performed for the first time (it was marked "ne[w]" by Henslowe in his *Diary*) a play called "harey the vj" (fol. 7). It is generally admitted that this *Henry VI* was the first part of the *Henry VI* that has come down to us in the folio of 1623. This identification rests on a passage of Nash's in his *Pierce Pennyless* (Stationers' Register, August 8, 1592), where mention is made of the great success on the stage

9. The last being by J. D. Wilson, "Malone and the Upstart Crow," in *Shakespeare Survey*, *4*, 56–68.

of the role of "brave Talbot," which certainly can apply to what we call 1 *Henry VI*. But this play dramatizes incidents from the Thirty Years War; its principal characters are Talbot and Joan of Arc; King Henry, still a child, appears only in three scenes toward the end, and his role is without importance: it is highly improbable that such a play should ever have been entitled "Henry VI." And it will be seen in a subsequent volume that it is only after a considerable revision that it was later linked to the Shakespearean 2 and 3 *Henry VI* to form a trilogy on the reign of that king. The "harey the vj" which Lord Strange's company performed in 1592 was certainly 3 *Henry VI*, recently revised by Shakespeare as one of the new additions to the repertoire.

If this is correct it follows:

1. That it is not necessary to suppose, as has been done, that Shakespeare ever wrote for the company of Lord Pembroke. This assertion is based only on the fact that the title page of the quarto of *The True Tragedie* (which is not Shakespeare's) says that it was "acted by the Right Honourable the Earle of Pembrooke his seruants." As Henslowe's *Diary* shows, Shakespeare's revision of that old play belonged to the repertoire of Lord Strange's company, and it is for that company that the revision was made, naturally by one of its members.

2. That *The True Tragedie*, revised by Shakespeare, was at first given as a play complete in itself (as indeed it must have been after author B transformed the second part of *The Contention* into a so-called "tragedy"), for Henslowe's *Diary* again never mentions any first or second part of "harey the vj." And this strengthens the possibility that *The first part of the Contention* was revised by Shakespeare only after *The True Tragedie*, as the percentages of feminine endings seem to show.

CHAPTER TWO. TITUS ANDRONICUS

On February 6, 1594, five weeks before Millington felt sure of the right to publish *The Contention,* John Danter, the printer, registered with the Stationers' Company a manuscript entitled *A Noble Roman Historye of Tytus Andronicus.* Although Langbaine asserted in his *Account of the English Dramatick Poets* (1691) that he had held in his hands a quarto of this play dated 1594, Shakespearean critics for a long time had been convinced that Danter had not carried out his plan, when a copy of this edition was discovered in December 1904 at the home of a postal employee in Malmö, Sweden. Henry Folger, the well-known Shakespearean collector, hastened to acquire the precious volume, and it is now housed in the Folger Library in Washington, D.C. An excellent facsimile of this quarto was brought out with an introduction by John Quincy Adams in 1936.[1]

The title page of the quarto [2] states that the play, *The Most Lamentable Romaine Tragedie of Titus Andronicus,* was reproduced "As it was Plaide by the Right Honourable the Earle of Darbie,[3] Earle of Pembrooke, and Earle of Sussex their Seruants," an excellent illustration of the manner in which the repertoire was sometimes passed about from company to company in those days. The volume was sold by Edward White and Thomas Millington.

A Second Quarto, printed by James Roberts for Edward White, appeared in 1600. The title page was identical save that "and the Lord Chamberlaine" was added to the list of companies that had presented the play, and the order of the first two companies was transposed. This second edition reproduced the first so slavishly

1. In the present chapter I refer for the quotations to this facsimile. The numbering of acts, scenes, and lines is that of the Globe edition.

2. The title of the play must have been, at first, as the register of the Stationers' Company shows, "The noble Roman Historye of Titus Andronicus"; the word "Historye" was changed by the printer to the more fashionable "Tragedie." The change was more justified than in the case of 3 *Henry VI.*

3. That is to say Lord Strange, who had become earl of Derby in September 1593 before the book was published.

that, ignoring the addition made on the title page, it repeated the original head title and preserved several of the typographical peculiarities such as the unusual centering of the speech headings on A_3 recto, A_4 recto, and I_2 recto.

This quarto, nevertheless, shows two interesting changes. Three and a half lines after the words "Done sacrifice of expiation" (I.i.35) were omitted, a suppression to which I shall have occasion to return, and toward the end of the play there was a variant of a singular kind. Apparently the bottoms of the last three pages, K_2, K_3, and K_4, of the copy employed in printing the Second Quarto were defective, perhaps damaged by moisture, more probably torn away,[4] in any case partly illegible (V.iii.93–7,130,132,133,195–6, 200) or entirely missing (V.iii.165–9,201–4). Very likely the printer had secured the aid of some play-cobbler who supplied the deficiency as best he could and in conclusion added four unnecessary and platitudinous lines for good measure. This strange section was subsequently transferred to the folio and from it to all modern editions. If the copy of the First Quarto had not fortunately been discovered the substitution would probably never have been suspected.

A Third Quarto, printed by Edward Allde for the same bookseller White, appeared in 1611. This time the title page gave only "the Kings Maiesties Seruants" as the troupe that had performed the play. But this edition was also a reproduction of the Second Quarto, though with some corrections and some new errors. The typographical peculiarities that existed in Q_1 and had been copied into Q_2 were retained, and the original phrase "As it was Plaide by the Right Honourable the Earle of Darbie, Earle of Pembrooke and Earle of Sussex their Seruants" served again as head title, despite the alteration made on the title page.

The manner in which Q_2 and Q_3 followed the quarto that preceded them deprives these two texts of any value. Only the First Quarto can faithfully represent the form in which the play existed prior to 1594, and upon it the following study is based.

4. This sort of accident must have been frequent at that time, for the dramatic quartos were not bound but simply stitched and protected only by a paper cover.

THE QUARTO OF 1594

THE MANUSCRIPT reproduced by the quarto of 1594 had all the features of a fair copy, carefully written. It was free from most of the irregularities that disfigure the dramatic publications of that period and contained very few misreadings.[5] It must have been a transcript prepared for the use of the company, a promptbook, probably, for the work of the bookholder is obvious in several places where exits forgotten by the author have been added in the space left free after the last words said by the actor leaving the stage (I.i.55,495; II.ii.26; II.iii.208; III.i.186,206; IV.i.123,130; IV. ii.18,172,181; IV.iii.119). And it was the prompter, too, who supplied some gestures or movements for the players, some in the imperative mood (II.i.46; II.iii.116; IV.ii.145).

Yet in spite of the care with which it was written, this manuscript showed traces of modifications, the most striking of which was to be found at the very beginning. On the verso of page A_3 are three lines which, as I have already said, were omitted in the Second Quarto: Marcus, recalling previous returns of Andronicus, victorious but mourning the death of some of his sons, adds:

> and at this day
> To the Monument of that Andronicy
> Done sacrifice of expiation,
> And slaine the Noblest prisoner of the Gothes (I.i.35–8)

But the expiatory sacrifice mentioned by Marcus as already accomplished before Andronicus appears on the stage is the subject of a long episode a little later (I.i.96–149). It is intercalated in the action at the moment when Titus, after reproaching himself for leaving his sons, whose coffins he brings, "to houer on the dreadfull shore of Styx," prepares to unite them with their brothers previously slain. The tomb of the Andronici is open, and Titus asks that it receive these, the recently slain:

> There greete in silence as the dead are wont,
> And sleepe in peace, slaine in your Countries warres:

5. "Bereaud in blood" for "embrewed here" (II.iii.222), "drugges" for "grudges" (I.i.154), "yellowing" for "yelping" (II.iii.20). Latin words are generally distorted, but this need not cause any surprise.

> O sacred Receptacle of my ioyes,
> Sweete Cell of vertue and Nobilitie,
> How many sonnes hast thou of mine in store,
> That thou wilt neuer render to me more (I.i.90–5)

At this point Titus is interrupted in his invocation by Lucius, eldest of his sons, who solicits that there be given up to him

> the prowdest prisoner of the Gothes,
> That we may hew his limbs and on a pile,
> *Ad manus fratrum,* sacrifice his flesh:
> Before this earthy prison of their boanes,
> That so the shadows be not vnappeazde,
> Nor we disturbde with prodegies on earth (96–101)

And without discussion Andronicus then surrenders

> the Noblest that suruiues,
> The eldest sonne of this distressed Queene (102–3)

Despite the supplications of Tamora, queen of the Goths, who asks that her son be spared, Lucius and his brothers depart leading Alarbus, while Chiron and Demetrius, other sons of Tamora, vow to avenge him.

Now according to the stage direction describing the entrance of Titus Andronicus, the queen of the Goths appears in the cortege with only two sons, Chiron and Demetrius. Thus Alarbus is the "Noblest prisoner of the Gothes," said by Marcus at line 38 to have been sacrificed before the play opens, and is now brought back from the dead to be sacrificed a second time and so become the subject of a sensational episode. An interpolation is evident, so evident that it did not escape the not very wide-awake printer of the Second Quarto.

When Lucius and his brothers return, satisfied at having dismembered and burned Alarbus, Andronicus can resume his interrupted funeral oration:

> In peace and honour rest you here my sonnes,
> Roomes readiest Champions, repose you here in rest
> Secure from worldly chaunces and mishaps (150–2)

If lines 96–149 which describe the sacrificing of Alarbus are omitted, the two parts of Titus' speech fit exactly together—a proof that this passage is an interpolation and did not appear in the play as originally conceived.[6]

What follows in the same scene has certainly been mutilated, for the trend of events is somewhat broken. Upon Titus' recommendation Saturninus has been elected emperor, and as a proof of his gratitude he declares that he will make Lavinia his empress. In his turn, Titus gives the emperor his sword and his prisoners and, doing so, assures Tamora that she will be well treated. Saturninus endorses this promise and with courtly politeness asks Lavinia if she is displeased with this. Lavinia with equal politeness declares she is perfectly satisfied by this act of princely courtesy. So far, all is friendliness and agreement on all sides. But the emperor's brother, Bassianus, claims Lavinia as his betrothed. He is supported by Marcus and especially by Mutius, one of Titus' sons, who offers Bassianus his help in the abduction of Lavinia. Andronicus is indignant, alerts the emperor, and prepares to go and bring back his daughter; he kills his son Mutius, who tries to stop him, and is severely blamed by Lucius, his eldest son. At this moment (ll. 298–9) a stage direction says: "Enter aloft the Emperour with Tamora and her two sonnes and Aron the moor." Saturninus was still on stage at line 287 when Andronicus told him: "Follow my Lord, Ile soone bring her backe." How the emperor and his suite, for whom no exit is indicated, had time to leave the lower stage and appear so rapidly "aloft" is difficult to imagine, and more inexplicable still is the complete change in Saturninus' attitude. He declares that he does not want Lavinia, whom a few minutes before he had begged to be his wife, and that henceforth he will have nothing to do with Andronicus and his haughty sons whom he accuses of having dishonored him (299–305). Surely, some scene or part of a scene must have been deleted here that prepared the spectators for such a complete and insulting change in the emperor's intentions and of which we catch a faint echo in the words of Saturninus:

> Was none in Rome to make a stale
> But Saturnine? Full well Andronicus,
> Agree these deeds, with that prowd bragge of thine,
> That saidst I begd the Empire at thy hands (304–7)

6. This has been pointed out as a probable addition by W. W. Greg, *The Editorial Problem,* p. 118.

But that is not all. After those reproachful words Saturninus offers to marry Tamora, a proposal that Tamora dutifully and
humbly accepts, and the emperor asks the lords to accompany him
to the Pantheon where the marriage will be celebrated, leaving
Andronicus humiliated at not having been "bid to wait upon the
bride" (338–40). Whereupon "Enter Marcus and Titus sonnes,"
and the tribune exclaims:

> O Titus see: O see what thou hast done
> In a bad quarrell slaine a vertuous sonne (341-2)

as if Andronicus had already forgotten that tragic incident. A
scene follows in which the sons, supported by their uncle Marcus,
ask for permission to bury Mutius in the family vault; Titus stoutly
refuses but at last consents (343–91), and "all exit but Marcus
and Titus." Then in a short scene Marcus asks Titus whether he
knows the reason for "the advancement of the subtile Queene of
Gothes." Greg in *The Editorial Problem in Shakespeare* (p. 118)
finds this transition "abrupt"; I agree with him and also with J. D.
Wilson who, going further, believes that this is another interpolation. Marcus' remark is pointless following the dramatic burial
of Mutius but, on the contrary, is most appropriate coming upon
the departure of the emperor and the imminent marriage of
Tamora. As in the former interpolation, if lines 341–91 are omitted
all becomes perfectly natural and smooth.

Lines 98–101 of Act IV.sc.iii are a small addition to the clown's
part. Titus asks, "Tell mee, can you deliuer an Oration to the Emperor with a grace?" and the clown answers, "Nay truelie sir, I
coulde neuer say grace in all my life." Now, at line 107, Titus asks
the same question, "Sirra, can you with a grace deliuer up a Supplication?" to which this time the clown answers simply, "I sir."
The first redaction was evidently introduced for the sake of the
pun on the word "grace" but makes a clumsy duplication of the
second.[7]

Inconsistencies in the names of the characters also disclose that
the play underwent alterations. Aron the Moor is usually referred
to by name, but twice in the stage directions (II.i.1; II.iii.9–10)
and in many speech headings (II.i.1,37,46,60,75,90,97; II.iii.30,52;

---

7. Noted also by W. W. Greg and J. D. Wilson.

III.i.175,189; IV.ii.24; V.iii.11) he is called simply Moor. The son of Lucius appears in the stage directions sometimes as "Lucius' sonne" and sometimes as "young Lucius," but in the speech headings always as "Puer." The distinction of the Latin form "Saturninus" is conferred on the emperor all through the opening of the first scene, in the stage directions for II.ii.11 and II.iii.267–8, in two speech headings (II.iii.246,253), and twice in the dialogue (I.i.232; II.i.90). But he is given the Anglicized form "Saturnine" in the second part of the first scene, in one of the stage directions for II.iii.267–8, in the speech headings II.ii.14,18; IV.iv.1,113, and in the dialogue in lines I.i.208; II.i.23; III.i.298,301; IV.i.63; IV.iii. 34,56. This character enters as "Emperour" in the stage directions I.i.299–300,398–9; II.iii.246; IV.iv.1; V.iii.16–17, in the speech headings I.i.300; V.iii.64, and in the text I.i.258,296,299; IV.iv.111. That Saturninus should be called emperor, especially in the text, is natural enough, and it is admissible that an author who has imagined a Roman personage should have given him an Anglicized name; here again the exigencies of versification may fully justify certain liberties. But the transformation of an emperor into "king," which happens in four scenes (II.iii.47,87,260–304; III.i.154; IV. iv.70–104; V.iii.17–59), is surprising and explicable only by different ideas about the period in which the action takes place. The wars with the Goths occurred during the last years of the Roman Empire, whereas kings carry us back to the semilegendary times when Rome was under the domination of the Etruscans. So here two different authors must have juxtaposed exact knowledge and ignorance respectively—one author was familiar with classical history, the other ignorant of local color and speaking of Roman institutions in terms of the English Court. This supposition becomes a certainty when we see Tamora, who after her marriage to Saturninus is called by her own name or referred to as "Empress," reduced to the title of queen in II.iii.91,98,168 and V.iii.26, the same scenes in which her consort has become what he never was in the story—a king.

Apart from these peculiarities, the manuscript was of the same kind as the manuscripts of *The Contention* and *The True Tragedie*. It has most of their characteristics. The stage directions are unusually detailed, and some have the peculiarity of dividing the various groups of entrants by the conjunctions "and," "and then":

> Sound Drums and Trumpets, and then enter two of Titus sonnes, and then two men bearing a Coffin couered with black, then two other sonnes, then Titus Andronicus, and then Tamora the Queene of Gothes and her two sonnes Chiron and Demetrius, with Aron the More, and others as many as can be, then set downe the Coffin, and Titus speakes (I.i.69–70) [8]

They give details that are not in the dialogue:

> Sound Trumpets, and lay the Coffin in the Tombe (I.i.151–2) [9]

They fix the movements and the gestures of the actors:

> The brother and the sonnes kneele (I.i.369–70) [1]

They sometimes name the properties:

> Marcus Andronicus with the Crowne (I.i.17–18) [2]

One of the stage directions gives a detail of staging which links *Titus Andronicus* still more closely to *The Contention*. When the play begins the tribunes and the senators enter "aloft" in what is supposed to be the Senate House, while Saturninus and Bassianus, followed by their partisans, enter below from two different doors to state their right to the "Roman Empery" left vacant by the death of their father. After they have declared their candidacy we are told that "they go up to the Senate House." This is exactly the same piece of stage business as in *The Contention* when Elinor goes up to the Tower where she watches the invocation of the spirits. *Titus Andronicus* was therefore first performed in the theater that had a tower and a stairway leading to it from the stage. There cannot be any doubt that this play, as the title page of the quarto proclaims, belonged from the first to the repertoire of Lord Strange's men. And it will not be surprising if we discover besides

8. Cf. I.i.1,398–9; II.ii.10–11; III.i.1; IV.i.1; IV.ii.1; IV.iii.1; IV.iv.1.

9. Cf. I.i.89–90,387,389–90; II.iii.267–8; II.iv.1,10–11; III.i.22–3,192–3; IV.iii. 52–3; V.i.1.

1. Cf. II.i.25–6; II.ii.10–11; III.i.11–12,22–3; IV.i.1,68–9,76–7; IV.iv.45–6; V.ii.8–9,204; V.iii.25–6,63–4.

2. Cf. II.ii.1; IV.ii.1; IV.iii.1, 76–7; IV.iv.1; V.ii.166–7.

that it was written by the authors of *The Contention* and of *The True Tragedie.*

∫ ∫ ∫

THIS IS in fact proved by a study of the versification and style.

First, the characteristics of the versification and style of author A are in evidence throughout the play:

1. Verse lines of irregular length from one foot to six feet.[3]
2. A few five-stress verses with the first foot truncated.[4]
3. Trisyllabic feet.[5]
4. Excessive use of trochaic feet. Passages in which this type of rhythmic variation rises to a high proportion are numerous; for instance, I.i.276–95 (8.6%), II.iii.246–58 (8.5%), III.i.193–206 (12.3%), IV.i.1–129 (7.2%), IV.iii.52–76 (12%), V.ii.1–28 (8.3%), V.ii.81–108 (7.1%), V.ii.121–66 (8.0%), V.iii.26–66 (6.6%).
5. The internal pauses are still more numerous than in *The Contention* and *The True Tragedie;* averages varying from 60% to 70% are common, and higher percentages are not rare.
6. Commonplace style vulgarized by too many exclamations and interjections: Come come, why, I, nay, faith, how now, oh, ah, what, alas, look, soft, see see, marry, zounds, fie, hark ye, hold, I warrant you, tut.[6]
7. Obsolescent expressions and colloquialisms: "wot" (II.i.48, 56; III.i.139; V.ii.87), "for why" for "because" (III.i.230), "sith" (I.i.323), "tofore" for "hitherto" (III.i.294), "fere" for "companion"

3. Cf. One foot: IV.ii.19,64; V.i.53. Two feet: I.i.203; II.i.9,25,60,101; II.iii.259; IV.i.29; V.i.154; V.iii.25. Three feet: III.i.36,64; IV.iii.36,54; IV.iv.61; V.i.162,165. Four feet: I.i.62; II.iii.261; II.iv.12; IV.i.78,95;·IV.iii.2,35,54; IV.iv.74; V.i.46,132; V.ii.62,152. Six feet: I.i.219; II.iii.118; III.i.45,160,282; IV.i.28,122; IV.ii.65; IV.iii.8, 10,56; IV.iv.103; V.i.96; V.ii.22,155; V.iii.33,96.

4. Cf. IV.i.45; iv.ii.71; V.iii.156.

5. I.i.22,47,74,243; II.iii.256; III.i.235,262; IV.i.101,119; IV.ii.44,136; IV.iii.2,8, 54,58,120; V.i.46,84,165; V.ii.50; V.iii.43,142,154.

6. Cf. I.i.71,159,456,479; II.i.38,45,63,75,90,95,102,120; II.iii.86,88,89,118,136, 143,150,155,158,168,175,182,185,198,204,220,233,276,286; II.iv.22,34,38,52,57; III. i.23,27,30,33,63,64,82,87,88,110,139,142,148,157,171,175,203,207,215,247,260,268, 276,294; IV.i.5,45,54,55,58,77,83,110,113,117,122; IV.ii.52,57,59,71,97,116,117,126, 136,148,162; IV.iii.35,36,52,63,69,76,80,83,85,87,91,95,100,102,105,114,115; IV.iv.1, 40,47,72; V.i.89,95,122; V.ii.134,155,156,167,202; V.iii.17,53,60,137.

(IV.i.89), third person plural present indicative ending in *s* or *th*
(II.iii.13; II.iv.16–17; III.i.9; IV.iv.72; V.i.2–3).

The following passage is a good example of that versification and
style:

> Come to this geare, you are a good Archer Marcus,
> Ad Iouem, thats for you, here ad Apollonem,
> Ad Martem, thats for my selfe,
> Here boy to Pallas, here to Mercurie,
> To Saturnine, to Caius, not to Saturnine,
> You were as good to shoote against the winde,
> Too it boy, Marcus loose when I bid,
> Of my word I haue written to effect,
> Ther's not a God left vnsollicited.
>   MARCUS. Kinsemen, shoot all your shafts into the Court,
> Wee will afflict the Emperour in his pride.
>   TITUS. Now Masters draw, Oh well said Lucius,
> Good boy in Virgoes lappe, giue it Pallas.
>   MARCUS. My Lord, I aime a mile beyond the Moone,
> Your letter is with Iubiter by this.
>   TITUS. Ha, ha, Publius, Publius, what hast thou done?
> See, see, thou hast shot off one of Taurus hornes.
>   MARCUS. This was the sport my Lord, when Publius shot
> The Bull being galde, gaue Aries such a knocke,
> That downe fell both the Rams hornes in the Court,
> And who should finde them but the Empresse villaine:
> Shee laught, and tolde the Moore hee should not choose,
> But giue them to his Master for a present.
>   TITUS. Why there it goes, God giue his Lordship ioy (IV.iii.52–76)

Characteristics of author B's versification are also found here:
a strictly regular verse, end-stopped, strongly accented with a
high number of spondaic feet, oratorical in tone, hyperbolic in
sense:

> ARON. Sooner this sword shall plow thy bowels vp,
> Stay murtherous villaines will you kill your brother?
> Now by the burning tapors of the skie,
> That shone so brightly when this boy was got,
> He dies vpon my Semitars sharpe point,
> That touches this my first borne sonne and heire:
> I tell you yonglings, not Enceladus,
> With all his threatning band of Typhons broode,
> Nor great Alcides, nor the God of warre,

Shall ceaze this pray out of his fathers hands:
What, what, yee sanguine shallow harted boies,
Yee whitelimde walles, ye ale-house painted signes,
Cole-blacke is better than another hue,
In that it scornes to beare another hue:
For all the water in the Ocean,
Can neuer turne the swans blacke legs to white,
Although shee laue them howrely in the flood:
Tell the Empresse from mee I am of age
To keepe mine owne, excuse it how shee can   (IV.ii.86–104)

Passages like this one, it should be added, are not frequent and
they appear in short fragments:

III.i.242–63   Sorrow of Marcus and Lucius on discovering Aron's treach-
                ery.
IV.i.124–8   Marcus' compassion for Titus' sorrow.
IV.ii.87–105   Aron menaces with extermination those who would kill his
                child. (Passage quoted above.)
V.i.26–43   The Goth who found Aron with a child in his arms reports
                the Moor's speech to his child.
V.i.124–51   Aron brags about the crimes he has committed.
V.iii.144–55   Lucius "sheds obsequious tears" upon the body of Titus.

As this list shows, the passages attributable to author B seem to
center especially on the character of Aron, the only one in the play
—as already noted by several critics—visibly inspired by Marlowe,
being conceived upon the model of Barabas in *The Jew of Malta*.
But it is also possible that the most distinguishing characteristic
of author B, his preference for spondaic feet, may have disappeared in many places owing to the subsequent revision which I
am now going to study—the revision by Shakespeare.

There have been lively discussions over whether Shakespeare
wrote *Titus Andronicus:* a study of the style in the play leaves no
doubt on the subject. All the characteristics which in the *Poems*
permitted us to define Shakespeare's style and which we found in
the Shakespearean parts of 2 and 3 *Henry VI* appear and reappear
in *Titus Andronicus* in considerable number and with remarkable
continuity.

1. Division of the thought into symmetrical parts of more or
less equal length:

A Nobler man, a braver Warriour (I.i.25)

Your noble Emperour and his lovelie Bride (I.i.334) [7]

2. Repetition of a word or grammatical form to accentuate the symmetrical construction:

Here lurks no treason, here no envie swels,
Here grow no damned drugges, here are no stormes (I.i.153–4)

You that suruiue, and you that sleepe in fame (I.i.173) [8]

3. Marked preference for the association of two words expressing two aspects of the same idea and connected by a conjunction:

Ambitiously for Rule and Emperie (I.i.19)

For many good and great deserts to Rome (I.i.24) [9]

4. Antitheses:

Behold the poore remaines aliue and dead (I.i.81)

He liues in fame, that dide in vertues cause (I.i.391) [1]

5. Concetti:
a. Repetition of the sound of a word or jingle:

May fauour Tamora the Queene of Gothes,
(When Gothes were Gothes, and Tamora was Queene) (I.i.139–40)

And helpe to set a head on headles Roome (I.i.186) [2]

b. Concetti proper in the Italian manner:

I am the sea. Harke how her sighs doth flow:
Shee is the weeping welkin, I the earth:

7. Cf. I.i.1,54,65,173,181,217,218,300,378,403,416,442,452; II.i.3,12,18,32,118; II.ii.2; II.iii.27,38,97,123; II.iv.2,3; III.i.1,23,24,59–60,182,239,296; IV.i.33,57; IV.ii.60; IV.iii.11,15,50; IV.iv.27,28,91,92–3; V.i.1,10,11,18,64,66,83; V.ii.29,35,36,37,47; V.iii.5,14,67,148,156,184.

8. Cf. I.i.352–3,371–2,409–10; II.i.21–3,26,82–4; II.ii.4–5; II.iii.96, 100; II.iv.13–14; III.i.4–5,130–1,228–9; IV.ii.109–10; V.ii.22–5,93–7,100–4,195–6; V.iii.26–7,54, 71–2.

9. Cf. I.i.42,45,48,49,58,60,61,81,86,93,110,114,123,142,150,152,157,158,182,188, 197,201,202,230,247,275,375,443,469,470,493,494; II.i.11,76,104,114,116,121,129; II.ii.1,17,25; II.iii.27,39,90,94,102,183,210,216; II.iv.5,17,24; III.i.15,137,230,258, 259; IV.i.17,52,53; IV.ii.16,58,84,118; IV.iii.49; IV.iv.50,57,71,96,99; V.i.6,76,88,95, 133,148; V.ii.1,72,78,118,140,178,204; V.iii.38,43,48,67,75,77,88,95,122,159,165,180, 181,198.

1. Cf. I.i.123; II.iii.121,178; II.iv.25; III.i.45,46–7; IV.iii.28; V.i.10; V.ii.24,29; V.iii.173.

2. Cf. I.i.75–6,167,186,200,241,262,264,371–2,386; II.i.26,34,96,97; II.iii.8; II.iv.52–3; III.i.66–7,108–9,217–18,233; IV.ii.31,109–10; V.i.17,18; V.iii.66.

> Then must my sea be mooued with her sighs,
> Then must my earth with her continuall teares,
> Become a deluge: ouerflowed and drownd (III.i.226–30) [3]

6. Compound words after the Greek and Latin manner: highest piering (II.i.8), fowle spoken (II.i.58), counsaile-keeping (II.iii.24), deadlie standing (II.iii.32), well beseeming (II.iii.56), new transformed (II.iii.64), Rauen culloured (II.iii.83), nice preserued (II.iii.135), rude growing (II.iii.199), new shed (II.iii.200), bloodstained (II.iii.210), true diuining (II.iii.214), blood drinking (II.iii.224), bright burning (III.i.69), honie dew (III.i.112), brine pit (III.i.129), big swolne (III.i.224), selfe bloud (IV.ii.123), long tongude (IV.ii.150), wall-eyd (V.i.44), lurking place (V.ii.35), braine-sicke (V.ii.71), brest deepe (V.iii.179).

7. Words of French consonance: bonjour (I.i.494), closure (V.iii.134; cf. *Venus and Adonis,* 782), conduit (II.iv.30; cf. *Lucrece,* 1234), complot (II.iii.265; V.i.65; V.ii.147; cf. 2 *Henry VI* III.i.147), "repose" meaning "rest" (I.i.353; II.iii.8).

In addition to these mannerisms *Titus Andronicus* contains numerous images characteristically Shakespearean, precise and suggestive, the fruit of attentive observation; their authenticity, in many cases, is proved by the presence of a similar image in the *Poems,* sometimes expressed in words that are almost identical. In the following list I have added some of Shakespeare's favorite ideas though they are not similes in the strict sense of the word. [4]

> Lo as the Barke that hath dischargd his fraught,
> Returnes with pretious lading to the bay
> From whence at first shee wayd her anchorage (I.i.71–3)

> And intrals feede the sacrifising fire,
> Whose smoke like incense doth perfume the skie (I.i.145–6)

>   whose vertues will I hope,
> Reflect on Rome as Tytus Raies on earth (I.i.225–6) [5]

3. Cf. II.iv.29–32,44–6; III.i.16–22,212–14,268–70.
4. Most of those images have already been noted by T. M. Parrott, "Shakespeare's Revision of *Titus Andronicus,*" *Modern Language Review,* January 1919, Vol. 14, No. 1; A. K. Gray, "Shakespeare and *Titus Andronicus,*" *Studies in Philology,* July 1928; J. S. G. Bolton, *"Titus Andronicus,"* Studies in Philology, April 1933; and of course by J. D. Wilson in his edition of the play (New Cambridge Shakespeare).
5. The sun's light effects are often described by Shakespeare; cf. *Venus and Adonis,* 177–8.

There lie thy bones sweete Mutius with thy friends,
Till wee with Trophees doo adorne thy tombe (I.i.388–9) [6]

As when the golden suune salutes the morne,
And hauing gilt the Ocean with his beames,
Gallops the Zodiacke in his glistering Coach,
And ouer-looks the highest piering hills (II.i.5–8)

And I haue a horse will follow where the game makes
Makes way, and runnes like swallows ore the plaine (II.ii.23–4)

The birds chaunt melodie on euerie bush (II.iii.12) [7]

The snakes lies rolled in the chearefull sunne (II.iii.13)

And whilst the babling eccho mocks the hounds,
Replying shrillie to the well tun'd hornes,
As if a double hunt were heard at once (II.iii.17–19) [8]

Whiles hounds and hornes, and sweete mellodious birds
Be vnto vs as is a Nurces song
Of Lullabie to bring her Babe asleepe (II.iii.27–9) [9]

My fleece of wollie haire that now vncurles,
Euen as an adder when shee doth vnrowle,
To doo some fatall execution (II.iii.34–6) [1]

Upon whose leaues are drops of new shed blood,
As fresh as morning dew distil'd on flowers (II.iii.200–1) [2]

6. Cf. sonnet 31:
    Thou art the graue where buried loue doth live,
    Hung with the trophees of my lovers gone (9–10)
7. Cf. *Lucrece:*
    The little birds that tune their mornings ioy
    Make her moans mad with their sweet melodie (1107–8)
8. Cf. *Venus and Adonis:*
    Then do they spend their mouths, Echo replies,
    As if another chase were in the skies (695–6)
9. Cf. *Venus and Adonis:*
    By this far off she hears some huntsman hollo;
    A nurse's song ne'er pleased her babe so well (973–4)
1. Cf. *Venus and Adonis:*
    Whereat she starts, like one that spies an adder
    Wreathed vp in fatal folds just in his way (878–9)
2. Cf. *Venus and Adonis:*
    Whose blood vpon the fresh flowers being shed (665)

    No flower was nigh, no grass, herb, leaf or weed,
    But stole his blood and seem'd with him to bleed (1055–6)

A pretious ring, that lightens all this hole:
Which like a taper in some monument,
Doth shine vpon the dead mans earthy cheekes (II.iii.227–9) [3]

Alas, a crimson Riuer of warme blood,
Like to a bubling Fountaine stirde with winde,
Doth rise and fall betweene thy Rosed lips,
Comming and going with thy honie breath (II.iv.22–5) [4]

And notwithstanding all this losse of blood,
As from a Conduit with their issuing spouts,
Yet doe thy cheekes looke red as Titans face,
Blushing to be encountered with a Clowde (II.iv.29–32) [5]

Sorrow concealed like an Ouen stoppt,
Doth burne the hart to cinders where it is (II.iv.36–7) [6]

Oh had the monster seene those Lillie hands,
Tremble like aspen leaues vpon a Lute,
And make the silken strings delight to kisse them (II.iv.44–6) [7]

Or had he heard the heauenly Harmonie,
Which that sweete tongue hath made,

3. For a diamond illuminating darkness, see sonnet 27:
        Which like a jewel hung in ghastly night
        Makes black night beauteous (11–12)
4. Cf. *Lucrece:*
        And from the purple fountain Brutus drew
        The murderous knife, and as it left the place,
        Her blood, in poor revenge, held it in chase;

        And bubbling from her breast it doth divide
        In two slow rivers that the crimson blood
        Circles her body in on every side (1734–8)
The expression "honey breath" is also found in sonnet 65, l. 5.
5. Cf. *Lucrece:* Like ivory conduits coral cisterns filling (1234).
6. Cf. *Venus and Adonis:*
        An oven that is stopp'd, or river stai'd,
        Burneth more hotly, swelleth with more rage
        So of concealed sorrow may be said (331–3)
7. Cf. sonnet 128:
        How oft, when thou, my music, music play'st,
        Upon that blessed wood whose motion sounds
        With thy sweet fingers, when thou gently sway'st
        The wiry concord that mine ear confounds,
        Do I envy those jacks that nimble leap
        To kiss the tender inward of thy hand (1–6)

He would haue dropt his knife and fell asleepe,
As Cerberus at the Thracian Poets feete (II.iv.48–51) [8]

For these, Tribunes, in the dust I write
My harts deepe languor, and my soules sad teares (III.i.12–13) [9]

O earth I will befriend thee more with raine,
That shall distill from these two auntient ruines,
Than youthfull Aprill shall with all his showres (III.i.16–18) [1]

So thou refuse to drinke my deare sonnes blood (III.i.22) [2]

A stone is soft as waxe, Tribunes more hard than stones (III.i.46) [3]

What foole hath added water to the sea? (III.i.68) [4]

Or brought a faggot to bright burning Troy (III.i.69) [5]

Oh that delightfull engine of her thoughts,
That blabd them with such pleasing eloquence (III.i.82–3) [6]

                that prettie hollow cage,
Where like a sweete mellodious bird it sung,
Sweete varied notes inchaunting euerie eare (III.i.84–6) [7]

Oh thus I found her straying in the Parke,
Seeking to hide her selfe as doth the Deare

8. Cf. *Lucrece:*
    So his unhallow'd haste her words delays,
    And moody Pluto winks while Orpheus plays (552–3)
9. Cf. 3 *Henry VI:* Write in the dust this sentence with thy blood (V.i.56).
1. Cf. *Venus and Adonis:* So they were dew'd with such distilling showers (66)
The comparison of tears with rain is a figure often employed by Shakespeare; cf.
Venus and Adonis:
    Till he take truce with her contending tears
    Which long have rain'd making her cheeks all wet (82–3)
See also *ibid.*, 360, and *Lucrece*, 560, 1271, 1787–90.
2. Cf. 3 *Henry VI:* Thy brothers blood the thirsty earth hath drunk (II.iii.15).
3. Cf. *Lucrece:*
    For stones dissolved to water do convert.
    O, if no harder than a stone thou art,
    Melt at my tears, and be compassionate (592–4)
4. Cf. 3 *Henry VI:* With tearful eyes add water to the sea (V.iv.8).
5. Cf. *Lucrece:* Troy had been bright with fame and not with fire (1491).
6. Cf. *Venus and Adonis:* Once more the engine of her thoughts began (367).
7. Cf. 3 *Henry VI:*
    Ay, such a pleasure as incaged birds
    Conceiue when after many moody thoughts
    At last by notes of household harmony
    They quite forget their loss of liberty (IV.vi.12–15)

That hath receaude some vnrecuring wound.
    TITUS. It was my Deare, and he that wounded her,
Hath hurt me more than had he kild me dead (III.i.88–92) [8]

For now I stand as one vpon a rocke,
Inuirond with a wildernes of sea,
Who markes the waxing tide, grow waue by waue,
Expecting euer when some enuious surge,
Will in his brinish bowels swallow him (III.i.93–102) [9]

             fresh teares
Stood on her cheeks, as doth the honie dew,
Vpon a gathred Lillie almost withered (III.i.111–13) [1]

          to behold our cheekes,
How they are staind like meadowes yet not drie,
With mierie slime left on them by a flood (III.i.124–6) [2]

Did euer Rauen sing so like a Larke,
That giues sweete tidings of the Sunnes vprise (III.i.158–9) [3]

Or with our sighs wele breath the welkin dimme,
And staine the sunne with fogge, as sometime clowds,
When they doe hug him in their melting bosomes (III.i.212–15) [4]

When heauen doth weepe, doth not the earth oreflow?
If the winds rage, doth not the sea waxe mad,
Threatning the welkin with his bigswolne face? (III.i.222–4) [5]

8. Cf. the same play on the word "dear" in *Venus and Adonis:* I'll be a park and
thou shalt be my dear (231).
9. Cf. 3 *Henry VI:* III.ii.135–9 (passage quoted on p. 135).
1. Cf. *Venus and Adonis:*
    In his soft flank, whose wonted lily white
    With purple tears that his wound wept, was drench'd (1053–4)
2. Cf. *Lucrece:*
    Poor Lucrece's cheeks vnto her maid seem so
    As winter meads when sun doth melt their snow (1217–18)
3. The idea of contrasting the song of the lark with the croak of a raven probably
comes from author B (cf. *The Contention,* sc.x.21–3), but the second line was certainly added by Shakespeare, as is proved by sonnet 29:
    Like the lark at break of day arising
    From sullen earth, sings hymns at heaven's gate
Cf. further, pp. 169–70.
4. Cf. *Venus and Adonis:*
    I'll sigh celestial breath, whose gentle wind
    Shall cool the heat of this descending sun (189–90)
5. Cf. 2 *Henry VI:*
    And with the southern clouds contend in tears,
    Theirs for the earths increase, mine for my sorrows (III.ii.384–5)

For why, my bowels cannot hide her woes,
But like a drunkard must I vomit them (III.i.231–2) 6

that kisse is comfortlesse,
As frozen water to a starued snake (III.i.251–2) 7

And thy brother I,
Euen like a stony image cold and numme (III.i.258–9)

and be this dismall sight
The closing vp of our most wretched eies (III.i.262–3) 8

Besides this sorrow is an enemie,
And would vsurpe vpon my watrie eies (III.i.268–9) 9

My Lord kneele downe with me, Lauinia kneele

.   .   .   .

Mortall reuenge vpon these Traiterous Gothes (IV.i.88–93) 1

That hath more scars of sorrow in his hart,
Than foe-mens marks vpon his battred shield (IV.i.127–8)

And from your wombe where you imprisoned were,
Hee is infraunchised, and come to light (IV.ii.124–5)

Ile diue into the burning lake belowe (IV.iii.43) 2

Marcus we are but shrubs, no Cedars wee (IV.iii.45) 3

These tidings nip me, and I hang the head
As flowers with frost, or grasse beat downe with storms (IV.iv. 71–2) 4

Is the sunne dimde, that Gnats doe fly in it (IV.iv.82) 5

6. Cf. *Lucrece:* Drunken desire must vomit his receipt (703).
7. Cf. *2 Henry VI:* I fear me you but warm the starved snake (III.i.343).
8. Cf. *Lucrece:* When heauvy sleep had closed vp mortal eyes (163).
9. Cf. *Venus and Adonis:* Whereat a sudden pale . . . Usurps her cheek (589–91).
1. The vow that Marcus exacts from Titus, Lavinia, and young Lucius has its analogue in *Lucrece* (1842–8), and in this passage the name of Lucrece is mentioned.
2. Cf. *2 Henry VI:* Descend to darknesse and the burning lake (I.iv.42).
3. In setting down this line, Shakespeare was certainly thinking of one that he had added to a passage in *3 Henry VI* (V.ii.11–14) written by the author of *The True Tragedie* and enumerating the properties of the cedar that "kept low shrubs from winters powerful winds."
4. Cf. *Venus and Adonis:*
Whose blood vpon fresh flowers being shed
Doth make them droop with grief and hang the head (665–6)
and *2 Henry VI:* Like to the summers corn by tempest lodged (III.ii.176).
5. Cf. *Lucrece:* Gnats are unnoted wheresoe'er they fly (1014).

The Eagle suffers little birds to sing,
And is not carefull what they meane thereby,
Knowing that with the shadow of his winges,
He can at pleasure stint their melodie (IV.iv.83–5) [6]

          weele follow where thou leadst,
Like stinging Bees in hottest summers day,
Led by their Master to the flowred fields,
And be aduengde on cursed Tamora (V.i.13–15) [7]

Witnes these trenches made by greefe and care (V.ii.23) [8]

Ther's not a hollow Caue or lurking place,
No vast obscuritie or mistie vale,
Where bloodie murther or detested rape,
Can couch for feare (V.ii.35–6) [9]

Here stands the spring whome you haue staind with mud (V.ii.
171) [1]

This goodly sommer with your winter mixt (V.ii.172) [2]

You sad facde men, people and sons of Rome
By vprores seuerd as a flight of fowle,
Scatterd by winds and high tempestuous gusts (V.iii.67–9) [3]

But if my frostie signes and chappes of age,
Graue witnesses of true experience (V.iii.77–8)

6. Cf. *Lucrece:*
    Which like a falcon towering in the skies,
    Coucheth the fowl below with his wings' shade (506–7)
7. Cf. 2 *Henry VI:*
    The commons like an angry hiue of bees
    That want their leader, scatter vp and down
    And care not who they sting in his reueng [Gloucester's] (III.ii.125–7)
The comparison comes from one of the authors of *The Contention,* and the italicized words are Shakespeare's addition, which he repeats here. Cf. further p. 170.
8. Cf. sonnet 2:
    When forty winters shall besiege thy brow
    And dig deep trenches in thy beauty's field (1–2)
9. Cf. *Lucrece:*
    In men as in rough-grown grove, remain
    Cave-keeping evils that obscurely sleep (1250)
1. Cf. *Lucrece:* Mud not the fountain that gaue drink to thee (577).
Sonnet 35: Roses have thorns and silver fountains mud (2).
2 *Henry VI:* The purest spring is not so free from mud (III.i.101).
2. Cf. *Venus and Adonis:* Lust's winter comes ere summer half be done (802).
3. Cf. *Lucrece:* As lagging fowls before the Northern blast (1335).

> To beg reliefe among Romes enemies,
> Who drownd their enmetie in my true teares (V.iii.106–7)

> Teare for teare, and louing kisse for kisse,
> Thy brother Marcus tenders on thy lips,
> Oh were the summe of these that I should pay,
> Countlesse and infinite, yet would I pay them (V.iii.156–9) [4]

Thus *Titus Andronicus* stands in the same state of evolution as the second and third parts of *Henry VI*. It is an old play, written by author A (traces of his versification and style are found in practically all the scenes), first touched up by author B to give it a Marlovian flavor, and finally revised in an important way (as the mannerisms and images show) by Shakespeare. And judging by the manner in which Shakespeare revised the two preceding plays, *Titus Andronicus* must be composed of passages in which the old text has been preserved word for word, of mixed passages reproducing parts of the old text more or less modified, and of passages entirely Shakespearean.

But as the basic original has not come down to us it will not be possible to determine with absolute certainty, as we have done in the preceding chapter, all the portions that can be traced back to Shakespeare. It will of course be pretty easy to distinguish passages which are wholly pre-Shakespearean and those which are entirely Shakespearean in versification and style. But the study of 2 and 3 *Henry VI* has shown that in the case of mixed passages the versification has lost most of its value as a test. Having to deal with a text which was not his own, Shakespeare could sacrifice his rhythmic preferences and adopt the foreign pattern of the verse with remarkable facility. All depended upon the extent of the modification. If only a few words had been changed here and there without really affecting the form of the thought the versification might retain almost entirely its pre-Shakespearean character; if the form of the thought had been radically altered the versification might approach or depart from that of the pre-Shakespearean author depending upon how faithfully Shakespeare had preserved the mold of the altered line. The analysis of the rhythmical varia-

4. Cf. *Venus and Adonis:* and one sweet kiss shall pay this countless debt (84).

tions in *Titus Andronicus* discloses this fact once again, for it reveals widely different percentages.

But it will always be possible at least to draw up a list of the portions in the mixed passages that particularly held Shakespeare's
attention, and even to state the greater or smaller extent of their
revision. Here mannerisms and images lose nothing of their value
as a test. They trace out a road through the play along which one
can follow Shakespeare, noting the places he passed rapidly by
and those where he made a prolonged stay. And differences in
rhythmical variations will then, in their turn, bring their testimony
which, combined with the list of mannerisms and images, will
permit us to establish four degrees of importance for Shakespeare's
modifications.

1. If a passage clearly has the characteristic versification of
author A or author B and has neither mannerisms nor images, there
will be a good chance that it is a portion of the original play,
which has been preserved word for word in the definitive text.

2. If a passage has the versification characteristic of Shakespeare and at the same time contains his mannerisms and images,
it will be pretty certain that it was either rewritten or added by
Shakespeare.

3. If a passage has a versification somewhat resembling that of
authors A or B, yet contains a small number of Shakespearean mannerisms or images, it can be identified as a part of the original play
slightly modified by Shakespeare.

4. If a passage has a versification approaching that of Shakespeare and in addition exhibits a considerable number of his mannerisms and images, it will be a portion of the original play profoundly modified by Shakespeare.

Let us therefore begin by making a list of mannerisms and
images, as they are distributed in the various scenes:

I.i	64	mannerisms:	1,19,24,25,42,45,48,49,54,58,60,61,65,75–6,81,
975 lines			82–4,86,93,110,114,123,139–40,142,150,152,153–4,157,158,
			167,173,181,182,186,188,197,200,201,202,217,218,230,241,
			247,262,264,275,300,334,352–3,371–2,375,378,386,391,403,
			409–10,416,442,443,452,469,470,493,494.
	4	images:	71–3,145–6,225–6,388–9

II.i   20 mannerisms: 3,8,11,12,18,21–3,26,32,34,58,76,82–4,96,97,
135 lines   104,114,116,118,121,129
         1 image: 5–8

II.ii   5 mannerisms: 1,2,4–5,17,25
26 lines   1 image: 23–4

II.iii   27 mannerisms: 8,24,27,32,38,39,56,64,83,90,94,96,97,100,102,
306 lines   121,123,135,178,183,199,200,210,214,216,224,265
         7 images: 12,13,17–19,27–9,34–6,200–1,227–9

II.iv   9 mannerisms: 2,3,5,13–14,17,24,25,30,52–3
57 lines   5 images: 22–5, 29–32,36–7,44–6,48–51

III.i   28 mannerisms: 1,4–5,15,16–22,23,24,27,45,46–7,59–60,66–7,
302 lines   69,108–9,112,129,130–1,137,182,212–14,217–18,224,226–
                30,230,233,239,258–9,268–70,296
         20 images: 12–13,16–18,22,46,68,69,82–3,84–6,88–92,93–102,
                111–13,124–6,158–9,212–15,222–4,231–2,251–2,258–9,262–
                3,268–9

IV.i   5 mannerisms: 17,33,52,53,57
129 lines   2 images: 88–93,127–8

IV.ii   9 mannerisms:16,31,58,60,84,109–10,118,123,150
180 lines   1 image: 124–5

IV.iii   5 mannerisms: 11,15,28,49,50
180 lines   2 images: 43,45

IV.iv   4 mannerisms: 27,28,91,92–3
113 lines   3 images: 71–2,82,83–5

V.i   16 mannerisms: 1,6,10,11,17,18,44,64,65,66,76,83,88,95,133,148
165 lines   1 image: 13–15

V.ii   18 mannerisms: 1,22–5,24,29,35,36,37,47,71,72,78,93–7,100–4,
206 lines   118,140,178,195–6,204
         4 images: 23,35–6,171,172

V.iii   26 mannerisms: 5,14,26–7,38,43,48,54,66,67,71–2,75,77,88,95,
204 lines   122,134,148,156,159,165,173,179,180,181,184,198
         4 images: 67–9,77–8,106–7,156–9

This list leads to some important deductions. There is not one
scene in the play but has its share of mannerisms and images:
Shakespeare's revision in *Titus Andronicus*, as in *The Contention*
and *The True Tragedy*, has been extended over the whole play.

But the images are far less numerous than the mannerisms. The majority of them are concentrated in a few passages: II.iii.10–50, Tamora tries to entice Aron to the pleasures of love; II.iv.11–57, Marcus meets Lavinia just after she has been violated by Tamora's sons; III.i.1–149, distress of Titus who has vainly begged the tribunes to spare the life of his sons and who sees the state to which Lavinia has been reduced. Everywhere else the images are scattered and widely separated from one another, and moreover they are generally brief, lacking that profuseness of picturesque detail which in 2 and 3 *Henry VI* is sometimes excessive. The mannerisms, on the contrary, are more evenly distributed and often found in continuous groups. While reading the text he was revising Shakespeare rarely felt his imagination stirred, and his work consisted principally in purifying the versification and the style. The first act provides an excellent example of this, and it is no doubt owing to that preponderance of mannerisms—which, after all, belong for the most part to the Greek and Latin rhetoric—that this first act is the only portion of the play which has a classical atmosphere; in the other acts one may even forget that the action takes place in ancient Rome.

Let us now, with the help of the versification test, try to divide the text into the four classes established above.

I. PASSAGES OF THE OLD PLAY RETAINED VERBATIM

I.i.276–98. Bassianus carries Lavinia off; Titus kills Mutius, his son, who has sided with Bassianus. The versification and style are characteristic of author A: trochaic feet 9.6%, spondaic feet 1.7%. No trace of Shakespeare.

I.i.392–7. Marcus is surprised at Tamora's advancement. Though the proportion of rhythmic variations might be that of Shakespeare (trochees, 2.5%, spondees 2.5%), this passage was certainly written by author A. There is 1 trisyllabic foot.

II.iii.246–58. Saturninus learns that his brother has been slain. The versification and style are those of A: trochaic feet 9.2%, spondaic feet 0%, 1 trisyllabic foot. No trace of Shakespeare.

III.i.193–206. Titus has his hand cut off and sends it to the emperor. Versification and style characteristic of A: trochaic feet 12.5%, spondaic feet 1.4%. No trace of Shakespeare.

III.i.242–50. Marcus and Lucius give vent to their sorrow and indignation. Lines strongly accentuated, no enjambment, and a single internal pause. The hyperbolic style bears the stamp of author B. No trace of Shakespeare.

IV.ii.87–105. Aron threatens "to plough the bowels up" of anyone who touches his son. Another passage by author B (see pp. 151–2).

IV.iii.52–76. Titus, Marcus, and young Lucius dispatch arrows to the gods. Trochaic feet 12.9%, spondaic feet 7.7%. No trace of Shakespeare.

V.i.20–43. Aron is taken prisoner by a Goth. The passage is probably by B: trochaic feet 2.5%, spondaic feet 5.8%. No trace of Shakespeare.

V.i.152–62. Emilius invites Lucius to parley with the emperor. Trochaic feet 6.3%, spondaic feet 3.1%. No trace of Shakespeare.

II. PASSAGES SLIGHTLY MODIFIED BY SHAKESPEARE

I.i.234–75. Saturninus asks that Titus give him Lavinia's hand in marriage. He assures Tamora that she will be honorably treated. Trochaic feet 5.7%, spondaic feet 1.9%, 1 trisyllabic foot, but 5 mannerisms.

II.iii.1–9. Aron buries gold under a tree. Trochaic feet 6.2%, spondaic feet 2.2%. 1 mannerism.

IV.i.1–129. Lavinia reveals the names of her ravishers. Trochaic feet 7.4%, spondaic feet 3.5%. Many internal pauses, but 5 mannerisms and 2 images.

IV.ii.1–51. As a message from his grandfather, young Lucius brings weapons to Demetrius and Chiron. Trochaic feet 4.2%, spondaic feet 1.6%. 2 mannerisms.

IV.ii.52–86. A nurse brings Aron his child by Tamora, with the order to kill it. Trochaic feet 4.6%, spondaic feet 2.6%, irregular lines, 1 truncated decasyllabic verse. 3 mannerisms.

V.i.124–51. Aron boasts of the crimes he has committed. Trochaic feet 3.5%, spondaic feet 6.4%. The passage is by B, and the imitation of Marlowe's Barabas is striking. Only 2 mannerisms.

V.ii.1–28. Tamora, disguised as Revenge, comes to Titus. Trochaic feet 8.6%, spondaic feet 3.5%. 3 mannerisms, 1 image.

V.ii.81–120. Titus asks Tamora and her sons to slay a murderer and a ravisher if they meet them. Trochaic feet 6.8%, spondaic feet 3.4%. 3 mannerisms.

V.ii.121–66. Titus binds the sons of Tamora. Trochaic feet 8.0%, spondaic feet 2.2%. 1 mannerism.

III. PASSAGES MORE RADICALLY MODIFIED BY SHAKESPEARE

I.i.1–63 (plus three verses omitted in modern editions). Saturninus and Bassianus compete for the emperorship. Trochaic feet 5.9%, spondaic feet 1.4%, 3 trisyllabic feet in the omitted lines, but 12 mannerisms.

I.i.64–95. Arrival of Titus with the bodies of his sons killed in the war. Trochaic feet 6.2%, spondaic feet 3.7%. 6 mannerisms, 1 image.

I.i.150–233. Titus refuses to be elected emperor and suggests that the tribunes and the people choose Saturninus. Trochaic feet 4.5%, spondaic feet 4.5%. 17 mannerisms, 2 images.

II.i.1–25. Aron rejoices at the success of Tamora and promises himself that he will take advantage of it. Trochaic feet 4.2%, spondaic feet 2.5%. 6 mannerisms, 1 image.

II.i.26–135. Chiron and Demetrius are both in love with Lavinia. Aron reconciles them by suggesting that they satisfy their passion by violating her. As in the preceding passage the larger number of trochees (4.7%, spondees 3.6%) indicates a substructure by author A; but 15 mannerisms can mean only an extensive recasting.

II.iii.192–245. Quintus and Martius fall into the pit where lies the dead body of Bassianus. Trochaic feet 3.3%, spondaic feet 2.9%. The scene certainly was in the pre-Shakespearean play, but most of it must have been rewritten by Shakespeare: 6 mannerisms and 2 images.

III.i.251–88. Marcus asks Titus why he remains silent in view of so many atrocities; Titus replies. The trochees in the passage— 4.8% as compared with 3.7% for spondees—and 1 trisyllabic foot show that it was originally composed by A. But 2 mannerisms,

4 images, and the lines on the oath of revenge, which remind one of a similar situation in *Lucrece*, leave no doubt about the wide extent of the revision.

IV.ii.106–80. Aron kills the nurse and proposes to Tamora's sons an exchange of children to save the reputation of the empress. Trochaic feet 5.3%, spondaic feet 2.6%. 4 mannerisms, 1 image.

IV.iv.50–113. Saturninus learns that the Goths are marching on Rome under the leadership of Lucius. Tamora cheers him up and promises to deceive Titus. Trochaic feet 4.3%, spondaic feet 2.1%. 2 mannerisms, 3 images. The passage has been rewritten especially toward the end.

V.ii.29–80. Tamora offers her help to Titus to take vengeance on his foes. Trochaic feet 3.8%, spondaic feet 3.4%. 8 mannerisms, 2 images.

V.iii.1–66. Lucius and the emperor accept Titus' invitation. During the banquet Titus kills Lavinia, then Tamora. The emperor kills Titus, and Lucius kills the emperor. Trochaic feet 5.8%, spondaic feet 3.6%. 8 mannerisms.

V.iii.141–200. Marcus and the sons of Lucius pay the last honors to Titus; Aron is condemned to be buried breast-deep in the earth and Tamora's body is to be thrown off to beasts and birds of prey. Trochaic feet 5.3%, spondaic feet 3.3%, 1 truncated decasyllable, 11 mannerisms, 1 image.

IV. PASSAGES REWRITTEN OR ADDED BY SHAKESPEARE

I.i.96–149. Sacrificing of Alarbus. An interpolation (cf. pp. 144–6). Trochaic feet 2.6%, spondaic feet 3.0%. 5 mannerisms, 1 image.

I.i.299–340. Saturninus turns against Titus and offers to marry Tamora. Trochaic feet 1.4%, spondaic feet 2.9%. 2 mannerisms.

I.i.341–90. Marcus and his nephews beseech Titus to let them bury Mutius with his brothers. Another Shakespearean interpolation (cf. p. 147). Trochaic feet 3.2%, spondaic feet 3.0%. 5 mannerisms, 1 image.

I.i.399–495. Tamora pleads for Titus, Marcus, and Bassianus, and the emperor pardons them. Trochaic feet 3.5%, spondaic feet 3.7%. 10 mannerisms.

II.ii.1–26. Titus and his sons prepare for the chase and welcome the emperor and the Court. Trochaic feet 3.4%, spondaic feet 3.4%. 5 mannerisms, 1 image.

II.iii.10–54. Tamora tempts Aron with the pleasures of love, but he refuses her. Trochaic feet 3.5%, spondaic feet 3.5%. 5 mannerisms, 5 images. Many resemblances to the chief incident in *Venus and Adonis* of which this passage is a replica in miniature.

II.iii.55–88. Bassianus and Lavinia join in insulting insinuations against Tamora. Trochaic feet 2.9%, spondaic feet 3.5%. 3 mannerisms.

II.iii.89–117. Tamora asks her sons to avenge her, and they slay Bassianus. Trochaic feet 2.7%, spondaic feet 3.4%. 6 mannerisms.

II.iii.118–91. Tamora's sons tell their intention to violate Lavinia, and Tamora, despite Lavinia's pleading, allows them to satisfy their lust. Trochaic feet 3.5%, spondaic feet 4.0%. 5 mannerisms.

II.iii.260–306. Deaf to the entreaties of Titus, Saturninus sends Quintus and Martius to prison. Trochaic 2.9%, spondaic feet 4.7%. 1 mannerism.

II.iv.1–57. Demetrius and Chiron jeer at Lavinia after violating her. Marcus meets his niece and guessing what has happened, expresses indignation against the authors of this crime. Trochaic feet 3.1%, spondaic feet 3.5%. 9 mannerisms, 5 images.

III.i.1–58. Titus entreats the tribunes to spare his sons. Trochaic feet 3.1%, spondaic feet 3.7%. 8 mannerisms, 4 images.

III.i.59–149. Grief of Titus and Marcus. Trochaic feet 3.9%, spondaic feet 3.9%. 8 mannerisms, 8 images.

III.i.150–92. Aron offers Titus the life of his sons if he, Marcus, or Lucius will cut off his own hand and send it to the emperor. The three men vie with each other in generosity. Trochaic feet 2.8%, spondaic feet 3.3%. A probatory image from *The Contention,* already modified in 2 *Henry VI* (III.ii.40), has been repeated here and modified anew (158–9), showing that the passage must have been present in the old play and is here only rewritten.

III.i.207–41. Titus' lamentations. A messenger brings back the hand of Titus and the heads of his two sons. Trochaic feet 4.0%, spondaic feet 4.0%. 7 mannerisms, 3 images. A trisyllabic foot retained shows that this passage is also only rewritten.

III.i.289–301. Lucius bids farewell to his father and to his sister. Trochaic feet 3.0%, spondaic feet 3.0%. 1 mannerism.

IV.iv.1–38. Saturninus complains of Titus' abuse. Tamora calms him, but she is sure that she has touched Titus to the quick. Trochaic feet 3.1%, spondaic feet 3.1%. 2 mannerisms.

V.i.1–19. The Goths swear to follow Lucius and take revenge on Rome. Trochaic feet 3.1%, spondaic feet 4.0%. 6 mannerisms. One image in *The Contention,* modified in 2 *Henry VI,* is resumed here and modified again: the passage is only rewritten.

V.i.44–123. Aron discloses the part that he played in past events. Trochaic feet 3.0%, spondaic feet 3.0%. 8 mannerisms.

V.ii.167–206. Titus tells Tamora's sons that he is going to serve them up to their mother as pasties. Trochaic feet 3.0%, spondaic feet 3.0%. 3 mannerisms, 2 images.

V.iii.67–95. Marcus asks the Romans to remain united; a Roman lord calls on Lucius to speak. Trochaic feet 3.4%, spondaic feet 3.4%. 6 mannerisms, 2 images.

V.iii.96–140. Lucius recalls the part he took in the recent events, Marcus justifies the deeds of the Andronici, and Lucius is elected emperor. Trochaic feet 3.5%, spondaic feet 4.0%. 2 mannerisms, 1 image.

This classification makes precise the evidence from the combined list of images and mannerisms and confirms the fact that Shakespeare's revision was most important. The passages rewritten or added are by far the longest of the four categories; they comprise 1046 lines, nearly half of the play. The passages radically modified come next with 774 lines; if we could know the exact composition of those passages the number of lines entirely in the hand of Shakespeare would surely be considerably augmented, for it is noticeable that in many cases the percentages of rhythmical variations are almost like those of Shakespeare. How many additions proper, now invisible, will forever be hidden 'in those mixed passages? Now and then it is possible to identify some of those suspected corrections. Take for instance the two lines which I have included in the list of images:

> Did euer Rauen sing so like a Larke,
> That giues sweete tidings of the Sunnes vprise? (III.i.158–9)

As a matter of fact only part of it is Shakespeare's. The first line was probably in the original play where, strictly speaking, it was not an image. It had been used by author B when he wrote in *The Contention:*

> Came he euen now to sing a Rauens note,
> And thinkes he that the cherping of a Wren
> By crying comfort through a hollow voice
> Can satisfie my griefes, or ease my heart (sc.x.21–4)

and he must have repeated the idea, slightly modified, in *Titus Andronicus*. Shakespeare retained the first line as he had already done in 2 *Henry VI* (III.ii.40–4), and this time enriched it by the addition of the second line which presents to the mind a totally different kind of suggestion: the dry, matter-of-fact comparison between the songs of two birds has, at one bound, been transported to the plane of poetic rapture.

A similar instance is to be found in Act V.sc.i. In *The Contention* (sc.x.41–2) author A compared the excitement of the Commons on hearing that Duke Humphrey had been assassinated to that of a swarm of angry bees that "Run vp and downe caring not whom they sting." Shakespeare adopted this comparison in 2 *Henry VI* (III.ii.126–7) but amplified it with a detail which endowed the bees with a human sentiment: they were furious because they had lost their leader:

> The Commons like an angry Hiue of Bees
> That want their leader, scatter vp and downe,
> And care not who they sting in his revenge

This comparison was also repeated in *Titus Andronicus* and applied to the Goths when they promised to follow Lucius in his vengeful venture: "Like stinging Bees in hottest summers day" (V.i.14). Shakespeare kept this idea too; but I suppose with his addition to 2 *Henry VI* in mind he supplemented it with "Led by their Master in the flowred fields," without noticing, however, that the new line contradicted the first by substituting a promise of booty for a threat of revenge.

A careful search might discover some other examples, but they would be only a few among hundreds of such interesting details —adjustments of limping verses, substitutions of picturesque synonyms for banal expressions, small ornaments embroidered on a plain canvas, etc.

After all, these accessions would not be of prime consequence. A more important part of Shakespeare's work is happily more easily discernible—I mean the effort to humanize some of the characters. There are enough traces of the old play in the text of *Titus Andronicus* to enable us to imagine in most cases what the psychology of the characters was in their pristine form and thus to read the history of their transformations.

Saturninus, in the pre-Shakespearean play, was a despot, capricious and brutal. He unjustly turns against Titus simply to satisfy his desire for Tamora; he condemns Titus' sons though he has no proof of their guilt; he puts to death the clown, an innocent carrier of Titus' ironic petition. And such he is in some parts of *Titus Andronicus*. But in other parts this absolute ruler has no will of his own, and like Henry VI he is a pure instrument in the hands of his consort. Hearing that Lucius marches against Rome at the head of an army of Goths, he loses heart and shows himself incapable of acting (IV.iv.61–106). And this is how Shakespeare understood him.

Lavinia also presents a contradiction in her nature, and within a single scene, Act II.sc.iii. At the beginning, in her taunts at the empress, she uses a language the coarseness of which has excited the indignation of many critics from Arthur Symons to J. D. Wilson. In the last part of the scene, when she entreats the empress, whom she has just insulted, to preserve her from the indignity that Chiron and Demetrius have in store for her, she shows herself to be so delicate that she cannot even pronounce the word for the attack on her chastity; she becomes the sweet and sympathetic woman that she had been before. The whole scene is written in the versification of Shakespeare, but some probatory comparisons with the tiger, the lion, and the raven show that the supplication (an essential part in the action) was in the old play and that this passage is only rewritten. I am afraid the insults are an addition by Shakespeare.

Aron is substantially the same as in the old play, a perfect specimen of the Marlovian villain, a Machiavellian, proud of his power for evil. Even his redeeming sentiments as a father are inherited from the pre-Shakespearean form, for his defense of his "first borne sonne and heire" is one of the rare passages which have been retained verbatim. But the analysis of the versification has also shown that the character is present in passages radically modified (II.i.1–25,26–135; IV.ii.106–80) or rewritten or added (II.iii.10–54; III.i.150–92; V.i.44–123), a long list which indicates that among the personages in the play Aron is the one who has attracted most of Shakespeare's attention—a fact which, incidentally, can be guessed from the way this inhuman creation has been made to appear lifelike.

Andronicus is another character who appears in the Shakespearean play as he was in the pre-Shakespearean form—the victorious soldier, devoted to the safety of his country, modest, respectful toward his "King and Commander" (I.i.247) to the point of killing one of his sons who dared oppose this supreme ruler, but who under the cruelty of the wrongs he has to bear finally becomes intent solely on avenging those wrongs according to the current formula of the tragedy of revenge, scenes of madness, real or feigned, included. But as with Aron, most of the passages in which Titus acts belong to class III (I.i.64–95; I.i.150–233; III.i. 251–88; V.ii.29–80; V.iii.1–66) or to class IV (II.ii.1–26; II.iii.260– 306; III.i.1–58,59–149,150–92,207–41; V.ii.167–206): the entire role of Titus has been either rewritten or amplified. There is one trait that has been particularly developed: Titus' propensity to express his sorrow. Here again, from passage III.i.251–88, originally written by author A, it is certain that in his pristine dramatic existence Titus let the spectators know his sufferings in classical lamentations. But in the Shakespearean play, to tell the truth, his confidences are too frequent and too abundant; in the third act his tears have become a deluge. I shall not, however, go so far as some have and call this "bleating pathos." Shakespeare's intention was good even if the execution was too generous: he wanted, according to his habit, to tone down the "heroic" and vindictive disposition of the man by a pathetic display of sensibility.

Tamora is probably the character who was most thoroughly improved by Shakespeare's revision. Her son Alarbus having been tortured by the sons of Titus, she was bound to be an avenger in woman's clothes, and this did not lead to femininity. Something of her cruelty is obvious in Act II.sc.iii when, deaf to the supplication of Lavinia, she abandons her to the lust of Chiron and Demetrius. But in a series of touches Shakespeare gave her some of the defects which man considers distinctive of woman. She shamelessly lies in some of the details she rehearses to her sons to excite them against Bassianus and Lavinia (II.iii.91–108). With hatred in her heart she is in appearance pitiful and conciliatory. Twice, with an admirable power of dissimulation, she feigns to exculpate Titus (I.i.399–495; IV.iv.1–38); and her exclamation when the sons of Titus are suspected to have killed Bassianus

Oh wondrous thing!
How easily murder is discouered (II.iii.286–7)

uncovers a soul to its very depths and equals Queen Margaret's utterance when, with similar hypocrisy, she expresses the hope that Duke Humphrey will be found innocent. Lastly Shakespeare has exposed her lascivious temperament in the scene where in imitation of Venus she tries to satisfy her lust with her black Adonis. Tamora is already one of those subtle portraits of women which Shakespeare knew how to paint with such a deft hand.

Thus Francis Meres was not entirely wrong when, in his *Palladis Tamia* (Stationers' Register, September 7, 1598), he included *Titus Andronicus* among the tragedies by Shakespeare. And the tradition that prevailed in the theatrical circles down to the seventeenth century, transmitted by Edward Ravenscroft in the Address to his *Titus Andronicus or the Rape of Lavinia* (1687), according to which the play was "brought by a private Authour to be acted" and Shakespeare "only gave some Master-touches to one or two of the principal Parts or Characters," is not so far from the truth, if we make allowance for the deteriorations that hearsay always suffers in the course of time: it is a fact that in the list of passages rewritten or added by Shakespeare, the characters most often mentioned are Titus and Tamora.

As in the case of 2 and 3 *Henry VI*, these changes were not all made at the same time. The distribution of the feminine endings in the passages of class IV shows three distinct periods.

A first period is remarkable for the very small number of feminine endings:

	Feminine endings	Verse lines	Percentages
I.i.196–249	1	54	1.8
290–340	1	42	2.3
341–90	1	50	2.0
399–495	1	97	1.0
II.ii.1–26	1	26	3.8
II.iv.1–57	3	57	5.2
III.i.1–58	2	58	3.4
207–41	2	35	5.7
IV.iv.1–38	1	38	2.6
V.ii.167–206	2	40	5.0
V.iii.67–95	0	29	0.0

15 feminine endings in 526 lines or an average of 2.8%

The period when Shakespeare made this revision is certainly contemporaneous with or possibly a little anterior to that of the first revision of 3 *Henry VI* with its percentage of 5.7%.

A second period comprises three passages:

	Feminine endings	Verse lines	Percentages
II.iii.55–88	3	34	8.8
260–306	4	47	8.5
III.i.59–149	8	91	8.7

15 feminine endings in 172 verse lines or 8.7%

It is noticeable that the first passage is the scene in which Lavinia insults the empress, and the others set forth the lachrymose character of Titus' sorrow. The average number of feminine endings in the first revision of 2 *Henry VI* is 8.3%: the two plays must have been revised at about the same time.

It is difficult to classify one passage (III.i.150–92); the percentage is 6.9% and it may belong to the second revision or may be a portion of the first revision with an exceptionally high percentage.

A third period comprises the remaining passages:

	Feminine endings	Verse lines	Percentages
II.iii.10–54	5	45	11.1
89,117	4	29	13.7
118–91	9	74	12.1
III.i.289–301	2	13	15.3
V.i.1–19	3	19	15.7
44–123	14	80	17.5

37 feminine endings in 260 verse lines or an average of 14.2%

This revision must have taken place not very long after the second revision.

It is possible to fix a downward limit for these revisions. From the title page of the 1594 quarto it appears that the play, as published, was performed first by the Earl of Derby's men (i.e., Lord Strange, who had inherited the title on September 25, 1593), then by the Earl of Pembroke's men, and finally by the Earl of Sussex' men. The company of Lord Pembroke, according to the dramatic annals of that period, made their first appearance during the last three months of 1592 when they were at Leicester. After playing at Court on December 26, 1592, and January 6, 1592/3, they traveled again, visited Ludlow, Shrewsbury, Coventry, Bath, and Ipswich; in June they were at York, in July at Rye. And that was the end of that venture. From a letter dated September 28, 1593, from Henslowe to Alleyn we learn that the company was not able to pay its expenses and had to pawn its "apparel" and go home (E. K. Chambers, *Elizabethan Stage*, 2, 128). Lord Strange's men therefore, according to a transaction the details of which are unknown, must have handed over their play of *Titus Andronicus* to Lord Pembroke's men in October 1592 at the latest. And the play, as the quarto shows, had already received its third and final revision.[5]

The history of the play *Titus Andronicus* is then as follows. The company of Lord Strange had in its repertoire a play on the pseudohistorical subject of Titus Andronicus, written by author A; rejuvenated, with a Marlovian flavor added, by author B; first incompletely revised by Shakespeare early in 1591/2 and perfected during the period from March to October 1592. This play was ceded to the company of Lord Pembroke when it was formed and was trying to assemble a repertoire of its own for the intended tour of 1592. When Lord Pembroke's company went bankrupt *Titus Andronicus* passed to the company of the earl of Sussex,

5. In *A Knack to Know a Knave,* a play acted by Strange's men at the Rose on June 10, 1592 (it was then "new"), is found an allusion to *Titus Andronicus:*

As Titus was vnto the Roman Senators,
When he had made a conquest on the Goths:
That in requitall of his seruice done,
Did offer him the imperiall Diademe

I believe the allusion is to Shakespeare's *Titus Andronicus* in its final revision, but it may also be a recollection of the older play.

and when the latter troupe, which had been on tour in 1593, came back to London and played for a six-week season (December 27, 1593–February 6, 1593/4) in Henslowe's theater, it gave three performances of *Titus and ondronicus.* On February 6, the day of the last performance, the manuscript of *Titus Andronicus* was registered for publication and appeared in the same year.

But this manuscript, reproduced by the quarto of 1594, was not necessarily the only manuscript. In transferring the play to Lord Pembroke's actors the company of Lord Strange did not abandon its right to retain it in its repertoire: no company would part so easily with a successful play. And indeed when it was reorganized in the spring of 1594 under the patronage of Lord Hunsdon, the lord chamberlain, "Andronicous" was one of the first plays to be presented in Henslowe's theater, on June 5 and 12, 1594. The manuscript ceded to Lord Pembroke's company was only a transcript of the company's promptbook, and this, by the by, is proved by the description I gave of it on page 144; the manuscript itself had remained in the hands of its owners.

ʃ ʃ ʃ

I HAD HOPED to obtain a few facts from two plays on the subject of *Titus Andronicus,* one German, the other Dutch, permitting us to get a clearer idea of the pre-Shakespearean play revised by Shakespeare. The former, *Eine sehr klägliche Tragoedia von Tito Andronico und der hoffertigen Kaiserin, darinnen kentwürdige actiones zubefinden,* is one of a collection of tragedies and comedies taken into Germany by English players about 1600; it gives fundamentally the same scenes as the Shakespearean version but is shorter, varies in a number of details, and with the exception of Titus and Saturninus the names of the characters are different. It is manifestly an adaptation for a German public rather than a translation of Shakespeare's play, and it is therefore impossible to say whether the places where it differs are peculiarities of the original or inventions of the adapter.[6]

The Dutch play, *Aran en Titus, of Wraak en Weerwraak* (or "Vengeance and Countervengeance," Amsterdam, 1641), by Jan

6. Albert Cohn, *Shakespeare in Germany,* London and Berlin, 1865.

Vos, follows Shakespeare more closely. Except for Titus' daughter, who is called Rozeline, the principal characters bear the same names: two incidents are found only in the Shakespearean and Dutch plays: the use made of a copy of Ovid's *Metamorphoses* in revealing the rape, and the allusion, in the dispute with the empress, to the classical story of Diana and Acteon. But *Aran en Titus* contains also a certain number of events from the German play that are not in Shakespeare's form, so that here again we come up against the same difficulty: we cannot know where the imitation ends and the invention of the adapter begins. Nothing certain can be based upon such uncertainties.[7]

The German play, however, yields a suggestive fact: the son of Titus is called Vespasian. Now it happens that from April 11, 1591/2, until June 2, 1592, Lord Strange's company gave seven performances of a play entitled *Titus and Vespacia* (Henslowe, fol. 7v), and it was formerly supposed by many critics that this was the old play revised by Shakespeare. Such a conjecture is not in favor just now, and recent commentators prefer to imagine that this was a dramatization of a story on the siege and conquest of Jerusalem by Titus, the son of Emperor Vespasian.

I am far from sure that these doubters are right. For I note that *Titus and Vespacia* was given for the first time on April 11, 1591/2 (it was marked by Henslowe "ne"), and that the analysis of the versification has shown that Shakespeare's first revision was probably made during the winter of 1591/2 (cf. pp. 173–4). This looks as if we had here that first revision under a title possibly still preserved from the pre-Shakespearean play. And I note also that in 1592/3 the same company gave three performances (January 23, 28, February 6) of a play entitled *Titus*—not *Titus and Vespacia*—which might be the Shakespearean play in its final form and with a new title. All this, to be sure, cannot be proved, and if it could be proved it would not do away with the fact that the German and the Dutch plays cannot be used for a reconstruction of the pre-Shakespearean play. So the best thing to do is probably to leave the question open.

7. For more details, see the article by Harold de W. Fuller, "The Sources of *Titus Andronicus*," *Publ. Mod. Lang. Assoc.*, 1901, *16*, 1–15.

THE TEXT OF THE FOLIO

ACCORDING TO a generally accepted belief the text of *Titus Andronicus* in the folio of 1623 was printed from a copy of the quarto of 1611; certain resemblances, especially errors, make this most probable; but it cannot be said that the two texts are identical throughout, for there are differences, some of them not unimportant.[8]

The folio contains two lines (I.i.398; IV.i.36) which are not in the quarto [9] and 69 textual variants. Thirty-one speech headings are changed, generally to make the nomenclature uniform in the cases of Saturninus, Tamora, Aron, and young Lucius. The word "Goth" has been substituted for "Romane Lord" (V.iii.73).

Seventeen stage directions are somewhat different, though fundamentally the same. But nineteen are new. Five of them are exits that had been forgotten and later were supplied by the prompter (II.iii.306; II.iv.10; III.i.16; V.ii.166; V.iii.204). The majority were intended to augment, as in *Henry VI*, the musical stage effects by the addition of flourishes (I.i.63–4, 151–2,398–9; IV.ii.48–9; V.i.1; V.iii.15). It was particularly specified that a long flourish must accompany the emperor and his suite as they came down from the Senate House, probably to fill up the interval until they were again on the stage instead of "aloft." Twice a direction was given in the imperative to "Winde Hornes" (II.ii.10–11; II.iv.10–11), although the addition in the first case was useless, for another direction which follows immediately after repeats in a more precise way: "Heere a cry of houndes, and winde hornes in a peale." Evidently the prompter expected a great deal from this effect already produced ten lines before: "Enter Titus Andronicus and his three sonnes, making a noyse with hounds and hornes." In the last scene, as the guests of Andronicus were going to take their seats at the banquet table, "hautboyes" were heard whose mournful notes were no doubt intended to prepare the

8. A minute comparison of the two texts has been made by Joseph S. G. Bolton, "The Authentic Text of *Titus Andronicus*," *Publ. Mod. Lang. Assoc.*, Sept. 1929, *44*, No. 3, 765–88.

9. On the other hand, the quarto has five lines (II.i.101; IV.ii.8,77; V.ii.162; V.iii. 52) that are not in the folio, but these were undoubtedly accidentally omitted by the compositor.

spectators for the lugubrious events that were to follow. This is
exactly the kind of changes, the addition of hautboys included,
that were made in the folio text of 2 *Henry VI*, probably by the
same prompter. And as in 2 *Henry VI* one of the stage directions
shows that *Titus Andronicus* came to be performed in a different
theater from the one for which it had first been written. At the
beginning of the banquet scene, in the last act, the quarto has the
following stage direction:

> Trumpets sounding, Enter Titus like a Cooke, placing the dishes, and
> Lauinia with a vaile ouer her face (V.iii.25–6)

Evidently the table was already on the stage, or rather in the alcove or inner stage, where probably part of the scene was performed. In the folio there is the same direction,[1] but it is preceded
by another: "A Table brought in." In this theater, as in the one
where 2 *Henry VI* was performed, there was no alcove, and they
had to bring in the table before the spectators when needed, in the
same primitive way that they brought in the bed for Henry VI to
see that Duke Humphrey had been assassinated (cf. p. 103).

But the folio text has another difference that is more important
—a scene of 85 lines which is not in the quarto, Act III.sc.ii in the
modern editions. It has naturally been supposed that this scene
must have been added after the publication of the quarto, and that
it was written by Shakespeare or by some other dramatist. A proof
that it did not exist in the original manuscript has been sought in
the facts that it is the only part of the play where "An." is used instead of "Titus" in the speech headings and where Tamora is
called Tamira.[2] An analysis of the versification and of the style
shows clearly that the scene was written by author A. All his characteristics are assembled: an excessive number of trochaic feet, 32 in
418 feet or 7.6%; lines of irregular length, one foot (75), three feet
(11); one truncated decasyllable (76)—unless this be a four-
stress line with a trisyllabic foot; many exclamations, so, so (1),
fie (21), how now (23), why (24), oh (29), fie, fie (31), come
(34), hark (35), alas (48, 59, 79).

On this pre-Shakespearean foundation has been built a super-

1. With this difference, however: "placing the meat on the Table."
2. This is not very significant for Tamira occurs only once; it may be a misprint.

structure whose Shakespearean characteristics are equally certain:

1. Division of the thought into symmetrical parts:

> There's for thyselfe, and that's for Tamira (74)

2. Repetition of a word or grammatical form to accentuate the symmetrical construction:

> Wound it with sighing, girle, kil it with grones (15)
>
> Breu'd with her sorrow: mesh'd vppon her cheekes (38)

3. Antitheses:

> He takes false shadowes, for true substances (80)

4a. Concetti consisting in the repetition of a word, or jingles:

> O handle not the theame, to talke of hands,
> Least we remember still that we haue none,
> Fie, fie, how Frantiquely I square my talk
> As if we should forget we had no hands:
> If Marcus did not name the word of hands (29–33)
>
> At that that I haue kil'd my Lord, a Flys.
> Out on the murderour: thou kil'st my hart (53–4)
>
> Peace tender Sapling, thou art made of teares,
> And teares will quickly melt thy life away (50–1)

b. Concetti in the Italian manner:

> This poore right hand of mine,
> Is left to tirranize vppon my breast
> Who when my hart all mad with misery,
> Beats in this hollow prison of my flesh,
> Then thus I thumpe it downe (7–11)
>
> That all the teares that thy poore eyes let fall
> May run into that sinke, and soaking in,
> Drowne the lamenting foole, in Sea salt teares (18–20)

5. Compound words in the Latin and Greek manner: sorrow-wreathen (4), Sea salt (20).

And there are images whose Shakespearean character is all the more unquestionable as several have an analogue in *Venus and Adonis,* in *Lucrece,* or in the *Sonnets:*

She saies, she drinkes no other drinke but teares (37) [3]

Thou Map of woe, that thus dost talk in signes (12) [4]

Or get some little knife betweene thy teeth,
And iust against thy hart make thou a hole,
That all the teares that thy poore eyes let fall
May run into that sinke . . . (16–19) [5]

thou art made of teares,
And teares will quickly melt that life away (50–1) [6]

He takes false shadowes, for true substances (80) [7]

Lavinia, goe with me,
Ile to thy closset, and goe read with thee
Sad stories, chanced in the times of old (81–3) [8]

Come boy, and goe with me, thy sight is young,
And thou shalt read, when mine begin to dazell (84–5) [9]

Unquestionably this scene was in the play from the beginning; it differs in no way from the other revised scenes, and it is even possible to say that it belongs to the second revision by Shakespeare, for it has 7 feminine endings in 85 lines or 8.2%. It was a

3. Cf. *Venus and Adonis:* Dost thou drink tears that thou provokest such weeping? (949).
4. The word "map" in combination with words of all sorts is one of Shakespeare's familiar images: "map of Death" (*Lucrece,* 402), "The face, that map which deep impression bears/Of hard misfortune" (*Lucrece,* 1712–13), "his cheek the map of days outworn" (sonnet 68, l. 1).
5. Cf. *Lucrece:*
    And whiles against a thorn thou bearest thy part
    To keep thy sharp woes waking, wretched I,
    To imitate thee well, against my heart
    Will fix a sharp knife to affright my eye (1135–8)
6. Cf. *Lucrece:* Melt at my teares and be compassionate (594).
7. Cf. sonnet 53:
    What is your substance, whereof are you made,
    That millions of shadows on you tend? (1–2).
See also sonnet 37: Whilst that this shadow doth such substance give (10).
    It should be said that this antithesis was at that time a commonplace.
8. A taste for stories or songs of the past is a trait that Shakespeare has given to several of his characters: Richard II, V.i.40–2; Orsino (*Twelfth Night*), II.iv.6; Lear, V.iii.12.
9. Cf. *Venus and Adonis:*
    Upon his hurt she looks so steadfastly,
    That her sight dazzling makes the wound seem three (1063–4)

part of the augmentation of Titus' lamentations, which is the distinctive character of that period of revision.

It is not difficult to guess the origin of the text of that addition. From the fact that the text of the folio was printed from the quarto of 1611, it has been supposed that the manuscript of the company had been lost or destroyed, and that a copy of the quarto had received the necessary additions and afterward served as a promptbook. There is no need to imagine such catastrophic contingencies. The reason why the King's company sometimes used quartos instead of a manuscript for the printing of the folio is simpler. When the text of a quarto was practically the same as that of the actual promptbook, and this was the case for *Titus Andronicus*, it was cheaper to spend the sixpence which was usually the price of those pamphlets than to call in a scrivener to transcribe the whole play. This was surely the course chosen by Heming and Condell: the text of the scene, as well as the additions or modifications to the stage directions enumerated above, were supplied from the promptbook which the actors of Lord Strange had kept for their own use and which still served them in 1622.

Of this the text of the scene affords a proof. It contains one of those Shakespearean additions which sometimes can be discovered in the mixed texts (cf. above, pp. 169–70). The incomplete lines 63 and 66 in the folio are the remnants of two verses: Shakespeare struck out the last three feet of the former and the first three feet of the latter in order to introduce an image of his own on the melodious buzzing of the fly (ll. 64, 65), which he interlineated between the two fragments. But as an afterthought he wrote two other lines above (61, 62) which indeed are better, forgetting, as was usual with him, to delete the rejected lines. When the scrivener prepared the foul papers and made a transcription which was to be the promptbook, he did not notice that lines 61 and 62 made an awkward repetition with lines 64 and 65, and he copied the two redactions the one after the other, thus:

How would he hang his slender gilded wings	61
And buz lamenting doings in the ayer,	62
Poore harmlesse Fly,	63
That with his pretty buzing melody,	64
Came heere to make vs merry,	65
And thou hast kil'd him	66

The compositor of the folio faithfully reproduced this disposition, which today tells the tale of its composition. The scene missing in the quarto was certainly supplied from the very first prompt-book of the play.

But then, it may be asked, if this scene existed from the first, and in Shakespeare's revised form as well, why was it not included in the quarto of 1594? I see but one explanation: it must have been omitted from the performances that Lord Strange's company were giving at the time when the play was ceded to Lord Pembroke's men. There were many good reasons for this suppression. Titus was shown in a fit of madness, but there is another scene of the same kind and infinitely more striking when he launches arrows before the emperor's palace. Moreover, this was also a banquet scene that could look flat compared to the final scene with its accumulated horrors. Lastly, and I believe this to have been the chief reason, the scene of the fly was meant to be pathetic but was apt to excite laughter from the commoners in the audience—the public in a theater is not composed solely of discerning people—so great is the discrepancy between the insignificance of the fly and the importance Titus attaches to its death.

A few words should be said about the textual variants. When they are listed in detail their number may be impressive, but a closer examination materially reduces their importance. For the most part they are misprints—a singular for a plural and vice versa, the article *the* for a possessive adjective, words or letters added or omitted, inversions of words, and so on. They are attributable to the haste or to the whim of a compositor, and they are devoid of any significance for the composition of the play. When these are disregarded there remain hardly a dozen real variants.

In some of these it is easy to discover why a line has been modified: to correct an irregular line (II.ii.17; V.ii.206); to suppress an oath in conformity with the law forbidding the use of profane language on the stage (V.ii.72); to avoid the repetition of a word (I.i.217); to correct a misreading in the quarto (I.i.154; II.iii.20). But for others (I.i.391; II.iv.41; III.i.281; V.ii.18; V.iii.199) I confess that I see no reason for the change.

It is quite possible that upon the occasion of some revival of *Titus Andronicus* Shakespeare may have read the text over again and endeavored to improve it, but it is difficult to understand why he was satisfied with so few and unnecessary corrections, while he left so many irregular lines just as they stood in the quarto. I am inclined to believe that those uninteresting variants are attributable to the man who regularized the nomenclature in the speech headings, who in the stage direction which I have quoted on pages 148–9 replaced the conjunctions "and then," "then," of which the pre-Shakespearean author had been prodigal, by the expression "after them," which no doubt he considered more literary; the same man who divided the play into acts, sometimes to the detriment of logic [1]—to the editor, in a word, whom the players entrusted with the duty of preparing the text of the folio.

This task was rather carelessly discharged. It never occurred to this editor to collate the text of the quarto, line by line, with the text of the company's promptbook as any scholar worthy of the name would do today; he would not otherwise have left untouched the apocryphal passages at the bottom of the last pages, which certainly were not in the promptbook (see above, p. 143), though this was one of the specially needed corrections.

To conclude, the only advantage possessed by the folio text is that it supplies a whole scene that is not in the quartos and affords the proof that after 1594 the staging of the play received more attention. But, on the other hand, the suspicion attaches to this text that some of its variants must be referred to the doubtful taste of the editor, and the certainty that about twenty lines toward the end are not authentic.

1. The second act begins with a passage which really pertained to the end of the first act. I suppose it is unnecessary to recall that *Titus Andronicus* like the plays of that period was divided only into scenes.

CHAPTER THREE. RICHARD II

$\mathcal{T}$he play of *Richard II* must have had a considerable success; before being included in the 1623 folio it appeared five times: in 1597 (Q_1), twice in 1598 (Q_2 and Q_3), in 1608 (Q_4), and in 1615 (Q_5).[1]

The first three quartos do not contain the abdication scene. This important scene was published for the first time in 1608. Aside from this difference all the quartos give essentially the same text, the variants representing either corrections of obvious faults in the preceding edition or new errors. On the other hand, since it seems that the folio was printed from Q_5 (perhaps from Q_3) the First Quarto represents the text having the greatest chance of approaching the original manuscript.

THE 1597 QUARTO

ON AUGUST 29, 1597, Andrew Wise registered with the Stationers' Company "The Tragedye of Richard II," and that same year the First Quarto appeared under the title of *The Tragedie of King Richard the second. As it hath beene publikely acted by the right Honourable the Lorde Chamberlaine his seruants.*[2]

There is no reason for supposing that the manuscript of Q_1 was obtained surreptitiously; Andrew Wise later published several other Shakespearean quartos—*Richard III* (1597), 1 *Henry IV* (1598), *Much Ado about Nothing* (1600), 2 *Henry IV* (1600)— without any protest on the part of Shakespeare's company.[3] There are, on the contrary, very good reasons to believe that the company

1. Q_1 excepted, all the editions attribute the play to Shakespeare on the title page.
2. In this chapter references are to William Griggs' facsimile, reproducing the duke of Devonshire's copy (Shakespeare Quarto Facsimiles, 1890, No. 17). The numbering of lines is about the same as that of the Globe edition.
3. *Much Ado,* it is true, was first entered in the Stationers' Register by Roberts on August 4, 1600, with the notation "to be staied." It has been supposed that the company made use of Roberts to forestall a pirated edition. But a few days later Wise in turn registered the same play and under normal conditions. There must have been some arrangement pending between Roberts and Wise.

sold the manuscript to the publisher. During the summer of 1597 the actors did, in fact, find themselves in a precarious position. The production of *The Isle of Dogs* had displeased the Privy Council and all performances had been prohibited in London. In July Shakespeare's company was obliged to undertake a tour outside London, a not very profitable business, and it is reasonable to think that needing money it had to part with some of its manuscripts.

The manuscript used for the printing of the First Quarto had, indeed, the characteristics of a playhouse book, and especially of one close to the original manuscript. There is a peculiarity which leaves no doubt in this respect: most of the proper names are abbreviated in the text as well as in the stage directions, sometimes making identification difficult:

> sc.vi(II.ii).119–20: Exeunt Duke, Qu man, Bush. Green

> sc.vi.131: Brist. Castle

> sc.xi(III.iii).35: H. Bull[ingbroke]

> sc.xiii(IV.i).101: Why B[ishop] [4]

A compositor would not have been guilty of such negligences unless he had found them in his copy, nor would a scribe have taken such liberties with the text. These abbreviations, on the other hand are quite natural if they emanate from an author in the heat of composition.

The stage directions are, in fact, an author's directions. They simply mark the entrances and exits of the characters at the moment they take place; when they are descriptive it is only to furnish the actors with information which the dialogue does not supply: "Enter Duke of Hereford appellant in armour" (sc.iii.25–6), "Enter Iohn of Gaunt sicke" (sc.v.1), "The trumpets sound, Richard appeareth on the walls" (sc.xi.60–1). Often an "&c." or some other indefinite expression leaves the task of fixing the number of supernumeraries up to the prompter—the decisive proof, be it remembered, that the direction is really the author's.

This manuscript, however, was not the author's foul papers. Lines badly divided are few (sc.v.186–8,277–8; sc.xii.56–8; sc.xiii.

4. Cf. sc.iii(I.iii).110; sc.v(III.ii).60; sc.x(III.ii).62–3; sc.xi(III.iii).44,100; sc.xii (III.iv).85; sc.xiii(IV.i).156–7; sc.xiv(V.i).6; sc.xv(V.ii).28; sc.xvii(V.iv).1; sc.xix (V.vi).17.

65–6), which is surprising since, as will be seen, the play had undergone many changes. The manuscript, moreover, was well written for there is practically no misreading in Q_1; the only phrase pointing to an indecipherable passage is "This sweares he, as he is princesse iust" (sc.xi.118).

Nor was it a transcript of the promptbook, though it may have been a fair copy prepared for the prompter to annotate. Several entrances were omitted by the author, which have not been added; and only rarely is there a mention of sound effects or of the use of properties.

A peculiarity of this manuscript permits us to hazard a hypothesis on the name of the scribe. A considerable number of words or phrases are in parentheses, where normally commas would be the punctuation:

> Throw downe (my sonne) the Duke of Norfolkes gage (sc.i.161)

> Then (dear my Liege) mine honour let me trie (sc.i.186)

> Who hither come ingaged by my oath
> (Which God defende a Knight should violate) (sc.iii.17–18)

> And al too soone (I feare) the King shall rew (sc.iii.205) [5]

This unusual use of parentheses is to be noted in the manuscripts in the hand of Ralph Crane, one of the scriveners of Shakespeare's company. It is true that the extant manuscripts which we know to have been written by him are posterior to 1619; but in the last years of the sixteenth century he held office as clerk of the Privy Council and of the Signet Office, and it seems that all his life he utilized his calligraphic talent in making copies for lawyers, authors, theatrical amateurs, etc. The way in which he spoke of the King's men in his poem *Workes of Mercy* (1621) suggests that his relation with Shakespeare's company had been of long duration, and it is not impossible that from 1597, and even before, he had worked for it.

Whatever may have been the care with which the manuscript was purged of its most obvious blemishes, traces of revision are not lacking. In sc.iii there is a double redaction of one and the

5. Cf. sc.i.45; sc.iii.64,97,181,205,206; sc.iv.57; sc.v.87; sc.vi.24,88,100; sc.ix.42; sc.xi.15,16,24,139,159; sc.xiii.41,52,61; sc.xiv.20,37,71,82; sc.xv.7,53; sc.xvi.6,8,52, 53,74; sc.xviii.73.

same idea. Having stopped the combat between Bolingbroke and
Mowbray the king gives his reason for this unexpected decision:

> For that our kingdomes earth should not be soild   125
> With that deare bloud which it hath fostered:
> And for our eies do hate the dire aspect
> Of cruell wounds plowd vp with neighbours sword,
> And for we thinke the Egle-winged pride
> Of skie-aspiring and ambitious thoughts,   130
> With riuall hating enuy set on you
> To wake our peace, which in our Countries cradle
> Draw the sweet infant breath of gentle sleepe,
> Which so rouzde vp with boistrous vntunde drummes,
> With harsh resounding trumpets dreadfull bray,   135
> And grating shocke of wrathfull yron armes,
> Might from our quiet confines fright faire Peace,
> And make vs wade euen in our kinreds bloud,
> Therefore we banish you our territories

As Pollard pointed out in the introduction to his publication of Q₃
(p. 91), Shakespeare cannot have read over this passage "or he
would not have left the 'Peace' of line 137 to be frighted by the
'peace' of line 132." This conflict of the two "peaces" through a
grammatical muddle suggests that we have here two different explanations of the same fact, a duplication made evident by the
use of the same words "And for" at lines 127 and 129. A former
redaction was probably the one that has been restored by the folio.
Richard explains his decision thus: The kingdom should not be
soiled by civil war (125–6); I dislike the dire aspect of civil strug-
gles (127–8) which with their sounds of trumpets and shock of
arms might frighten peace and shed the blood of kinsfolk (135–8):
therefore I banish you. Shakespeare must have thought that the
reason given by Richard that he personally disliked civil war was
too devoid of political urgency and by no means justified the decision taken, rather made it tyrannical; so he substituted a reason
that a king could acknowledge: the pride, ambition, or hatred of
Bolingbroke and Mowbray might awaken peace which, for the
moment, was like an infant gently sleeping (129–34). These lines
were probably written in the margin opposite lines 127 and 128
which they were to replace, but the scribe, taking them for an
addition, inserted them without omitting the rejected lines, thus

breaking up the logical development of the thought. That lines 129–34 are a correction by Shakespeare cannot be doubted: they contain an image borrowed from familiar life, the only such image in the passage; three compound words in the Greek and Latin manner; and their versification, especially in line 133, has a harmonious sweetness in marked contrast to the harsh sonority of the lines by which they are surrounded.

Numerous also are the traces of cuts made in the texture of the plot. Several times in the play we hear of incidents which can be understood only by one to whom the chronicles are familiar. For instance, there is frequent talk (sc.i.100,132–4; sc.v.126–31,182; sc.vi.101; sc.xiii.10–13) of the assassination of Thomas of Woodstock, duke of Gloucester and uncle of the king. There is even a whole scene (ii) in which the duchess of Gloucester beseeches her brother-in-law, John of Gaunt, to avenge this death. Sc.xiii also revolves around this affair when Parliament is assembled to judge Aumerle, who is accused of having been an accomplice of the king in the assassination of the duke. It is not usual with dramatic writers to pose problems to the spectators that they cannot solve without knowing the minutest details of the history of their country. If this assassination is recalled with such insistence the scene in which it was prepared or executed must have been cut.

The same is true of another incident mentioned in sc.v.167–8, "the preuention of poore Bullingbrooke,/About his mariadge." Holinshed tells us that Bolingbroke, at the time of his exile, took refuge in France where he was honorably received by King Charles VI, so much so that there was some plan for him to marry the daughter of the duke of Berry, the king's cousin. As soon as Richard got wind of this he sent the earl of Salisbury to Paris to oppose any marriage with "such a traitor as Bolingbroke," and the project was wrecked. Here again a scene must have existed setting in action this duplicity of Richard.

Indeed the omission of such a scene has left a gap which it was impossible to mend. A clumsy solution to the continuity exists between sc.iv (I.iv) and sc.v (II.i). At the end of sc.iii Bolingbroke bids farewell to England, takes leave of his father, John of Gaunt, and departs. At the beginning of sc.iv Aumerle tells the king that he has accompanied Bolingbroke to the nearest highway and left him there.[6] The king then says a few words recalling Bolingbroke's efforts to make himself popular, and Bushie comes in to announce that Gaunt is very ill and would like to see the king. This call the king answers at once, and the following scene shows his arrival with the queen, his ill-concealed bad humor in the face of advice from Gaunt, who retires after having done his duty. A few words from York, excusing the bluntness of his brother, are immediately followed by the news that Gaunt has expired. Whereupon Richard announces his intention of seizing Gaunt's goods and leaves saying that he goes to make preparations for his departure to Ireland. Left alone, the lords deplore the king's conduct, and Northumberland then reveals to them that Bolingbroke, commanding an army of three thousand men, has embarked from Port Blanc in Brittany and shortly intends to touch the northern coast of England. All these events have taken place on the very day on which Bolingbroke was exiled; he cannot have left England and here he is already returning from Brittany! The theater has conventions which one readily admits, but no dramatic writer would dare toy in that manner with the credulity of the spectators. A scene analogous to that in 3 *Henry VI*, where Queen Margaret obtained aid from the French king in the form of an army to reconquer the kingdom, must inevitably have come to the mind of an author not wishing to upset too grossly the sequence of historical events; not only did such a scene render those events natural but it also served to bridge the rather short interval of time that elapsed between Bolingbroke's departure and his return.[7]

In the same scene in which this important event is revealed York alludes to his "owne disgrace" (sc.v.168). There are no traces of this disgrace in the play any more than of the evil influence of Richard's favorites, to which Bolingbroke refers in another scene (ix). Condemning Bushie and Green to be executed, he gives the reasons for his decision by accusing those favorites of having turned the king from his duties, and he upbraids them principally for having by their dissolute ways

6. This is contrary to what took place in sc.iii, where Aumerle definitely bids farewell to Bolingbroke (249–50).

7. According to some chroniclers Bolingbroke was banished in August, according to others in September 1398, and he returned in July 1399.

Made a diuorce betwixt his Queene and him,
Broke the possession of a royall bed,
And stainde the beutie of a faire Queenes cheekes
With teares, drawen from her eies by your fowle wrongs
(sc.ix.12–15)

In the play as we read it, the queen loves her husband with charming idolatry and calls him "my fair rose." But there must have been, at one time, a scene or scenes which set in evidence a debauched side of Richard. Holinshed has reported that during this king's rule there "reigned abundantlie the filthie sinne of lecherie and fornication, with abominable adulterie, especially in the king." It is particularly surprising that the favorites, whom the nobles as well as the people held responsible for Richard's instability of conduct, do not play a more important role in the action. Actually they are not much more than supernumeraries, and there is not one scene in which they exercise over Richard that nefarious influence of which Bolingbroke speaks.

At the end of sc.ix Bolingbroke announces that he is going to fight Glendower and his accomplices. According to Holinshed the Welsh had raised an army of forty thousand men to defend Richard. Nothing remains of this incident but a short scene (viii) in which a Welsh captain reports that he has tried in vain to prevent his men from disbanding, but they believe the king is dead and therefore are dispersing.

The end of the play is particularly loose. It is only indirectly that we learn that a plot had been hatched against the new king, when in scenes xv and xvi York denounces his own son, Aumerle, as one of the conspirators. And yet the basis for an entire subplot had been laid down in the last lines of sc.xiv, when the abbot of Westminster promises some of Richard's adherents that he will reveal to them the plot he is preparing, a promise which is not followed up in the play. This promise, however, was kept, since Bolingbroke at the end of sc.xvi announces that he intends to pursue the abbot of Westminster and his own brother-in-law (a personage we hear of for the first time); and in sc.xix Fitzwater reports that he has sent to London the heads of Broccas and Sir Benet Seely, "Two of the daungerous consorted traitors,/That sought at Oxford thy dire ouerthrow" (sc.xix.13–16). And lastly,

sc.xvii has literally lost its beginning. It opens with the stage direction: "Exeunt. Manet sir Pierce Exton." The word "Manet" cannot
refer to sc.xvi, which it follows, because in that scene the king at
Aumerle's request dismissed his suite, and at the end only Aumerle,
York, and the duchess of York remained with him on the stage.
The words "Manet . . . Exton" must then have come after a
scene that has disappeared.

It is difficult to understand how certain critics have been able to
speak with enthusiasm of the unity of *Richard II*. No other play
of Shakespeare's exists that leaves such an impression of having
been composed of fragments whose interrelationship has been destroyed. An analysis of the versification and of the style will help
to discover the reasons for these mutilations.

$$\int \quad \int \quad \int$$

THREE TYPES of versification and of style can be easily distinguished. First of all a considerable portion of the play—more than
five hundred lines—is in rhymed verse. Of these about a hundred
have certainly been either added or touched up by Shakespeare;
all the others are of such an inferior quality that they could not
have been perpetrated except by a man who may have understood something of the theater but who was not a poet. These
verses are distributed in passages of variable length, ranging from
simple distichs to long developments, one of which has sixty lines
(sc.xvi.68–135 or V.iii.70–136). This passage seems to be given
exactly as it was written, and it is long enough to yield valid conclusions and percentages.

The verse adopted is a strictly decasyllabic iambic pentameter.
The number of rhythmic variations in trochees as well as in spondees is high, with a marked preference for spondees (trochees
6.3%, spondees 9.3%). This combination of opposite rhythmic
effects no doubt enabled the actors to deliver the lines with easy
contrasts between flippant lightness and ponderous gravity (and
that is why, I imagine, this passage was preserved). But the general impression that remains is that of a verse mechanically monotonous, each line being a unity within itself, and in this long
passage there is but one enjambment or a proportion of 1.5%.

If some value can be granted to this versification from the point of view of dramatic diction, the same cannot be said from the point of view of style. The author—let us call him C—no doubt prided himself on cultivating the ornate language of his time; it is true enough except that his style is a caricature of that language. The only effects he seeks consist of a monotonous repetition of two rhetorical devices:

1. Antitheses:

> Mine honour liues when his dishonour dies (68)
>
> The traitor liues, the true man's put to death (71)
>
> His words come from his mouth, ours from our breast (100)
>
> He prayes but faintly, and would be denied (101)
>
> His weary ioynts would gladly rise I know,
> Our knees still kneele till to the ground they grow (103–4)
>
> His prayers are full of false hypocrisie,
> Ours of true zeale and deepe integritie (105–6)

2. Concetti-jingles:

> A beggar begs that neuer begd before (76)
>
> This festred ioynt cut off, the rest rest sound,
> This let alone wil all the rest confound (83–4)
>
> Loue louing not it selfe, none other can (86)
>
> And neuer see day that the happy sees (91)
>
> Till thou giue ioy, vntil thou bid me ioy (92)
>
> Vnto my mothers prayers I bend my knee.
> Against them both my true ioynts bended be (95–6)
>
> The word is short, but not so short as sweete (115)
>
> Dost thou teach pardon pardon to destroy? (118)
>
> That sets the word it selfe against the word (120)
>
> Good aunt stand vp.
>   I do not sue to stand (127)
>
> I pardon him as God shall pardon me (129)
>
> Twice saying pardon doth not pardon twaine,
> But makes one pardon strong (132–3)

These are the only mannerisms on which author C might be confused with Shakespeare. But all the other Shakespearean mannerisms are absent,[8] especially those which require some facility of invention. This versifier totally lacked imagination; the few expressions that might be considered as metaphors are either old clichés or are drawn from the familiar stock of comparisons borrowed from husbandry, like those knees that will "kneele till to the ground they grow" (103–4) or that ear which the duchess of York asks Bolingbroke "to plant" in his "piteous heart." And these would-be images are less absurd than that "tongue" which is to be "set" in an "eye" that "begins to speak" (123). The rhymes are not always of good quality: "liege" rhymes with "beseech," "pierse" with "rehearse"; and if it is difficult to find a rhyme any make-rhyme will do, however senseless it may be:

> We pray with heart and soule, and all beside (102)

or some acrobatic inversion:

> More sinnes for this forgiuenes prosper may (82)

> Shall thy old dugs once more a traitor reare? (88)

The rhymed verses of author C are found in all the scenes but two, the fourth (Richard describes the efforts of Bolingbroke to render himself popular) and the ninth (Bolingbroke gives the reasons why he ordered the execution of Bushie and Green). They are too mediocre to make us suppose that they were meant to raise the dialogue in moments of particularly poetic tension. Unquestionably they are the remnants of an old play written entirely in rhymed verse and belonging to a period when the English drama was not yet using blank verse. This is so true that if we bring together those dispersed fragments we shall ipso facto reconstruct the skeleton, so to speak, of this primitive play.

> sc.i.43–6   Bolingbroke accuses Mowbray of treason and asks permission to back up his accusation with his sword.

8. In the whole passage there are three examples of words linked by a conjunction —"heart and soule." (102), "true zeale and deepe integritie," and "plaints and prayers" (125). But that small number, compared with the number of antitheses and concetti-jingles, shows that this type of mannerism was not a characteristic of this author's style, only the lapse of a tautological mind.

133–4 Mowbray acknowledges that he neglected his duty at the time of Gloucester's assassination but swears that he is not guilty.

154–81 Richard asks Bolingbroke and Mowbray to be reconciled.

184–97 They refuse.

202–7 Richard then orders that a judicial combat take place.

sc.ii.54–7 Gaunt and the duchess of Gloucester part.

60–1,63–4,66–7,69–74 The duchess begs Gaunt to bid York come to see her at Pleshy, then changing her mind she asks him not to do anything about it, for York would find only an empty house and sadness.

sc.iii.55–58 Richard wishes success to Bolingbroke.

59–62,65–6 Bolingbroke is full of confidence in his good cause.

93–8 Bolingbroke feels calm and joyous; the king bids him farewell.

172–7 Mowbray finds the king's sentence equivalent to a death sentence, but he obeys.

206–7 Mowbray says farewell to the king.

221–4 Gaunt thinks that he will not live long enough to see his son again.

247–50 The king and Aumerle say farewell to Bolingbroke.

251–2 The lord marshal offers to accompany Bolingbroke to the port of embarkation.

304–9 Bolingbroke bids farewell to England; although banished he will remain a true Englishman.

sc.v.7–11 Gaunt believes that the words of a dying man will have some value for Richard.

135–8 Gaunt curses Richard and asks to be borne to his bed to die.

143–6 York apologizes for his brother's bluntness.

150–4 Gaunt's death is announced. Different impressions that this event makes on York and on Richard.

209–14 Richard seizes Gaunt's possessions. York predicts that nothing good can come from such acts.

296–9 Northumberland asks Ross and Willoughby to keep secret the return of Bolingbroke; he himself is ready to act. Ross and Willoughby promise to follow him.

sc.vi.31–2 The queen is full of anxious thoughts.

sc.vii.168–71 York does not know what he should do.

sc.viii.16–17 The Welsh disband, believing that the king is dead.

sc.x.71–4 Salisbury informs Richard that the Welsh have abandoned him.

76–81   Richard turns pale on learning this piece of news
            and realizes that those seeking safety are fleeing
            his side.

139–42   Scroop affirms that the favorites, Bushie and Green,
            have been executed.

sc.xi.179–82   Richard feels that he is debased.

sc.xii.96–101 Having learned that Richard is Bolingbroke's pris-
            oner, the queen decides to join him in Lon-
            don. She hopes that the plants grafted by the
            gardener who brought the news will never grow.

sc.xiii.158–61 The bishop of Carlisle predicts that the day on
            which Richard abdicated prepares woes for the
            future; Aumerle would like to know whether
            there are no ways of ridding the realm of this
            pernicious blot.[8a]

sc.xiv.81–102 The queen wishes to follow Richard in his exile; he
            answers that they must separate, and they part
            with a kiss.

sc.xv.36–40   York thinks that Heaven has had a hand in the past
            events and therefore will follow Bolingbroke.

sc.xvi.47–8   York shows Bolingbroke (now Henry IV) the pledge
            signed by the conspirators.

68–71   York wants no pardon for his son.

73–135   The duchess of York begs Bolingbroke to pardon
            her son in spite of her husband's opposition.

141–5   Henry IV consents, but will punish the plotters.

sc.xvii.10–11 Exton wants to rid the king of his foe.

sc.xviii.95–8 The keeper of the Tower obliges Richard's devoted
            groom to leave.

108–11   Richard is struck down by Exton and dies.

112–17   Exton's remorse.

sc.xix.7–12   News of the execution of the plotters is announced.

17–18   The king will not forget the merit of Fitzwater who
            brought this news.

22–9   Bolingbroke pardons the bishop of Carlisle.

31–52   Henry IV disowns Exton and announces that he is
            going to undertake a pilgrimage.

The simple enumeration of these fragmentary passages shows
that the historical events essential to a play on Richard II were
to be found in the play in rhymed verse: Bolingbroke's accusation
against Mowbray, the judicial combat, the banishment of Bolingbroke and of Mowbray, Gaunt's death, Richard's confiscation of

8a. These lines prove that the abdication scene existed in the rhymed verse play.

Gaunt's property, the discontent of the nobles, Bolingbroke's return, the desertion of the Welsh, the execution of the favorites, Richard's discouragement, his abdication, the role of Exton in the murder of Richard. And there were also numerous sentimental incidents such as the parting of Gaunt and the duchess of Gloucester, the sadness of the queen, the scene between the queen and the gardener, the last meeting of the queen and Richard, the visit of the faithful groom to Richard in the Tower, episodes which one might seek for in vain in the accounts of the chroniclers. The sentimental element is so important in fact that it is safe to suggest that author C, as a dramatist, had a marked preference for the picturesque byways of history rather than for history itself.

∫ ∫ ∫

THE REMAINDER of the play is entirely in blank verse. But not all the blank verse is of the same quality. In many passages are noticeable the characteristics of the versification and style of our old acquaintance, author A.

1. Verse lines of irregular length from one foot to eight feet.[9]
2. Trisyllabic feet:

    sc.i.20,118,139
    sc.iii.84,269
    sc.iv.15
    sc.v.247
    sc.vi.58,90,108,113,116,131,136,137
    sc.vii.134
    sc.x.3,55
    sc.xi.10,20,30,103,172
    sc.xii.10,67,73
    sc.xiii.112,114,155

9. One foot: sc.iv.55; sc.v.147; sc.xi.31; sc.xviii.103. Two feet: sc.iii.123; sc.iv.56; sc.vi.91; sc.vii.86; sc.xi.22,185,186,188; sc.xii.6,12,71; sc.xiii.156; sc.xv.80,95; sc.xvi. 14,23; sc.xviii.15. Three feet: sc.v.148; sc.vii.2,23,25,28,30; sc.xii.3,24,54; sc.xiii.19, 101; sc.xv.54,69,73,76,87,88; sc.xvi.12,39; sc.xviii.81; sc.xix.24. Four feet: sc.ii.44; sc.iii.26,80,124,191–2,279; sc.iv.1; sc.vi.117; sc.vii.20; sc.ix.42; sc.x.133,175,176; sc.xi.10; sc.xiii.102; sc.xv.53,64; sc.xvi.37,143; sc.xviii.66,97; sc.xix.5. Six feet: sc.iv. 11; sc.v.141,250,254; sc.vi.25,53,108; sc.vii.56,87,124,168; sc.viii.6; sc.ix.9,29; sc.x.90; sc.xi.23–4,27,69,119; sc.xii.56,57,74; sc.xiii.1–2,17–18,18–19,89,129; sc.xv.52,65,70, 71,97,101,117; sc.xvi.40,44; sc.xvii.2; sc.xviii.74,101. Seven feet: sc.v.283,284; sc.vi. 60,119; sc.xviii.14. Eight feet: sc.vi.122.

sc.xv.57,59,73,78
sc.xvi.1,52,55
sc.xviii.100,105

3. Excessive use of trochaic feet:

sc.iii.78–92 (7.0%)
sc.vi.73–122 (7.6%)
    123–37 (8.2%)
sc.x.121–40 (8.0%)
sc.xiii.113–56 (5.4%)
sc.xv.72–94 (11.5%)
sc.xvi.24–46 (7.4%)

4. Commonplace style vulgarized by too many exclamations and interjections: Why, why then, oh, oh then, ah, ha ha, nay, yea, faith, well, well well, come, come come, now, now by my soul, sirrah, alas, soft, tut, what, afore God, oh God, oh God forfend.[1]

5. Obsolescent expressions and colloquialisms: trow (sc.v.218), wot (sc.v.250; sc.vi.40; sc.vii.60), Me rather had ("Me" a dative, sc.xi.191), The nobles they are fled, the commons they are colde (sc.vi.87), Richard he is in the mightie hold (sc.xii.83), Your husband, he is gone (sc.vi.79), twenty shadowes,/Which shewes like griefe (sc.vi.14–15).

6. Figures of speech borrowed from bestiaries or books of husbandry: cormorant (sc.v.38), Pellican (sc.v.126), Lyon, lambe (sc.v.173–4), curs (sc.vi.135), caterpillers (sc.vii.166), Spiders (sc.x.14), toades (sc.x.15), nettles (sc.x.18), Dogs (sc.x.130), Snakes (sc.x.131), Serpent (sc.xvi.56), weedes (sc.xii.38–9,44,49–50,56–7,64).

In the preceding chapters author A has appeared as responsible for the invention of the subject; this time he shows himself in the role of reviser of a play written by someone else. The revision must have been comprehensive enough since traces of his manner are visible in the majority of scenes. Probably the reason for his intervention was to bring the play up to date: the rhymed verse of author C must have looked antiquated and particularly stiff from the moment the superiority of blank verse as a means of expression

1. Sc.ii.44; sc.iii.5,69,253,268,294,300; sc.iv.5,37,61; sc.v.5,93,104,184,186,187,230,238,273; sc.vi.51,52,74,89,104,115,131,141,145; sc.vii.25,87,103,152; sc.xi.20,131,135,169; sc.xii.72,98; sc.xiii.42,101,129,145; sc.xiv.7,26,46,93; sc.xv.50,57,76,88; sc.xvi.72,85,109; sc.xviii.41,54,104,113.

in the drama was recognized. The fact that author A retained so many of the rhymed verses which he had undertaken to eliminate proves, however, that this was not his only aim. If we judge from *The Contention* and *The True Tragedie* he was, in contrast to author C, more interested in the historical events which he carefully collected from the chroniclers. He was certainly not the one who suppressed the events whose disappearance has been revealed by the study of the manuscript. It is, on the contrary, most probable that he added those events. What lends weight to that supposition is, for instance, the incongruous uselessness of the small scene at the beginning of Act IV(1–90) in which Aumerle is accused of having had a hand in Gloucester's assassination. It adds nothing to the action and only an author anxious not to leave out any historical event in the period he is dramatizing could have the idea of introducing it at a moment when the interest of the spectators is concentrating on Richard's sufferings. The taste for history of author A is also manifest in the care with which obscure pamphlets of the time such as *La Chronicque de la trahison et la mort de Richard deux*, *l'Histoire du Roy d'Angleterre Richard II* by Jean Créton, as well as *The Cronycles of Syr Johan Froyssart*, translated by Berners, were searched for details on Richard's life.[2]

Thus when Shakespeare decided to improve the play on Richard II preserved in the archives of his company (the rest of this chapter will prove superabundantly that Shakespeare's blank verse is mingled with the blank verse of author A), he had before him a play that must have resembled *The Contention* and *The True Tragedie*—a chronicle play, setting in action the political events of the last years of Richard II, his fall, and the accession of Henry IV. This source play has not reached us and we are left with the impossible task (as in the case of *Titus Andronicus*) of disengaging Shakespeare's part. Certainty is impossible; we must be content with the approximations that can be obtained through the aid of the method already applied to *Titus Andronicus*.

But before drawing up the list of Shakespearean mannerisms and images we must make a reservation. Antitheses and jingles

2. Cf. Paul Reyher, "Notes sur les sources de *Richard II*," *Revue de l'enseignement des langues vivantes*, Jan.–April 1924; J. D. Wilson, introduction to his edition, pp. xxxviii ff.

cannot always be counted as Shakespearean mannerisms since the author of the rhymed verses uses them constantly. We cannot know whether they were introduced by author C, retained by author A, or added by Shakespeare. The safest way will be not to take them into account, and I shall not include them in the tabulation of Shakespeare's mannerisms, even though this will no doubt deprive us of the help of a considerable number of these figures by means of which we could with more certainty identify Shakespeare's stylistic work.

MANNERISMS

1. Division of the thought into symmetrical parts, of more or less equal length:

> My gratious soueraigne my most louing liege (sc.i.21)
>
> Like a false traitour, and iniurious villaine (sc.i.91) [3]

2. Repetition of a word or grammatical form to accentuate the symmetrical construction:

> Nor neuer looke vpon each others face,
> Nor neuer write, regreete nor reconcile (sc.iii.185–6) [4]

3. Marked preference for the association of two words expressing two aspects of the same idea and connected by a conjunction:

> Hast thou according to thy oath and bande (sc.i.2)
>
> From my giuing reines and spurres to my free speech (sc.i.55) [5]

4. Concetti in the Italian manner:

> Each substance of a griefe hath twenty shadowes,
> Which shewes like griefe it selfe, but is not so:
> For Sorrowes eyes glazed with blinding teares,
> Diuides one thing entire to many obiects,
> Like perspectiues, which rightly gazde vpon

3. Cf. sc.i.19; sc.ii.68,69; sc.v.52,54; sc.vi.12; sc.vii.4,59,87,109; sc.viii.13–14; sc. ix.23; sc.x.93,111,163; sc.xi.127; sc.xii.17–18; sc.xiii.167; sc.xviii.42,86; sc.xix.20,25.
4. Cf. sc.v.40–3,45–6,50–1; sc.xi.143–4,147–51; sc.xviii.78–9,86.
5. Cf. sc.i.96,97,115,202; sc.ii.24,43; sc.iii.19,39,89,106,111,183; sc.iv.25; sc.v.130, 139,142,175,189,190,199,208,237,258; sc.vi.32,79; sc.vii.7,12,43,44,63,85,90,120,131, 167; sc.viii.12,14,15,16,22; sc.ix.9,10; sc.x.46,74,79,119,145,184,196; sc.xi.5,26,38,78, 80,83,101,109,110,183,200; sc.xiii.67,89,128; sc.xiv.26,27,77; sc.xv.6,8,40,52; sc.xvi. 10,23,31,57,59,125; sc.xviii.46.

Shew nothing but confusion; eyde awry,
Distinguish forme: so your sweet maiestie,
Looking awry vpon your Lords departure,
Finde shapes of griefe more than himselfe to waile,
Which lookt on as it is, is naught but shadows
Of what it is not (sc.vi.14–24) [6]

5. Compound words after the Greek and Latin manner: time
honoured (sc.i.1), High stomackt (sc.i.18), soone beleeuing (sc.
i.101), Wrath kindled (sc.i.152), beggar-feare (sc.i.191), daring,
hardy (sc.iii.43), Egle-winged (sc.iii.129), skie-aspiring (sc.iii.
130), riuall-hating (sc.iii.131), harsh resounding (sc.iii.135), oile-
dried (sc.iii.221), time bewasted (sc.iii.221), party verdict (sc.iii.
234), leane-witted (sc.v.115), rugheaded (sc.v.156), life-harming
(sc.vi.3), fiery red (sc.vii.59), pale fac't (sc.vii.94; sc.viii.10),
leane-lookt (sc.viii.11), long parted (sc.x.8), heauy-gated (sc.x.
15), care tunde (sc.x.92), double fatall (sc.x.117), maid-pale (sc.
xi.97), lie-giuer (sc.xiii.68), plume-pluckt (sc.xiii.108), still-breed-
ing (sc.xviii.8), al-hating (sc.xviii.65), neuer quenching (sc.xviii.
107).

IMAGES

sc.i.19 In rage, deafe as the sea, hastie as fire

41–2 Since the more faire and cristall is the skie,
      The vglier seeme the cloudes that in it flie

55–6 From giuing reines and spurres to my free speech,
      Which else would post vntill it had returnd

103 Slucte out his innocent soule through streames of bloud

109 How high a pitch his resolution soares

155 Deepe malice makes too deepe incision

182–3 A iewell in a ten times bard vp chest,
       Is a bold spirit in a loyall breast

203 The swelling difference of your setled hate

sc.ii.7–8 Who when they see the houres ripe on earth,
           Will raine hot vengeance on offenders heads

11–12 Edwards seuen sonnes whereof thy selfe art one,
       Were as seuen viols of his sacred bloud

6. Cf. sc.xi.57–59,163–8; sc.xv.12–17; sc.xviii.6–29,50–9.

17–19   One violl full of Edwards sacred bloud,

.   .   .   .   .   .

Is crackt, and all the precious liquor spilt

sc.iii.48–9   For Mowbray and my selfe are like two men,
That vow a long and wearie pilgrimage

67–8   Loe, as at English feasts so I regreet
The daintiest last, to make the end most sweet

79–82   Be swift like lightning in the execution,
And let thy blowes doubly redoubled,
Fall like amazing thunder on the caske
Of thy aduerse pernitious enemy

91–2   More than my dauncing soule doth celebrate
This feaste of battle with mine aduersarie

132–3   To wake our peace, which in our Countries cradle
Draw the sweet infant breath of gentle sleepe

145–7   That Sunne that warmes you here, shall shine on me,
And those his golden beames to you heere lent,
Shall point on me, and guilde my banishment

161–5   And now my tongues vse is to me, no more
Than an vnstringed violl or a harpe,
Or like a cunning instrument casde vp,
Or being open, put into his hands
That knowes no touch to tune the harmonie

166–9   Within my mouth you haue engaold my tongue,
Doubly portculist with my teeth and lippes,
And dull vnfeeling barren ignorance
Is made my Gaoler to attend on me

187   This lowring tempest of your home-bred hate

195–6   One of our soules had wandred in the aire,
Banisht this fraile sepulchre of our flesh

200   The clogging burthen of a guiltie soule

202   My name be blotted from the booke of life

208–9   Vncle, euen in the glasses of thine eyes,
I see thy grieued heart

213–15   How long a time lies in one little word,
Foure lagging winters and foure wanton springes,
End in a word, such is the breath of Kinges

227–8   Shorten my daies thou canst with sullen sorrowe,
        And plucke nights from me, but not lend a morrow

229–30 Thou canst helpe time to furrow me with age,
        But stoppe no wrinckle in his pilgrimage

236   Things sweet to taste, prooue in digestion sowre

265–7   The sullen passage of thy weary steps,
        Esteeme as foyle wherein thou art to set,
        The pretious Iewell of thy home returne

271–4   Must I not serue a long apprentishood,
        To forreine passages, and in the end,
        Hauing my freedome, boast of nothing else,
        But that I was a iourneyman to griefe

288–91 Suppose the singing birds musitions,
        The grasse whereon thou treadst, the presence strowd,
        The flowers, faire Ladies, and thy steps, no more
        Then a delightfull measure or a dance

302–3   Fell sorrowes tooth doth neuer ranckle more,
        Then when he bites, but launceth not the soare

sc.iv.14 That words seemd buried in my sorrowes graue

24   How he did seeme to diue into their harts

59–60   The lining of his coffers shall make coates
        To decke our souldiers for these Irish warres

sc.v.5–6 Oh but they say, the tongues of dying men,
          Inforce attention like deepe harmony

12–13   The setting Sunne, and Musike at the close,
        As the last taste of sweetes is sweetest last

28   Where will doth mutiny with wits regard

46   This precious stone set in the siluer sea

61–3   England bound in with the triumphant sea,
        Whose rockie shoare beates backe the enuious siege
        Of watry Neptune, is now bound in with shame

75   Within me Griefe hath kept a tedious fast

97–9   And thou too carelesse pacient as thou art
        Commitst thy annoynted body to the cure
        Of those Physitions that first wounded thee

100   A thousand flatterers sit within thy Crowne

117–19   Darest with thy frozen admonition
         Make pale our cheeke, chasing the royall bloud
         With furie from his natiue residence

133–4   And thy vnkindnes be like crooked age,
         To crop at once a too long withered flower

149   His tongue is now a stringlesse instrument

263–5   But Lords we heare this fearefull tempest sing,
         Yet seeke no shelter to auoid the storme:
         We see the wind sit sore vpon our sailes

270–1   Not so, euen through the hollow eies of death,
         I spie life peering . . .

291   Impe out our drowping countries broken wing

292–3   Redeeme from Broking pawne the blemisht Crowne,
         Wipe off the dust that hides our Scepters guilt

sc.vi.10   Some vnborne sorrow ripe in Fortunes wombe

14–24   See pp. 200–1, concetti

61–4   So Greene, thou art the midwife to my woe,
         And Bullingbrooke my sorrowes dismall heire,
         Now hath my soule brought forth her prodigie,
         And I a gasping new deliuerd mother

83   Now comes the sicke houre that his surfet made

97–8   God for his mercy, what a tide of woes
         Comes rushing on this wofull land at once!

sc.vii.66–8   Euermore thanke's the exchequer of the poore,
         Which till my infant fortune comes to yeares,
         Stands for my bounty

128   To rowze his wrongs and chase them to the baie

sc.viii.18–20   Ah Richard! with the eies of heauy mind
         I see thy glory like a shooting starre
         Fall to the base earth from the firmament

21–2   Thy sunne sets weeping in the lowly west,
         Witnessing stormes to come

sc.ix.12–13   Made a diuorce betwixt his Queene and him,
         Broke the possession of a royall bed

20   And sigh't my English breath in forren cloudes

sc.x.8–9   As a long parted mother with her childe
           Plays fondly with her teares and smiles in meeting

37–46   That when the searching eie of heauen is hid,
           Behind the globe that lights the lower world,
           Then theeues and robbers range abroad vnseene,
           In murthers and in outrage bouldly here,
           But when from vnder this terrestriall ball,
           He fires the proud tops of the easterne pines,
           And dartes his light through euery guilty hole,
           Then murthers, treasons and detested sinnes,
           The cloake of night being pluckt from off their backs,
           Stand bare and naked trembling at themselues?

47–52   So when this thiefe, this traitor Bullingbrooke,
           Who all this while hath reueld in the night,
           Whilst we were wandring with the Antipodes,
           Shall see vs rising in our throne the east,
           His treasons will sit blushing in his face,
           Not able to endure the sight of day

54–5   Not all the water in the rough rude sea,
           Can wash the balme off from an annointed King

67–8   One day too late I feare me noble Lo:
           Hath clouded all thy happy daies on earth

81   For time hath set a blot vpon my pride

105–10   To beare the tidings of calamity,
           Like an vnseasonable stormie day,
           Which makes the siluer riuers drowne their shores,
           As if the world were all dissolude to teares:
           So high aboue his limits swels the rage
           Of Bullingbrooke couering your fearefull land

124–5   That they haue let the dangerous enemy,
           Measure our confines with such peacefull steps

146–7   Make dust our paper, and with rainy eies,
           Write sorrow on the bosome of the earth

153–4   And that small modle of the barren earth,
           Which serues as paste, and couer to our bones

160–6   All murthered, for within the hollow crowne
           That roundes the mortall temples of a king,
           Keepes death his court, and there the antique sits,
           Scoffing his state and grinning at his pompe,

Allowing him a breath, a litle sceane,
To monarchise be feard, and kil with lookes,
Infusing him with selfe and vaine conceit

167–8   As if this flesh which wals about our life,
Were brasse impregnable

169–70 Comes at the last, and with a little pin
Boares thorough his Castle wall, and farewell King

217–18 Discharge my followers, let them hence away,
From Richards night, to Bullingbrookes faire day

sc.xi.32–4 Go to the rude ribbes of that ancient Castle,
Through brazen trumpet send the breath of parlee
Into his ruinde eares

42–3   And lay the summers dust with showres of bloud,
Rainde from the wounds of slaughtered English men

45–6   such crimson tempest should bedrench
The fresh greene lap of faire King Richards land

48–9   Go signifie as much while here we march
Vpon the grassie carpet of this plaine

53–6   Me thinkes King Richard and my selfe should meete
With no lesse terrour than the elements
Of fire and water, when their thundring shocke
At meeting teares the cloudie cheekes of heauen

61–6   See see King Richard doth himselfe appeare,
As doth the blushing discontented Sunne,
From out the fierie portall of the East
When he perceiues the enuious cloudes are bent
To dimme his glorie, and to staine the tracke
Of his bright passage to the Occident

67–8   Yet lookes he like a King, beholde his eye,
As bright as is the Eagles, lightens forth

92–3   he is come to open
The purple testament of bleeding warre

95-9   Ten thousand bloudy crownes of mothers sonnes,
Shall ill become the flower of Englands face,
Change the complexion of her maid-pale peace,
To scarlet indignation and bedew
Her pastors grasse with faithfull English bloud

106–7   And by the roialties of both your blouds,
        Currents that spring from one most gratious head

160–2   Weele make fowle weather with despised teares;
        Our sighs and they shall lodge the summer corne,
        And make a dearth in this reuolting land

177–8   Downe, downe I come, like glistring Phaeton:
        Wanting the manage of vnrulie Iades

189–90 faire coosen, you debase your princely knee,
        To make the base earth proud with kissing it

sc.xii.29–31 Go bind thou vp yong dangling Aphricokes,
        Which like vnruly children make their sire,
        Stoope with oppression of their prodigall weight

33–5   Go thou, and like an executioner
        Cut off the heads of two fast growing spraies,
        That looke too loftie in our common-wealth

75–6   What Eue? what serpent hath suggested thee
        To make a second fall of cursed man?

85–9   In your Lo. scale is nothing but himselfe,
        And some few vanities that make him light:
        But in the ballance of great Bullingbrooke,
        Besides himselfe are all the English peeres,
        And with that oddes he weighs King Richard downe

sc.xiii.72 How fondly doest thou spurre a forward horse?

sc.xiv.8–10 My faire Rose wither, yet looke vp, behold,
        That you in pittie may dissolue to deaw,
        And wash him fresh againe with true loue teares

12–13   Thou mappe of honour, thou King Richards tombe,
        And not King Richard

13–15   thou most beauteous Inne,
        Why should hard fauourd greife be lodged in thee,
        When triumph is become an alehouse guest?

20–2   I am sworne brother (sweet)
        To grim necessitie, and he and I,
        Will keepe a league till death

31–2   and wilt thou pupill-like
        Take the correction, mildly kisse the rod

46–50   For why, the senselesse brands will simpathize
        The heavy accent of thy moouing tong,
        And in compassion weepe the fire out,
        And some wil mourne in ashes, some cole blacke,
        For the deposing of a rightfull King

55–6   Northumberland, thou ladder wherewithall
        The mounting Bullingbrooke ascends my throne

58–9   ere foule sinne gathering head
        Shall breake into corruption

78–80   My wife to Fraunce, from whence set forth in pomp
        She came adorned hither like sweete Maie,
        Sent backe like Hollowmas or shortst of day

sc.xv.23–8   As in a Theater the eies of men,
        After a well-graced Actor leaues the stage,
        Are ydly bent on him that enters next,
        Thinking his prattle to be tedious;
        Euen so, or with much more contempt mens eies
        Did scowle on gentle Ric.

32–3   His face still combating with teares and smiles,
        The badges of his griefe and patience

46–7   who are the violets now
        That strew the greene lap of the new come spring

sc.xvi.59–61   Thou sheere immaculate and siluer Fountaine,
        From whence this streame, through muddy passages,
        Hath held his current, and defild himselfe

66–7   And he shall spend mine honour, with his shame,
        As thriftles sonnes, their scraping Fathers gold

sc.xviii.6–8   My braine Ile prooue, the female to my soule,
        My soule the father, and these two beget
        A generation of still-breeding thoughts

12–16   As thoughts of things diuine are intermixt
        With scruples, and do set the word it selfe
        Against the word, as thus: Come little ones, & then againe
        It is as hard to come, as for a Cammell
        To threed the posterne of a small needles eie

17–20   Thoughts tending to ambition they do plot,
        Vnlikely wonders: how these vaine weake nailes
        May teare a passage thorow the flinty ribs
        Of this hard world my ragged prison walles

22–7 Thoughts tending to content flatter themselues,
   That they are not the first of fortunes slaues,
   Nor shall not be the last like seely beggars,
   Who sitting in the stockes refuge their shame,
   That many haue, and others must set there.
   And in this thought they find a kind of ease

41–7 Ha ha keepe time, how sowre sweete Musicke is
   When time is broke, and no proportion kept,
   So is it in the musike of mens liues:
   And here haue I the daintinesse of eare
   To checke time broke in a disordered string:
   But for the concord of my state and time,
   Had not an eare to heare my true time broke

49–59 For now hath time made me his numbring clocke;
   My thoughts are minutes, and with sighes they iarre,
   Their watches on vnto mine eyes the outward watch
   Whereto my finger like a dialles poynt,
   Is pointing still, in cleansing them from teares.
   Now sir, the sound that telles what houre it is,
   Are clamorous groanes which strike vpon my hart,
   Which is the bell, so sighs, and teares, and grones,
   Shew minutes, times, and houres: but my time,
   Runnes posting on in Bullingbrokes proud ioye,
   While I stand fooling heere his iacke of the clocke

64–5   and loue to Richard,
   Is a strange brooch in this al-hating world

sc.xix.29 High sparkes of honour in thee haue I seene

50 To wash this bloud off from my guiltie hand

Such are the signs of the Shakespearean revision in the First Quarto. But this edition is not complete. The folio and all modern editions have a scene following the Parliament scene in Act IV (ll. 162–318), which was published for the first time in the 1608 quarto. And the question arises whether it existed in 1597 or was an addition made after the publication of the first edition.

In fact, this problem does not really exist. One can hardly imagine a play concerning the last years of Richard II's reign that would not include the principal event in the existence of that king —his abdication. And the First Quarto itself proves that the scene of the abdication had been suppressed before the First Quarto was

printed. After the bishop of Carlisle's arrest (150–3) the lines in
which Bolingbroke asks that Richard be led before the Parliament
in order to surrender his crown publicly have been deleted and
replaced by two and a half lines fixing the date for the coronation
on the next Wednesday. But when this deletion was made the following line, spoken by the abbot of Westminster, was left: "A
wofull Pageant have we heere beheld," which can scarcely apply
to the dispute between Aumerle and his accusers. The study of
the versification and of the style corroborates the supposition that
this scene was suppressed. The portion devoted to Richard's abdication is, like the rest of the play, composed of rhymed verses
(174–5,188–99,214–21,317–18)[7]—fragments retained from the
original version (which, although rewritten by Shakespeare, still
have some of the characteristics of author C)—and of blank verse,
most of which is unquestionably Shakespearean as is proved by
the usual mannerisms—division of the thought into symmetrical
parts (251–2), repetition of a word or grammatical form to accentuate the symmetrical construction (207–10,212–13,214–15),
marked preference for the association of two words expressing
two aspects of the same thought (173,179,225,237), and numerous
images (166,184–9,228–9,237–8,242,260–2,273–5,277–9,283–4,298).
It can be stated positively that the text published in the 1608
quarto emanated from the same manuscript that provided the
text for the First Quarto, for an example of that peculiarity which
is attributable to the scrivener Ralph Crane is found also in the
abdication scene: in line 239 the words "with Pilat" are set in
parentheses.[8] There is therefore no reason to suppose that the text
of this scene was obtained by devious means or through the aid
of some imaginary pirate. The truth is that it was supplied from
a manuscript having the same origin as that which was used for
the printing of Q_1, and this manuscript was of course the promptbook of the company.

Having disposed of that mooted question, we can now try to dis-

7. The numbering of the lines in this scene is that of the Globe edition.
8. If the spelling at that epoch were not so erratic, it could be added that the word
"coosen" or "cousin" has here that peculiar form (181,304–5) exactly as in numerous
lines of Q_1 (sc.i.188; sc.iii.247; sc.iv.1,19; sc.x.36; sc.xi.159,189,203).

cover the nature of Shakespeare's revision. I shall first draw up a
recapitulative list of Shakespeare's mannerisms and images:

sc.i(I.i)   15 mannerisms: 1,2,18,19,21,41,55,91,96,97,101,115,152,
207 lines   191,202
                  8 images: 19,41–2,55–6,103,109,155,182–3,203

sc.ii(I.ii)   4 mannerisms: 24,43,68,69
74 lines   3 images: 7–8,11–12,17–19

sc.iii(I.iii)   12 ·mannerisms: 19,39,43,89,106,111,129,130,131,135,183,
309 lines   185–6
                 21 images: 48–9,67–8,79–82,91–2,132–3,145–7,161–5,166–
                     9,187,195–6,200,202,208–9,213–15,227–8,229–30,236,
                     265–7,271–4,288–91,302–3

sc.iv.(I.iv)   1 mannerism: 25
63 lines   3 images: 14,24,59–60

sc.v(II.i)   17 mannerisms: 40–3,45–6,50–1,52,54,115,130,139,142,156,
299 lines   175,189,190,199,208,237,258
                 15 images: 5–6,12–13,28,46,61–3,75,97–9,100,117–19,133–
                     4,149,263–5,270–1,291,292–3

sc.vi(II.ii)   5 mannerisms: 3,12,14–24,32,79
145 lines   5 images: 11,14–24,61–4,83,97–8

sc.vii(II.iii)   15 mannerisms: 4,7,12,43,44,59,63,85,87,90,94,109,120,131,
171 lines   167
                  2 images: 66–8,128

sc.viii(II.iv)   8 mannerisms: 10,11,12,13–14,14,15,16,22
24 lines   2 images: 18–20,21–2

sc.ix(III.i)   3 mannerisms: 9,10,23
44 lines   2 images:13,20

sc.x(III.ii)   14 mannerisms: 8,15,46,74,79,92,93,111,117,119,145,163,
218 lines   184,196
                 13 images: 8–9,37–46,47–8,54–5,67–8,81,105–10,124–5,
                     146–7,153–4,160–71,167–8,169–70

sc.xi(III.iii)   17 mannerisms: 5,26,38,57–9,78,80,83,97,101,109,110,127,
208 lines   143–4,147–51,163–8,183,200
                 13 images: 32–4,42–3,45–6,48–9,53–6,61–6,67–9,92–3,95–
                     9,107,160–2,177–8,189–90

sc.xii(III.iv)   2 mannerisms: 17–18,32
107 lines   4 images: 29–31,33–5,75–6,85–9

sc.xiii (IV.i)	13	mannerisms: 67,68,89,108,166,173,179,207–10,212–13,
334 lines		214–15,225,237,251–2
	11	images: 72,166,184–9,228–9,238,242,260–2,274–5,277–
		9,284,298
sc.xiv (V.i)	3	mannerisms: 26,27,77
102 lines	9	images: 8–10,12,13–15,20–2,31–2,46–9,55–6,58–9,78–80
sc.xv (V.ii)	5	mannerisms: 6,8,12–17,40,52
117 lines	3	images:23–8,32–3,46–7
sc.xvi (V.iii)	6	mannerisms: 10,23,31,57,59,125
145 lines	2	images: 59–61,66–7
sc.xvii (V.iv)	0	mannerisms
11 lines	0	images
sc.xviii (V.v)	9	mannerisms: 6–29,8,42,46,50–9,65,78–9,86,107
117 lines	7	images: 6–8,12–16,17–20,22–7,41–7,49–59,64–5
sc.xix (V.vi)	2	mannerisms: 20,25
52 lines	2	images:29,50

A comparison of this list with a similar list in the preceding chapter (pp. 162–3) shows striking differences. In *Titus Andronicus* the images, generally short, were numerous only in a few scenes, and from this fact it could be concluded that Shakespeare's imagination had not been greatly stimulated, that the purpose of the revision had been primarily to give vividness to the trite style of the pre-Shakespearean play. In *Richard II*, on the contrary, the images are distributed profusely among the scenes (with only one exception, of little importance), just like the mannerisms, which they equal and sometimes exceed in number. And they do not differ only by their quantity or by the regularity with which they are distributed throughout the play; they are also developed at greater length, evincing the ease with which the author spun out the facts which they illustrate beyond their material existence. One feels that Shakespeare was not content with the modest role of corrector of style: the creator within him awoke. The subject took hold of him completely, he thought the thoughts over again, relived the incidents with the design of giving them a form of his own.

This does not mean that all the scenes have been treated with equal originality. The old play has left its imprint on the versification. As in 2 and 3 *Henry VI*, as in *Titus Andronicus*, there are mixed passages which have kept something of the pre-Shakespearean verses. And this is easily understandable. Shakespeare was working on a text overladen with trochees coming from two sources—author C having almost as much fondness for this type of rhythmic variation as author A—so that his versification was doubly exposed to contamination. In exceptional cases the mannerisms and especially the images will happily bring a decisive element of certainty by their number, and one can, without too many chances of error, divide the text into four classes according to the importance of the Shakespearean modifications.

I. PASSAGES OF THE OLD PLAY RETAINED VERBATIM

The number of such passages is small. Besides the rhymed lines which I have listed on pages 194–6, there are very few passages in blank verse which may be said to have been written entirely by author A. I see only three passages in a style characteristically un-Shakespearean and bearing no trace of Shakespeare's hand:

sc.v.273–89   Northumberland announces that Bolingbroke returns at the head of an army.
Trochees 8.3%, spondees 3.5%, 3 irregular lines.

sc.xv.72–117   York rushes to warn Henry IV that Aumerle is one of the conspirators.
Trochees 7.1%, spondees 5.3%, 9 irregular verses, 2 trisyllabic feet.

sc.xvi.37–56   York denounces his son as a traitor to Henry IV.
Trochees 8.3%, spondees 2.0%, 4 irregular verses, 2 trisyllabic feet.

sc.xvii.1–9   Sir Pierce Exton believes that the king would like to be rid of Richard.
Trochees 2.4%, spondees 0%, O mannerisms, 0 images.

II. PASSAGES SLIGHTLY MODIFIED BY SHAKESPEARE

sc.iii.1–53   Bolingbroke and Mowbray present themselves for the judicial combat.
Trochees 4.5%, spondees 1.1%, 3 mannerisms, 1 image.

99–123   The adversaries are armed by the heralds; the king stops the combat.

Trochees 6.5%, spondees 4.9%, 1 truncated decasyllable, 2 mannerisms, 0 images.

sc.v.224–61   Some lords criticize the king's actions.

Trochees 5.7%, spondees 1.0%, 1 trisyllabic foot, 2 mannerisms.

sc.vi.41–71   Green tells the queen that Bolingbroke has returned to England.

Trochees 1.2%, spondees 5.0%, 1 trisyllabic foot, 3 irregular verses, 0 mannerisms, 1 image.

73–119   York does not know which way to turn.

Trochees 8.2%, spondees 1.7%, 4 trisyllabic feet, several irregular verses, 1 mannerism, 2 images.

120–41   The favorites understand that all is lost.

Trochees 5.6%, spondees 1.8%, 3 trisyllabic feet, but 2 antitheses which seem to be Shakespeare's.

sc.vii.137–67   York will remain neutral though he recognizes that Bolingbroke has been unjustly treated.

Trochees 0.6%, spondees 4.5%, 1 mannerism, 0 images.

sc.x.1–35   On his return from Ireland Richard salutes his native soil and calls on it to repel the invader.

Trochees 5.5%, spondees 5.7%, 1 trisyllabic foot, several bookish comparisons, but 2 mannerisms, and 1 image.

63–70   Salisbury brings bad news.

Trochees 2.5%, spondees 15.0%, 0 mannerisms, 1 image.

121–38   Scroop announces to Richard that the favorites have been executed.

Trochees 7.8%, spondees 6.7%, 0 mannerisms, 1 image.

We have here a visible proof that this passage was modified. In lines 122–5 Richard wonders where the earl of Wiltshire, Bagot, Bushie, and Green can be:

that they have left the dangerous enemy
Measure our confines with such peacefull steps

which is a Shakespearean image; but a few lines further he is indignant against those "Three Iudasses, each one thrise worse then Iudas" (132), and this is in a passage in which there are several pre-Shakespearean comparisons. It is this last passage which is correct, for Bagot at that time was in Ireland (cf. sc.vi.137) and therefore could not be executed at Bristol with the other favorites.

194–218   More bad news makes Richard sink into despair.
           Trochees 1.7%, spondees 5.1%, 14 rhymed verses
           touched up by Shakespeare, 1 mannerism, 0
           images.
sc.xi.1–30   Percy comes to Bolingbroke announcing that Flint
           castle is royally manned and will not surrender.
           Trochees 4.7%, spondees 3.3%, 3 trisyllabic feet, 2
           mannerisms, 0 images.
sc.xii.1–23   The queen cannot get rid of her presentiments.
           Trochees 4.7%, spondees 2.8%, some irregular verses,
           1 trisyllabic foot, 1 mannerism, 0 images.
sc.xiii.91–183   The bishop of Carlisle reports that Mowbray died in
           Venice after fighting for Jesus Christ. He is op-
           posed to Richard's deposition.
           Trochees 6.6%, spondees 5.0%, 2 trisyllabic feet, 1
           mannerism, 0 images.
sc.xv.41–117   York discovers that his son, Aumerle, is one of the
           conspirators.
           Trochees 5.3%, spondees 4.7%, 4 trisyllabic feet, ir-
           regular verses, 1 mannerism, 1 image.
sc.xvi.1–21   Henry IV asks if anyone has seen his "unthriftie son."
           Percy tells the last fanfaronade of the heir to the
           throne.
           Trochees 2.9%, spondees 4.9%, 1 trisyllabic foot, 1
           mannerism, 0 images.
22–56   Aumerle asks the king to pardon him. York arrives
           and denounces his son as a traitor.
           Trochees 6.0%, spondees 3.0%, 2 trisyllabic feet,
           some irregular verse, 2 mannerisms, 0 images.
sc.xviii.66–93   A faithful groom visits Richard in the Tower.
           Trochees 4.2%, spondees 7.7%, 2 mannerisms, 0
           images.
99–107   Richard beats his keeper, kills two servants, and is
           in his turn struck down by Exton.
           Trochees 17.0%, spondees 4.8%, 2 trisyllabic feet, 1
           mannerism.

III. PASSAGES RADICALLY MODIFIED BY SHAKESPEARE

sc.i.1–42,47–83   Bolingbroke accuses Mowbray of treason.
           Trochees 4.6%, spondees 5.1%, 1 trisyllabic foot, 7
           mannerisms, 3 images.
sc.iii.69–92   Bolingbroke asks his father to pray for him. Mowbray
           with "a quiet breast" agrees to fight.
           Trochees 5.0%, spondees 3.3%, 1 trisyllabic foot, 2
           mannerisms, 2 images.

178–204   Richard asks Bolingbroke and Mowbray to swear that
they will never meet to plot against England.
Trochees 5.2%, spondees 1.4%, 2 mannerisms, 4
images.
J. D. Wilson in his edition of the play (p.lxxi) thinks
that he can in several passages distinguish what he
calls "fossil-rhymes," which are not explainable except on the supposition that "Shakespeare was rewriting rhymed verse," and as an instance he quotes
from the present passage the following lines (the
words rhyming together are in italics):

> You never shall, so help you truth and God,
> *Embrace* each other's love in banishment,
> Nor never look upon each other's *face*
> Nor never write, *regreet*, nor reconcile
> This louring tempest of your home-bred
> *hate,*
> Nor never by advised purpose *meet,*
> To plot, contrive, or complot any ill,
> 'Gainst us, our *state,* our subjects, or our
> land.

208–20   Richard reduces Bolingbroke's exile to six years.
Trochees 7.6%, spondees 4.6%, 0 mannerisms, 2
images, 2 rhymed verses touched up by Shakespeare.

sc.v.1–30   Gaunt on his deathbed wants to see Richard in order
to give wholesome counsel to the unsteady youth.
Trochees 5.3%, spondees 4.6%, 0 mannerisms, 3
images, 16 rhymed verses rewritten by Shakespeare.

sc.vi.1–30,33–40   The queen has a presentiment that some misfortune
is imminent.
Trochees 3.9%, spondees 4.9%, 4 mannerisms, 2
images, 2 rhymed verses.

sc.viii.1–15,18–24   A Welsh captain says that his men, hearing that the
king is dead, will disperse.
Trochees 8.0%, spondees 4.0%, 8 mannerisms, 2
images.

sc.ix.1–44   Bolingbroke has the favorites Bushie and Green executed.
Trochees 5.9%, spondees 3.2%, 2 irregular verses, 3
mannerisms, 2 images.

sc.x.82–118   Richard for a moment has faith in his kingly power,
but Scroop brings the news that both young and
old rebel.

Trochees 4.8%, spondees 4.8%, 4 mannerisms, 1 image.

sc.xi.31–60 Bolingbroke respectfully offers to meet Richard.

Trochees 4.0%, spondees 6.1%, 2 mannerisms, 5 images.

The high proportion of spondaic feet is probably due to the influence of author C's versification, the sonorous rhythm of which is noticeable especially at the beginning.

171–8,183–208 When Bolingbroke presents himself Richard welcomes him ironically, then suddenly yields to Bolingbroke's will.

Trochees 4.4%, spondees 11.0%.

This passage is singularly composite: 10 rhymed verses and a high proportion of spondaic feet suggest that it was primarily written by author C and that some part of this has been preserved; on the other hand a trisyllabic foot shows that the blank verse was by author A; lastly 2 mannerisms and 2 images indicate that the whole has been revised by Shakespeare.

sc.xii.24–95 The queen overhears the gardener saying that Richard will be deposed.

Trochees 5.0%, spondees 5.6%, 1 trisyllabic foot, 1 truncated decasyllable, but 2 mannerisms and 4 images.

sc.xiv.1–80 Richard and the queen part.

Trochees 3.7%, spondees 5.5%, 3 mannerisms, 9 images.

sc.xv.1–36 York describes the coming of Bolingbroke and Richard into London.

Trochees 3.8%, spondees 8.8%, 3 mannerisms, 2 images.

sc.xviii.1–65 Richard compares his prison to the world. Music which he hears reminds him that he has not known how to check the concord of his state and time.

Trochees 2.1%, spondees 7.0%, 6 mannerisms, 7 images.

IV. PASSAGES REWRITTEN OR ADDED BY SHAKESPEARE

sc.i.84–132,135–49 Richard asks Bolingbroke to make his accusation precise; Mowbray defends himself and asks that a day be fixed for a judicial combat.

Trochees 2.2%, spondees 2.3%, 1 trisyllabic foot, 6 mannerisms, 2 images.

sc.ii.1–53   The Duchess of Gloucester begs Gaunt to avenge the assassination of her husband.

Trochees 3.3%, spondees 3.7%, 2 mannerisms, 3 images.

This passage is followed by 4 rhymed verses written by author C.

sc.iii.124–71   Richard banishes Bolingbroke and Mowbray.

Trochees 2.9%, spondees 3.3%, 4 mannerisms, 4 images.

225–32,235–46   Gaunt feels sure that he will never see his son again.

Trochees 3.0%, spondees 4.0%, 0 mannerisms, 2 images.

With the exception of 2 lines this passage is in rhymed verse (Shakespearean) and is in the vicinity of other passages in the characteristic style of author C; as a matter of fact it has preserved something of the stiffness of the older author (only one enjambment).

258–303   Gaunt vainly tries to alleviate the grief of his son.

Trochees 3.5%, spondees 3.9%, 0 mannerisms, 4 images.

The versification is extremely supple (14 enjambments); but 4 rhymed verses (292–3,302–3) indicate that the passage has only been rewritten and probably amplified.

sc.iv.1–62   Richard reminds Aumerle of Bolingbroke's efforts to make himself popular; he announces his intention to conduct the Irish war personally and to "farm" the realm.

Trochees 3.0%, spondees 4.0%, 1 mannerism, 3 images.

The versification, as in the preceding passage, is very supple (10 enjambments); but 1 trisyllabic foot and several irregular verses show that this has only been rewritten.

sc.v.31–68   Gaunt describes the shameful state into which England has degenerated.

Trochees 2.6%, spondees 3.6%, 5 mannerisms, 5 images.

69–134   Gaunt makes Richard ashamed of the way in which he mismanages the kingdom, a rebuke which Richard takes very much amiss.

Trochees 3.3%, spondees 3.9%, 2 mannerisms, 5

images. 1 trisyllabic foot and an excessive use of conceits of the jingle kind show that the passage has only been rewritten.

139–42,147–9   York beseeches Richard to excuse Gaunt's bluntness. Northumberland announces that Gaunt has died. Trochees 2.8%, spondees 2.8%, 2 mannerisms, 1 image.
The interbedded rhymed verses make it sure that this passage was at first written by author C.

155–208   Richard says that he is going to seize Gaunt's property; York protests violently. Trochees 1.8%, spondees 3.3%, 6 mannerisms, 0 images.
It is here possible to see how Shakespeare modified the old play. Holinshed says simply: "The Duke of York was therewith [the confiscation of York's property] sore moved," and it is not likely that in the pre-Shakespearean play York spoke so openly, independence of mind not being one of his qualities. His frankness is probably an addition by Shakespeare.

sc.vii.1–83   Bolingbroke arrives before Berkeley castle, where Percy, Ross, and Willoughby join him. A messenger from York comes and asks him why he breaks thus the peace of the country. Trochees 3.2%, spondees 3.2%, 7 mannerisms, 1 image.
This passage may be a long amplification by Shakespeare (cf. further p. 224).

84–136   Bolingbroke enumerates to York, who upbraids him, the wrongs he has suffered. Trochees 3.3%, spondees 3.7%, 7 mannerisms, 1 image. 1 trisyllabic foot indicates that the passage has only been rewritten.

sc.x.36–62   Richard is sure that God will defend his deputy elect and that Bolingbroke will "tremble at his sin." Trochees 1.4%, spondees 3.7%, 1 mannerism, 3 long images. 2 rhymed verses, 1 trisyllabic foot indicate that the passage was in the old play.

143–183   Richard, hearing that the favorites have been executed, wants to talk only of graves and of the death of kings. Trochees 2.5%, spondees 4.4%, 2 mannerisms, 5 images. Probably Shakespeare's addition.

sc.xi.61–167   Richard at first receives Northumberland haughtily

and ends by promising to grant Bolingbroke all that
he asks. Afterward he is somewhat ashamed of this
weakness but finally is reconciled to the idea of
losing his throne.

Trochees 1.8%, spondees 2.4%, 11 mannerisms, 6
images. 1 trisyllabic foot and 6 rhymed verses show
that the passage is only rewritten.

sc.xiii.1–90   Aumerle, in a session of Parliament, is accused of
having taken part in the assassination of the duke
of Gloucester.

Trochees 2.2%, spondees 2.4%, 3 mannerisms, 1
image, very supple versification (20 enjambments).

162–317   Richard abdicates.

Trochees 3.6%, spondees 4.3%, 9 mannerisms, 10
images.

sc.xvi.57–67   Henry IV compares the character of York and that of
Aumerle. In this short passage there are neither
trochees nor spondees, but it is composed of two
long characteristically Shakespearean images and
contains 2 mannerisms.

sc.xix.22–52   Henry IV pardons the bishop of Carlisle, disavows
Exton, and announces that to wash this blood off
his hands he will undertake a pilgrimage to the
Holy Land.

Trochees 3.2%, spondees 3.9%, 1 mannerism, 2
images.

This passage is in rhymed verse and had been primarily written by author C, whose characteristics
it has preserved (jingles, inversions, antitheses,
strained constructions), but the versification has
been deeply modified.

Shakespeare's intentions are now clear enough. It is noticeable
first that in the second class most of the slightly modified passages
dramatize historical events, while in the third and fourth classes
most of the passages radically modified, rewritten, or added, that
is to say those which represent Shakespeare's creative contribution, concern much more what the personages were as individuals
than the role they played in the political pattern. It is evident that
Shakespeare was less interested in the intrigues of the rulers of
his country than in the signs they could give that under the mask
of the politician there lived a human being as capable of weeping
or laughing as the generality of mankind. This was already dis-

cernible in the chapter on the first and second parts of *Henry VI;* but what was then an impression has become a fact in *Richard II.* The case of Richard is particularly striking. There are in the third and fourth classes 14 passages which have to do with this character and of these only 4 show him in the discharge of his royal duties: he superintends preparations for the judicial combat (sc.i.84–153), he banishes Bolingbroke and Mowbray (sc.iii.124–71), he confiscates Gaunt's property (sc.v.155–208), he reduces Bolingbroke's time of exile to six years (sc.iii.208–20).[9] All the other passages contribute some detail to the portrait of a king constantly vacillating between displays of energy or pride and moments of depression which plunge him into a state of fatalistic helplessness; they emphasize Richard's sentiments when he sees himself threatened by the man whom he has banished in a fit of jealous suspicion; they report at length his tearful lamentations which at times remind one of Titus Andronicus, at other times make him speak, as Northumberland says, "like a frantike man" (sc.xi.183–4); they stress, in a word, the chief trait of this character, the astonishing lack of strength in one naturally self-willed but who cannot bear the vicissitudes of Fortune. Richard is a first sketch of Hamlet with this difference—the unhappy prince of Denmark was paralyzed by an excess of thinking, while words with Richard serve only to compose attitudes.

This conception of the character was not entirely original with Shakespeare. It had been suggested by Holinshed in one of those attempts at psychological appreciation in which he indulged occasionally. Speaking of Richard this chronicler said: "He doubted not to revenge himselfe of his adversarie and so at first he passed with good courage; but when he understood as he went thus forward, that all the castels, even from the borders of Scotland unto Bristow were delivered unto the duke of Lancaster, and that likewise the nobles and commons, as well of the south parts as of the north, were fullie bent to take part with the duke against him, and further hearing how his trustie councellors had lost their heads at Bristow, he became so greatlie discomforted, that sorrowfullie

9. It would be more correct to say 3 passages, for the last mentioned might be joined to the second group; it shows that Richard, in spite of his light-mindedness, is not quite devoid of sensibility, since it is on seeing Gaunt's sadness that he reduces Bolingbroke's sentence.

lamenting his miserable state, he utterlie despaired of his owne safetie, and calling his armie together, which was not small, licenced everie man to depart to his home." This manner of explaining the course of events had surely been exploited in the pre-Shakespearean play, as is proved by a few rhymed verses retained in sc.xi(167–70,173–4,179–82), precisely in the passage in which Richard, downhearted, surrenders to Bolingbroke.

Shakespeare, therefore, simply expanded this idea, expressed, we may be sure, briefly and dryly by his predecessor, but he did so with such abundance that the part of Richard is, I believe, with that of Hamlet, one of the longest he ever wrote.[1] Above all, he illuminated it with the splendor of an inexhaustible mint of images which make of Richard one of the most brilliant and poetical [2] protagonists of the Shakespearean drama.

In giving such an exceptional development to the character of Richard, Shakespeare completely changed the nature of the play. From what has been preserved of the pre-Shakespearean play it is easy to see that it was a characteristic chronicle play of the same kind as *The Contention* and *The True Tragedie,* in which historical facts alone mattered. Its subject was not Richard II but the last seventeen months of the reign of Richard II and the first two months of the reign of Henry IV. There was no prominent character, but two rivals, of whom one triumphed while the other was eliminated. It was certainly Shakespeare who suppressed the historical events whose disappearance is revealed by a study of the text (cf. pp. 189–92). He destroyed the state of balance established between the two men by the facts, and the chronicle play was transformed into a tragedy—*The Tragedie of King Richard the Second* said the title—in which one character monopolizes the attention of the public and the other characters are, to a greater or less extent, cogs in the mechanism of the plot.

1. The part of Richard has 744 lines, which is about a third of the whole play.
2. This overflow of images has made some critics believe that Shakespeare meant to present Richard as a poet. This is to forget that the images are Shakespeare's and are of the same kind as those with which all his great protagonists are endowed. Richard is not a poet; he is simply a man who hides his lack of decision under loquacity and plays with words when it is necessary to act.

∫ ∫ ∫

THE PROPORTIONS of feminine endings in the passages of class IV, the only ones which can be considered as almost entirely in the hand of Shakespeare, indicate three distinct periods of revision.[3]

1. Six passages have a proportion of feminine endings varying from 0 to 5%:

	Feminine endings	Blank verses	Percentages
sc.v.69–134	2	62	3.2
155–208	2	54	3.7
sc.x.36–62	0	25	0.0
143–183	1	41	2.4
sc.xi.61–170	5	104	4.8
sc.xiii.1–90	5	90	5.5

15 feminine endings in 376 lines, average 3.9%

2. Six other passages, with a remarkable regularity, have a proportion somewhere about 9%:

	Feminine endings	Blank verses	Percentages
sc.ii.1–53	5	53	9.4
sc.iii.258–303	4	42	9.5
sc.iv.1–62	6	62	9.6
sc.v.31–68	4	38	10.5
sc.xiii.162–317 (abdication scene)	12	132	9.0
sc.xvi.57–67	1	11	9.0

32 feminine endings in 338 lines, average 9.4%

3. Three passages have proportions somewhere about 18%:

	Feminine endings	Blank verses	Percentages
sc.i.84,132,135–49	11	60	18.3
sc.vii.1–83	15	83	18.0
84–136	9	53	16.9

35 feminine endings in 196 lines, average 17.8%

The first revision with its percentage of 3.9% must have been

3. Sc.iii.124–71 contains a double redaction, one of which may not be Shakespeare's; for this reason it has not been included. The few rhymed verses, even though rewritten by Shakespeare, have of course been deducted from the total lines of the passages.

made at about the same period as the first revision of *Titus Andronicus* (average 2.8%) and somewhat earlier than the first revision of 3 *Henry VI* (average 5.7%). In that group all the passages except one (where Aumerle is accused of having taken part in the assassination of Gloucester) show Richard in some of his distinctive moods, and the portrait is nearly complete; the traits suggested by Holinshed—his absolutism, his blind confidence in the power he held from God, followed by fits of discouragement, his tendency in such moments to eloquent lamentations—have been amply developed.

The second revision has a percentage of feminine endings slightly higher than that of the first revision of 2 *Henry VI* and of the second revision of *Titus Andronicus;* it is marked by a further development, in the abdication scene, of Richard's plaintive loquacity, to which is added this time an instinctive taste for striking histrionic attitudes. And Gaunt's eloquent description of the degradation of England is certainly there to emphasize the blameworthy side of the king.

The third group is not, properly speaking, a revision but the outcome of a single intention. The three passages of that group concern Bolingbroke, and each of them contributes to the comeliness of his character. The authority with which he cites the proofs of Mowbray's treason gives evidence of his own truthfulness and courage, all the more so as it is contrasted with his opponent's admission of delinquency. In his conversation with his partisans before Berkeley castle there is a tone of courtly refinement unique in the play and which suggests the charm and elegance of the man. His dispassionate enumeration of the wrongs he had to suffer is so convincing that it nonpluses York who has come to reprimand him. And to these passages should no doubt be added sc.xix.8–52, entirely written in Shakespearean rhymed verse, which stresses other qualities of Bolingbroke, his clemency, his gratefulness, his piety. The reason those passages were modified or introduced is evident: Shakespeare wanted to enlist the sympathies of the spectators on the side of this character. These modifications with an average of feminine endings of 17.8% must belong to a period somewhat later than that of the first two revisions.

Though the play existed in a Shakespearean form as early as in 1591–92, there are good reasons to believe that it never was performed publicly before 1595. In a letter of that year dated December 9 Sir William Hoby, the son of the translator of *Il Cortegiano*, inviting Sir Robert Cecil to visit him at his residence in Canon Row, promised his guest that "a gate for your supper shall be open and King Richard shall present himself to your view." (Hatfield MSS, published in *Review of English Studies, 1*, 75.) So the play was being performed at that time, or the company would not have been able to give a private performance of it thus, at a moment's notice, and furthermore Sir William would not have chosen such a play as an after-supper treat if it had not been a sensational novelty that Cecil had not yet seen. How it happened that the company had to wait so long before they were able to perform it is not hard to imagine. The time had not yet come when the supporters of the earl of Essex would use *Richard II* as a rallying sign against Queen Elizabeth; but government circles had early found a disturbing analogy between a King Richard ill advised by his favorites and a queen who listened too much to some of her courtiers who knew how to flatter her. In a letter of January 9, 1578, Sir Francis Knollys, refusing to give the queen unwelcome counsel, said that he would not "play the partes of King Richard the Second's men." The phrase seems to have been current for it is found again, before 1588, in another letter of Henry Lord Hunsdon, later the patron of Shakespeare's company, who asserted that he "never was one of Richard the II's men." [4] Moreover the reign of Richard II was full of unpleasant implications in the minds of those who had a share in the government of England. The triumph of Bolingbroke was the first blow dealt at the constitutional organization of the country: Bolingbroke was a usurper and was still considered one by all who knew the record of the past. Now he was a Lancaster, and the head of the Tudor dynasty, Henry VII, had based his claim to the crown on being heir to the house of Lancaster; Bolingbroke, the usurper, was consequently an ancestor of the present occupant of the throne. It was hardly opportune to revive the memory of those facts at a time when the watchword was that the Tudor dynasty had restored the blessings of peace through the establishment of a legitimate government. From whichever side it was considered, the subject of Richard II for a play was politically dangerous; and the spectacle of an English king deposed and

4. E. K. Chambers, *William Shakespeare* (Oxford, Clarendon Press, 1930), *1*, 353.

murdered was so intolerable as to pass for seditious. When one remembers the jealous care with which the Privy Council kept watch upon the doings of the actors' companies, the punctilious zeal with which Sir Edmund Tilney, the Master of the Revels, sifted the most innocent political allusion, it is not mere guessing to be convinced that the company of Lord Strange could never obtain the authorization to perform this play upon the public stage. We know pretty well what their repertory was in 1591–93, and although they had a *Henry VI* they never gave a *Richard II* during their seasons in Henslowe's theater. But in 1595 the situation was quite different: since 1594 their protector had been Henry Lord Hunsdon who, as lord chamberlain, exercised authority over the office of the revels. It was difficult for Sir Edmund to refuse an authorization if the lord chamberlain thought that his players should have it. The price for this favor was no doubt the promise that the abdication scene should be left out and, possibly, that Bolingbroke would be represented in such a favorable light as to obliterate his guilt.[5]

The Text of the Folio

THE COMPARISON of the text of the First Quarto with the text of the folio yields results very similar to those obtained by comparison of the quarto and folio texts of *Titus Andronicus*. It seems that the text of the folio was printed from a copy of Q_5 (1615) or of Q_3[6] that had been collated with the company's manuscript, as is shown by the hundred or so readings of F which agree with Q_1

5. 1595 is the date generally admitted for the *composition* of *Richard II*. It is based upon resemblances between the play and *The Civil Wars of Lancaster and York,* a poem by Samuel Daniel published in 1595 (Stationers' Register, Oct. 11, 1594). This question has given rise to numerous discussions, certain critics believing that Daniel had imitated Shakespeare, other critics being sure that Shakespeare had imitated Daniel, a third group refusing to find imitation anywhere. Most of the supposed resemblances, notably the two most striking—the scene in which Richard bids adieu to the queen and the one where Exton realizes that the king wants to be rid of Richard—were in the pre-Shakespearean play, so that Shakespeare need not have gone to Daniel as a source; and Daniel, if he had seen the old play performed, may have been inspired by it.

6. In the introduction to his edition of the Third Quarto, Pollard is inclined to believe that the folio may have been printed from the MS in the library of William Augustus White (*A New Shakespeare Quarto, Richard II,* 1916, pp. 52–3 and 74).

and thus with the manuscript from which Q₁ was set.[7] Some fifty
lines are missing in the folio text; they are evidently cuts made
after 1597. The omission of three single lines (sc.vi.76; sc.x.49;
sc.xvi.97) may have been due to carelessness, though in the second
case (Ireland being assimilated to the Antipodes) this geographical
oddity may have seemed too fantastic and have been suppressed.
But in the following passages the omissions were certainly made
for a set purpose:

sc.iii.129–33. This is the passage I have quoted (p. 188) as containing an interpolation which made the meaning obscure; the
disappearance of the lines interpolated has cleared up the
sense.

sc.iii.239–42. This is a passage written by author C which heavily
repeats an idea just expressed; a cut was necessary.

sc.iii.263–98. This is one of those poetical amplifications, more
ingenious than dramatic, in which Shakespeare indulged at the
beginning of his career and which came at the end of a long scene.

Four verse lines, some too short, some too long in the quarto,
are strictly decasyllabic in the folio:

Q. Our selfe and Bushie,
    Obserued his courtship to the common people (sc.iv.22–3)
F. Our selfe, and Bushy: heere Bagot and Greene
    Obseru'd his Courtship to the common people (I.iv.23–4)

Q. Three Iudasses, each one thrice worse then Iudas,
    Would they make peace? terrible hel,
    Make war vpon their spotted soules for this (sc.x.132–4)
F. Three Iudasses, each one thrice worse then Iudas,
    Would they make peace? terrible Hell make warre
    Vpon their spotted Soules for this Offence (III.ii.132–4)

Q. Which our prophane houres heere haue throwne downe
    (sc.xiv.25)
F. Which our prophane houres here haue stricken downe (V.i.25)

Q. What newes from Oxford, do these iusts & triumphs hold?
    (sc.xv.52)

7. Pollard noticed those correspondences and supposed that before sending the
copy for the folio to the printer it had been collated with the First Quarto. But if the
First Quarto was printed from a copy of the original it stands to reason that every
time a reading of the promptbook (itself a copy of the original) was substituted it
would be in agreement with the First Quarto.

F. What newes from Oxford? Hold those Iusts & Triumphs?
(V.ii.52)

Some of the stage directions are different in the two texts. In
the First Quarto they were often insufficient; the prompter's work
is now visible in the folio. The number of supers, when left unde-
termined, has been fixed: for instance two ladies-in-waiting have
been assigned to the queen and two assistants to the head gardener
in Act III.sc.iv. The musical effects have been augmented by the
addition of "flourishes" (I.iii.6,248–9; III.ii.1; III.iii.209). In some
cases the military calls have been accompanied with displays of
flags (III.ii.1; III.iii.1).

Lastly there are textual variants. Again, as in *Titus Andronicus,*
a complete list of these is impressive; but most of them are misprints or misreadings, and if those mistakes are set apart there
remain scarcely thirty variants proper (the first word is the reading of Q_1, the second the reading of F): month: time (I.i.157),
throw vp: throw downe (I.i.186), Woodstockes: Glouster (I.ii.1),
right: iust (I.iii.55), aduerse: amaz'd (I.iii.82), paine of life: paine
of death (I.iii.140), grieuous sicke: verie sick (I.iv.54), life-harming: selfe-harming (II.ii.3), cousin: Kinsman (II.iii.125), power:
friends (III.ii.35), light: Lightning (III.ii.43), coward: sluggard
(III.ii.84), and decay: Losse, Decay (III.ii.102), wound: hand
(III.ii.139), nere sit and waile their woes: ne're waile their present
woes (III.ii.178), partie: Faction (III.ii.203), he standes: he is
(III.iii.91), laugh: mock (III.iii.171), tale: fall (V.i.44), men:
friends (V.i.66), wife: Queene (V.i.78), Aumerle: Sonne (V.ii.81),
yeares: dayes (V.iii.21), walke: kneele (V.iii.93), word: Faith
(V.v.13 and 14), checke: heare (V.v.46), (Oxford: Spencer (V.
vi.8).

Among those variants I see only two for which there is some
justification: in I.ii.1 Woodstock, the name by which the duke of
Gloucester was first known, might not have been known to the
readers of the folio, for the modification was evidently made for
them; in V.vi.8 Oxford on the list of the executed conspirators is
an error, for the earl did not take part in the plot, while Spencer
(Thomas Despencer) was really one of the conspirators. One may
wonder why the other variants were ever made. As Pollard justly
said, they are "petty tinkerings, sometimes giving a slightly easier

reading, more often a harmless alternative, but never one which strongly demands assent" (introduction to his publication of Q₃, p. 80). I will go even further: not only were the corrections of the folio uncalled for, but the readings of the quarto are as a rule preferable for they are racier.

It is most unlikely that Shakespeare would have wasted his time making such useless changes. The actors are of course out of the question. There remains only the man who prepared the text of the folio for printing. We have already suspected his unnecessary intervention in the case of *Titus Andronicus*. A similarity of method—the corrections are of the same kind—shows that he is again at work. And his personality which so far has remained vague begins to assume some distinctness. He seems to have been a man of little imagination, puzzled by original expressions, preferring words in current use understandable by anyone. He was not totally devoid of literary pretensions, for he did not hesitate to rewrite after a fashion a verse that was not in accordance with the rules of the time. I do not think he was the prompter, as has been supposed; he must have been a third-rate poetaster. To be sure he had some knowledge of history: he never fails to correct facts that do not agree with what is to be found in the chroniclers, whom he seems to know well, better indeed than Shakespeare did. He has fixed ideas on what should be the language of a person of rank: Richard says (V.i.78) "my wife"; a king does not say "my wife" like a commoner, hence the substitution of "my queen." In a word, this editor is as different as possible from Shakespeare and that is why he wants to modernize that aging writer. Living in the seventeenth century, he is thinking more of future readers of the folio than of the spectators of the Globe. So far he has not done too much havoc, but he is a dangerous collaborator and will have to be watched.

To sum up, the text of the folio has only one advantage: it has the abdication scene, the most important scene in the play, which is missing in the First Quarto, but it lacks some fifty lines which the quarto has. Its defects are due to the combined insufficiencies of the compositor and of an editor without refinement. The text of the quarto is certainly nearer the original text as it was when Shakespeare had completed his revision.

Note on *Thomas of Woodstock*

A MANUSCRIPT preserved in the British Museum (Egerton 1994) contains among other things a play sometimes known as *The First Part of Richard II*, sometimes as *Thomas of Woodstock* from the name of the principal character (the title page is missing). Two or three phrases on the pillage and taxes inflicted upon the nation and the expression "pelting farm" common to the two plays have led some critics to suppose that Shakespeare may have known this play. But those ideas are also mentioned by the chroniclers. Besides, *Richard II* and *Thomas of Woodstock* are very different. *Thomas of Woodstock* begins with the marriage of Richard with Ann of Bohemia (1382) and ends with the murder of the duke of Gloucester in 1397; thus it covers a different period from the Shakespearean version. The chief theme in the action is the revolt of the people and the nobles against Richard's favorites. A lawyer, Tresilian by name, inspires the king's depredations, and the way his emissaries carry out his orders is the occasion for comic scenes that remind one of those in which Jack Cade and his followers appear in *The Contention*. *Thomas of Woodstock* is of no significance for the study of the composition of Shakespeare's *Richard II*.

CHAPTER FOUR. RICHARD III

$\mathcal{R}$ichard III was another of Shakespeare's plays that was among the great successes of its day. It appeared six times in quarto editions: in 1597, 1598, 1602, 1603, 1612, and 1622. These quartos present virtually the same text, for each one save Q_5 is reprinted from its predecessor; hence the first is probably the most authentic version. The folio of 1623 gives on the whole the same text but with a considerable number of differences in details.

THE QUARTO OF 1597

THE MANUSCRIPT was entered on the Stationers' Register on October 20, 1597, by Andrew Wise, the bookseller who had just published *Richard II*, and the first edition appeared in that same year under the title *The Tragedy of King Richard the third. Containing, His treacherous Plots against his brother Clarence: the pittiefull murther of his innocent nephewes: his tyrannicall vsurpation: with the whole course of his detested life, and most deserued death. As it hath beene lately Acted by the Right honourable the Lord Chamberlaine his seruants.*

According to the title page this quarto was issued from the press of Valentine Simmes, who had also printed *Richard II*. But from signature H on a different type was employed, and according to Colonel Frank Isaac, quoted by Greg in his *Editorial Problem in Shakespeare* (p. 88, n. 4), the work from III.vii.54 on was completed by Peter Short.

The manuscript reproduced by this quarto was of the same nature as the one that served as copy for the First Quarto of *Richard II*, and possessed the same characteristics, including that unusual peculiarity of having the proper names of the characters or their titles often abbreviated: Exit Has (I.i.144), Exit Clar. (I.i.

116), manet Gl. (I.ii.228).[1] "Lord" and "My Lord" are almost uniformly shortened to "Lo" and "My Lo."

The stage directions are author's directions: they are simple, mention only the names of the characters, are rarely descriptive and this only when they provide details which the dialogue does not make clear:

Enter Lady Anne with the hearse of Harry the 6 (I.ii.1)

Enter Duke of Glocester and Buckingham in armour (III.v.1)

Enter Rich. with two bishops a lofse (III.vii.94–5)

Enter Buckingham to execution (V.i.1)

Apart from these few cases instructions on the properties and sound effects are scanty. Several entrances are followed by "&c.," leaving to the company the task of fixing the number of supernumeraries (III.i.1; V.iii.18–19,46–7).

This manuscript had been cleared of irregularities in the same way as that of *Richard II*. It contained only four ill-divided lines that may be considered as marginal corrections (II.ii.23–4; IV.ii. 46–7) and but one passage in prose (I.iv.84–161) printed as though it were verse. It did not give the compositor much trouble for I have found only seven misreadings: "loue" for "luth" (I.i.13), "I am strong in fraud" for "I am strongly framed" (I.iv.154), "my eire" for "my deare" (II.ii.71), "Ans" for "Ambo" (II.ii.145), "Ryu" for "Bi"[shop] (III.iv.6), "He laid" for "He liud" (III.v.32), "ease dropper" for "eaues dropper" (V.iii.221); and it is possible that some of those misreadings may have been caused by a moment's inattention on the part of the compositor. It was certainly well written, a fair copy made by a professional scrivener—in fact by the same scrivener who transcribed *Richard II*, for it has eight examples of Ralph Crane's habitual use of parentheses as a mark of punctuation instead of commas (I.i.97,126; I.iii.58,136; III.ii. 104; IV.iv.412; V.v.32).

But here the resemblances cease. We have seen that the manuscript from which the First Quarto of *Richard II* was printed was

1. Cf. I.iii.74,323; II.ii.145; II.iv.1,38; III.i.96; III.i.150–1; III.iv.81–2; III.v.106; IV.i.1; IV.iv.8–9,126,440; V.iii.46–7,117–18,250–1.

The references in this chapter are to the Griggs facsimile (Shakespeare Quarto Facsimiles, 1886, No. 11).

a fair copy of the author's foul papers which had not been adapted
for performance; the manuscript of *Richard III*, on the contrary,
bore many marks of the prompter's work. The rule in the manuscript was to center the entrances; many had been omitted; they
were all added in the space vacant at the end of the verse preceding the entrance:

> I feare our happines is at the highest. *Enter Glocester* (I.iii.41) [2]

or, if the space was not sufficient, at the ends of two consecutive
lines thus:

> To be thus taunted, scorned, and baited at: *Enter Qu.*
> Small ioy haue I in being Englands Queene.   *Margaret* (I.iii.109–10) [3]

It was likewise the prompter who added certain movements or
gestures of the actors, in the same way, at the ends of one or two
lines:

> But twas thy heauenly face that set me on: *Here she lets fall*
> Take vp the sword againe or take vp me   *the sword*   (I.ii.183–4) [4]

Unquestionably, the manuscript from which the First Quarto of
Richard III was printed was a transcript of the company's promptbook; it was probably sold to the bookseller by the actors and for
the same reason that they sold the manuscript of *Richard II*.

ʃ   ʃ   ʃ

IT HAS ALREADY been pointed out by several critics that *Richard
III* is a continuation of *The True Tragedie*. At the end of the latter play, after slaying Henry VI, Gloucester lets it be known in a
monologue that his role is not yet finished, and announces, as
though in a serial, what his first crime will be in a play that is to
follow:

> Clarence, beware, thou keptst me from the light
> But I will sort a pitchie daie for thee.

---

2. Cf. I.iii.16; II.i.94; II.iv.37; III.ii.111; III.iv.23,60; III.v.11; III.vii.57,84; IV.ii.
45,66; V.iii.78.
3. Cf. II.ii.88–9; II.iii.5–6; III.ii.34–5; III.iv.46–7,82–3; III.v.20–1.
4. Cf. I.iv.92,276; III.ii.108–9,113; IV.ii.2–3; IV.iv.150; V.iii.276,302–3.

> For I will buz abroad such prophesies,
> As Edward shall be fearefull of his life,
> And then to purge his feare, Ile be thy death.
> Henry and his sonne are gone, thou Clarence next,
> And by one and one I will dispatch the rest,
> Counting myself but bad, till I be best
>
> (sc.xxv.75–82; 3 *Henry VI* V.vi.84–97)

Richard III does in fact open with a scene in which the duke of Clarence, whose name is George, is taken off to prison by order of the king because Gloucester has spread abroad the rumor that "G." according to a prophecy, will be the murderer of Edward's heirs (I.i.39).

And just as *The True Tragedie* announces what is to happen in the coming play, so *Richard III* recalls some of the most striking incidents in *The True Tragedie*. Thus Act I.sc.ii opens with the removal of the body of Henry VI, whom Gloucester murdered in *The True Tragedie*, and in line 95 Lady Anne invokes the evidence of Queen Margaret, who had seen the blood-stained sword used by Gloucester in dispatching the son of Henry VI—the very weapon with which he had threatened Queen Margaret herself in *The True Tragedie* (sc.xxiv.78). Queen Margaret recalls also the murder of her husband (sc.iv.119–20) and of her son (sc.iv. 270–2). Gloucester for his part mentions Clarence's treachery (I.iii.135–6) and alludes (I.iii.174–87) to the torture undergone by his father, the duke of York, when Queen Margaret placed a crown of paper on his head and gave him a handkerchief wet with the blood of young Rutland (sc.iv.66–70) with which to wipe away his tears. He remembers also (IV.ii.98–102) that Henry VI had foretold (sc.ix.76–82) that young Henry of Richmond would one day be king.

And it is not these links alone that show a connection between the two plays. There are words and phrases that are employed in *Richard III* in a rather particular way as they are in *The True Tragedie* and in *The Contention* as well:

To play the orator (an expression which is found also in Marlowe):

> Feare not, my Lord, Ile play the Orator (*Richard III* III.v.95)
> Full well hath Clifford plaid the Orator (*The True Tragedie* vi.42)

Off with his head:

> Off with his head. Now by Saint Paule
> > (*Richard III* III.iv.78)
> Off with the crowne, and with the crowne his head
> > (*The True Tragedie* iv.92)
> Off with his head and set it on York gates (*ibid.iv.*164)

Troublous (to describe the uncertainties of the political situation):

> I feare, I feare, twill prooue a troublous world (*Richard III* II.iii.5)
> Then masters looke to see a troublous world (*ibid.* II.iii.8)
> But in this troublous time, whats to be done?
> > (*The True Tragedie* v.127)

Empty air:

> Kept in my soule, and would not let it foorth,
> To seeke the emptie vast and wandering aire (*Richard III* I.iv.37–8)
> And dead mens cries do fill the emptie aire (*The Contention* xxii.12)

Withered (applied to Richard's shrunken arm):

> behold mine arm
> Is like a blasted sapling withered vp (*Richard III* III.iv.70–1)
> To drie mine arme vp, like a withered shrub
> > (*The True Tragedie* xii.122)

Burthened (applied to the feelings):

> Vsurpe the iust proportion of my sorrow,
> Now thy proud necke, beares halfe my burthened yoke
> > (*Richard III* IV.iv.110–11)
> And methinks my burthened heart would breake
> > (*The Contention* x.156)

Protector (in a pun):

> I meane the Lord Protector.
> The Lord protect him from that Kinglie title
> > (*Richard III* IV.i.19–20)
> Protector, protect thyself (*The Contention* x.48)

Thus a mere reading of *Richard III* suggests the existence of another play, a sequel to *The True Tragedie* and written by the same authors, from which the Shakespearean play derives its subject and even some stylistic peculiarities.

A study of the versification and style fully confirms this presupposition. There are abundant traces of the versification of author A:

1. Excessive use of trochaic feet: [5]

	Trochaic feet	Feet	Percentages
I.i.62–78	6	85	7.0
84–116	10	165	6.0
I.ii.141–51	8	55	14.5
I.iii.188–214	10	135	7.4
320–338	10	95	10.5
II.i.99–120	12	110	10.9
II.ii.79–111	11	102	10.7
II.iii.1–47	17	225	7.5
III.v.72–102	17	152	11.1
IV.i.66–97	14	160	8.7
IV.ii.68–96	14	133	10.5
IV.iv.9–34	9	100	9.0
196–287	26	380	6.8
343–68	12	130	9.2
500–19	11	101	10.8
IV.v.1–20	6	95	6.3
V.i.1–29	13	141	9.2
V.ii.1–24	11	120	9.1
V.iii.1–18	11	87	12.6
47–82	27	158	17.0
117–76	22	293	7.5
177–222	19	224	8.4
V.iv.1–13	5	65	7.6

2. Verse lines of irregular length from one foot to seven feet.[6]

5. The following list is far from being complete; I have not included passages too short to give safe percentages.

6. One foot: I.i.210; I.iii.279; II.ii.2,32; III.i.124; III.vii.241; IV.iii.44; IV.iv.266, 442,452–3; IV.v.20; V.iii.67,207. Two feet: I.i.134; I.ii.219; I.iii.92,99,137; II.ii.106, 145; II.iii.6; II.iv.32,37,45; III.i.59,80,90,112,143,189; III.ii.1,2,4,42; III.iv.36; III.v. 5,16,27,40,97; III.vii.83; IV.i.14,18; IV.ii.67,85,114; IV.iii.35; IV.iv.154,257,387; V.i. 11; V.iii.4,44,47,55,58,208,223,276. Three feet: I.ii.193–203; I.iv.281; II.i.28; II.iii. 46; II.iv.43,68; III.i.169; III.ii.5,61,111,124; III.iv.33; III.v.15,17; III.vii.43; IV.i.36; IV.ii.21,41,50,83,89,102,111,113; IV.iv.100,422,457; V.i.2; V.iii.226,235,344. Four feet: I.i.67,92,142–3; I.iii.308,323; I.iv.276; II.i.138; II.ii.23,60; II.iii.16; II.iv.13,21, 63; III.i.74,136,149; III.ii.3,9,17,60,92,96,108,119,120; III.iv.37,60,61,77,78; III.v. 18,21,72; III.vi.11; III.vii.41,59,70,82,114,198; IV.i.25,38,57; IV.ii.11,20,81,98,117; IV.iv.75,388,430,521; IV.v.8; V.iii.53,62,143,148,220,298,303,343. Six feet: I.i.105;

3. Trisyllabic feet:

I.i.71,95,98,103
I.ii.101,192,226
I.iii.280,313,350
I.iv.64,249,276
II.i.39,108
II.ii.25,105
II.iii.28
II.iv.13,20,26,63
III.i.52,149,191
III.ii.17,61,82,91,92,99,100,108
III.iv.9,28,45,52,54,61,77
III.v.35,36,108,109
III.vii.3,9,45,52,55,81,221,229,240
IV.ii.71,81,124
IV.iv.183,269,496,506,513
V.i.2
V.iii.7,75,186,220
V.v.11

4. Commonplace style vulgarized by too many interjections and exclamations such as: alack, alas, ay me, oh, ah, why, what, well, now, come, come come, yea, nay, go to, lo, tush, tut, fie, soft, how now, marry, faith, zounds, by saint Paul, by heaven.[7]

5. Obsolescent expressions and colloquialisms: moe (IV.v.13), spake (II.i.108; III.vii.33), God he knows (III.vii.235), Thy Edward, he is dead, Yong Yorke, he is but boote, Thy Clarence he is dead (IV.iv.63,65,67).

I.ii.64,141,238; I.iii.344; I.iv.65,98,218; II.i.133; II.ii.24; II.iii.8; II.iv.25; III.i.37,39, 158,192,198; III.ii.46,80,114; III.iii.23; III.iv.9; III.v.6; III.vi.9; III.vii.55,58; IV.i. 27; IV.ii.45,71; IV.iv.361,368,512,513,523,537; V.iii.22,29,52,68,72,78,187,196,209, 280,299,305,319. Seven feet: II.i.55; III.ii.112; III.iv.12,48; III.v.70; III.vii.7,131; IV.iv.235.

7. Cf. I.i.47,49,62,71,114,138,139; I.ii.12,36,41,44,55,62,63,78,89,91,92,104,140, 142,175,180,182,188,197,239; I.iii.11,45,74,98,113,126,163,183,188,196,234,237,239, 257,263,266,271,280,289,297,299,313,339,340,350; I.iv.2,43,44,66,88,89,101,111, 124,129,149,154,158,162,232,239,247; II.i.9,77,131,133,137; II.ii.29,34,47,71,72,80, 86; II.iii.27,31; II.iv.16,21,27,35,49,66,73; III.i.22,102,106,116,118,140,143,149,154, 157,199; III.ii.66,74,90,111,114,117,119; III.i.1,9,18,23; III.iv.9,22,58,78,89,94,98; III.v.1,5,21,33,40,47,85; III.vi.10; III.vii.1,2,23,56,58,71,81,82,204,219,220,224,246; IV.i.32,34,39,53,54,64,71,78,88; IV.ii.12,13,14,22,45,73,88,114,116,121,122,125; IV. iii.9,16; IV.iv.22,31,34,35,59,79,116,124,179,180,205,215,284,362,366,374,377,448, 457,460,467,496,515; V.i.12,28; V.iii.5,11,50,108,169,178,185,186,189,208,212,214, 215,236,285,289.

It is not so easy to distinguish the part written by author B in the text that has come down to us. To be sure, there are many passages in which the rhythm is exceptionally spondaic, but nearly all are too short to furnish reliable percentages. In some scenes, notably in those marked by a tone of lamentation or malediction, a vigorous, declamatory, hyperbolic verse recalling author B's imitation of Marlowe's style is apparent. Richard's oration to his army (V.iii.314–41) is fairly representative of this kind, but even here some feminine endings and a few enjambments break up the monotonous stiffness characteristic of author B's verse. His versification—suppleness and poetic pulsation set apart—had regularity after all, in common with Shakespeare's. It did not require such a thorough recasting of the rhythm as the versification of author A, and I am convinced that many passages which could have been attributed to him are today no longer recognizable beneath the sweetness and flexibility with which Shakespeare must have endowed them.

For no matter what some critics have said, Shakespeare revised that pre-Shakespearean *Richard III* just as he revised the other plays that I have been discussing so far. This is clear from the presence of his habitual mannerisms and images.

MANNERISMS

1. Division of the thought into symmetical parts of more or less equal length:

> With curses in her mouth, teares in her eies (I.ii.233)
>
> So full of vgly sights, of gastly dreames (I.iv.3) [8]

2. Repetition of a word or grammatical form to accentuate the symmetrical construction:

> Our bruised armes hung vp for monuments,
> Our sterne alarmes changd to merry meetings,
> Our dreadfull marches to delightfull measures (I.i.6–8)

8. Cf. I.ii.52; I.iii.29; I.iv.172; II.i.50; II.ii.24,35,55,61,112; III.iv.30; III.v.100; III.vii.16,25,26,32,39,40,100,189,226,231,235,247; IV.iii.7; IV.iv.114,151,206,464, 491; V.iii.54, 264; V.v.34.

> Curst be the hand that made these fatall holes,
> Curst be the heart that had the heart to doe it (I.ii.14–15) [9]

3. Marked preference for the association of two words expressing two aspects of the same idea and connected by a conjunction:

> And that so lamely and vnfashionable (I.i.22)
>
> As if thou wert distraught and mad with terror (III.v.4) [1]

4. Antitheses:

> Now is the winter of our discontent
> Made glorious summer by this sonne of Yorke (I.i.1–2)
>
> He cannot liue I hope, and must not die (I.i.145) [2]

5. Concetti:

a. Repetition of the sound of a word or jingle:

> Curst be the heart that had the heart to do it (I.ii.15)
>
> More direfull hap betide that hated wretch,
> That makes vs wretched by the death of thee (I.ii.17–18) [3]

b. Concetti proper in the Italian manner:

> Inestimable stones, vnualued Iewels,
> Some lay in dead mens sculs, and in those holes,
> Where eies did once inhabite, there were crept

9. Cf. I.ii.62–3,228–9; I.iii.56,228–33; I.iv.22–3,27,217,229–30; II.ii.74–9; III.i.
158–9; III.iii.17–18; III.vii.118–21; IV.i.92–4; IV.iv.40–5,63–4,92–6,98–102,169–71,
364–5,370–2,470–1; V.v.25–6.
1. Cf.   I.i.33,36,54,91,92,136,161;   I.ii.22,23,59,60,136,171;   I.iii.5,47,48,51,55,
141,281; I.iv.213,264; II.i.117; II.ii.18,34; II.iii.14,28; II.iv.52,53,55,59,63–4; III.i.5,
31,45,54,67,134,153; III.ii.31; III.iii.10; III.iv.49,54,93; III.v.1,23,41,63; III.vii.14,
38,92,138,172,175,185,187,188,205,208,217,234; IV.i.95; IV.iii.1,20; IV.iv.18,160,
168,169,170,193,204,243,347,353,362,363,397,416,449,512,513,538; IV.v.13; V.ii.6;
V.iii.24,46,79,126,127,128,130,135,138,140,144,146,148,150,153,154,163,171,238.
2. Cf. I.i.10–13,28–31,36–7; I.iii.69,73–4,81–4,87–8,89–90,91–2,108–9,153,168; I.
iii.23–4, 338; I.iv.77,79,172,232,255; II.i.8,9–10,35,50,88–9,102–3; II.ii.43,81; III.i.
93,146–7; III.iv.54; III.vii.72–7; IV.i.73; IV.iv.16,26,27,29,86,98–102,118–22,124,
201,343–4,353–4,401; V.i.22; V.iii.117.
3. Cf. I.ii.60–1,80,87–8,190,200–1,206; I.iii.7–8,81–2,94–100,319; I.iv.274; II.i.4,
92; II.ii.11; II.iv.65; III.i.85–6, 87; III.ii.43–4; IV.iv.217–20,355–6,420–1,426–7; V.i.
29; V.iii.185–90,193–5,196–8,202–3,266.

As twere in scorne of eies reflecting gems,
Which woed the slimy bottome of the deepe,
And mockt the dead bones that lay scattered by (I.iv.27–33) [4]

6. Compound words after the Greek and Latin manner: grim-visagde (I.i.9), night-walking (I.i.72), hell-gouernd (I.ii.67), false boading (I.iii.247), numbcold (II.i.117), hart-sorrowing (II.ii.112), all-ending (III.i.78), boare-speare (III.ii.74), care-crazd (III.vii.184), beauty-waining (III.vii.185), foule-fac't (III.vii.231), iron witted (IV.ii.28), teare falling (IV.ii.66), arch-act (IV.iii.2), snail-pact (IV.iii.53), woe-wearied (IV.iv.18), hel-hound (IV.iv.48), bunch-backt (IV.iv.81), toong-tide (IV.iv.132), al-seer (V.i.20), smooth-faste (V.v.33).

7. French words or words of French consonance: semblance (II.ii.51), complots (III.i.192,200), closure (III.iii.11), fete (V.iii.19).[5]

IMAGES

I.i.1–4   Now is the winter of our discontent,
            Made glorious summer by this sonne of Yorke:
            And all the cloudes that lowrd vpon our house,
            In the deepe bosome of the Ocean buried

9   Grim-visagde warre, hath smoothde his wrinkled front

12–13   He capers nimbly in a Ladies chamber
            To the lasciuious pleasing of a loue

17   To strut before a wanton ambling Nymph

147–8   Ile in to vrge his hatred more to Clarence,
            Which lies well steeld with weighty arguments

I.ii.12–13 Lo in those windowes that let foorth thy life,
            I powre the helplesse balme of my poore eies

55–6   Oh gentlemen see, see dead Henries woundes,
            Open their congeald mouthes and bleede a fresh

204–5   Looke how this ring incompasseth thy finger,
            Euen so thy breast incloseth my poore heart

4. Cf. I.iv.36–41; IV.iii.12–13.
5. "Fete" is the reading in the quarto; the folio has "set," and modern editors have followed the latter. But "fete" or "fête" is the French word for "feast" and makes perfect sense.

I.iii.49   Ducke with French nods and apish courtesie

122–3   I was a packhorse in his great affaires,
A weeder out of his proud aduersaries

140   I would to God my heart were flint like Edwards

158–9   Heare me you wrangling Pyrats that fall out,
In sharing that which you haue pild from me

259–60   They that stand high haue many blast to shake them,
And if they fall they dash themselues to pieces

264–5   Our aiery buildeth in the Cedars top,
And dallies with the winde, and scornes the sunne

267–9   Witnes my son, now in the shade of death,
Whose bright outshining beames, thy cloudy wrath
Hath in eternall darkenes foulded vp

I.iv.247–8   O doe not slaunder him for he is kind,
Right as snow in haruest, thou deceiu'st thy selfe

II.ii.51–4   But now two mirrours of his Princely semblance,
Are crackt in pieces by malignant death:
And I for comfort haue but one false glasse,
Which grieues me when I see my shame in him

68–70   All springs reduce their currents to mine eies,
That I being gouernd by the watry moane,
May send foorth plenteous teares to drowne the world

101–2   al of vs haue cause
To waile the dimming of our shining starre

148–9   For by the way Ile sort occasion,
As index to the story we late talkt of

II.iii.33   When great leaues fall, the winter is at hand

44   The waters swell before a boistrous storme

III.ii.87–8   And they indeed had no cause to mistrust:
But yet you see how soone the day ouercast

III.iv.86–8   Three times to day, my footecloth horse did stumble,
And startled when he lookt vpon the tower,
As loath to beare me to the slaughterhouse

100–3   Who buildes his hopes in aire of your faire lookes,
Liues like a drunken sayler on a mast,

Ready with euery nod to tumble downe
Into the fatall bowels of the deepe

III.v.29   So smoothe he daubd his vice with shew of vertue

95–7   Feare not, my Lord, Ile play the Orator,
As if the golden fee for which I pleade
Were for my slefe

III.vii.125–6   This noble Ile doth want her proper limbes,
Her face defac't with scars of infamie

128–9   And almost shouldred in the swallowing gulph,
Of blind forgetfulnesse and darke obliuion

162–4   Beeing a Barke to brooke no mightie sea,
Then in my greatnes couet to be hid
And in the vapour of my glorie smotherd

167–8   The roiall tree hath left vs roiall fruit,
Which mellowed by the stealing houres of time [6]

185–7   A beauty-waining and distressed widow,
Euen in the afternoone of her best daies
Made prise and purchase of his lustfull eye

228–9   Since you will buckle fortune on my backe,
To beare her burthen whether I will or no

231–2   But if blacke scandale of foule-fac't reproch
Attend the sequell of your imposition

IV.i.53   O ill dispersing winde of miserie

83–4   For neuer yet, one houre in his bed,
Haue I enioyed the golden dew of sleepe

IV.ii.62   Or else my kingdome stands on brittle glasse

IV.iii.12–13   Their lips were foure red Roses on a stalke,
Which in their summer beautie kist each other

51–4   Come I haue heard that feareful commenting,
Is leaden seruitour to dull delaie,
Delaie leades impotent and snaile-pact beggerie
Then fierie expedition be my wing

IV.iv.1–2   So now prosperitie begins to mellow
And drop into the rotten mouth of Death

6. The first line was probably in the pre-Shakespearean play; only the melodious
line is Shakespeare's addition.

9-10   Ah my young princes, ah my tender babes!
        My vnblowne flowers, new appearing sweets

15-16   saie that right for right,
        Hath dimd your infant morne, to aged night

37   And let my woes frowne on the vpper hand

58   And makes her puefellow with others mone

111-13 Now thy proud necke, beares halfe my burthened yoke,
        From which, euen here, I slippe my wearie necke,
        And leaue the burthen of it all on thee

127-30 Windie atturnies to your Client woes,
        Aerie succeeders of intestate ioies,
        Poore breathing Orators of miseries,
        Let them haue scope

132-4   If so, then be not toong-tide, go with me
        And in the breath of bitter words lets smother
        My damned sonne

195   Shame serues thy life, and doth thy death attend

208   Throw ouer her the vale of infamie

384-6   And both the princes had bene breathing heere,
        Which now, two tender plaie-fellowes for dust,
        Thy broken faith, hath made a praie for wormes

413   Be the atturney of my loue to her

V.ii.2 Bruisd vnderneath the yoake of tyrannie

7-10   The wretched, bloudie, and vsurping bore,
        That spoild your somer-fieldes, and fruitfull vines,
        Swils your warme bloud like wash, and makes his trough,
        In your inboweld bosomes

23   True hope is swift, and flies with Swallowes wings

V.iii.19-21 The wearie sonne hath made a golden fete,
        And by the bright tracke of his fierie Carre,
        Giues signall of a goodlie day to morrow

85-6   The silent houres steale on,
        And flakie darkenesse breakes within the east

116   Eare I let fal the windowes of mine eies

209-10   the earlie village cocke,
        Hath twise done salutation to the morne

241–2   The praiers of holy Saints and wronged soules,
        Like high reard bulwarkes, stand before our faces

250–1   A base foule stone, made precious by the foile,
        Of Englands chaire, where he is falsely set

282–4   The sunne will nor be seene to day,
        The skie doeth frowne, and lowre vpon our armie,
        I would these dewie teares were from the ground

317–18 A scum of Brittains and base lacky pesants,
        Whom their orecloied country vomits forth

Mannerisms and images are distributed among the different scenes as follows:

I.i   17 mannerisms: 1–2,6–8,9,10–13,16,22,28–31,33,36,36–7,54,72,
162 lines   91,92,136,145,161
          5 images: 1–4,9,12–13,17,147–8

I.ii   28 mannerisms: 14–15, 15, 17–18,22,23,52,59,60,60–1,62–3,67,
259 lines   69,73–4,80,81–4,87–8,89–90,91–2,108–9,136,153,168,171,
             190,200–1,206,228–9,233
          3 images: 12–13,55–6,204–5

I.iii   17 mannerisms: 5,7–8,23–4,29,47,48,51,55,56,81–2,94–100,141,
350 lines   228–33,247,281,319,338
          7 images: 49,122–3,140,158–9,259–60,264–5,267–9

I.iv   15 mannerisms: 3,22–3,27,27–33,36–41,77,79,172,213,217,229–
277 lines   30,232,255,264,274
          1 image: 247–8

II.i   10 mannerisms: 4,8,9–10,35,50,54,88–9,92,102–3,117
138 lines 0 images

II.ii   12 mannerisms: 11,18,24,34,35,43,51,55,61,74–9,81,112
133 lines 4 images: 51–4,68–70,101–2,148–9

II.iii   2 mannerisms: 14,28
47 lines   2 images: 33,44

II.iv   7 mannerisms: 52,53,55,59,63–4,65,69
72 lines   0 images

III.i   15 mannerisms: 5,31,45,54,67,78,85–6,87,93,134,146–7,153,
197 lines   158–9,192,200
          0 images

III.ii   3 mannerisms: 31,43–4,74
123 lines 1 image: 87–8

III.iii   3 mannerisms: 10,11,17–18
23 lines   0 images

III.iv   4 mannerisms: 30,49,54,93
105 lines 2 images: 86–8,100–3

III.v   6 mannerisms: 1,4,23,41,63,100
104 lines 2 images: 29,95–7

III.vi   0 mannerisms
14 lines   0 images

III.vii   27 mannerisms: 14,16,25–6,32,38,39,40,72–7,92,100,118–21,
227 lines   138,172,175,184,185,187,188,189,205,208,217,226,231,234,
              235,247
           7 images: 125–6,128–9,162–4,167–8,185–7,228–9,231–2

IV.i   3 mannerisms: 73,92–4,95
90 lines   2 images: 53,83

IV.ii   2 mannerisms: 28,66
125 lines 1 image: 62

IV.iii   6 mannerisms: 1,2,7,12–13,20,53
57 lines   2 images: 12–13,51–4

IV.iv   49 mannerisms: 16,18,26,27,29,40–5,48,63–4,81,86,92–6,98–
455 lines   102,114,118–22,124,132,149,151,160,168,169,170,193,201,
              204,206,217–20,243,343–4,347,353,353–4,355–6,362,363,
              364–5,370–2,397,401,416,420,426–7,449,464,470–1,491,512,
              513,538
           12 images: 1–2,9–10,15–16,37,58,111–13,127–30,132–4,195,
              208,384–6,413

IV.v   1 mannerism: 13
20 lines   0 images

V.i   3 mannerisms: 20,22,29
29 lines   0 images

V.ii   1 mannerism: 6
24 lines   3 images: 2,7–10,23

V.iii   28 mannerisms: 19,24,46,54,79,117,126,127,128,130,135,138,
349 lines   140,144,146,148,150,154,163,171,185–90,193–5,196–8,202–
              3,238,264,266,334
           9 images: 19–21,85–6,86,116,209–10,241–2,250–1,282–3,318

V.iv   0 mannerisms
13 lines   0 images

V.v   3 mannerisms: 25–6,33,34
41 lines   0 images

The mannerisms are distributed among all the scenes except
two, III.vi and V.iv, which are very short (14 and 13 lines respectively): Shakespeare's revision has therefore been a total one from
beginning to end, and the number of mannerisms is rather high
(262), much higher than in *Richard II* (156). The images, on the
other hand, are remarkably few: 62 in 3536 lines, hardly more than
half the number in *Richard II*, which has 125 in only 2357 lines.
They are scattered in small groups, often singly, throughout only
17 scenes out of the 25 into which modern editions are divided. As
in *Titus Andronicus* they are short and to the point, metaphors
rather than pictures. There are few of those vignettes, typical of
the poet whose mind was full of visions of the world, that Shakespeare loved to insert in the dialogue of *2 Henry VI*. Shakespeare's
imagination, which heretofore had been prodigal of its riches, appears to have suffered a partial eclipse.[7]

The analysis of the rhythmical variations will help us to define
and explain this phenomenon.

I. There are only seven passages of any length with characteristically pre-Shakespearean versification and bearing no trace of
revision by Shakespeare that can be supposed to have been retained verbatim from the pre-Shakespearean play:

I.iii.339–55   Richard gives his instructions to the murderers of Clarence
                Trochees 1.2%, spondees 6.1%, 1 trisyllabic foot
II.iv.1–37   Young duke of York makes smart remarks about his uncle
                Richard
                Trochees 4.4%, spondees 5.3%, 3 trisyllabic feet
III.vi.1–14   Remarks of the scrivener who had copied the indictment rela-
                tive to Hasting's execution

7. Like *The Contention* and *The True Tragedie*, *Richard III* comparisons borrowed for the most part from books of husbandry—arboriculture (I.iii.259–60,263–5;
II.ii.41–2; II.iii.33; III.iv.70–1), gardening (I.iii.123; II.iv.12; III.i.103; III.vii.167,
216), harvesting (I.ii.248; I.iv.249; II.ii.115–16; V.ii.8,15). Bestiaries furnished a
long list of cruel or repugnant animals that were insultingly identified with Richard:
the wolf (IV.i.23), the tiger (II.iv.50), the wild boar (III.ii.11,28–9,33; IV.v.2; V.ii.
7), the hog (V.ii.10), the cockatrice (IV.i.55–6), the spider (I.ii.10; I.iii.242; IV.iv.
81), the hedgehog (I.ii.102), the toad (I.ii.19; I.iii.240; IV.iv.145), the dog (IV.iv.
49,78; V.v.2), the cur (IV.iv.56), the owl (IV.iv.509). These Shakespeare found in
the pre-Shakespearean play.

Trochees 2.8%, spondees 7.1%

IV.ii.67–85   Tyrrell agrees to kill Edward's children

Trochees 8.0%, spondees 4.1%, 2 trisyllabic feet

86–126   Buckingham claims the reward promised by Richard

Trochees 5.7%, spondees 2.6%, 1 trisyllabic foot

V.iii.1–18   Richard pitches his tent in Bosworth Field

Trochees 12.6%, spondees 5.7%

V.iv.1–13   Richard's courage in battle

Trochees 7.5%, spondees 1.5%

These passages total 158 verse lines.

    II. Thirty-five passages totaling 1680 verse lines seem to have been slightly modified:

I.i.42–116   Richard meets Clarence who is being led to the Tower

Trochees 5.1%, spondees 2.4%, 4 trisyllabic feet, 4 mannerisms, 0 images

I.iii.111–87   Queen Margaret rebukes Richard for his crimes

Trochees 4.4%, spondees 2.7%, 1 mannerism, 3 images

188–251   Queen Margaret's imprecations

Trochees 5.0%, spondees 6.2%, 2 mannerisms, 0 images

304–23   Richard hypocritically confesses he was wrong

Trochees 5.5%, spondees 3.3%, 1 mannerism, 0 images

324–38   Richard is proud of his skill in dissimulating

Trochees 9.3%, spondees 1.3%, 1 mannerism, 0 images

I.iv.166–99   Clarence argues with his murderers

Trochees 4.0%, spondees 1.3%, 1 mannerism, 0 images

238–90   The murderers tell Clarence, who cannot believe it, that they have been sent by Richard

Trochees 3.9%, spondees 2.1%, 2 trisyllabic feet, 3 mannerisms, 1 image

II.i.95–139   King Edward's lamentations on hearing that Clarence is dead

Trochees 6.1%, spondees 3.0%, 1 trisyllabic foot, 2 mannerisms, 0 images

II.ii.1–32   The duchess of York tells Clarence's children of their father's death

Trochees 4.7%, spondees 3.4%, 1 trisyllabic foot, 3 mannerisms, 0 images

66–154   Lamentations of the duchess of York and of the queen; Richard's insolence to his mother; Buckingham suggests sending for the heir to the throne

Trochees 6.2%, spondees 5.5%, 1 trisyllabic foot, 3 mannerisms, 3 images

II.iii.1–47   Citizens comment on the news

Trochees 7.5%, spondees 6.2%, 1 trisyllabic foot, 2 mannerisms, 2 images

III.i.95–150 The young duke of York wittily scoffs at Richard
Trochees 4.2%, spondees 2.6%, 1 trisyllabic foot, 2 mannerisms, 0 images

151–200 Richard sends Catesby to sound Hastings
Trochees 4.2%, spondees 3.8%, 1 trisyllabic foot, 4 mannerisms, 0 images

III.ii.74–124 Hastings believes himself more powerful than ever
Trochees 5.0%, spondees 3.7%, 6 trisyllabic feet, 1 mannerism, 1 image

III.iv.1–43 Meeting of the council
Trochees 0.9%, spondees 2.3%, 2 trisyllabic feet, 1 mannerism, 0 images

44–81 Richard accuses the queen and Lady Shore of witchcraft; he gives orders to have Hastings beheaded
Trochees 5.9%, spondees 1.0%, 5 trisyllabic feet, 2 mannerisms, 0 images

82–109 Hastings realizes that Margaret's curse has come home to him
Trochees 5.0%, spondees 4.1%, 1 mannerism, 1 image

III.v.1–40 Richard convinces the lord mayor of London that Hastings is a traitor
Trochees 5.7%, spondees 5.2%, 2 trisyllabic feet, 3 mannerisms, 1 image

72–109 Richard sends Buckingham to win over the mayor and the citizens
Trochees 9.8%, spondees 2.3%, 2 trisyllabic feet, 1 mannerism, 1 image

IV.i.1–97 The duchess of York, Lady Anne, and the queen meet before the Tower of London; lamentations of the three women
Trochees 5.3%, spondees 6.2%, 3 mannerisms, 2 images

IV.ii.1–65 Richard gives Buckingham to understand that he wants to be rid of Edward's children; Buckingham being cold to the idea, he sends for Tyrrell
Trochees 5.6%, spondees 4.6%, 1 mannerism, 1 image

IV.iii.44–57 Receiving bad news, Richard decides on prompt action
Trochees 3.0%, spondees 7.5%, 1 mannerism, 1 image

IV.iv.196–368 Richard offers to marry the queen's daughter, Elizabeth
Trochees 12.3%, spondees 5.5%, 1 trisyllabic foot, 13 mannerisms, 1 image

433–57 Hearing that Richmond has arrived Richard is somewhat bewildered
Trochees 5.4%, spondees 3.6%, 1 mannerism, 0 images

500–40   Bad news continues to arrive; Richard's agitation and decision
         Trochees 8.8%, spondees 5.3%, 1 trisyllabic foot, 3 mannerisms, 0 images
IV.v.1–20 Stanley notifies Richmond that he cannot help him
         Trochees 6.3%, spondees 4.2%, 1 mannerism, 0 images
V.i.1–29   Execution of Buckingham
         Trochees 8.2%, spondees 6.4%, 1 trisyllabic foot, 3 mannerisms, 0 images
V.ii.1–24 Richmond encourages his followers
         Trochees 9.1%, spondees 7.5%, 1 mannerism, 3 images
V.iii.19–46 Richmond sends Blunt to Stanley with a letter and prepares for battle
         Trochees 6.5%, spondees 8.9%, 3 mannerisms, 1 image
47–78   Richard's vigil before the battle
         Trochees 16.8%, spondees 5.0%, 2 trisyllabic feet, 1 mannerism, 0 images
118–76   The ghosts of Richard's victims pass judgment on him and encourage Richmond
         Trochees 7.5%, spondees 4.7%, 14 mannerisms, 0 images [8]
177–222 Richard wakes up, profoundly stirred by the visitation of the ghosts
         Trochees 8.4%, spondees 7.3%, 2 trisyllabic feet, 4 mannerisms, 1 image
271–313 Richard courageously prepares for battle
         Trochees 4.2%, spondees 3.4%, 0 mannerisms, 1 image
314–51   Richard's oration to his soldiers
         Trochees 5.8%, spondees 6.3%, 1 mannerism, 1 image
V.v.1–41   Richmond kills Richard and is crowned king; end of the Wars of the Roses
         Trochees 5.3%, spondees 5.3%, 1 trisyllabic foot, 3 mannerisms, 0 images

III. Nine passages totaling 573 verse lines seem to have been more substantially modified by Shakespeare, but they have preserved many traces of author A:

I.ii.1–32 Lady Anne accompanies the body of Henry VI
         Trochees 5.1%, spondees 3.7%, 5 mannerisms, 1 image
33–109   Richard refutes the accusations of Lady Anne
         Trochees 4.3%, spondees 3.5%, 1 trisyllabic foot, 14 mannerisms, 1 image
110–227 Richard declares his love for Lady Anne

8. The large number of mannerisms in this passage results from a repetition of the same form of curse; Shakespeare certainly modified the passage only slightly.

Trochees 2.9%, spondees 2.3%, 2 trisyllabic feet, 7 mannerisms, 0 images

III.vii.1–58   Buckingham describes the way the citizens received his speech
Trochees 5.7%, spondees 4.1%, 5 trisyllabic feet, 7 mannerisms, 0 images

220–47   Richard accepts the burden which the citizens buckle on his
back
Trochees 3.8%, spondees 5.3%, 3 trisyllabic feet, 5 mannerisms, 2 images

IV.iii.1–23   Tyrrell describes the murder of Edward's children
Trochees 3.4%, spondees 6.9%, 5 mannerisms, 1 image

IV.iv.1–135   Lamentations of Queen Margaret, Queen Elizabeth, and the
duchess of York
Trochees 4.9%, spondees 5.5%, 16 mannerisms, 8 images

136–95   The duchess of York curses Richard
Trochees 5.0%, spondees 4.3%, 1 trisyllabic foot, 7 mannerisms, 1 image

458–99   Richard suspects Stanley
Trochees 4.4%, spondees 5.3%, 1 trisyllabic foot, 3 mannerisms, 0 images

IV. Twenty-one passages totaling 1125 verse lines have percentages of rhythmic variations that are distinctly Shakespearean.
A few have retained a trisyllabic foot, which proves that the passage was in the pre-Shakespearean play and was merely rewritten;
in all the other cases it was probably added or, at least, constitutes
an important amplification:

I.i.1–41   Richard's monologue
Trochees 2.9%, spondees 4.3%, 10 mannerisms, 4 images

117–44   Richard congratulates Hastings on having been set at
liberty
Trochees 3.8%, spondees 3.8%, 1 mannerism, 0 images

145–62   Richard discloses his plan in a monologue
Trochees 3.3%, spondees 3.3%, 2 mannerisms, 1 image

I.ii.228–64   Richard's monologue
Trochees 3.8%, spondees 3.8%, 1 trisyllabic foot, 2 mannerisms, 0 images

I.iii.1–41   The king's illness makes the queen anxious
Trochees 3.4%, spondees 3.9%, 1 trisyllabic foot, 4 mannerisms, 0 images

42–110   Richard complains of the hostility of the queen and of her
family
Trochees 3.5%, spondees 4.4%, 7 mannerisms, 1 image

255–303   Queen Margaret tells Buckingham that she does not include him in her curse
Trochees 3.7%, spondees 3.7%, 1 trisyllabic foot, 1 mannerism, 3 images

I.iv.1–83   Clarence's dream
Trochees 2.8%, spondees 3.9%, 1 trisyllabic foot, 7 mannerisms, 0 images

200–37   Clarence threatens his murderers with God's punishment
Trochees 1.6%, spondees 3.2%, 4 mannerisms, 0 images

II.i.1–94   Reconciliation scene; Richard announces that Clarence is
dead
Trochees 3.2%, spondees 4.5%, 1 trisyllabic foot, 8 mannerisms, 0 images

II.ii.34–65   Grief of the queen at the king's death
Trochees 2.5%, spondees 3.1%, 6 mannerisms, 1 image

II.iv.38–73   The queen learns that Rivers and Grey have been sent to
Pomfret
Trochees 3.4%, spondees 3.4%, 1 trisyllabic foot, 7 man-
nerisms, 0 images

III.i.1–94   The heir to the throne shows his intelligence and wisdom
Trochees 3.0%, spondees 4.1%, 1 trisyllabic foot, 9 mannerisms, 0 images

III.ii.1–73   Catesby sounds Hastings
Trochees 2.6%, spondees 3.8%, 2 trisyllabic feet, 2 mannerisms, 0 images

III.iii.1–25   Execution of Rivers, Grey, and Vaughan
Trochees 1.7%, spondees 3.4%, 3 mannerisms, 0 images

III.v.41–70   Richard deludes the lord mayor
Trochees 1.3%, spondees 2.6%, 2 mannerisms, 0 images

III.vii.59–219   Richard has to be pressed to accept the crown
Trochees 2.4%, spondees 2.7%, 2 trisyllabic feet, 15 mannerisms, 5 images

IV.iii.24–43   Richard plans to marry Princess Elizabeth
Trochees 2.0%, spondees 2.0%; this passage has no mannerisms and no images, due probably to its shortness

IV.iv.369–431   Richard asks the queen for Princess Elizabeth's hand in
marriage
Trochees 3.8%, spondees 3.8%, 6 mannerisms, 2 images

V.iii.83–117   Derby brings news from Richmond's mother
Trochees 3.4%, spondees 4.5%, 1 mannerism, 3 images

223–270   Richmond's oration to his soldiers
Trochees 4.2%, spondees 4.2%, 3 mannerisms, 2 images

The first class, containing the passages of the old play which
seem to have been retained verbatim, is not important and does

252

not contradict the impression formed from the tabulation on pages 244–6 that the revision covered practically the whole play. The class of passages which seem to have been rewritten or added by Shakespeare represents 1125 lines out of 3536 or about a third of the play. The class which is the most important is that of the passages slightly modified, 1680 lines; and if we add the 573 lines of class III, passages more thoroughly modified, we reach a total of 2253 lines of mixed verse, which is about two-thirds of the play.

Here we might be tempted to draw the conclusion that Shakespeare's revision was after all superficial. But if we examine these latter two classes more closely a significant peculiarity becomes apparent, which throws a good deal of light on the subject. In only some 10 or 12 passages out of 44 are the rhythmical variations those of author A or author B; in all the other passages they are not so far removed from Shakespeare's habitual proportions. The trochees often stand at about 5% and a few may sometimes be as low as 4%, while the proportion of spondees is often around 3 or 4%, which are the most usual figures for Shakespeare. If the revision of the style was slight, the revision of the versification, on the contrary, was more thorough than usual. Shakespeare must have retained much of the language of the original version. This is quite apparent, for instance, in the numerous scenes of insults, lamentations, and maledictions.[9] Their vulgarity and noisy bluster have nothing in common with the sober sweetness that is so temperamentally characteristic of Shakespeare; dramatic truth collapses to give way to a flow of words which in no manner helps the action. It was by making the dialogue more fluent that Shakespeare tried to improve the original play, and this he achieved by changing the rhythm of the verses: he regulated the halting verse of author A and broke the rigidity of author B. The dialogue is probably not very different from that in the pre-Shakespearean play; its sole novelty must have been in the ease and fluidity that prevail in scenes where Shakespeare's style is not recognizable.

There were many good reasons why Shakespeare should not feel obliged to carry out a more extensive revision. The history of Richard III's reign had been amply treated by the chroniclers.

9. As well as in the frequent use of stichomythy, which belongs to a classical technique that is not Shakespeare's.

Sir Thomas More had written a fully documented life of this king, in which he assembled the most varied pieces of information communicated to him by those who had played a role in the politics of this turbulent period, Cardinal Morton among them. This biography, extensively employed by Hall and Holinshed, had been supplemented by Polydore Vergil and amplified by the malevolence of the anti-Yorkists or the credulity of the common people to such a degree as to make it an ideal subject for a melodrama. Author A had only to draw on the chroniclers, Hall in particular, who themselves reflected those popular distortions, to find already dramatized the incidents for a play full of sensational turns of events. Even the episodic scenes, which contain nothing historical and which one might suppose to have been invented by the author —such as those in which the citizens express their apprehensions at the king's death (II.iii) [1] or in which the scrivener comments on the proclamation that he had had to transcribe [2]—were indicated or suggested by Hall.

Hall seems to have had some literary aspirations far exceeding the resources of his dull and awkward style. He wrote the history of his country in the classical manner, never hesitating to invent conversations, and some of these were transferred to the dialogue of the play. For instance, Hastings is made to say to Lord Stanley's messenger:

> A good lord (q^d the lord Hastynges) to the messenger, leaneth my lorde thy maister so much to suche tryfles, and hath suche faithe in dreames, whiche either his awne feare phantasieth, or do ryse in the nightes rest by reason of the dayes thought. Tell him it is playne wichcraft to beleue in such dreames, which if they were tokens of thinges to

1. "Then began here & there some maner of mutterynge emongest the people, as though all thyng should not long be well, though thy wyst not what they feared nor wherefore: were it, that before suche greate thynges, mennes hertes (of a secrete instinct of nature) misgiueth theim, as southwynde sometyme swelleth of hym selfe before a tempeste, or were it that some one manne happely somewhat per[c]eauyng, filled many men with suspicio-thoughe he shewed fewe menne what he knewe." (*Chronicle*, in Furness ed., p. 472.)

2. "Nowe was thys proclamacion made within twoo houres after he was beheaded, and it was so curiously endyted and so fayre writen in Parchement in a fayre sette hande, and therewith of it selfe so long a processe, that euery chyld might perceyue that it was prepared and studyed before . . . So that vpon the proclaimyng thereof one that was scolemayster at Paules standyng by and comparyng the shortenesse of the tyme with the length of the matter sayed to theim that stoode about hym, here is a gaye goodly cast, foule cast awaye for hast . . ." (*Chronicle*, in Furness ed., p. 477.)

come, why thynketh he not that we might as likely make theim true by
oure goyng yf we were caught and brought backe . . . for then had
the bore a cause lykely to race vs with his tuskes . . . (Hall, *Chronicle*,
quoted in the Furness edition of *Richard III* [Philadelphia, J. B. Lippin-
cott, 1908], p. 475)

In the play this has become:

> Go fellow go, returne vnto thy lord
>
> .   .   .   .   .   .
>
> Tell him his feares are shallow, wanting instance,
> And for his dreames, I wonder he is so fond,
> To trust the mockery of vnquiet slumbers,
> To flie the boare, before the boare pursues vs,
> Were to incense the boare to follow vs,
> And make pursuite where he did meane no chase (III.ii.19–30)

Hall cited also the imaginary orations that Richmond and
Richard are supposed to have delivered before the battle of Bosworth Field, and these were imitated in the play (V.iii.237–70,314–
41). He drew a picture of Richard as complete as it was malevo-
lent, bringing out that mixture of virtue and vice that made of this
prince, born to be a great king, a murderous tyrant whose cruelty,
audacity, political sense, ambition, insidious eloquence, clever dissimulation, seductive familiarity even with those whom he hated,
prodigality, and feigned religiosity appear by turns in the description of this blending of contradictions. So complete was the presentation that it included Richard's favorite oath, "By Saint Paul's,"
and the habit of biting his lip when he was angry. Author A had
only to render in dialogue what he had read, and here he was
not lacking in skill, as we have seen.

Thus a word that one would confidently proclaim a stroke of
Shakespeare's genius is often the echo of a word uttered by Richard, spread by tradition and picked up by the chronicler. When
Richard directs Buckingham to insinuate that King Edward had
been an adulterine child,

> But touch this sparingly as it were farre off,
> Because you know, my Lord, my mother liues (III.v.94–5)

this astonishingly suggestive restriction merely reproduced a remark by Hall who had pointed out the impropriety of circulating
the rumor, even in a vague and indirect form:

To lay bastardy in kyng Edward sounded openly to the rebuke of the
protectours awne mother, whiche was mother to them bothe. For in that
poinct could be none other coloure, but to pretende that his awne mother
was an auoutresse, but neuerthelesse he would that poinct should be lesse
and more fynely & closely handled, not euen fully playne and directely,
but touched a slope craftly, as though men spared in that poinct to speake
all the trueth for feare of his displeasure (*Chronicle,* in Furness ed.,
pp. 478–9)

Similarly, in Act IV.sc.iii, when on the eve of the battle that was
to decide his fate Richard said to Ratcliff:

> I haue not that alacrity of spirit
> Nor cheere of mind that I was wont to haue (73–4)

the word "alacrity" reminds us immediately of Falstaff, who employed it in a memorable passage (*Merry Wives of Windsor,* III.
v.13); but this moment of discouragement had been noted (or
imagined) by Hall, and the two lines uttered by Richard in the
play are merely a reproduction in verse of the prose passage of the
chronicler:

> For incontynent after, his heart beynge almost damped, he prognosti-
> cated before the doubtfull chaunce of the battaile to come, not vsynge
> the alacrite and myrth of mynde and of countenaunce as he was ac-
> customed to do before he came toward the battaile (*Chronicle,* in Furness
> ed., p. 494)

So when Shakespeare undertook to improve the original *Richard III* he had before him a play that exploited to the full everything that was known about this king. There was nothing to be
added to the incidents, for the play contained an accumulation
of crimes and Machiavellian machinations that would satisfy to
the limit the taste of the period for tragedies of horror; nor was
it necessary to enrich the principal character whose psychology
was rudimentary but infinitely various in the manifestations of
its perversity. It was excellent melodrama, an inferior dramatic
form that nevertheless always exerts its fascination on audiences
whether or not they admit its power, and the company needed
such plays because of the large receipts they brought in. Shakespeare therefore took it as it was, just as he had accepted all the
horrors in *Titus Andronicus.* He did not alter the construction itself, loose and awkward though it sometimes was, nor did he at-

tempt to dissipate the somber atmosphere with poetical embellishments which would have weakened its crudity; all this belonged
to the nature of the play. He merely infused into the dialogue that
lifelike vitality which is probably the main feature of his dramatic
manner, making us almost forget the gross exaggerations in this
melodrama. Did Shakespeare take a supreme pleasure in this kind
of work? I wonder: he would not have allowed so many prosodic
irregularities if he had. Perhaps his revision was as hurried as it
was restricted.

The whole revision, however, was not completed at the same
time. From the proportions of feminine endings in the passages
which seem to have been rewritten or added by Shakespeare two
periods are distinguishable:

	Feminine endings	Lines	Percentages
I.i.117–44	3	28	10.7
I.iii.255–303	7	49	14.2
I.iv.200–37	3	38	7.8
II.i.1–94	11	94	11.7
II.iv.38–73	3	36	8.3
III.i.1–94	9	94	9.5
III.iii.1–25	3	25	12.0
III.v.41–70	4	30	13.3
III.vii.59–219	17	144	11.8
IV.iv.369–431	8	62	12.9
V.iii.83–117	5	35	14.2

73 feminine endings in 635 verse lines give an average of 11.4%

This first revision must have followed pretty closely after the first
revision of 2 *Henry VI* and the second of *Titus Andronicus*.

In a second group the proportions of feminine endings are nearly
twice as much as in this first group:

	Feminine endings	Lines	Percentages
I.i.1–41	10	41	24.3
I.ii.228–64	8	35	22.8
I.iii.41–110	13	69	18.8
I.iv.1–83	16	76	21.0
III.ii.1–73	13	73	17.8
II.ii.34–63	6	30	20.0
IV.iii.24–43	5	20	25.0
V.iii.223–70	9	48	18.7

81 feminine endings in 392 lines, average 20.6%

This second revision seems to have been less thorough than the first; it may have been made between the third revision of *Richard II* (average 17.8%) and the second of 2 *Henry VI* (average 23.7%). It is not without importance to note that out of the 8 passages on the list 5 affect the character of Richard, for that is perhaps the reason why this second revision was undertaken on the occasion of some revival.

Two passages, I.i.145–62 and I.iii.1–41, have higher percentages, 33.3% and 34.1% respectively. It is hardly plausible that Shakespeare revised *Richard III* once more for such a trifle, especially as these higher figures are perhaps due to the repetition at the end of a line, twice of the word "father" in the first case and three times of the word "Darby" in the second case.

THE TEXT OF THE FOLIO

THE FOLIO and the quarto present the same play: the scenes follow in the same order and most of the dialogue is identical. Hence it has been supposed that the folio was printed from a copy of the quarto of 1622, corrected from a manuscript. But there are differences between the two texts so great in number if not in importance that some commentators have been led to assert that Q_1 and F should be considered as distinct. On the basis of this assertion two contradictory theories have arisen; for some the folio text is the text of the quarto corrected and augmented by Shakespeare, while for others the quarto is an incomplete and corrupt reproduction of the folio text, the result of a defective memory.

An exact comparison, made in the absence of any preconceived ideas, shows that these two theories are equally wrong. There are so many differences in details, amounting to more than 500 mere textual variations alone, that a small volume would be required to examine them all.[3] I shall therefore merely cite the more important differences, those that have real significance for the conclusions to which they lead.

3. A minute comparison has been made by David Lyall Patrick in a doctoral dissertation, *The Textual History of Richard III*, Stanford University Publications, Language and Literature, 1936, Vol. 6. I cannot accept the thesis that this study was intended to support, but I gladly acknowledge that the complete listing of all the variants has considerably facilitated my own work.

The stage directions are practically the same in the two texts, though in the folio they are often more detailed and tend to contribute graphic and explanatory notes:

I.ii.1   Q. Enter Lady Anne with the hearse of Harry the 6
          F. Enter the Coarse of Henrie the sixt with Halberds to guard it, Lady Anne being the Mourner

I.iii.1 Q. Enter Queene, Lord Rivers, Gray
          F. Enter the Queene Mother, Lord Riuers, and Lord Gray

II.ii.33–4 Q. Enter the Quee.
             F. Enter the Queene with her haire about her ears, Riuers & Dorset after her

III.iv.1 Q. Enter the Lords to Councell
           F. Enter Buckingham, Darby, Hastings, Bishop of Ely, Norfolke, Ratcliffe, Louell, with others, at a Table

III.v.1   Q. Enter Duke of Glocester and Buckingham in armour
           F. Enter Richard, and Buckingham, in rotten Armour, maruellous ill-fauoured [4]

Stage directions like these, describing the scene as it was performed, are not such as prompters were accustomed to enter in their books; they were found only in manuscripts copied for collectors of dramatic plays or prepared especially for publication. But it was certainly the prompter who supplied the names of the entering characters whenever they were missing in the quarto, as in III.iv.1,[5] and ordered new musical effects. When Richard ascends the throne after his coronation his entrance is preceded by the words "Sound a Sennet" (IV.ii.1), where the quarto has merely "The Trumpets sound"; and when the young prince makes his exit (III.i.150) he also is saluted by a sennet. Again, in order to drown the abuse heaped upon him by his mother Richard cries to his troops, "A flourish trumpets, strike alarum drummes" (IV.iv.

4. The words "maruellous ill-fauoured" were suggested by a passage from Sir Thomas More: "The Protector . . . sent in al the hast for many substauncial men out of the city into the Tower. And at their comming, himself with the Duke of Buckingham, stode harnessed in old il faring briganders, such as no man shold wene that thei wold vouchsafe to haue put vpon their backes" (quoted in Furness edition, note to III.v.1, pp. 241–2). This may therefore have been a stage direction of the author's; but it is probable that its eminently graphic character is attributable to whomever corrected the other directions rather than to the author.
5. Cf. II.i.1; II.ii.88; V.iii.18–19.

148), which in the quarto was judged sufficient; the folio, as a precaution no doubt, has between the lines, where they would be clearly visible, the words "Flourish. Alarums."

In several cases parts of the dialogue are not assigned to the same characters:

I.iv. In the quarto Clarence, as prisoner, enters with Brokenbury, the lieutenant of the Tower, whereas in the folio it is with a keeper.

II.iv.37–48. In the quarto Dorset brings the news that the relatives of the queen have been sent as prisoners to Pomfret; in the folio the part is given to a messenger. In the same scene a cardinal accompanies the queen when she goes to take refuge in a sanctuary; and it is a cardinal, no doubt the same, who goes (III.i) and fetches the young duke of York from the sanctuary to which the queen had retired. In the folio this role is played by an archbishop in II.iv and by a cardinal in III.i.

III.iv.82–109. Catesby takes it upon himself to lead Hastings to his execution; in the folio Richard expressly charges Lovel and Ratcliff with this duty.

IV.iii.43–8. In the quarto Catesby tells Richard that Buckingham and the bishop of Ely have revolted, but in the folio it is Ratcliff who brings the news.

V.i.1–29. Buckingham is led to his execution by Ratcliff in the quarto, by a sheriff in the folio.

V.iii.2. In the quarto Richard asks Catesby why he seems so dejected, but in the folio the king asks the same question of Lord Surrey.

It has been maintained that these changes were made in the quarto by a small troupe in order to reduce the number of actors. By so doing they could dispense with a keeper of the Tower, a messenger, an archbishop, and two lords, Lovel and Surrey. At first sight the supposition seems reasonable, but it is at variance with the facts. In the first place, I do not see any economy in substituting Ratcliff for Catesby, since these two characters appear in both texts up to the end of the play, and together in Act V.sc.iii. The keeper of the Tower, the messenger, and the archbishop, who are supposed to have been eliminated, all have minor roles and never appear together, so that the same actor could have played those three parts if necessary. As a matter of fact, the company

did not lack utility men: in Act IV.sc.iv four messengers were on
the stage, three of whom enter one after the other (499, 504, 507,
519).

There are proofs, on the contrary, that these changes were made
by a company more numerous than the one that gave the play in
its pre-Shakespearean form and that by so doing it was availing
itself of its resources in personnel to eliminate improbabilities in
the action. It was really not natural that the marquis of Dorset,
the son of the queen, should be used to carry news or that the
lieutenant of the Tower should have to keep the prisoners himself.

The last example furnishes the best of proofs that such a change
did represent an innovation in the folio, for the replacement of
Brokenbury by a keeper has given rise to an improbability that is
infinitely greater than the one it was supposed to remove. In the
quarto the scene unfolds naturally. Clarence relates to the lieutenant of the Tower the dream that he had during the night and ends
the narration with a confession that his conscience is not easy. He
begs Brokenbury to stay with him, for his heart is heavy and he
wants to sleep. He falls asleep and Brokenbury, moved by the
confession, discourses in a monologue on the situation of princes,
to whom the cares of the common man are not unknown. In the
folio the conversation proceeds with the keeper in exactly the same
way, and it is only when Clarence has fallen asleep that the
lieutenant enters, one knows not why, and although he has not
heard Clarence's confession he delivers his little lecture just as it
appears in the quarto, without the alteration of a single word.

The intention of removing another improbability in the action
of the quarto also explains the substitution of Lovel and Ratcliff
for Catesby in Act III.sc.iv of the folio. In a fit of feigned anger
Richard has condemned Hastings to be beheaded immediately.
"Come see it done," he says, and Catesby, understanding that he
must undertake that task, leads the condemned man away. Sc.v
opens forthwith. Buckingham and Richard are waiting for the
lord mayor, who actually enters a little later. While Buckingham
is welcoming him and the accompanying citizens, Richard, pre-
tending to fear an attack, calls out: "Looke to the drawbridge
there," "Catesby ouerlooke the wals." But at that moment Catesby
is busy having Hastings beheaded and he does not arrive until

two lines later, bearing the head as Richard had commanded.

It was an absurd situation in the quarto. The spectators had seen Catesby leave with Hastings and return under conditions recalling his absence in a manner which could not pass unnoticed. What was the meaning of that summons by Richard, who knew that it would be impossible for Catesby to carry out the order? It was therefore necessary to find something that would not overstep dramatic probability, and so it was done. The improbability does not exist in the folio. And here we are sure that the correction was made in the folio, for it involved the recasting of an entire passage. Instead of issuing a vague order Richard charges two of his trusted followers, Lovel and Ratcliff, with seeing that Hastings is executed. The scene opens as in the quarto, but after a short exchange of ideas between Richard and Buckingham the latter suddenly notices—a remark surely unexpected—that Catesby is absent, and he exclaims, "But what, is Catesby gone?" "He is," answers Richard and adds, "and see he brings the Maior along." Then follows a stage direction: "Enter the Maior, and Catesby." And all the probabilities being satisfied, Richard can call out to Catesby, who now is really present, "Catesby, o're-looke the Walls."

The greater importance given to Ratcliff here and in Act IV.sc.iii is an improvement in the distribution of parts. Like Catesby, he was one of Richard's closest adherents; yet in the text of the quarto he does not appear before Act IV.sc.iv, and after that only in the first and third scenes of Act V. It was strange that the spectators should not have been made to realize the importance of this character until the last moments; Ratcliff's share in the action was then made more continuous and more natural by having him appear as early as Act III, as well as by substituting him for Catesby in Act IV.

These modifications in the distribution of the roles may have been made during the rehearsals, with or without Shakespeare's assent. But I very much doubt that either he or the company could have been responsible for changing one of the cardinals in the quarto to an archbishop, for here it was a question of correcting a slight error. According to the chroniclers it was Thomas Rotheram, archbishop of York, who accompanied the queen in her search for a sanctuary, and Cardinal Bourchier who had to persuade her to let the young duke of York rejoin his brother, the heir to the throne, in London. Actors as a rule do not show such an unquenchable thirst for historical accuracy, and I am afraid that we perceive here the editor of the folio casting his shadow over the text.

Passing now to a comparison of the dialogue in the two texts we find lacunae on both sides. The quarto has about forty lines that are not in the folio. The absence of some is easily explained. Two were omitted in conformity with the edict of 1606 which forbade the use of profane language on the stage (I.iv.195; III.vii.220). Eight (I.ii.203,226; I.iii.114; I.iv.243; II.ii.145; III.iii.1; III.iv.60; IV.iv.39) may have been carelessly overlooked by the compositor of the folio, since most of them are essential to an understanding of the context. In four lines a few words were left out of the folio in order to rectify irregular lines of the quarto: Looke ye my Lo: Maior (III.v.27), by nothing (IV.iv.368), sir my mind is changed (IV.iv.456), as you gesse (IV.iv.467). In the last two cases the correction was far from felicitous, for they are repetitions meant by the author, a sort of habit assigned above all to Richard, but also to Hastings, to the duchess of York, and to Queen Margaret. Once more I cannot believe that the actors would have given up such an interesting bit of characterization.[6]

None of the preceding omissions is of real importance. It is not so with one rather long passage (IV.ii.102–19). It occurs in the quarto toward the end of the scene in which Buckingham asks Richard to carry out his promises and Richard pretends at first not to understand; losing patience finally, he snubs the petitioner roughly by saying he is not in a giving mood. This passage was in the pre-Shakespearean play: it is one of those that seem to have been preserved in their entirety (see p. 247). The style, that of author A, shows no trace of revision by Shakespeare. Its omission leaves a blank for it is necessary to the understanding of the words "I am not in the vain," which are in both texts and refer to a phrase in the excluded passage, "I am not in the giuing vaine." It ends a scene without distinction of style though excellent from a dramatic point of view, for it brings out the brutal side of Richard's char-

6. Cf. I.i.70; I.iii.261; II.iii.5; III.i.154; III.ii.37,66; III.iv.94; IV.ii.102,122; IV.iv. 73,145; V.iii.214,289.

acter. I can see but one reason for its exclusion from the folio: there is nothing in it of Shakespeare.

On the other hand the folio has over 200 lines that are not in the quarto. About 30 of these are single lines, and their absence in the quarto may be explained in the same way as the absence of the single lines from the folio—by a moment of inattention on the part of a compositor. I would explain similarly the absence from the quarto of two lines that appear in the folio, though in this case such a lapse seems less probable. In Act III.sc.vii, when Richard appears flanked by two bishops, Buckingham says:

> And see a Booke of Prayer in his hand,
> True Ornaments to know a holy man (98–9)

But these two lines were certainly in the play before the First Quarto was printed, for in line 47 of that quarto Buckingham says to Richard, apropos of the meeting with the lord mayor that is about to take place, "And looke you get a praier booke in your hand." Only an accident can have caused the disappearance of a detail of staging so carefully prepared.

Conversely line 68 of Act II.sc.i was cut from the text before the printing of the quarto. Proclaiming his desire to live in peace with the whole world, Gloucester names specifically those whom he regards as his most important enemies. In the folio he says:

> Of you and you, Lord Riuers and of Dorset,
> That all without desert haue frown'd on me:
> Of you Lord Wooduill, and Lord Scales of you (II.i.66–8)

From a dramatic point of view the third line was excellent, as it allowed the actor to strike attitudes by which he could express the aggressive vivacity of the character; but it was pure nonsense for Woodville and Scales were both names of Lord Rivers, already mentioned in the first line, who was Woodville by birth and Scales because of his marriage to the daughter and heiress of Lord Scales. This blunder was surely discovered at the first rehearsal, for the simple reason that there was no character in the play who could thus be challenged by Richard.

Among the longer passages that are only in the folio text the following can also be considered as early cuts made to shorten the play. They are too long for their disappearance to be explained by a moment of inattention on the part of a scrivener or compositor, and when their versification is examined it is evident that they were part of the text as revised by Shakespeare. In certain cases it can even be said whether they belonged to the first or the second revision.

I.ii.156–67. In courting Lady Anne Richard compares his previous lack of feeling with the tears he now sheds for his love of her. This passage is inserted in one of those that have been substantially revised by Shakespeare (cf. p. 249); it has the same proportion of trochees as the rest of the passage, several mannerisms, a charming and characteristically Shakespearean image, "Like Trees bedash'd with raine," and a conceit that is repeated in sonnet 148: "Thy Beauty hath, and made them blinde with weeping." [7] Having but one feminine ending the passage belongs to the first revision.

I.iv.69–72. After expressing his remorse Clarence adds this prayer:

> O God! if my deepe prayres cannot appease thee,
> But thou wilt be aueng'd on my misdeeds,
> Yet execute thy wrath in me alone:
> O spare my guiltlesse Wife, and my poore children

The stiff awkward versification and clumsy style suggest that this may be a verbatim remainder of the pre-Shakespearean play, a possible reason for its suppression.

I.iv.266–70. In reply to Clarence's exhortations the second murderer says in the quarto: "What shall we doe?" "Relent, and saue your soules," answers Clarence. "Relent, tis cowardly and womanish," objects the first murderer, and to these words Clarence replies, "Not to relent, is beastly, sauage, diuelish." This piece of dialogue with its quick retorts is perfectly easy and clear. In the folio to the words "Relent and saue your soules" Clarence adds a question:

> Which of you, if you were a Princes Sonne,
> Being pent from Liberty, as I am now,
> If two such murtherers as your selues came to you,
> Would not intreat for life, as you would begge
> Were you in my distresse

To this no attention is paid and the first murderer answers, as in the quarto, "Relent? no: 'Tis cowardly and womanish." Several

7 Sonnet 148 has: O cunning love, with tears thou keep'st me blind.

explanations have been offered for this solution of continuity; they are mentioned in the Furness edition (pp. 144–6). The most satisfactory is that of Staunton: "These six lines were apparently the poet's first sketch of a speech for Clarence and which he no doubt intended to be superseded by his after-thought and this retention has reduced the trialogue to chaos." The copyist who prepared the text for the printing of the First Quarto rightly left the passage out.

II.ii.89–100. Dorset reproaches the queen for not having submitted to God's will, and Lord Rivers advises her to have her son crowned without delay. The versification is characteristically pre-Shakespearean (trochees 6.6%, spondees 8.3%). Two inept metaphors, "to drown sorrow in a grave" and "to plant joys in a throne," prove that the original play had victoriously resisted Shakespeare's revision. Moreover it is one of those useless passages that a troupe wishing to shorten a play would willingly delete.

II.ii.123–40. Buckingham suggests that the heir to the throne be brought to London with a small escort, and after having asked the reason for this recommendation Rivers falls in with it. The versification is definitely Shakespearean (trochees 3.3%, spondees 4.4%). This passage is linked to the preceding one by the question of the coronation. Three feminine endings in 16 lines indicate that it was added at the time of the second revision.

III.vii.144–53. These lines are part of Richard's speech to the lord mayor and to the citizens of London; they amplify the idea expressed in the preceding lines. One feminine ending, or a proportion of 10%, shows that they, like the rest of the speech, belong to the first revision. The style is distorted and does not add anything to the sense and might very well tax the patience of the spectators. The text was certainly improved by its elimination.

IV.i.98–104. Queen Elizabeth's apostrophe to the wall of the Tower of London. Shakespeare seems to have touched it up a little but not enough to do away with its old-fashioned tone and the stiffness of the versification. It was a remnant of the pre-Shakespearean play; the suppression by the company is understandable.

IV.iv.221–34. Queen Elizabeth reproaches Richard for having arranged the murder of her children. This is a passage that has retained traces of the pre-Shakespearean play in the style. Shakespeare, however, modified it extensively (trochees 2.8%, spondees

5.6%), and it contains one of his familiar images, that of a disabled bark dashed to pieces on a rocky shore, while 3 feminine endings in 13 lines (i.e., 23.0%) are an assurance that it was part of the second revision. Only the necessity for shortening the play can explain why it was cut.

IV.iv.288–342. Richard holds before Queen Elizabeth's eyes the glittering prospect of the advantages that she and hers would gain if she had a king for a son-in-law. The proportions of rhythmic variations are nearer to those of author A than of Shakespeare. But there is no trace of the pre-Shakespearean play, whereas there are five mannerisms and three images, one of which,

> The liquid drops of Teares that you haue shed,
> Shall come againe, transform'd to Orient Pearles

occurs almost word for word in sonnet 34. Furthermore, the line "With the sweet silent houres of Marriage ioyes" has the haunting melody that is so characteristic of Shakespeare. The proportion of feminine endings, 12 in 55 lines, or 21.8%, makes these lines fall into the category of passages extensively modified in the second revision. It is an important one, for its aim seems to have been to make the queen's too rapid submission to Richard's request appear more credible. But it came at the end of a scene that was already too long and was a repetition of the one in which Richard had gained Lady Anne's consent to marry him. Its omission reduced the play by 55 lines, and that was probably a decisive reason for this cut—a reason that holds for most of the cuts mentioned above, for *Richard III* is, next to *Hamlet*, the longest of Shakespeare's plays.

But all the passages that are only in the folio are not parts of the action which were deleted by the company on grounds of expediency at some time or other, probably early and certainly before 1597. Some, manifestly, were introduced into the folio text in order to correct defects or errors in the quarto text.

III.i.172–3. Buckingham sends Catesby to sound out Hastings in order to know whether he will consent to Richard's projects. In the quarto his instructions are precise and clear:

> Sound thou Lo: Hastings, how he stands affected   171
> Vnto our purpose, if he be willing,

> Encourage him, and shew him all our reasons:
> If he be leaden, icie, cold, vnwilling,
> Be thou so too: and so breake off your talke   175

In the folio after the words "for our purpose" follows an invitation to be present at the meeting that is to take place:

> And summon him to morrow to the Tower,
> To sit about the Coronation

That these two lines were interpolated in the text of the quarto is not doubtful, for not only do they interrupt the development of the thought but their introduction involved an alteration of the whole context. Line 171 had to be cut in two and the first part remained hanging in the air while the words "if he be willing" were transformed into a whole line, "If thou do'st finde him tractable to vs," to restore the prosodic regularity. And in the following scene, where Catesby carries out Buckingham's instructions, he never mentions the invitation to the council meeting, the best proof that this invitation was not in the revised form of the text: the first interpolation necessitated a second which the interpolator forgot to make. The reason for this addition is easily understood. Lord Hastings had to be present at the meeting since it was at this meeting that Richard was to accuse him of treason. But the spectators (or the readers of the folio) might be surprised to find him present at an assembly for the purpose of fixing the date of Richard's coronation (III.iv) when they knew that in an earlier scene Hastings had expressed his irrevocable intention to remain faithful to the legitimate heir to the throne.

The same intention of forestalling the possible surprise of spectators or of readers accounts for the presence in the folio of three lines that are not in the quarto:

I.iii.167-9. Queen Margaret heaps abuse upon Richard, and the latter interrupts her in the middle of her tirade with the question:

> Wert thou not banished, on paine of death?

to which the queen replies:

> I was: but I doe find more paine in banishment,
> Then death can yeeld me here, by my abode

This is not very convincing, is even nonsensical; but after such an assertion anyone who remembered that Margaret was sent back

to France at the end of 3 *Henry VI* could not be astonished at the
presence of the old queen in this play, where historically she does
not belong.

IV.iv.274–6. Queen Elizabeth, recalling one of the incidents
that I have noted (see p. 234), ironically advises Richard to pay
his court to Princess Elizabeth in imitation of the manner adopted
by Queen Margaret toward the duke of York. The quarto has:

> Therefore present to her as sometimes Margaret
> Did to thy father, a handkercher steept in Rutlands bloud,
> And bid her drie her weeping eies therewith

Assuredly this passage is excessively concise; it contains, moreover, an irregular line. The text of the folio develops the allusion
in an endeavor to render perceptible the connection between
situations as different as that of the duke of York, tortured by his
mortal enemy, and the son of that duke who is trying to win over
a young girl. The long line was adjusted, but at the price of awkward syntax that increases rather than removes the obscurity of
the allusion:

> Therefore present to her, as sometime Margaret
> Did to thy Father, steept in Rutlands blood,
> A hand-kercheefe, which say to her did dreyne
> The purple sappe from her sweet Brothers body,
> And bid her wipe her weeping eyes withall

III.vii.5–8. Richard asks Buckingham if he emphasized the bastardy of Edward's children in his speech to the citizens. In the
quarto Buckingham answers:

> I did, wyth the insatiate greedinesse of his desires,
> His tyranny for trifles, his owne bastardy,
> As beying got, your father then in Fraunce

The folio text, after the words "I did, with," has:

> his Contract with Lady Lucy,
> And his Contract by Deputie in France

which recalls the arguments invoked at the time against Edward's
children. According to a report that had been spread King Edward
had once been engaged to Lady Elizabeth Lucy by what was
called a "pre-contract," and a second time to Princess Bona, an

THE TEXT OF THE FOLIO

event which is one of the incidents in *The True Tragedie;* in accordance with the canon law of the period these two contracts made his marriage to Lady Grey doubly void. The addition certainly missed its aim, for it hardly said more than the "I did" of the quarto; besides, it introduced a repetition in the same scene with lines 177–91, which express the same argument clearly and logically.

Finally there are two cases where a need for clarity is not comprehensible:

I.iv.9. In telling of his dream Clarence begins thus in the quarto: "Me thoughts I was imbarkt for Burgundy," a line that is not in the least obscure or mysterious. Yes, but Clarence is a prisoner in the Tower; how can he say that he is leaving for Burgundy? Somebody was shocked by this defect and corrected it in the folio text where Clarence, logical even in his dream, begins "Me thoughts that I had broken from the Tower," and continues with the line in the quarto slightly modified, "And was embark'd to crosse to Burgundy." Precision carried to this excess is truly mere lumpishness.

A few lines further (I.iv.34–7) is found a correction of the same kind. Clarence is describing the wreckage at the bottom of the sea into which he has fallen; the amazed Brokenbury asks him in the quarto:

> Had you such leasure in the time of death,
> To gaze vpon the secrets of the deepe?

Clarence accounts for his strange experience as follows:

> Methought I had, for still the enuious floud
> Kept in my soule, and would not let it foorth

which is not remarkably well expressed but is understandable. A corrector, evidently the same, thought it was not, and changed the answer to:

> Me thought I had, and often did I striue
> To yeeld the Ghost: but still the enuious Flood
> Stop'd in my soule, and would not let it forth

with no better result than the addition of a platitude.

IV.i.2–6. The duchess of York, accompanied by Queen Eliza-

beth, sees Lady Anne, now duchess of Gloucester, coming like
herself to the Tower, and, surprised, exclaims, "Who meets vs
heere, My neece Plantagenet?" Here again the corrector of the
preceding passages thought he had discovered an error: how could
the duchess of York use in this circumstance the words "my niece"?
The duchess of Gloucester was her daughter-in-law. And though
from the stage direction (the same in the two texts) it was plain
that the duchess of Gloucester entered alone, this guardian of
precision imagined that there must have been a child, the daughter of Clarence, for instance, for whom the word niece was appropriate, and he boldly added to the text of the folio the line,
"Led in the hand of her kind Aunt of Gloster?" And to strengthen
his correction he supplied two more lines that ended in such a
way as to leave no doubt on the relationship between the two
women:

> Now, for my Life, shee's wandering to the Tower,
> On pure hearts loue, to greet the tender Prince.
> Daughter, well met

Now the error existed only in the mind of the corrector, who doubtless was not aware that the duchess of York was the aunt of the
earl of Warwick, father to the duchess of Gloucester, and that
therefore the latter was the grand-niece of the duchess of York before being her daughter-in-law. Moreover, all through the sixteenth century the word "niece" could be applied to any female
relative, no matter how distant, so that this appellation, in this
case, was doubly correct and the modification unnecessary in
every way.

Indeed, the same thing might be said of most of the corrections
cited above. The sentences in the quarto that were questioned
were never so obscure or inexact as to puzzle an audience or even
a reader. Indeed the concise dialogue of the quarto is often preferable to the diluted and "clarified" text of the folio.

Lastly there are the textual variants. As in the preceding chapters I shall not take into account words added, omitted, or transposed in the same sentence, plurals used in place of singulars or
vice versa, definite articles that replace possessive or demonstra-
tive adjectives, differences in the mode or tense of verbs, and so
on—all mistakes attributable to a compositor or to a copyist

memorizing passages too long to be accurately retained. I shall silently pass over changes that seem useless, such as the substitution of "tell" for "say" (I.iii.330) or of "day" for "time" (I.iii.245). But even when typographical errors or useless changes are disregarded the list of real textual variants is still long, much longer than that for *Titus Andronicus* or for *Richard II;* in fact I have counted 360, and I do not claim to have found them all.

When those variants are considered, detached from the sense of the passage in which they occur, the first impression is that chance alone can have given rise to so many differences. But when they are restored to their context it becomes apparent that they fall into a few groups serving the same purpose—to purge the text of prosodic irregularities and stylistic imprecisions.

Most of the irregular lines are changed to decasyllables; this is the largest group and contains more than a hundred examples:

Q. And so brake off and came away
F. And euen here brake off, and came away (III.vii.41)

Q. My Lord, he doth intreat your grace
F. He doth entreat your Grace, my Noble Lord (III.vii.59)

Q. God and our innocence defend vs
F. God and our Innocencie defend, and guard vs (III.v.20)

In this regularization of the versification the elimination of many trisyllabic feet is an important part:

Q. By heauen I thinke there is no man is securde
F. By heauen, I thinke there is no man secure (I.i.71)

Q. Tush feare not my Lo: we will not stand to prate
F. Tut, tut, my Lord, we will not stand to prate (I.iii.350)

Q. No marueile my Lo: though it affrighted you
F. No maruell Lord, though it affrighted you (I.iv.64) [8]

Repetitious words or phrases in the same passage—a frequent fault with author A—have been weeded out:

Q. Why then they are not dead,
But dead they are, and diuelish slaue by thee

8. Cf. I.i.103; I.ii.192,226; I.iii.280; I.iv.249,276; II.i.108; II.ii.25; II.iii.28; II.iv.13,20,26,63; III.i.149; III.ii.17,82,91,92,99,100,108;III.iv.9,21,28,45,52,54,61,77; III.v.35,36,108,109; III.vii.3,45,52,55,114,221,224,229,240; IV.ii.20,71,81,124; IV.iv.269,496,513; V.i.2; V.iii.7.

F. Then say they were not slaine:
   But dead they are, and diuellish slaue by thee (I.ii.89–90)

Q. Stabd by the selfesame hands that made these holes,
   Lo in those windowes that let foorth thy life,
   I powre the helplesse balme of my poore eies.
   Curst be the hand that made these fatall holes
F. Stab'd by the selfesame hand that made these wounds.
   Loe, in these windowes that let forth thy life,
   I powre the helplesse Balme of my poore eyes.
   O cursed be the hand that made these holes (I.ii.11–14) [9]

The search for weaknesses of this kind in the quarto was conducted with more than ordinary care; repetitions so far apart that
they really pass unnoticed have been nevertheless corrected. Thus
in line 85 of Act I, sc.iv Brokenbury, surprised at seeing two
strangers enter Clarence's cell, asks, "In Gods name what are
you." A long scene follows between the two men who have come
to murder Clarence, at the end of which he wakes (l. 169) and
exclaims, almost in Brokenbury's words, "In Gods name what art
thou." In line 85 of the folio Brokenbury's question has been
changed to "What would'st thou Fellow?"

Two identical phrases, still farther apart in the quarto, are assigned to Richard. When he dispatches Catesby to sound out
Lord Hastings he ends his instructions by asking, "Shall we heare
from you Catesby ere we sleepe?" (III.i.188). Nine scenes later,
after Richard has obtained Tyrrell's promise to murder King Edward's children he dismisses him with exactly the same words,
"Shall we heare from thee Tirrel ere we sleep?" (IV.ii.84). The
folio simply omits this last line.

We have seen that author A sometimes used word forms that
were already obsolescent in Shakespeare's day. The language had
changed considerably in the years that had followed, and some
of these must have sounded archaic for they were replaced in the
folio with more modern expressions—whilest:while (I.iii.226),
betwixt:between (I.iv.82; III.vii.48), wert:wast (I.iv.213; IV.ii.
217; IV.iv.88,107), spake:spoke (II.i.108; III.vii.33), laments:com-
plaints (II.ii.67), Yee:you (II.iii.39), God he knowes:God doth

9. Cf.I.ii.75–81,105–8,237–9; I.iii.326–7,332; I.iv.18,229–30,235–7,289–90; II.i.
9–10,33–5; II.iii.5–9; II.iv.9–31; III.ii.28; III.v.24–5; III.vii.46–57,239–40; IV.i.13–
15; IV.ii.52–8; IV.iv.37–9, 511–15.

know (III.vii.235), grauen:branded (IV.iv.141), moe:other (IV. v.13).

The quarto had many negligences of style—slips, inexactitudes, absurdities—which are amended in the folio:

II.ii.57–9. The duchess of York compares her grief with that of Queen Elizabeth who has lost her husband but still has her children, whereas the duchess has not even this consolation:

> But death hath snatcht my children from mine armes,
> And pluckt two crutches from my feeble limmes,
> Edward and Clarence

It is obvious that if the comparison is to bear on all the points of resemblance between the two cases the duchess should have said "my husband" instead of "my children," and such is the reading in the folio.[1]

A similar mistake is to be found in IV.iv.41 of the quarto. This time it is Queen Elizabeth who is comparing her misfortunes, one by one, with those of the duchess of York: her husband and her son had both been killed by Richard:

> I had an Edward, till a Richard kild him:
> I had a Richard, till a Ricard kild him

Queen Margaret's consort was not a Richard but Henry VI; in the folio the slip was corrected in the same way:

> I had a Husband, till a Richard kill'd him.[2]

IV.iv.130–1. Queen Elizabeth thinks it is better to let sorrow find some assuagement in words, for "those orators of miseries"

> though what they do impart,
> Helpe not at al, yet do they ease the hart

which is pure nonsense and recalls the phrase by Shakespeare that Ben Jonson in his *Timber of Discoveries* found ridiculous: "Caesar never did wrong but with just cause." The folio cautiously says:

> though what they will impart,
> Helpe nothing els, yet do they ease the hart

which is a pretty clever correction for once.

---

1. It is possible that this was a slip attributable to the compositor of the quarto.
2. This may also have been a slip of the compositor of the quarto.

Other corrections bear witness to a singularly punctilious turn of mind:

II.ii.150. Buckingham and Richard take steps to have the heir to the throne brought to London in a way that would avoid popular demonstrations, and Buckingham will find a way "To part the Queenes proud kindred from the King." But as the prince had not yet been crowned he could not be called "king," and the word in the folio was replaced by "Prince."

III.vii.58. No less serious appeared Buckingham's error in making Catesby the servant of Richard: "Here coms his seruant." William Catesby, the son-in-law of Lord Zouch of Harringsworth, was an important man whom More recognized to be well versed in the law. Named chancellor of the exchequer in 1483, he was appointed by Richard in the following year to the position of speaker of the Parliament that was about to convene. The folio left out the whole sentence, "Here comes his servant," an easy way to efface the degradation inflicted upon the character.

A respect for the rules of etiquette dictated several other corrections. There were polite formulas in Court circles that had to be observed according to the rank of the person addressed, and in the quarto those ceremonious formalities were often lost sight of. Its queens employed the quarrelsome language of a scold, while Richard's subjects spoke to him in a tone that sometimes bordered on disrespect. Thus in IV.iv.445 Richard, having met with one misfortune after another, issues contradictory orders and in the quarto says roughly to Catesby, who does not execute one of them promptly enough, "Why standst thou still? and goest not to the Duke"; to which Catesby replies with equal bluntness, "First mightie Soueraigne, let me know your minde." This, in spite of the "mighty sovereign," seemed an inconceivable lack of respect, and the folio gives a response more in keeping with the distance separating Catesby from the king: "First, mighty Liege, tell me your Highnesse pleasure." Even the duke of Buckingham, though himself of royal blood, was not supposed to speak familiarly to his sovereign. When he comes to ask Richard for the promised reward the king pretends not to understand. In the quarto (IV.ii.120) the duke, incensed at such bad faith, says, "Whie then resolue me whether you wil or no?" In the folio Buckingham, like Catesby, is made to adopt a more deferential attitude: "May it please you to resolue me in my suit."

This by no means exhausts the list of such corrections, for every time that Richard himself uses some familiar expression (III.i.184, 193, for example) it is changed in the folio to one more in keeping with his rank. I will give only one other example, for I have noted the very same correction in *Richard II* (see p. 229). In Act IV.sc.ii Richard orders Catesby to spread abroad the rumor "That Anne my wife is sicke and like to die." In the folio Richard says with more dignity: "That Anne, my Queene, is sicke, and like to dye."

The number and kind of these additions and variants make it clear that the text of the quarto or the manuscript from which it derived has been the object of a thorough and methodical revision. The question arises as to who made this revision. Naturally one thinks first of Shakespeare himself. It is of course possible that he may have had a desire to perfect the recasting that he had made incompletely years before. But this is not likely. The patient and minute labor involved in making minor and often useless changes is not of the sort to be expected of an author whose facility prompted him to improvise on the spur of the moment. He may have felt obliged, as his dramatic experience increased, to make over a scene or a passage, but it is highly improbable that he ever subjected himself to the task of proofreader. Besides, many of those modifications are far from happy, and the prosodic quality of some modified lines reveal in their author a complete lack of the sense of melody: lines which in the quarto were not melodious but were at least not ear splitting were sometimes replaced by others that are actually cacophonous. For example:

> Ah Aunt! you wept not for our Fathers death (II.ii.62)
>
> Be not you spoke with, but by mightie suit (III.vii.46)
>
> There, take thou that, till thou bring better newes (IV.iv.510)

Never did Shakespeare, who had the almost miraculous gift of writing lines that seem to glide over the lips of the actors, assemble so many harsh sounds in ten syllables.

Finally, and this seems to me a decisive argument, throughout this long and tiresome revision there is not one of those images that mark Shakespeare's style; in fact, among all the variants there is not one indifferently good metaphor.

Nor was it the actors who introduced those changes. They were not men to worry over historical inaccuracies or imprecisions, for they knew that the stage perspective has no need for truth. They did not want graphic stage directions either: these were for readers.

Once more we must turn to the one who was charged with the task of preparing the text for the printing of the folio, and here we find ourselves on familiar ground. The corrections in *Richard III* are of the same type as those noted in the chapter on *Richard II;* one is even common to both plays (see above, p. 275). It was certainly the same poetaster, devoid of imagination and obsessed by precision, who tampered with both plays. The only difference is that the imperfect revision of *Richard III* offered innumerable possibilities for "improvements," which he seized without restraint so that his character, of which we had caught only a glimpse in *Richard II,* now appears in full view. This detestable corrector was none other than he who made the fair copy of Shakespeare's revision of the play years earlier (see p. 232), Ralph Crane, the scrivener of the King's men, for his signature—the parentheses which he liked to use—is on practically every page of the folio. We have seen that the First Quarto had only 8 of those peculiar signs of punctuation, the folio has 72 (the 8 of the quarto included) in 32 pages.[3]

Indeed, for those who know Crane—and he is pretty well known thanks to a small volume of verse that he published in 1621 under the title *The Workes of Mercy, both Corporal and Spiritual,* thanks especially to the introduction to this volume, in which he relates his life—it is impossible to resist the conviction that this is the very man we are seeking. There is so much similarity between the mind of the man who conceived the kind of corrections I have cited

3. Cf. I.i.24,60,87,97,99,126,127; I.ii.75,78,150,214,241,245,254; I.iii.45,58,65, 136,151,276,301; I.iv.19,31,45,58,61,65,67,91,144,279; II.i.87,99,106,115,117,125, 127; II.ii.42,60; II.iii.39; II.iv.27,54; III.ii.69,90,104,109,170; IV.i.72,87; IV.ii.39; IV.iii.9,10,15,30; IV.iv.139,161,206,282,363,412; V.i.10,26; V.ii.8; V.iii.33,36,243, 330,331; V.v.11,32.

and the mind which we guess to have been this calligrapher's that the identity of the two men is obvious.

Ralph Crane [4] was the son of a London merchant draper. As he wrote a beautiful hand he served at first, for seven years, as a "painful Clarke" under Sir Anthony Ashley, secretary of the Privy Council and later in the office of the Signet and Privy Seal. He worked also for learned and famous men of law. Meticulous by nature, as is shown by the care he took with the smallest details of his florid script, accurate as he had to be in his administrative functions where the slightest error in the wording of a document might have been followed by serious consequences, he had acquired the habit of precision, a habit that may easily become a mania. In his professional contacts he had learned to realize the importance of titles and the respect that was their due in a solidly hierarchical society, and his deference was doubled by a real admiration that he artlessly acknowledged: the years spent in the offices of the Privy Council, he wrote, were the happiest of his life, for there he had experienced

> The goodness and nobilitie o'th' Peeres,
> Those reverend Lords, those Counsellers of State,
> Vpon whose vertues I must meditate
> While I haue breath; and praise while I am able

This man, imbued with the necessity of regularity and accurateness, enemy through his calling of fantasy and invention, believed he was a poet. To increase the happiness of mankind, in his *Workes of Mercy* he proposed antithetically, as in a geometrical theorem, fourteen precepts, parallel and equal, seven of which were material and seven spiritual. He chose the rhymed distich to convey them in this philanthropic poem which I have read through to the end, and I can say that I have rarely seen so prosaic a poetical form. For Crane a verse consisted of ten syllables, expressing a complete thought whenever possible, and squeezed into a rigid mold with the help of facile syncopations. His sentences with their lame syntax admit only ultrabanal metaphors ("the circuit of

4. Crane's life will be found first in the *Dictionary of National Biography* and more fully in an article by F. P. Wilson, "Ralph Crane, Scrivener to the King's Players" (*The Library*, 1926–27, *4*, 7), which contains also studies of the manuscripts which he prepared.

years," "a thankful river that doth send his tribute to the Ocean," "a field of honour," "Fame's trumpet," and so on) and are totally devoid of any musical quality. The following lines:

> Is not extinguish'd yet, though I am old
> Whilst Fame a trumpet hath, or I a tongue

are entirely comparable in their cacophony with those cited on page 275.

Now suppose the text of *Richard III* is set before a man of this intellectual make-up with a view to presenting it to the greater glory of Shakespeare; his precise and compact mind will want to do what the editor of the folio actually did. He will replace words that he thinks vague with others that are commonplace but which seem to him more exact, correct historical errors, seek out repetitions as signs of weakness, substitute clarity for what he judges ambiguity, and see that each character in the play is treated with the respect to which his rank entitles him. Trusting his "muse" he will not hesitate to adjust irregular lines, even at the cost of syntax and melody, and as the plays in the folio are to be read by men of the seventeenth century he will modernize expressions that are too reminiscent of a bygone day.

About 1620, when the idea arose of publishing Shakespeare's Complete Works, as those of Ben Jonson had been published a few years before, Ralph Crane seems to have held a regular position with the King's men. In 1619 he had made a fair copy of *Barnavelt,* played by them in that year. Some changes having been decided upon by the actors, according to F. P. Wilson, it was Crane himself who made them, which seems to show that he was employed more than occasionally by the company. In 1621 in *Workes of Mercy* he referred to the King's men with words of gratitude:

> And some employment hath my vseful Pen
> Had 'mongst those ciuill, well-deseruing men,
> That grace the Stage with honour and delight,
> Of whose true honesties I much could write,
> But will compris't (as in a Caske of Gold)
> Vnder the kinglie Seruice they doe hold

Crane at that time was in want. His career as a calligrapher had not brought him wealth, and he was reduced to copying manuscripts which he sent with a dedication to collectors in the hope that such compliments would be suitably rewarded. Cannot one of the "honesties" [5] alluded to by Crane have been that the King's men entrusted to his "useful pen" the remunerative task of editing the works of Shakespeare?

The connection between the quarto text and the folio text seems now clear enough. The two texts do not provide distinct plays; they derive, on the contrary, from the same manuscript, the fair copy of Shakespeare's complete revision established to serve as promptbook for the company. The quarto was printed from a copy of this promptbook which had numerous cuts made to shorten this particularly long play. The folio was printed from another copy of the same promptbook which included the passages omitted at performances and the alterations introduced after 1597, such as the different distributions among the actors of certain parts of the dialogue and a few details of stage setting—changes which, having been made by the actors themselves, did not affect the composition of the play.[6] But it also contains a rather important element added by a well-intentioned editor who was unable to approach his task with the requisite understanding. The text of the quarto, typographical errors apart, faithfully reproduces *Richard III* as it was performed until 1597 and probably after; and it has, besides, preserved for us an interesting fragment of a scene whose absence from the folio cannot be easily explained. The text of the folio, on the other hand, permits a more complete idea of the state in which the play must have been when Shakespeare had completed his revision, but it contains arbitrary additions and variants, and this posthumous collaboration prevents it from being an authoritative text. For it is the folio which gives a corrupt version of Shakespeare's original and not the quarto as it has sometimes been maintained.

5. In the sixteenth century one of the meanings of the word honesty was liberality, generosity. Cf. *Timon of Athens* III.i.29: "a Noble Gentleman 'tis, if he would not keep so good a house . . . every man has his fault, and honesty is his."

6. It is of course possible that a quarto of 1622, on which had been entered the deleted passages and other modifications, may have been the copy sent to the printer; but this, it seems to me, is not likely, for the work of collation would have been so long and so complicated that it was infinitely more simple to make a transcript of the promptbook.

CHAPTER FIVE. ROMEO AND JULIET

Several quartos giving the text of *Romeo and Juliet* have come down to us. The first (Q_1), published in 1597, was followed by a second (Q_2) in 1599 and a third (Q_3) in 1609. A fourth (Q_4) was undated and a fifth (Q_5) bears the date 1637. From Q_3 on each one reproduced its predecessor in all but a few unimportant variants; and as the text of the 1623 folio is almost identical with that of Q_2, only Q_1 and Q_2 are of any value in tracing the history of the composition of *Romeo and Juliet*.

THE FIRST QUARTO (1597)

THE FIRST QUARTO was printed by John Danter, who never deposited the manuscript at Stationers' Hall for registration. It appeared under the title *An Excellent conceited Tragedie of Romeo and Iuliet, As it hath been often (with great applause) plaid publiquely, by the right Honourable the L. of Hunsdon his Seruants.* Shakespeare's company was called "Lord Hunsdon's servants" only from July 22, 1596—the date of the death of its patron, Henry Carey, the lord chamberlain and first Lord Hunsdon—to March 16, 1596/7, when the second Lord Hunsdon was in turn appointed lord chamberlain. The First Quarto was therefore printed between these two dates, and as the title page is dated 1597 it must have appeared shortly before March 25, 1597, or very soon afterward.[1]

Now at that time John Danter was in serious trouble with Stationers' Hall. The records of the Stationers' Company show that during the Lenten season 1596/7, that is, between February 9

---

1. There are many modern reproductions of this quarto: the facsimiles of Edmund W. Ashbee, 1866; of C. Praetorius, with introduction by Herbert A. Evans (Shakspere Quarto Facsimiles, 1886, No. 85); the reprints by George Steevens (*Twenty Plays of Shakespeare*, 1766, Vol. 4); of P. A. Daniel (New Shakspere Society, 1874); of Horace Furness (Variorum Shakespeare, 1871); of Appleton Morton (Bankside Shakespeare, 1889, Vol. 5); and of W. A. Wright (Cambridge Shakespeare, 1893, Vol. 9).

References in the present chapter are to the Praetorius facsimile.

and March 27, two presses and various fonts of type that had been used in Danter's printing house for illegal printing of the *Jesus Psalter* were confiscated. This seems to have interrupted the work on *Romeo and Juliet* so that Danter was obliged to entrust the completion of the volume to another printer, and this explains the two sizes of type used in the First Quarto. Sheets A–D (up to line 81 of Act II.sc.iii) are in a type corresponding to modern 7 point, and the normal page has 32 lines; whereas sheets E–K are in smaller type, comparable with modern 9 point, and there are 36 lines to a page.[2]

This untoward event in Danter's printing house renders suspect the way in which the manuscript used for printing the First Quarto was obtained, but it throws no light on the composition of the play. Fortunately the manuscript had peculiarities so significant that it is possible to give a particularly detailed description of it.

It was composed of two parts very different from one another. The first comprised roughly the first nine scenes (I.i–II.iv). It was in many places hard to decipher, for I have found a considerable number of misreadings:

I.i.135,136	"honor" for "humour"
178	"without lawes giue path-waies" for "without eyes get pathways"
I.ii.4,5	"they" for "you"
I.iv.90	"Elfeldcks" for "Elflocks"
I.v.107	"though: grant nor praier forsake" for "though grant for praiers sake"
II.i.13	"young Abraham: Cupid" for "young Adam Cupid"
II.ii.16	"doe enter at" for "to entreat"
52	"beskrind" for "bescreened"
74	"thee" for "mee"
188	"I were sleep and peace of sweet to rest" for "I were sleep and peace so sweet to rest"
II.iii.6	"darke" for "dank"
34	"my" for "thy"
II.iv.73	"Swits and spurres, swits & spurres" for "switch and spurres" (twice)
91	"faire and wide" for "farre and wide"
153	"roperipe" for "ropery"

2. For more details on the career of John Danter, and more especially on the printing of the First Quarto of *Romeo and Juliet,* see the first chapter of Harry R. Hoppe, *The Bad Quarto of Romeo and Juliet,* Cornell University Press, 1948.

It had also several marginal corrections, ill-divided verse lines or verses printed as though they were prose (notably a long speech of the nurse): I.ii.67–73; I.iii.2–5,8–11,13–15,16–49,59–61,63–5, 67–8,75–6; I.iv.100–1; I.v.44–5,67–8,115–18,138–9,144–5; II.i.8–21,23–29; II.ii.26–7,92–4,168–71.

The stage directions (except one at the beginning, describing the fight between the Montague and Capulet factions) are brief, mentioning only the names of the characters entering or leaving the stage:

> Enter Conntie Paris, old Capulet (I.ii.1)
>
> Enter Benuolio and Romeo (I.ii.44–5)

Lastly, in this first part Juliet's father (here again with the exception of the very first stage direction) is called Capulet, sometimes old Capulet, as in all the English versions of the story.

The second part of the manuscript, beginning with Act.II.sc.v, comprises all the rest of the play. It was perfectly legible, for it caused no difficulty to the compositor: I have not found one error which could indisputably be called a misreading, and it has only misprints, wrong letters, added letters, or words omitted or added, etc.

In this second part there are very few corrections; many scenes have none at all; and with the exception of another speech of the nurse printed as prose they are short, generally affecting one or two lines, rarely three, and four lines only once: III.i.64–5,72–4; III.iii.158–61; III.v.122–4,194–5,226–7; IV.v.1–16.

The stage directions here are descriptive and have, besides, that picturesque way of indicating how the scene was performed in the theater, which is found only in transcripts made for collectors of dramatic literature or in manuscripts prepared for publication:

II.iv.140–1	He walkes by them, and sings
162–3	She turns to Peter her man
II.vi.15–16	Enter Iuliet somewhat fast, and embraceth Romeo
III.i.93–4	Tibalt vnder Romeos arme thrusts Mercutio in and flyes
III.ii.4–5	Enter Nurse wringing her hands, with the ladder of cordes in her lap
III.iii.108–9	He offers to stab himselfe, and Nurse snatches the dagger away
III.iv.11–12	Paris offers to goe in, and Capolet calles him againe
III.v.1	Enter Romeo and Iuliet at the window

39–40	She goeth downe from the window
59–60	Enter Nurse hastely
161–2	She kneeles downe
234–5	She lookes after Nurse
IV.iii.59	She fals vpon her bed within the Curtaines
IV.iv.1	Enter Nurse with hearbs, Mother
12–13	Enter Seruingman with Logs & Coales
IV.v.55–6	All at once cry out and wring their hands
90–1	They all but the Nurse goe foorth, casting Rosemary on her and shutting the Curtens
V.i.11–12	Enter Balthasar his man booted
V.iii.1	Enter Countie Paris and his Page with flowers and sweete water
11–12	Paris strewes the Tomb with flowers
17–18	Boy whistles and calls. . . . Enter Romeo and Balthasar, with a torch, a mattocke, and a crow of yron
43–4	Romeo opens the tombe
120–1	Enter Fryer with a Lanthorne
137–8	Fryer stoops and lookes on the blood and weapons
170	She stabs herselfe and falles

And Juliet's father, in this part, is consistently called Capolet, which seems to be an Anglicized form of some Italian word like *capoletto*.[3]

It is no wonder that the second part of the manuscript was legible, for it was surely in the handwriting of Ralph Crane. The graphic character of the stage directions is, as we have seen in a preceding chapter, a mark of the manuscripts prepared by this scrivener for collectors of dramatic literature, and the singular use of parentheses instead of commas appears here and there in the last half of the play:

II.iv.189	(as I take it)
II.vi.14	(Cloasd in Nights mysts)
16	(if I be Day)
III.iii.26	(Taking thy part)
IV.i.77	(rather than marrie Paris)
IV.ii.11	(my Lord)
V.i.7	(Strange dreames that giue a dead man leaue to thinke)
51	(Whose present sale is death in Mantua)
V.iii.202	(loe)

3. The same use of the double form Capulet, Capolet is also found in the German play, *Die Tragoedie von Romio und Julietta*, published in Albert Cohn's *Shakespeare in Germany*, 1855. This similarity is tantamount to a proof that the German play is an adaptation of the text of the First Quarto of *Romeo and Juliet*.

237   (Loathing a second Contract)
243   (tutord by mine arte)
250   (Frier John)

It should be added that in the prologue and in one of the first lines of the play there are three more instances:

Prologue.2   (In faire Verona, where we lay our Scene)
   10–11   (Through the continuing of their Fathers strife,
           And death-markt passage of their Parents rage)
  I.i.13   (of my word)

which added to the descriptive stage direction (I.i.65) and the spelling "Capolet" (I.i.1) permit the deduction that before the corrections were made the entire manuscript must have been in the handwriting of Crane.

This manuscript in its original form was a transcript of a play already old in Shakespeare's time. It had a prologue [4]; and prologues or choruses, pronounced by a messenger or a nuntius, announcing at the beginning of the play or of each act what was going to happen, were part of the technique of the interludes such as *Jack Juggler* or *New Custom* or even plays like *Cambyses* or *Damon and Pythias* belonging to the period around 1560. There were also several instances of the habit in the same period of calling the characters by generic terms instead of by their family names. In two entrances Capulet was introduced by the word "Oldeman" (IV.iv.3; IV.v.20); likewise Lady Capulet is "Mother" (III.v; IV.iii; IV.iv). Other characters with generic names are Nurse, Friar, Apothecary, Watch, etc.

In this hybrid form, however, the play had been performed. It is not that I believe entirely the assertion of crafty Danter on the title page that the play he was publishing had been acted by Lord Hunsdon's servants; this was probably an attempt to create a confusion with the play actually performed by Lord Hunsdon's men at the time of publication, which was different, as we are going to see. But the hand of the prompter is visible in 21 exits and 2 en-

---

4. It is even probable that there were other "choruses" marking the development of the action, such as the one that has been retained in the folio at the beginning of what is in modern editions the second act. This chorus is rhymed and in the form of an English sonnet. The versification is stiff and mechanical, the style awkward and old-fashioned; it certainly is not Shakespeare's.

trances omitted in the manuscript and added, as usual, at the end
of the last line preceding the actor's exit or for the entrances at
the end of the first available line.[5]

To sum up, the manuscript reproduced by the First Quarto was
a copy made by Crane, possibly for some collector. It had been
acquired by Lord Strange's men under circumstances which we
shall probably never know, had been corrected heavily in the
first two acts, very lightly touched up in some four places in the
last half of the play, and had been presented in that form. At the
point we have reached it is impossible to say more.

$$\int \quad \int \quad \int$$

ABOUT THREE HUNDRED verses of the First Quarto are rhymed.
Several passages are composed of a simple distich and a few others
of four verses. Of these it is impossible to say whether the rhymes
were intentional or accidental. But there are longer rhymed passages of 6 lines (I.i.162–7,199–204; I.ii.46–51; I.v.60–5; II.ii.185–
90; II.vi.36–41), 10 lines (I.iv.44–53; I.v.46–55; III.i.147–56), 12
lines (the prologue), 14 lines (III.i.181–204), 16 lines (I.ii.91–
106), 20 lines (I.ii.16–37), 22 lines (I.v.91–112), 86 lines (II.iii.
1–92); and in these we must presume that the rhymes were deliberately employed. A great many of these passages, as we shall
see later, were recast by Shakespeare; nothing definite can be
based upon them for the moment. But there is one passage, the
longest of all (II.iii.1–92), which (though it begins with four
verses indubitably Shakespearean and contains two blank verses,
an obvious interpolation) [6] has certainly preserved its original form
which is not in the least Shakespearean. This long dissertation by
the friar on the virtues of plants is that of a man who was accustomed to see nature only through herbaries and books of rural
economy; the style and versification are mediocre. When the
four Shakespearean verses and the two blank verses interpolated
are omitted, there remains a passage long enough to provide certain facts giving an idea of the author.

5. Cf. I.i.64,222; I.iii.5; I.v.147; II.iii.92; II.iv.231,232; II.v.82; II.vi.41; III.ii.143;
III.v.59,197,205; IV.ii.47; IV.iii.5,13; IV.v.148,149; V.i.86; V.ii.23,31.

6. In line 58 there is also the spelling "Capulet."

The five-stress iambic line is strictly decasyllabic; the rhymes are often satisfactory though plainly imperfect at times—lies:qualities, remedies:lies, how:vowes, sit:yet; the rhythmic variations are numerous, with a strong preponderance of spondaic feet (8.2%) which produces a heavily grandiloquent tone, though the number of internal pauses is rather high (61.2%). The frequency of enjambments is variable (15% in the present passage), but in other passages—the prologue, for instance—it may fall as low as 0%, for this author has a decided tendency to consider the line as a unit in itself.

The style is of a definitely inferior quality. The language is without distinction of any sort and sentences are often involved, even incorrect:

> Vertue it selfe turnes vice being misapplied,
> And vice sometimes by action dignified (21–2)

> Being tasted slaies all sences with the hart (26)

> both our remedies
> With in thy help and holy phisicke lies (51–2)

where "lies" is at once a faulty rhyme and a colloquialism.

Not that this author was devoid of literary pretensions. Like Shakespeare and many others he followed the literary fashions of the period, but his imitation was limited to two mannerisms which he repeated to sickening satiety; antitheses and plays on words of the jingle kind.

Antitheses:

> With balefull weeds, and precious iuyeed flowers (8)

> Nor nought so good, but straind from that fair vse,
> Reuolts to vice and stumbles on abuse:
> Vertue it selfe turnes vice being misapplied (19–21)

> Within the infant rinde of this small flower,
> Poyson hath residence, and medecine power (23–4)

> Two such opposed foes incampe them still,
> In man as well as herbes, grace and rude will (27–8)

> Is Rosaline whome thou didst loue so deare
> So soone forsooke, lo yong mens loue then lies
> Not truelie in their harts, but in their eyes (66–8)

> Women may fal, when ther's no strength in men (80)

Jingles:

> For nought so vile, that vile on earth doth liue (17)
>
> Care keepes his watch in euerie old mans eye,
> And where care lodgeth, sleep can neuer lie (35–6)
>
> I haue forgot that name, and that names woe (46)
>
> Where on the sodaine one hath wounded mee
> Thats by me wounded . . . (50–1)
>
> Ridling confession findes but ridling shrift (56)
>
> As mine on hers, so hers likewise on mine
> And all combind, saue what thou must combine (59–60)
>
> To season loue, that of loue doth not taste (72)
>
> If euer thou wert thus, and these woes thine,
> Thou and these woes were all for Rosaline (77–8)
>
> Doth grace for grace, and loue for loue allow (86)

If the reader will now go back to pages 193–4 he will see that the rhymed verse in *Romeo and Juliet* and the rhymed verse of the old play, which has been partly preserved in *Richard II*, were written by the same author, whom I have called author C. They have in common the same versification with the same percentages and types of rhythmic variations, the same sprinkling of imperfect lines, the same flat style with involved sentences, and the same exclusive taste for antitheses and jingles. The resemblance is really striking; and the mind that conceived the dissertation on the virtues of medicinal herbs is the same mind that compared the government of a state with the management of a garden in which the trees are carefully pruned.

And like the rhymed verse of *Richard II* the rhymed verse of *Romeo and Juliet* is embedded within the blank verse in which most of the play is written. There is no reason why it should be there at all, for it is an integral part of the idea of the surrounding blank verse and there is no change in the dramatic tone by which its existence might be justified. As in *Richard II* these rhymed fragments are remnants of a pre-Shakespearean play, the old play which the examination of the manuscript has led us to expect— possibly the play that Arthur Brooke, in the introduction to his

Romeus and Juliet, published in 1562, said he had seen "lately set forth" on the same subject as his own poem.

∫ ∫ ∫

THE BLANK VERSE in which the greater part of the play is written is not of the same quality throughout. For the sixth time I have to note the presence of author A, who more and more appears to have been the regular purveyor of plays to Shakespeare's company before Shakespeare himself, for all the characteristics of versification and style which distinguish this author are found in the play from beginning to end.

1. Excessive use of trochaic feet (I cite only the most important passages):

	Trochees	Feet	Percentages
I.iii.1–15	6	70	8.5
III.iii.74–108	18	151	11.9
III.iv.1–19	7	59	11.8
III.v.43–59	8	84	9.5
66–124	13	170	7.6
147–57	4	48	8.3
IV.ii.10–47	11	153	7.1
IV.iii.1–24	8	76	10.5
IV.v.17–50	11	109	10.0
V.ii.1–30	7	91	7.6
V.iii.18–73	19	206	9.2
74–120	8	112	7.1
174–96	7	60	11.4

2. Verse lines of irregular length from one foot to seven feet.[7]

7. One foot: I.v.135; II.vi.19; III.iii.172; V.iii.17. Two feet: II.ii.92; II.vi.16; III. iii.163; III.v.66,139; IV.ii.36; IV.v.17; V.ii.22; V.iii.186. Three feet: I.i.206; I.ii.66; I.v.88,129; II.v.79; III.i.159,179; III.ii.90; III.iv.29; III.v.47,160,188,228,230; IV.v. 24; V.i.65; V.ii.17,26; V.iii.129,190,213,299. Four feet: I.i.207; I.ii.34,65; I.iii.14; I.iv.8,43; I.v.130; II.i.40,41; II.ii.107; II.iv.201; III.i.118; III.ii.40,41; III.iii.46,99; III.iv.33; III.v.140,152,177,192,226,234; IV.i.17,33; IV.v.23,25; V.ii.1; V.iii.103–5,110,140,141,201. Six feet: I.iii.40,47; I.iv.49; I.v.22–3,34,84–5; II.i.4,17–18; II.v.47–8; III.i.143,204; III.ii.85,91,112; III.iii.20–1,138; III.iv.12,13,23,27–8,31; III.v.105,157,162,176,182,200,227; IV.iv.13; V.i.79; V.iii.50–3,134,197,205,274–5, 307. Seven feet: II.ii.94; II.iv.1; III.iii.103; III.v.131,143–4,220; IV.i.109; IV.ii.12; V.i.22,78–9; V.iii.2.

3. Trisyllabic feet:

I.ii.34
I.iii.8
II.ii.90,183
II.iv.232
III.i.59,60,61,63,69,151
III.ii.130
III.iii.77,99,105
III.iv.3,12,31,35
III.v.153,173,179,206,207,221,227,229,233
IV. ii.38
V.i. 49
V.iii.24

4. Commonplace style vulgarized by too many interjections or exclamations. There are no less than 240 examples of the free use of those forms of speech: ay, nay, come, why, why then, tut, what, now, how now, faith, well, go to, marry, but soft, loe, sirrah, trust me, look ye, ah, oh, fie, alas, alack.

5. Obsolescent expressions and colloquialisms: III.v.226, As for your husband he is dead; IV.iv.16, I haue a heade I troe to choose a Log; V.iii.135, And not for to disturbe him; 153, Paris he is slaine; 258, for to see his loue.

These characteristics of author A appear in most of the scenes: his intervention, therefore, as in *Richard II*, resulted in a nearly complete recasting that was meant to replace with blank verse the rhymed verse of his predecessor. And it is worth noticing, by the way, that these characteristics are less numerous in the first two acts, which the examination of the manuscript has shown to have been corrected: these corrections must have been made upon the text of author A.

$$\int \quad \int \quad \int$$

IT IS PRECISELY in the first two acts that the characteristics of Shakespeare's versification and style are more often found, as the list of Shakespearean mannerisms and images will indicate. In drawing up this list we come upon the same difficulty we met in *Richard II*. It is possible that some of the mannerisms that author

C had in common with Shakespeare may have been retained; to tabulate the antitheses and jingles would assuredly magnify Shakespeare's share unduly; I have accordingly omitted those two types of mannerisms, even though by so doing I have diminished the importance of a valuable "detector" of his presence.

MANNERISMS

1. Division of the thought into symmetrical parts of more or less equal length:

> That most are busied when th'are most alone (I.i.134)
>
> Beautie too rich for vse, for earth too deare (I.v.49) [8]

2. Repetition of a word or grammatical form to accentuate the symmetrical construction:

> O're Courtiers knees: who strait on cursies dreame
> O're Ladies lips who dreame on kisses strait (I.iv.72–3) [9]

3. Marked preference for the association of two words expressing two aspects of the same idea and connected by a conjunction:

> To scorne and ieere at our solemnitie (I.v.59)
>
> Now by the stocke and honor of my kin (I.v.60) [1]

4. Concetti in the Italian manner:
I.v.95–113. The conversation between Romeo and Juliet at the Capulets' feast is a long-drawn-out concetto.
II.ii.1–22. The monologue of Romeo admiring Juliet as she appears at her window is another series of concetti.
5. Compound words after the Greek and Latin manner: best seeming (I.i.185); Saint seducing (I.i.220); Earth treadding (I.ii.25); dew-dropping (I.iv.103); bow-boyes but-shaft (II.iv.17).
6. French words: pardonmees (II.iv.36); bon iour (II.iv.47).

---

8. Cf. I.ii.33; I.v.21,75; II.i.15,18,19; II.ii.34,68; III.iii.24; III.v.28.
9. Cf. I.i.197–8; I.iv.77–83, 84–5; I.v.83; III.iii.68; III.v.19–22.
1. Cf. I.i.176; I.ii.37,57; I.iii.16; I.v.70; II.i.10,28; II.ii.5,8,40,41,63,140; III.i.173, 197,198,199; III.iii.16,87,99,143; III.v.114,116,178; IV.i.64,72,87,96; IV.iii.29; IV.v.25,66,81; V.ii.12.

IMAGES

I.i.125–6   before the worshipt sunne
              Peept through the golden window of the East

169   . . . what sorrow lengthens Romeos houres?

196–8   Loue is a smoke raisde with the fume of sighes
Being purgde, a fire sparkling in louers eyes:
Being vext, a sea raging with a louers teares

218–19   Shee'le not abide the siedge of louing tearmes,
Nor ope her lap to Saint seducing gold

222   That when she dies with beautie dies her store

I.ii.10   Let two more sommers wither in their pride

25   Earth treadding stars, that make darke heauen light

27–8   When well apparaild Aprill on the heele
Of lumping winter treads

50–1   Take thou some new infection to thy eye,
And the ranke poyson of the old will die

101–2   But in that Cristall scales let there be waide,
Your Ladyes loue

I.iv.35–6   let wantons light of hart
Tickle the senceles rushes with their heeles

97–8   True I talke of dreames,
Which are the Children of an idle braine

100–3   the winde,
Which wooes euen now the frosē bowels of the north,
And being angred puffes away in haste,
Turning his face to the dew-dropping south

112–13   But he that hath the steerage of my course
Directs my saile

I.v.44–5   What Ladie is that that doth inrich the hand
Of yonder Knight?

47–8   It seemes she hangs vpon the cheeke of night,
Like a rich iewell in an Aethiops eare

50   So shines a snow-white Swan trouping with Crowes

97–8   My lips two blushing Pilgrims ready stand,
       To smooth the rough touch with a gentle kisse

II.ii.1–5   He iests at scars that neuer felt a wound:
            But soft, what light forth yonder window breakes?
            It is the East, and Iuliet is the Sunne,
            Arise faire Sunne, and kill the enuious Moone
            That is alreadie sicke, and pale with griefe

15–17   Two of the fairest starres in all the skies,
        Hauing some busines, doe enter at her eyes
        To twinckle in their spheares till they returne

20–2   As day-light doth a Lampe, her eyes in heauen,
       Would through the airie region streame so bright,
       That birdes would sing, and thinke it were not night

27–32   For thou art as glorious to this night beeing ouer my head,
        As is a winged messenger of heauen
        Vnto the white vpturned woondring eyes,
        Of mortals that fall backe to gaze on him,
        When he bestrides the lasie pacing cloudes,
        And sailes vpon the bosom of the aire

52–3   What man art thou, that thus beskrind in night,
       Doest stumble on my counsaile?

58–9   My eares haue not yet drunk a hundred words
       Of that tongues vtterance

66   By lones light winges did I oreperch these wals

75   I haue nights cloak to hide thee from their sight

82–4   I am no Pilot: yet wert thou as farre
       As that vast shore, washt with the furthest sea,
       I would aduenture for such Marchandise

85   Thou knowst the maske of night is on my face

107–8   By yonder blessed Moone I sweare,
        That tips with siluer all these fruit trees tops

119–20   Too like the lightning that doth cease to bee
         Ere one can say it lightens

157–8   Loue goes toward loue like schoole boyes from their bookes,
        But loue from loue, to schoole with heauie lookes

159–63   O for a falkners voice,
         To lure this Tassell gentle backe againe:

Bondage is hoarse and may not crie aloud,
Els would I teare the Caue where Eccho lies
And make her airie voice as hoarse as mine

177–82   I would haue thee gone,
But yet no further than a wantons bird,
Who lets it hop a little from her hand,
Like a pore prisoner in his twisted giues,
And with a silke thred puls it backe againe,
Too louing jealous of his libertie

II.iii.1–4   The gray ey'd morne smiles on the frowning night,
Checkring the Easterne clouds with streakes of light,
And flecked darkenes like a drunkard reeles,
From forth daies path, and Titans fierie wheeles

II.iv.201–3   The cordes, made like a tackled staire,
Which to the hightop-gallant of my ioy
Must be my conduct in the secret night

II.v.4–6   Loues heralds should be thoughts,
And runne more swift, than hastie powder fierd,
Doth hurrie from the fearfull Cannons mouth

II.vi.13–14   As doo waking eyes
(Cloasd in Nights mysts) attend the frolicke Day

17   Come to my Sunne: shine foorth, and make me faire

III.i.119–20   Thy beautie makes me thus effeminate,
And in my temper softens valors steele

129   And fier eyed fury be my conduct now

III.ii.1–4   Gallop apace you fierie footed steedes
To Phoebus mansion, such a Waggoner
As Phaeton, would quickly bring you thether,
And send in cloudie night immediately

64   What storme is this that blowes so contrarie

83–4   Was neuer booke containing so foule matter,
So fairly bound

III.iii.5   What Sorrow craues acquaintance at our hands

20–1   Calling death banishment,
Thou cutst my head off with a golden axe

55   Aduersities sweete milke, philosophie

83   There on the ground, with his owne teares made drunke

103–4 As if that name shot from the deadly leuel of a gun
Did murder her

107–8   Tell me that I may sacke
The hatefull mansion?

142 Happines Courts thee in his best array

III.v.2–3 It was the Nightingale and not the Larke
That pierst the fearfull hollow of thine eare

7–10   See Loue what enuious strakes
Doo lace the senering clowdes in yonder East.
Nights candles are burnt out, and iocond Day
Stands tiptoes on the mystie mountaine tops

13–15 It is some Meteor that the Sunne exhales,
To be this night to thee a Torch-bearer,
And light thee on thy way to Mantua

19–23 Ile say yon gray is not the Mornings Eye,
It is the pale reflex of Cynthias brow.
Ile say it is the Nightingale that beates
The vaultie heauen so high aboue our heads,
And not the Larke the Messenger of Morne

34 Hunting thee hence with Huntsvp to the day

71 I thinke thoult wash him from his graue with teares

132–5 For this thy bodie which I tearme a barke,
Still floating in thy euerfalling teares,
And tost with sighes arising from thy hart:
Will without succour shipwracke presently

198–9 Is there no pitty hanging in the cloudes,
That lookes into the bottom of my woes?

IV.i.8 For Venus smiles not in a house of teares

30–1 The teares haue got small victory by that,
For it was bad enough before their spite

62–5 Twixt.my extreames and me, this bloodie Knife
Shall play the Vmpeere, arbitrating that
Which the Commission of thy yeares and arte
Could to no issue of true honour bring

V.i.1 If I may trust the flattering Eye of Sleepe

3   My bosome Lord sits chearfull in his throne

64–5   As suddenly as powder being fierd
From forth a Cannons mouth

V.iii.45–7   Thou detestable maw, thou womb of death,
Gorde with the dearest morsell of the earth.
Thus I enforce thy rotten iawes to ope

102–3   O I beleeue that vnsubstanciall death,
Is amorous, and doth court my loue

109   With wormes, that are thy chambermayds

117–18   Come desperate Pilot now at once runne on
The dashing rockes thy sea-sicke weary barge

Distribution of Shakespearean mannerisms and images among the different scenes:

I.i.126–222   Benvolio seeks the reason for Romeo's strange mood.
5 mannerisms: 134,176,185,197–8,220
5 images: 125–6,169,196,218–19,222

I.ii.1–37   Capulet authorizes Paris to make love to his daughter Juliet.
3 mannerisms: 25,33,37
3 images: 10,25,27–8

46–106   Benvolio tries to cure Romeo of his love for Rosaline.
1 mannerism: 57
2 images: 50–1,101–2

I.iii.16–99   Chatter of the nurse. Lady Capulet asks Juliet what she thinks of marriage with Paris.
1 mannerism: 16
0 images

I.iv.1–113   Romeo and his friends prepare to go masked to the Capulets' feast.
4 mannerisms: 72–3,77–83,84–5,103
4 images: 35–6,97–8,100–2,112–13

I.v.1–113   The Capulets' feast. First meeting of Romeo and Juliet.
8 mannerisms: 21,49,59,60,69,75,83,95–113
4 images: 44–5,47–8,50,97–8

II.i.1–42   Mercutio conjures Romeo to show himself.
5 mannerisms: 10,15,18,19,28
0 images

II.ii.1–190   Scene in the orchard.
9 mannerisms: 1–22,5,8,34,40,41,63,68,140
15 images: 1–5,15–17,20–2,27–32,52–3,58,66,75,82–4,
85,107–8,119–20,157–8,159–62,177–82

II.iii Scene attributable to the author of the rhymed lines.
   0 mannerisms
   1 image: 1–4

II.iv.1–48 Mercutio makes fun of Tybalt and vies in wit with Romeo.
   3 mannerisms: 17,36,47
   0 images

191–232 Romeo sends his instructions to Juliet by the nurse.
   0 mannerisms
   1 image: 201–3

II.v.1–6 Juliet impatiently awaits the return of the nurse.
   0 mannerisms
   1 image: 4–6

62–82 The nurse returns with Romeo's answer.
   0 mannerisms
   0 images

II.vi.1–27 The friar marries Romeo and Juliet.
   0 mannerisms
   2 images: 13–14,17

III.i.114–204 Infuriated by Mercutio's death, Romeo kills Tybalt.
   4 mannerisms: 173,197,198,199
   2 images: 119–20,129

III.ii.1–90 Juliet learns that Romeo has killed Tybalt.
   0 mannerisms
   3 images: 1–4,64,83–4

92–143 Juliet is inconsolable at the thought that Romeo is banished.
   1 mannerism: 198
   0 images

III.iii.1–108 Romeo, hearing that he has been banished, gives way to despair.
   6 mannerisms: 16,24,68,87,99,143
   6 images: 5,20–1,55,83,103–4,107–8

109–57 The friar puts Romeo to shame for his lack of courage and bids him take leave of Juliet as had been agreed.
   1 mannerism: 143
   1 image: 142

III.iv.1–36 Capulet names a day for the wedding of Paris and Juliet.
   0 mannerisms
   0 images

III.v.1–59 Romeo and Juliet part at dawn.
   2 mannerisms: 19–22,28
   5 images: 2–3,7–10,13–15,19–23,34

64–125 Juliet learns that she is to marry Paris and refuses.
   2 mannerisms: 114,116
   1 image: 71

130–97   Capulet's anger at her refusal.
        1 mannerism: 178
        1 image: 132–5

198–233   Juliet implores her mother not to abandon her.
        0 mannerisms
        1 image: 198–9

IV.i.1–42   Paris and Juliet meet in the friar's cell.
        0 mannerisms
        2 images: 8,30–1

43–109   The friar gives Juliet the means of avoiding marriage with Paris.
        4 mannerisms: 64,72,87,96
        1 image: 62–5

IV.ii.16–40   Juliet feigns to submit.
        0 mannerisms
        0 images

IV.iii.1–58   Juliet drinks the potion given her by the friar.
        1 mannerism: 29
        0 images

IV.iv.1–24   Preparations for the wedding.
        0 mannerisms
        0 images

IV.v.1–91   Juliet is discovered lifeless on her bed. Lamentations of the Capulets.
        3 mannerisms: 25,66,81
        0 images

V.i.1–86   Hearing that Juliet is dead, Romeo decides to kill himself.
        0 mannerisms
        3 images: 1,3,64

V.ii.1–30   The friar learns that the letter addressed to Romeo has not been delivered.
        1 mannerism: 12
        0 images

V.iii.45–70   Paris and Romeo meet before the tomb of the Capulets.
        0 mannerisms
        1 image: 45–7

74–120   Romeo lays the slain Paris beside Juliet and drinks poison.
        0 mannerisms
        3 images: 102–3,109,117–18

The distribution of those traces of Shakespeare's style thoroughly confirms what the examination of the manuscript has led us to expect. More than half the mannerisms (39 in a total of 64) and half the images (34 in a total of 68) are to be found in the part of the manuscript which the handwriting and marginal corrections show to have been strongly corrected. In the part supposed to have been lightly touched up (II.v–V.iii) the characteristics of Shakespeare's style are rare and interspersed, especially in the last two acts, which have only 9 mannerisms and 10 images in 579 lines. Several passages (II.v.62–82; III.iv.1–36; IV.ii.16–40; IV. iv.1–24) have neither mannerism nor image. Only a few incidents —the duel between Romeo and Tybalt, Romeo's despair on having to leave Verona, the separation of the two lovers—have really held Shakespeare's attention.

The analysis of the rhythmical variations adds further precision. Most of the passages having the normally Shakespearean percentages are in the first two acts:

I.ii.4–37   Capulet authorizes Paris to woo Juliet (partly rhymed).
              Trochees 3.3%, spondees 3.3%.
    87–106   Benvolio advises Romeo to love another woman (partly rhymed).
              Trochees 3.3%, spondees 3.3%.
I.iii.20–99   Chatter of the nurse. Lady Capulet asks Juliet what she thinks
              of marriage with Paris.
              Trochees 3.3%, spondees 3.7%.
I.iv.96–113   Mercutio gives his definition of dreams. Romeo has presentiments of death.
              Trochees 4.3%, spondees 4.3%.
II.ii.1–190   Scene in the orchard.
              Trochees 3.7%, spondees 4.6%.
II.v.66–82   The nurse brings Romeo's instructions to Juliet.
              Trochees 2.9%, spondees 4.4%.

If to these we add three passages in the first scene that have percentages approaching those of Shakespeare and which can therefore be supposed to have been extensively revised,

I.i.88–110   The prince promises to punish the fomenters of disorder.
              Trochees 5.7%, spondees 5.7%.
   111–165   Benvolio tells Lady Montague how he met Romeo that morning.
              Trochees 4.8%, spondees 4.8%.
   166–221   Romeo describes his love for Rosaline.
              Trochees 4.5%, spondees 4.5%.

we see that the first two acts are in great part the work of Shakespeare.

In the last three acts I have found only one passage that has Shakespeare's rhythmical variations:

IV.v.51–90   Lamentations in the Capulet home when Juliet is believed to be
          dead.
          Trochees 3.0%, spondees 3.8%.

Two other passages have percentages that approach this:

IV.i.1–42   Paris and Juliet meet in the friar's cell.
          Trochees 3.3%, spondees 2.4%.

  44–110   The friar gives Juliet a means of avoiding marriage with Paris.
          Trochees 4.4%, spondees 4.0%.

In this part of the play Shakespeare's revision has been superficial
even in the passages which have a notable number of mannerisms
or images, since it has not affected the versification which has
continued to predominate. Here again the indications of style and
versification agree. The text reproduced by the First Quarto was
certainly composed of two parts, the first mainly by Shakespeare,
the second containing only a few passages having a Shakespearean
ring.

It is now possible to sum up the history of the composition of
this first text. An old play, written in rhymed verse about 1562,
was first recast in blank verse by author A. Shakespeare assumed
the task of revising this revision. He had completed about a third
of his project when he had to suspend his work of emendation for
a reason that may be advanced without too great a risk of error:
the urgent need in a difficult moment of a play that would bring
the company large receipts. So Shakespeare, turning to what was
most essential, touched up only a few passages in Act III where
the dramatic interest became tense. In Act IV he modernized the
technique of the lamentations in the Capulet home, which probably smacked too much of the drama of a bygone day. He bright-
ened up the denouement with some images and left the rest much
as he found it.[2] The text of the First Quarto is not, as has long
been believed, a first draft by Shakespeare of his play about Romeo
and Juliet; it is still less a badly reported text of the play we have

2. It might be added that the revision even in the first two acts was hastily made,
as two curious lapses bear witness. In the scene of the feast at the Capulets' home,
when Romeo discovers that the person with whom he has been talking is the daughter
of the house, he exclaims in great astonishment: "Is she a Montague?" In Act IV.sc.i
Paris is talking with the friar about his projected marriage when Juliet unexpectedly
arrives, and the stage direction says: "Enter Paris." These two examples show that
Shakespeare did not take the time to read over his revision.

in the First Folio. It is simply an unfinished revision of a pre-Shakespearean play, set aside by the company when, as we shall see, Shakespeare provided an entirely revised form.

This imperfect revision was made at a very early period in Shakespeare's career. In the six passages that have the normal percentages of Shakespeare's rhythmical variations (see above, p. 298), I have counted only 3 feminine endings in 235 blank verses or 1.2%. This is probably the first attempt made by Shakespeare to improve one of the plays belonging to his company.

An allusion in the play enables us to propose a fairly precise date. Speaking of the time when Juliet was weaned, the nurse says: "Tis since the Earth quake nowe eleuen yeares." There was a memorable earthquake in London on the evening of April 6, 1580, and "almost generally throughout all England," which, according to Holinshed, "caused such an amazedness among the people as was wonderful for the time and caused them to make their prayers to Almighty God." This puts the production of the play in the year 1591. The critics who would have it that Shakespeare wrote *Romeo and Juliet* in 1595 or 1596 refuse to admit the validity of the allusion; this, they say, is giving the accuracy of the nurse an improbable value. But it is the author, not the nurse, who, by recalling such an event, introduced a realistic note into the action and thus tried to awake in the audience a remembrance of their own experience. At any rate, the date 1591 agrees perfectly with the type of versification to be found in this form of the play.[3]

∫ ∫ ∫

SEVERAL PASSAGES, four of which introduce servants of the Capulets, are written in prose:

3. Recently this date has been contested once again. Sidney Thomas (*Modern Language Notes,* June 1949, pp. 417–19) has expressed his belief that the earthquake in question was the one that shook Switzerland on March 1, 1594, and was mentioned by William Covell in *Polimanteia* (1595). Sarah Dodson (*Modern Language Notes,* Feb. 1950, p.144) was inclined to accept this opinion. But this is to forget that in the sixteenth century there was neither telegraph nor radio to transmit such a piece of news to the whole world within a few hours. Communications between countries was infrequent and slow, and when it took place by correspondence it had but a limited circulation within narrow circles. One may be sure that the audience at *Romeo and Juliet* saw in the words of the nurse an allusion to an event with which they were familiar.

I.ii.38–44,68–86   A servant is sent to deliver invitations to the feast at the Capulets'.
I.iii.100–3   A servant announces to Lady Capulet that dinner is served.
IV.ii.1–9   Capulet orders one of his servants to find good cooks.
IV.v.98–149   One of Capulet's servants asks facetious questions of the musicians who have come to play at Juliet's wedding.

In these four cases the servant is the usual type of clown, and he is so called in the speech heading of I.iii.100. He is a simpleton who excites laughter with his silly utterances, and it is highly probable that those passages were in the pre-Shakespearean play.

In I.i.65, according to the stage direction, two serving men of the Capulets wrangle with two serving men of the Montagues. But these belong to a different class. They carry swords like gentlemen and thus should be included among the attendants who were attached to the household of a lord and stood midway between partisans and protégés under the name of retainers. The conversation between the two servants of Capulet is entirely made up of puns, and one might be inclined to attribute this passage to the author of the rhymed verse. I believe, however, that this part of the scene, which contains no less than eight exclamations, was written by author A.

As these five passages are comic in nature, the use of prose is normal, but this is not true of four others in which Mercutio (II. iv.10–106; III.i.5–110) and the nurse (II.iv.108–90; II.v.25–69) have the principal roles. Mercutio and the nurse speak in verse throughout the rest of the play, and these passages in prose are inserted in scenes that begin and end in verse: evidently they are interpolations or corrections. This is proved by irreconcilable differences in the conception of those characters. In Act I.sc.iv, where Mercutio makes his first entrance, he is an amiable and kindly man who tried to beguile Romeo's sorrow by taking his friend to the feast at the Capulets'. By nature he is decidedly inclined to reverie; he thinks he sees in Romeo the influence of Queen Mab and complacently describes this creation of popular mythology. To the objection that he speaks of nothing, he readily admits that he has been talking of dreams and goes on to describe poetically these "Children of an idle braine" (I.iv.98–103). This character conforms to the Mercutio of Arthur Brooke's poem, *The Tragical History of Romeus and Juliet*, where he is presented as

A courtier that eche where was highly had in price,
For he was courteous of his speeche, and pleasant of devise [4]

In the two prose passages, on the contrary, he is a brilliant but uncongenial man. Cynical, ironical, he sees everything from the comic side and is incapable of understanding the weaknesses of sensibility and of love. Intelligent, and conscious of it, he spends his wit in a continuous flow of jests, and his facile talk on mere nothings is not a tendency to dream but proof of a deep-seated levity of which he cannot be cured even by the shadow of death. As Romeo says, he is "a gentleman that God hath made for himself to marre . . . a gentleman that loves to hear himself talk, and will speak more in an hour than he will stand to in a month." This is the Mercutio of the marginal corrections to Act II.sc.i.8–21 and 23–30, in other words the Mercutio of Shakespeare.

So it is with the nurse. Her indefatigable loquacity, with its licentious undertones, is found only in the prose passages or in the marginal corrections to I.iii.2–76 and IV.v.1–16. In the portion that Shakespeare revised slightly, that is in the pre-Shakespearean play, this character was of a conventional type—a nurse sincerely attached to the young girl she had reared, treating her with maternal tenderness and familiarity, quick to defend her even against her father (III.v.169–73). It was from pure affection that she acted as go-between for the two lovers and kept watch on their wedding night (III.v.39–40). A woman who had seen life, she had the unflattering idea that all men are alike, and that is why she advised Juliet to marry Paris since Romeo, having been banished, could be of no further use to her. There is no comedy in all this: this nurse is not the delightfully garrulous woman of Shakespeare; she is vulgar and experienced, well suited to the utilitarian milieu of the Capulets.

The style of these prose passages has some of the mannerisms which Shakespeare used freely in his early productions, those at least that Lyly too had appropriated to adorn his own style: parallelism, antitheses, plays on words. There is every reason to

4. The Mercutio of the poem belonged to the Capulet faction, for in the scene of the feast he is present as a guest. Such he must have been in the pre-Shakespearean play, for his name appears on the list of those to whom Capulet sent invitations (I.ii.71).

suppose that these prose passages belong to the same period as the verse in Shakespeare's first revision. Why Shakespeare wrote the additions to the roles of Mercutio and of the nurse sometimes in verse, sometimes in prose, is difficult to say. I am inclined to believe that under pressure prose flowed more easily from his pen than verse.

THE SECOND QUARTO (Q₂)

THE SECOND QUARTO appeared in 1599 under the title: *The Most Excellent and lamentable Tragedie, of Romeo and Iuliet. Newly corrected, augmented, and amended: As it hath bene sundry times publiquely acted, by the right Honourable the Lord Chamberlaine his Seruants.* The volume was printed by Thomas Creede for Cuthbert Burby, and the manuscript, like that of the First Quarto, was not registered at Stationers' Hall. But this does not imply in the least that this time the publication was fraudulent; on the contrary, it is highly probable that the players themselves delivered to the printer the text of the play as they were performing it, seeking thus to avert any damage that might be done them by the existence of the incomplete Shakespearean version. For what did the statement on the title page mean, that the lamentable tragedy had been "corrected, augmented, and amended," unless it contrasted the new edition with the preceding one of 1597, the only text with which readers could compare it?

The text of the Second Quarto is indeed a complete revision of the incomplete and premature one published as the First Quarto. Of this we have the most irrefragable proof: several passages in which Shakespeare is caught in the very act of correction. He is seen beginning to repeat words that are in the First Quarto, suddenly stopping in the middle of a sentence, no doubt because the idea was not developing as he had hoped, then beginning over again and substituting a second version, to which he finally held. But under the pressure of inspiration, or perhaps in accord with a habit that I have already pointed out several times, he did not take the trouble to cross out the rejected form, and so these constitute an evident repetition but preserve forever, as in a photograph, the image of Shakespeare's own manuscript.

II.ii.41–2. Juliet ponders that the man with whom she is in love
belongs to the hostile house of Montague. She tries to drive out
the memory of this fact, pregnant with tragic consequences, by
telling herself that a name means nothing after all. The First
Quarto expresses this as follows:

> Whats Montague? It is nor hand nor foote,
> Nor arme, nor face, nor any other part.
> Whats in a name?

Not only are these lines prosaic, the words "nor any other part"
are ambiguous. Shakespeare must have thought so after having
first adopted them, and he made them intelligible by the addition
of "Belonging to a man." The obscure phrase was clarified but the
platitudinous nature of the idea was accentuated, not to mention
the fact that in a play where obscene jokes are frequent the addition might be the occasion of indecent interpretations. Something
else had to be found, and then the phrase that was finally chosen
offered itself; Shakespeare removed the word "part," sole cause
of the difficulty, and the line became

> Nor arme nor face, ô be some other name

The solution had been found, and the new line blended well with
the next words: "Whats in a name?" But the half line "Belonging
to a man" was not expunged and remains to this day hanging in
the air, interrupting the easy flow of the idea and transforming it
into a truism:

> Whats Mountague? it is nor hand nor foote,
> Nor arme nor face, o be some other name
> Belonging to a man.
> Whats in a name . . .

II.iii.1–4. In the First Quarto the friar, setting out at dawn to
gather medicinal herbs, speaks the following lines:

> The gray ey'd morne smiles on the frowning night,
> Checkring the Easterne clouds with streakes of light,
> And flecked darkenes like a drunkard reeles,
> From forth daies path, and Titans fierie wheeles

which were an addition by Shakespeare at the time of the first
revision. In the Second Quarto the scene opens with the same four

lines, but slightly changed, "checkring" having been replaced by "checking," "flecked" by "fleckeld" (typographical errors), and "fierie" by "burning," a questionable variant. But these lines occur also at the end of the preceding scene, after the last verse spoken by Romeo as he leaves Juliet and before the verse in which he tells his intention of going to the friar's cell to announce his good fortune. And this time the text of the four verses has received a more important and better correction:

> The grey eyde morne smiles on the frowning night,
> Checkring the Easterne Clouds with streaks of light,
> And darknesse fleckted like a drunkard reeles,
> From forth daies pathway, made by Tytans wheeles.

It goes without saying that Shakespeare never wanted such a glaring repetition, and it is not difficult to imagine how it happened. At first he tried to improve the text of Q_1 by replacing "fierie" with "burning" but the new version still did not satisfy him. The idea of departing night reeling away from the day's pathway and Titan's wheels is neither an appropriate nor a happy one. Hence the correction of the fourth line, making the image coherent, which Shakespeare wrote in the margin. As the margin was already occupied by the word "burning" he put the new form a little higher up so that the printer or the copyist thought it was an addition to the end of the preceding scene. Such is the explanation advanced by some critics, P. A. Daniel, for example, in his revised edition of the Second Quarto (New Shakespere Society, 1875, p. 114). It is a possible one; but there is another which seems to me preferable. Even with the word "burning" in the margin opposite the fourth line, there was still enough room for Shakespeare to write his correction opposite the first three lines, especially as he had, in addition, the wide space separating sc.ii from sc.iii. And what necessity had he to rewrite the four lines? No compositor could by any possibility mistake the place where the marginal correction was intended to go. I rather believe that Shakespeare decided to transfer the four verses to the end of the second scene, in order to suggest that Romeo was so happy that he could not wait for a more timely hour to bring the good news to the friar. And he must have actually rewritten the four verses opposite the place where they were finally to stand.

II.v.13–14. Juliet is impatiently awaiting the nurse, who is to bring back a reply from Romeo. If the nurse were younger, she thinks,

> She would be as swift in motion as a ball,
> My words would bandie her to my sweete loue (13–14)

This is a new rendering in Q₂ replacing the text of Q₁ which is quite different, and Shakespeare was going to continue with a word beginning with the letter *M;* he had just written that letter when he changed his mind. So he did not complete the word and went on as follows:

> And his to me, but old folks, many fain as they wer dead (16)

The printer thought that the letter, which had not been erased, was an abbreviation of "Mother" and made a speech-heading of it:

> M. And his to me . . .

But Juliet is alone in the scene; an interruption by the mother is absurd.

III.iii.33–42. Hearing that he has been banished, Romeo is in despair; life far away from Juliet seems to him intolerable. The lowest creature in Verona, he exclaims in Q₁, dwells in heaven, since it may look on Juliet:

> More validitie,
> More honourable state, more courtship liues
> In carrion flyes, than Romeo: they may seaze
> On the white wonder of faire Iuliets skinne,
> And steale immortall kisses from her lips;   37
> But Romeo may not, he is banished.
> Flies may doo this, but I from this must flye

This passage had already been revised in the First Quarto: the rhythm of the verses is excellent and has the sweetness that is distinctive of Shakespeare. It lacks, however, one of those flights of the imagination always shown by his characters in moments when their feelings are strained to the breaking point, and it is this lack which Shakespeare tried to rectify. After line 37, improved by the change of "kisses" to "blessing," he introduced a charming conceit and expanded the thought by comparing exile with death:

> And steale immortall blessing from her lips, 37
> Who euen in pure and vestall modestie
> Still blush, as thinking their owne kisses sin.
> This may flyes do, when I from this must flie;
> And sayest thou yet, that exile is not death?

and he ended by repeating the two verses of Q₁:

> But Romeo may not, he is banished.
> Flies may do this, but I from this must flie

without noticing that he had already used the concetto-jingle "flies":"fly" in his addition. And that this was really an oversight there is no question, for he has in a way bolstered up the repetition by adding to the last line another repetition:

> They are free men, but I am banished

in which the antecedent of "they" is "flies."

III.iii.75–6. A stage direction has deeply puzzled commentators. In the scene where the nurse knocks for admission to the friar's cell there is another stage direction: *"Slud knock."* What can this Slud mean? An actor? One of the personnel of the company? Edward Dowden discovered, I believe, the correct explanation, and I borrow it from him: "The original word in line 76 was not *study; stud* was written above, but the word could not be completed, being interrupted by *knock; study* was then written in the margin, and *stud* was not erased; which the printer misrepresented by Slud" (Arden Edition, p. 112, n. 75).

IV.i.110–11. Here the text of Q₂ contains another example of double redaction. The friar is telling Juliet what will take place while she is under the influence of the soporific draught, and one of the details relates to her supposed burial:

> Then as the manner of our countrie is,
> Is thy best robes vncouered on the Beere,
> Be borne to buriall in thy kindreds graue (109–11)

"Be borne" is a future whose auxiliary verb occurs six lines above in the phrase "Thou shalt continue." But five lines were inserted between, which prevent the mind from connecting "be borne" with its auxiliary, and Shakespeare corrected line 110 by the simple expedient of repeating "thou shall" and modifying the line to avoid a twelve-stress line:

Thou shall be borne to that same auncient vault

But once more he forgot to delete the line he had corrected, and the text of Q₂ has the two versions, one after the other.

V.iii.101–20. In this passage there are no less than three places that show signs of false starts immediately corrected. These changes are especially interesting because they reveal the rapidity and lucidity with which Shakespeare criticized his own expressions whenever they sprang more spontaneously than appropriately. Romeo, wondering at the beauty of Juliet whom he believes to be dead, says in Q_1:

> Ah deare Iuliet,
> How well thy beauty doth become this graue?
> O I beleeue that vnsubstanciall death,
> Is amorous, and doth court my loue (101–4)

These lines were unquestionably an addition made by Shakespeare in the text of the First Quarto: the idea of Death in love with Juliet, the epithet "vnsubstanciall" to qualify Death, and the limpidity of the style are far beyond the capabilities of the pre-Shakespearean author. But the passage lacks the supreme attribute of poetry—suggestion. The idea is arresting but a frigid supposition; it is not an image. Nevertheless it was worth preserving. Shakespeare rewrote it, therefore, and this time it was animated by the identification of Death with a hideous monster, imprisoning the one he wished to subdue:

> Ah deare Iuliet
> Why art thou yet so faire? I will beleeue,
> That vnsubstanciall death is amorous,
> And that the leane abhorred monster keepes
> Thee here in darke to be his parramour?

The image was now striking, but at the same time there is an expression—"I will beleeue"—that psychologically is faulty: in a moment like this could Romeo be master of his will? Only agonizing doubt could be capable of forming such a supposition. So Shakespeare replaced "I will" with "shall I," which suggests in Romeo a feeling of horror. But as he had written the correction in the left-hand margin of the manuscript, the compositor thought that it should be put at the beginning of the following line, which thus gained two extra feet:

> Why art thou yet so faire? I will beleeue,
> Shall I beleeue that vnsubstanciall death is amorous (Q₂ 102–3)

The First Quarto continued:

> Therefore will I, O heere, O euer heere,
> Set vp my euerlasting rest
> With wormes, that are thy chambermayds

The first line was really bad, for the adverb "therefore" is much too coldly decisive in this moment of desperate resolve, and the words "O heere, O euer heere" are too cacophonous by far. Shakespeare accordingly replaced this faulty and stilted line with an image that prolonged the ideas of terror and of night suggested in the preceding correction:

> For feare of that I still will staie with thee,
> And neuer from this pallat of dym night.
> Depart againe, come lye thou in my arme,
> Heer's to thy health, where ere thou tumblest in (Q₂ 106–9)

after which he had Romeo repeat essentially the line and a half by which he hailed his deliverance from life in the First Quarto:

> O true Appothecarie!
> Thy drugs are quicke. Thus with a kisse I die (110–11)

But on reflection Shakespeare found this change insufficient; it provided a too rapid end for the protagonist of the play, while to drink the health of one already dead came perilously near to comedy. Furthermore, two images in the First Quarto had disappeared that were certainly his own—the comparison with chambermaids of the worms that will swarm on the dead body of Juliet, or of a shattered life with a ship that has been dashed to pieces on the rocks. Shakespeare took up the text again at the point where he had stopped, and around the two neglected images, now restored, Romeo expressed at greater length his will to join forever the one he loved:

> Depart againe, here, here, will I remaine,
> With wormes that are thy Chamber-maides: O here

Will I set vp my euerlasting rest:
And shake the yoke of inauspicious starres,
From this world wearied flesh, eyes looke your last:
Armes take your last embrace: And lips, O you
The doores of breath, seale with a righteous kisse
A datelesse bargaine to ingrossing death:
Come bitter conduct, come vnsauoury guide,
Thou desperate Pilot, now at once run on
The dashing Rocks, thy seasick weary barke:
Heeres to my Loue (108–19)

And Shakespeare ended with the same words as in the first form:

O true Appothecary
Thy drugs are quicke. Thus with a kisse I die (119–20)

Thus in the Second Quarto Romeo's last speech has two conclusions, differing in length and expression but having the same final exclamation.

If I have insisted so much—perhaps more than was necessary —upon these details of the revision, it is not solely because this is the only text in which we can so clearly see Shakespeare at work, but above all because those false starts with their rectifications put it beyond doubt that Q₂ is a complete revision of the first imperfect quarto, and they permit us to detect how this work was done.

ʃ ʃ ʃ

WHEN SHAKESPEARE decided to complete his revision he had as a starting point the choice between two written forms of the text: a) the manuscript made by Crane with its corrections—I shall call this M in order to distinguish it from those that are to follow —which was to serve as copy for the printing of the First Quarto; b) the fair copy of this manuscript (M₁) that was used as a temporary promptbook. Wisely Shakespeare chose the latter, in the virtually free margins of which he could write his corrections. This manuscript he read over, and so long as he worked on the part already corrected by him at the time of the first revision, he had to enter only brief modifications or a few additions, and he wrote them on the manuscript. Thus it is that in the first two acts of Q₂ are found traces of marginal corrections—verses ill divided

(II.i.27–8,42–3), verses printed as prose (I.iv.55–91, description of Queen Mab), and a number of misreadings in places where the manuscript was partly illegible, probably because the corrections had been squeezed into spaces that were too small:

I.ii.29	"Fennell buds" instead of "female buds"
I.iii.98	"Endart" instead of "endear"
I.iv.39	"I am dum" instead of "I am done"
42	"Or saue you reuerence loue" instead of "Of this sir-reuerence loue"
66	"man" instead of "maid"
113	"Sute" instead of "saile"
II.i.10	"prouaunt" instead of "pronounce"
13	"Abraham: Cupid" instead of "Adam Cupid"
38	"Et cetera" omitted by the compositor
II.ii.31	"puffing cloudes" instead of "pacing clouds"
101	"haue coying to be strange" instead of "have . . . cunning to be strange"
168	"My Neece" instead of "Madame"
II.iv.29	"affecting phantacies" instead of "affecting fantasticoes"

In this portion the two texts are fairly similar and there are even some identities that are absolutely complete. In their article on "The Stolen and Surreptitious Texts" J. D. Wilson and Alfred W. Pollard (London *Times Literary Supplement,* Aug. 14, 1919) showed that in some passages not only the text is the same but the spelling, punctuation, and capitalization as well. As an example they cited III.v.25–37. Lines 40–48 of Act II.sc.iv exhibit a singularity that is even more surprising. Mercutio is recalling the names of some women celebrated in literature for their great love, and in both texts Helen, Hero, Thisbe, and Laura are in italics, whereas Dido and Cleopatra are in roman type; the verse lines of the nurse in I.iii are printed as prose and in italics [5] in both texts; two misreadings in Q₁, "Abraham:Cupid" (II.i.13) and "Swits and spurres" (II.iv.73), are also common to both texts. These resemblances have puzzled many commentators; they are natural since both texts are derived from the same original text. [6]

5. It is impossible to give a reason for this unusual employment of italics. Several explanations have been advanced, some of which are inappropriate or impossible. I might add my own, but as I have not the slightest proof of its validity, I prefer to keep it to myself.

6. Some critics have also concluded from these resemblances or links between the two quartos that Q₂ was in part printed from Q₁. The First Quarto had not yet been printed at the time of the second revision.

When Shakespeare came to the part of the manuscript which he had touched up slightly in his first revision and where he had to rewrite the dialogue almost entirely, especially in the last two acts, the additions were so numerous that there could not possibly have been enough room in the blank spaces of the prompt-book M_1. The easiest and surest course, surely, was to transcribe the whole text on fresh sheets of paper. This is what Shakespeare did, as is shown first by the false starts cited above, where fragments of Q_1 adhere to the new matter; secondly, by the extremely small number of marginal corrections and misreadings; [7] thirdly, by the disappearance of Crane's parentheses [8] and stage directions.

So in its final form the manuscript of the second revision, M_2, was composed of two parts which corresponded to the two parts of M, the original manuscript of Crane: a) a fragment of M_1 covering roughly the first two acts and which could still be used; b) a portion entirely new, in the hand of Shakespeare, and which properly speaking was the rough draft or foul papers of Shakespeare.

Such a manuscript, made up partly of a corrected one and partly of loose sheets, could not well be used as a playhouse promptbook, and the company had to provide a fair copy, M_3, which then became their promptbook and was probably still in use in 1599.

In the interval between the date when this fair copy was made and 1599, the history of Shakespeare's company was marked by a number of events—changes in personnel, changes in playhouses—and some of these events resulted in modifications that were recorded in their promptbook. An apparently insignificant correction, for instance, proves that the text of Q_2 was not performed in the same theater as that of Q_1. In the First Quarto Juliet says to the friar:

> Oh bid me leape (rather than marrie Paris)
> From off the battlements of yonder tower (IV.i.77–8)

and as he pronounced the word "yonder" the actor evidently

---

7. The only marginal corrections that I have found in this second part are II.v. 60–1; III.iv.34–5; and V.iii.265–6. The misreadings are: "chapels sculls" for "chapless skulls" (IV.i.83), "good father" for "good faith" (IV.iv.21), and "loue" for "long" (IV.v.41).

8. One parenthesis (V.iii.243), however, remained, which was in the text of Q_1.

pointed to a tower that was in view of the audience. In the Second Quarto Juliet says:

> Oh bid me leape, rather than marrie Paris,
> From off the battlements of any Tower

the actor evidently no longer had a tower at which to point.

Two stage directions in Q_1 show that in this same theater there was also an alcove or inner stage in which scenes could be performed. When Juliet takes the sleeping draught she is seen falling "vpon her bed within the curtains" (IV.iii.58); and when her supposedly dead body was discovered after the Capulets and Paris had expressed their sorrow

> They all but the Nurse goe foorth, casting Rosemary on her
> and shutting the Curtens (IV.v.90–1)

In the corresponding scenes of Q_2 no mention of curtains is made. In the first case Juliet drinks the potion and no stage direction follows; in the second case the Capulets and Paris simply "Exeunt," leaving the nurse behind to dismiss the musicians who have come for the wedding: according to the text of Q_2 the theater had no inner stage.

Now we have seen (pp. 101–2) that *The Contention* was played in a theater having a tower to which access was obtained, in full view of the audience, by way of a staircase, and that the same theater also had an inner stage, and that neither tower nor inner stage existed in the theater where according to the folio text *2 Henry VI* was performed. There cannot be any doubt that the imperfect revision of *Romeo and Juliet* was played in the same theater as *The Contention* and that the complete revision was made with another theater in view.

In 1599 Shakespeare's company was richer in minor personnel, for in the text of the Second Quarto several examples prove that a large body of supernumeraries were needed. Thus in Act I.sc.i the prince enters with his retinue; in I.iv Romeo and his friends arrive at the Capulets' feast "with fiue or six other Maskers, torchbearers"; in III.i.37–8, the duel scene, Tybalt is accompanied by "Petruchio and others"; and in the same scene, when the prince enters with Montague, Capulet, and their wives, the addition to the stage direction of the words "and all" indicates that they were followed by a crowd.

Also the staging was more artfully carried out. The Second
Quarto makes use of a procedure, employed only once in the text
of Q₁ (III.iii.71), that always produces in the theater a striking
physical effect on the audience—the use of unexpected, insistent,
off-stage sounds in a moment of especially dramatic tension. As
Juliet learns that the young man with whom she has just fallen in
love belongs to the hostile family of the Montagues, "one calls
within Juliet" (I.v.144–5). In the orchard scene, while Romeo and
Juliet are plighting their troth, a call is heard twice, "Madam,
madam" (II.ii.148,150). Finally, when the despairing Romeo rolls
on the floor in the friar's cell, the nurse knocks for admittance, and
while the friar begs Romeo to rise and hide himself, she knocks
thrice impatiently (III.iii.70–1,73–4,75–6), augmenting with each
stroke the excitement of the friar.⁹

In 1599 when Shakespeare's company decided to publish the
complete and amended text of *Romeo and Juliet,* two manuscripts
were available: their promptbook and the manuscript of the
second revision (M₂). To part with the promptbook of a successful
play that was still on the boards was entirely out of the question;
only a transcript was possible. But was not the promptbook itself
a copy of M₂? Why not hand this manuscript over to the printer?
It would be easy to transfer from the promptbook the few changes
that had been made, and Shakespeare's foul copy would be as
complete as the promptbook. This apparently is what was done.
And it was Ralph Crane who was entrusted with the task of bringing the foul copy up to date.

There is always some danger in being too positive when under-
taking the solution of a problem such as this one, where so much
of the unknown may remain concealed; but certain features in
the text of the Second Quarto permit us to suppose beyond any
reasonable doubt that it was really Crane who edited the foul
papers of Shakespeare to serve as copy for the printing of the
Second Quarto. For in parts of Q₂ are found some of those odd
parentheses which have been recognized as a mark of Crane's
calligraphy. Shakespeare never used parentheses as a means of
punctuation: as we have seen, in his final revision he retained only

9. In this case the modification must have been made with Shakespeare's help, for
it has involved a new redaction of the dialogue.

one from Crane's manuscript M (cf. p. 312), and we cannot ascribe to him the following which have the unusualness that distinguished those of Crane:

I.i.154   Is to himselfe (I will not say how true)

235   Tis the way to call hers (exquisit) in question more

I.ii.44–5   and can neuer find what names the writing person hath here writ
(I must to the learned) in good time

I.v.106   They pray (grant thou) least faith turne to dispaire

II.ii.151   I do beseech thee (by and by I come)   Madam

74   Hark how they knock (whose there) Romeo arise

It is to be noted, besides, that three of them (I.i.154; I.i.235; and II.ii.151) are in important additions of 11, 22, and 9 lines respectively, and two others (I.ii.44; III.iii.74) occur in passages that have been almost entirely rewritten by Shakespeare.[1] All these long fragments had probably been squeezed into inadequate spaces and consequently there was some risk that they might not be easily deciphered or inserted in the right place.

On the other hand, as the above list shows, all those parentheses were found in the corrected part of manuscript M_2; in the part entirely in Shakespeare's hand Crane seems to have transcribed only III.iii.74–81, one of the passages in a scene which had been touched up by Shakespeare (cf. p. 296). From all this we can, I think, infer that Crane's work as an editor was limited to tidying up passages hard to decipher or to the addition of some stage directions. He certainly did not collate all the foul papers with the book of the company. For it is impossible that after the first rehearsal the actors should have retained all the false starts with their consequent double redactions and lapses, like the name Horatio instead of Benvolio,[2] that made some roles unplayable as they were.

1. I.v.106 is found in a rewritten verse where "(grant thou)" replaced "yeeld thou" of Q_1.

2. This strange error attributes a speech to Horatio in I.iv.23. Romeo, Mercutio, and Benvolio are preparing to enter the Capulet home on the evening of the feast. The conversation is mainly between Mercutio and Romeo when a reply unexpectedly comes from Horatio. No doubt Shakespeare meant to have Benvolio answer. While revising *Romeo and Juliet* was he working on *Hamlet* also, and did he mix up in his mind two characters that are somewhat alike?

And thus it happened—it is not to be regretted, after all—that the Second Quarto is a faithful reproduction of Shakespeare's first draft, with all the untidiness in which he left it, supplemented only by a few details of staging.

$$\int \quad \int \quad \int$$

WITH THE DIFFERENCE that in the first nine scenes (I.i–II.iv) Shakespeare was often revising his own text, the relation of Q_2 to Q_1 is on the whole the same as that of 2 and 3 *Henry VI* to *The Contention* and *The True Tragedie:* we have a good part of the pre-Shakespearean play which Shakespeare revised, and we can therefore see with some precision what this revision consisted of.

As in 2 and 3 *Henry VI* three kinds of verses can be distinguished in the text of Q_2: a) verses retained verbatim; b) mixed verses or pre-Shakespearean verses more or less modified; c) verses entirely new, amplifications or additions.

I. VERSES RETAINED VERBATIM

As might be expected, the passages or scenes in the first two acts that had already been extensively recast in the First Quarto have carried over the largest number of verses reproduced word for word, 417 in the first eight scenes (II.iv is mostly in prose) in a total of 916 verses.[3] Beginning with II.v and continuing to the end the number of lines common to both texts diminishes greatly, forming a total of 264 in 1591 verses. Only in the parts of Act III already retouched in the first revision are they moderately numerous. In the rest of the play there are but a few.[4]

II. MIXED VERSES

This class is by far the most important of the three. The similarity of Q_1 to Q_2 in the first two acts has been greatly exaggerated.

3. I.i, 53 verses; I.ii, 68; I.iii, 54; I.iv, 39; I.v, 51; II.i, 25; II.ii, 79; II.iii, 48.
4. II.v, 3 verses; II.vi, 0; III.i, 23; III.ii, 12; III.iii, 70; III.iv, 4; III.v, 49; IV.i, 41; IV.ii, 3; IV.iii, 1; IV.iv, 1; IV.v, 2; V.i, 10; V.ii, 5; V.iii, 40.

It is true that, as I have shown, certain passages are identical; but it is no less true that in that part of the play there are 522 verses [5] that have been recast in the course of the second revision. And, on the other hand, the dissimilarity of Q_1 and Q_2 in the last three acts has been still more unduly magnified, and here the truth is that there are more than 600 mixed verses in a total of 1591 lines and that there is not any fundamental difference in the development of the action or in the meaning of the dialogue. The revision consisted principally in improving the wording of the speeches, which is sometimes so different as to constitute a complete rewriting of the passage. The long speech of the friar at the denouement (V. iii.229–69) is a good example.

The modifications in the mixed lines greatly resemble those that have been noted in 2 and 3 *Henry VI*. Many were inspired by the desire to purge the text of such deficiencies in style as had survived the first revision. Irregular lines, except three (I.i.206; II.i.4; III. v.228), were brought to the normal five feet, and the trisyllabic feet have disappeared; only three (I.iii.8; III.i.61; III.iv.34) have not been rectified. Repetitions of the same word in neighboring sentences have been avoided:

> Q_1 I drew towards him, but he was ware of me,
> And drew into the thicket of the wood
>
> Q_2 Towards him I made, but he was ware of me,
> And stole into the couert of the wood (I.i.131–2)

Many variants are motivated by the desire to substitute a word more precise or, as in the preceding instance, more suggestive:

> Q_1 And if thou doost, Ile giue thee remedie
> Q_2 And if thou darest, Ile giue thee remedie (IV.i.76)

The following example shows how Shakespeare took pains to have his images in keeping with reality. In Q_1 the pre-Shakespearean author had written

> So shines a snow-white Swan trouping with Crowes (I.v.50)

5. I must say that I cannot vouch for the absolute exactness of these totals. In many passages the mixture of verse and prose or other prosodic irregularities makes it often difficult to count the lines with precision; but errors, if there be any, cannot be very extensive.

Swans do not ordinarily flock with crows; Shakespeare in Q₂ changed the swan to a dove, which is at least possible, though such a spectacle, I suppose, is not frequent.

And last but not least, if we sought the inner meaning of most of those changes we should find that the real intention of Shakespeare was to replace ill-sounding lines with lines that could be more easily pronounced by the actors, as in the following:

> Q₁ Indeed I should haue askt thee that before.
> Q₂ Indeed I should haue askt you that before (I.ii.81)

> Q₁ And with a silke thred puls it backe againe
> Q₂ And with a silken threed, plucks it backe againe (II.ii.181)

III. VERSES ENTIRELY NEW, AMPLIFICATIONS OR ADDITIONS

This class of revisions, also numerous, reaches a total of nearly 600 lines. Most of them are short passages varying from one to four verses, simple details of an idea already expressed in Q₁. But there are also longer passages, a few of which exceed 14–20 lines, and these can be considered as added or really new material.[6]

Amplifications proper make up the greater part of this new material. An idea expressed concisely in Q₁, as a mere casual fact, becomes in Q₂ a long development in which all the details are fully explored; the sentences have, so to speak, dilated, particulars that had found no place in the original text open like buds under a warming sun, images flower. Of this the following passage is an excellent example (III.iii.115–49). Romeo wishes to destroy himself, but the friar shames him for his lack of spirit and proves that instead of despairing he has every reason to consider himself

6. Here is the list of those new verses: I.i.89–92,95,115–22,136–46,151–61,219, 223–43; I.ii.1–3,14–15,18–19; I.iii.49–57,69–73,79–95,105–6; I.iv.17–28,32–4,62,67–9; I.v.24–8,74,87,121–2; II.i.15–16; II.ii.10–11, 39,42,121–35,149–56, 167; II.iii.9–14, 93–4; II.iv.198; II.v.5–16,19–24,31–8,73–4; II.vi entirely rewritten; III.i.3–4,17–19, 34–7,40,53–8,74–5,81–3,85–8,90–3,135–6,155,160–7; III.ii.5–33,47–51,63,74–85,93–9,102–6,111,113–21,125–6,132–9; III.iii.38–9,42–3,102–3,118–34,139–40,164; III.iv. 6–7,10–11,14–17,21–2;   III.v.37–41,67–8,83–8,90,93–103,107,119–21,126–9,142, 145–6,150,158–9,161,207–14,217–18,222–3,225;   IV.i.47,52–60,82,99–103,106–10, 118–23,125–6; IV.ii.25–30,40–5; IV.iii.34–48; IV.iv.22–3; IV.v.27–32,66–78,83–95; V.i.13,20–1,44–5,61,63,83; V.ii.15–17,19; V.iii.38–9,48,60–1,66–7,80–6,111–16,162, 276–7,293–5,306.

fortunate. In the First Quarto the friar simply indicates a fact which he presents with the dryness of a mathematician demonstrating a theorem; Tybalt tried to kill Romeo, Romeo killed Tybalt, and Juliet, for whose sake Romeo was going to kill himself, still lives:[7]

> I thought thy disposition better temperd,
> Hast thou slaine Tybalt? wilt thou slay thy selfe?
> And slay thy Lady too, that liues in thee?
> Rouse vp thy spirits, thy Lady Iuliet liues,
> For whose sweet sake thou wert but lately dead:
> There art thou happy Tybalt would kill thee,
> But thou sluest Tybalt, there art thou happy too.
> A packe of blessings lights vpon thy backe,
> Happines Courts thee in his best array:
> But like a misbehaude and sullen wench
> Thou frownst vpon thy Fate that smilles on thee.
> Take heede, take heede, for such dye miserable

In Q_2 the situation is examined from its many sides, each of which affords reasons for hope and for condemnation of the act which Romeo would commit. Comparisons borrowed from real life support the arguments, make them irrefutable by these reminders of reality, and the demonstration has become eloquent, captivating, vivid:

> I thought thy disposition better temperd.
> Hast thou slaine Tybalt? wilt thou sley thy selfe?
> And sley thy Lady, that in thy life lies,
> By doing damned hate vpon thy selfe?
> Why raylest thou on thy birth? the heauen and earth?
> Since birth, and heauen, and earth all three do meet,
> In thee at once, which thou at once wouldst loose.
> Fie, fie, thou shamest thy shape, thy loue, thy wit,
> Which like a Vsurer aboundst in all:
> And vsest none in that true vse indeed,
> Which should bedecke thy shape, thy loue, thy wit:
> Thy Noble shape is but a forme of waxe,
> Digressing from the valour of a man,
> Thy deare loue sworne but hollow periurie,
> Killing that loue which thou hast vowd to cherish,
> Thy wit, that ornament, to shape and loue,

7. The pre-Shakespearean author belonged to a generation whose education was influenced by the syllogistic method of scholastic philosophy.

> Mishapen in the conduct of them both:
> Like powder in a skillesse souldiers flaske,
> Is set a fier by thine owne ignorance,
> And thou dismembred with thine owne defence.
> What rowse thee man, thy Iuliet is aliue,
> For whose deare sake thou wast but lately dead.
> There art thou happie, Tybalt would kill thee,
> But thou slewest Tibalt, there art thou happie.
> The law that threatned death becomes thy friend,
> And turnes it to exile, there art thou happie.
> A packe of blessings light vpon thy backe,
> Happines courts thee in her best array,
> But like a mis[be]haued and sullen wench,
> Thou puts vp thy fortune and thy loue:
> Take heede, take heede, for such die miserable

If such amplifications are accompanied by some transposition in the domain of poetry, the movement, the whole atmosphere of a passage can be changed. Several scenes were thus made more animated: Juliet's impatience as she awaits the answer that the nurse is to bring her (II.v.31–7,55–67); the scene in which she learns of Tybalt's death and Romeo's banishment (III.ii.43–51,74–85,93–99,132–7); and that in which her replies, by their mental reservations, lead her mother to think that she hates Romeo though every word is a confession of her love (III.v.83–104)—these scenes are almost doubled in Q_2. The speech of the prince threatening the fomenters of the brawls (I.i.89–92), Benvolio's accounts of the quarrels in which he has taken part (I.i.115–22; III.i.160–7), the objurgations of the friar as he scolds Juliet's parents (IV.v. 65–78), and his description of the effects of the sleeping draught (IV.i.99–103) have all gained in eloquence. We have already seen how Romeo's end has been made more "heroic" by that means.

The additions proper, that is, those that introduce entirely new matter, are not very numerous. By its very nature the subject hardly lent itself to the invention of a dramatic author. Born in an atmosphere of hatred, the love of Romeo and of Juliet was doomed from the first to a disastrous ending. Ordained by a superhuman power that could annihilate the best-laid plans, it was destroyed by unforeseen events, a quarrel and a letter that never reached its destination. Thus Shakespeare did not alter the plot. He invented only one scene: at the opening of Act I.sc.v he showed the Capulet servants grumbling as they went about their business of preparing the room where the ball was to be held, one of those scenes borrowed from ordinary life by which Shakespeare delighted to underline the most romantic happenings. Again, for the stage direction describing the quarrel at the beginning of the play he substituted a dialogue in which the adversaries challenge one another, followed by the arrival of Montague and Capulet who are joined by excited citizens, the whole giving a picture of the discord and hate which provides a background for the entire play.

Nor were the characters susceptible of an original psychological development. The minor ones, like Mercutio, Benvolio, Capulet, and the nurse had already attained full stature in the part of the First Quarto which had been extensively recast, and Shakespeare could only intensify their principal traits with a few touches: in Mercutio by inflating his excessive loquacity (II.i.15–16; III.i. 17–19,57–8,81–2), in Benvolio by giving other examples of his conciliatory, reasonable nature (I.i.72,231,233–4; I.iv.33–4; I.v. 121; III.i.53–6), in Capulet by furnishing other proofs of his dictatorial, choleric temperament (I.v.23–8,74,87; III.iv.14–17,21–2; III.v.142,144–6; IV.ii.23–30,40–5),[8] and in the nurse by adding to the licentious thoughts that obsessed her mind (I.iii.50–7,95; II. iv.210–32; III.iii.164; III.v.217–18).

Paris is perhaps the only one among the secondary characters that has been somewhat changed. He was a mere utility man, Romeo's rival for Juliet's hand and nothing more in the First Quarto, with this one exception, however, that in the end he shows how truly he loved Juliet. Nevertheless he was a rival on a very small scale and with nothing in his favor but Capulet's preference, which naturally did not endear him to the audience. A long addition in which Lady Capulet likens him to a fair and precious book, sumptuously bound, portrays him as an attractive man, morally no less than physically. Still I am not sure but that the change was intended to make Romeo's success with Juliet even more

8. In the case of Capulet one small addition shows Shakespeare's skill in turning even simple exclamations to account for the expression of feelings. When Capulet finds that Juliet will not marry Paris he is so furious that he can utter only barking sounds, as it were: "How, how, how how, chopt lodgick" (III.v.150).

remarkable since he was chosen above a man who was perfect in every respect, in addition to his elevated social standing.

As for the two protagonists, from the moment love strikes like a thunderbolt and possesses them utterly, their acts are never influenced by their characters. They are simply what the development of the plot requires. This is especially true of Juliet. The young girl, naïve and sincere at first, becomes dissimulative and given to lying; the child becomes a resolute woman who never shrinks from death voluntarily inflicted. To confer more breadth to her character Shakespeare could only intensify her various traits as in the case of the minor characters: her love (II.ii.121–35), her impetuosity (II.v.7–38; III.ii.44–51), her dissimulation (III.v.83–7,97–103), her determination (V.iii.164–7). I find only one new trait in the text of Q_2: love has awakened voluptuous desires in Juliet, which she voices with a crudity that must have seemed natural in Shakespeare's time, to judge from the number of licentious and even obscene allusions that are put in the mouth of Mercutio and of the nurse, but which are offensive today. Twice she lets it be seen that her love is not of the heart or the spirit alone and that she expects from marriage permissible pleasures. No such desires were expressed in Q_1. They appear for the first time in Q_2 in the opening lines of Act III.sc.ii when she awaits the arrival of Romeo and asks the night to

> Spread thy close curtaine loue-performing night,
> That runnawayes eyes may wincke, and Romeo
> Leape to these armes, vntalkt of and vnseene
>
> .   .   .   .
>
> And learne me how to loose a winning match,
> Plaide for a paire of stainlesse maydenhoods (III.ii.5–13)

She returns to the subject in equally unmistakable terms in the same scene when, having learned of Romeo's banishment, she believes that the pleasures she had expected of that night of love have also been banished. Ordering the nurse to take away the ropes that Romeo was to have used in coming to her, she adds:

> Take vp those cordes, poore ropes you are beguilde,
> Both you and I for Romeo is exilde:
> He made you for a highway to my bed,
> But I a maide, die maiden widowed.

> Come cordes, come Nurse, ile to my wedding bed,
> And death not Romeo, take my maiden head (III.ii.132-7)

And that Shakespeare made this addition deliberately is proved by a small but significant correction in II.ii.49, where Q_1 has "Take all I haue" and Q_2 "Take all my selfe." By introducing this realistic note he wanted no doubt to mitigate somewhat the excessive exaltation of her love.

The case of Romeo is analogous. The hero of the play is the personification of sublime love. Between him and Juliet there is even a parallelism to which the nurse once draws attention (III.iii. 84-5). There is the same exclusive, consuming love in both, with the same early foreboding (I.iv.106-11; II.ii.117-19), the same need to give all even to the final sacrifice, the same despair at the thought of separation, the same inflexible resolve not to survive the loved one. Shakespeare heightened these traits in Romeo as he did in Juliet, but he also made an addition which, in a certain degree, modifies the character. In Q_1 Romeo's love for Rosaline is more an intellectual sport than a passion. He speaks of it as a sonneteer:

> Loue is a smoke raisde with the fume of sighes
> Being purgde, a fire sparkling in louers eyes:
> Being vext, a sea raging with a louers teares.
> What is it else? A madnes most discreet,
> A choking gall, and a preseruing sweet (Q_1 I.i.196-200)

Shakespeare probably inserted these lines in his first revision (for they are certainly his own) to create a contrast with the deeper love that Romeo was to experience later. But on reflection the dramatist in him must have been dissatisfied with this antithesis, for in Q_2 there are some entirely new touches that represent Romeo as a man suffering deeply from the indifference of the woman he courts in vain. This new man appears first in old Montague's description of the inexplicable mood of his son, who sighs and weeps continuously and retires to his chamber far from human contact as soon as day has broken (I.i.137-46); he has been gently questioned but keeps closely the secret that gnaws at him:

> As is the bud bit with an enuious worme,
> Ere he can spread his sweete leaues to the ayre,
> Or dedicate his bewtie to the same (I.i.157-9)

Mercutio, who is not a man to take love seriously, advises him
ironically to borrow Cupid's wings; he will be able then to "bound
a pitch above a common bound." But Romeo protests against this
skepticism, and here, from his mouth, is a second definition of
love that contradicts the former:

> Is loue a tender thing? it is too rough,
> Too rude, too boystrous, and it pricks like thorne (I.iv.25–6)

After these few changes Romeo is no longer quite the same man:
from a character who spoke of love in a falsetto voice Shakespeare
has changed him into one of the great characters predestined to
the role of love's victims.

Shakespeare introduced a similar change into Act II.sc.vi. This
scene, a turning point in the plot, is the one in which the friar
marries Romeo and Juliet secretly; it has been entirely rewritten.
In Q_1 the gravity proper to the occasion is entirely lacking. Romeo
asks the friar to unite him to Juliet, which is agreed to forthwith.
Juliet arrives soon afterward, "somewhat fast," according to the
stage direction, and with a boldness surprising in a young girl who
has been strictly brought up, throws herself into Romeo's arms.
He responds gallantly to this proof of love with an image in which
reappears the man fed on the poetry of his time:

> My Iuliet welcome. As doo waking eyes
> (Cloasd in Nights mysts) attend the frolicke Day,
> So Romeo hath expected Iuliet,
> And thou art come.

Juliet, equally well versed in all the finesses of hyperbolic language,
responds

> I am (if I be Day)
> Come to my Sunne: shine foorth, and make me faire

Romeo, with the same gallantry, pays her a second compliment:

> All beauteous fairnes dwelleth in thine eyes

to which Juliet replies with another compliment

> Romeo from thine all brightnes doth arise

At this point the friar interrupts these "wantons" and takes them
away to regularize their premature embraces. The scene is pretty,

it must be granted—too pretty, for it was a prelude far too light for the tragedy that this marriage held in store. In a situation replete with dangers it lacked not only gravity but even seriousness; it was a witty scene at a moment when the shadow of a fate that was brewing should have been projected; and it was this that Shakespeare wanted to remedy when he rewrote the scene completely.

In the Second Quarto the friar introduces a disquieting note in the opening lines of the scene:

> So smile the heauens vpon this holy act,
> That after houres, with sorrow chide vs not (1–2)

and to Romeo's impatient demand that he be only united to his beloved, after which he will defy death, the friar makes answer: "violent delights haue violent endes." This somber warning has just been expressed when Juliet enters. As a young girl who has a knowledge of the ways of society, she first pays her respects to the friar and, only then, she addresses Romeo. He, now realizing the importance of the event that is to determine his life, tells his overwhelming joy at the very thought of the happiness he imagines is awaiting them:

> Ah Iuliet, if the measure of thy ioy
> Be heapt like mine, and that thy skill be more
> To blason it, then sweeten with thy breath
> This neighbour ayre and let rich musicke tongue,
> Vnfold the imagind happines that both
> Receiue in either, by this deare encounter

And Juliet, with equal fervor, though it is veiled with modesty as befits a woman, answers:

> Conceit more rich in matter then in words,
> Brags of his substance, not of ornament,
> They are but beggers that can count their worth,
> But my true loue is growne to such excesse,
> I cannot sum vp sum of halfe my wealth

Here the superficiality of sentiments imagined rather than felt has disappeared, to be replaced by the stammering sincerity of two beings enslaved by a love that is too deep to be easily expressed, two beings who are no longer mere characters in a play but real beings, each with his or her own existence, and who at that moment are one. The indifferent scene of the quarto has been replaced by one of the best scenes in *Romeo and Juliet*.[9]

When the longest passages on the list of entirely new verses are assembled, namely, I.i.136–46,151–61,223–43; I.iv.17–28; II.ii.121–35; II.v.5–16; II.vi.1–37; III.ii.5–33; III.iii.118–34; IV.iii.34–48, they form a total of 165 blank verses (I have of course not taken into account the few rhymed lines that are embedded in the blank verse). Out of these ten passages eight have no feminine endings; III.iii.118–34 has one, and II.vi (the marriage scene) has three. Even if we include the latter, the number of feminine endings in those additions is only 4 or 2.4%. But considering the more advanced dramatic skill of Shakespeare in this beautiful scene I am inclined to believe that it was rewritten later than the rest, possibly at the same period as the second revisions of *2 Henry VI* and *Richard II*.

In any case, the second revision of *Romeo and Juliet* followed close upon the first revision, and the tragedy on the subject of the lovers of Verona was one of the first plays, if not the first, that Shakespeare revised for his company.

The Text of the Folio

The text of the folio was printed from the Third Quarto (1609). Q_3 had been printed by John Smethwick who received the right to publish it from Nicholas Linge, who in turn had it from Cuthbert Burby. Apart from some fifty misprints that had been corrected, and the addition of some new ones, this quarto followed closely the text of Q_2, so closely as to retain some of the typographical peculiarities of that quarto—the misreadings "houre" for "honour" (I.iii.66), "prouaunt" for "pronounce" (II.i.10), and "Abraham:Cupid" for "Adam Cupid" (II.i.13); the part of the nurse and the description of Queen Mab in I.iv printed as prose; two badly divided lines (II.i.27–8 and V.iii.266–8); almost all the false starts with the consequent double redactions (II.ii.41–2; II.iii.1–4; IV.i.111; V.iii.102–3,106–20); and the error "Horatio"

9. It is interesting to note that this scene has the normal Shakespearean rhythmic variations (trochees 3.7%, spondees 3.7%).

as speech heading (I.iv.23).[1] All these imperfections passed over into the text of the folio, which added a good number of misprints of its own, for the compositor of this portion of the folio seems to have been especially careless.

The folio text is better only for the punctuation, which in general is satisfactory. One feels also that some care was devoted to the wording of the stage directions in order to make them more precise. Entrances and exits that had been omitted in Q_3 were added (I.ii.84,154; III.i.126; IV.v.16; V.i.57; V.iii.310). In several cases *Exit* is followed by the names of the characters leaving the stage (I.iii.104; II.iv.151,232; II.v.17; IV.i.43; IV.ii.48,97; V.i.32), and when several characters go off together *Exit* was changed to *Exeunt*. The word "Madam" (II.ii.148) is preceded by "within," and in the same scene when Juliet, hearing a noise, says "Anon good Nurse" "Cals within" was added between the lines. Such additions are without any importance and the prompter certainly did not waste his time inserting similar minutiae which to him were useless. As their only advantage lay in facilitating the reading of the play, they are attributable to the man who was charged with preparing the text for the printing of the folio—to the meticulous Crane.

Indeed, his intervention is proved, as in Q_2, by the presence of a number of parentheses. When the friar tells the prince what has just happened (V.iii.229–69), there are no less than five instances of this peculiarity of Crane's handwriting:

> For whom (and not for Tybalt) Iuliet pinde
>
> And (with wilde lookes) bid me deuise some meanes
>
> But when I came (some Minute ere the time
> Of her awaking) heere vntimely lay
>
> And she (too desperate) would not go with me,
> But (as it seemes) did violence on her selfe

This passage is the only one in the part of the manuscript written by Shakespeare that contains examples of this calligraphic whim, and this raises the question: why was the scrivener so moderate?

---

1. Only the wrong speech heading M. (II.v.15), the enigmatic stage direction "*Slud*" (III.iii.75), and the jingle "flyes": "flie" (III.iii.39) were corrected.

One explanation alone seems possible. The friar's speech was printed partly on the recto, partly on the verso of signature M, and that page is the last but one of the quarto; it, and perhaps the last one too, must have been lost, no doubt a frequent occurrence—as has already been shown in the case of *Titus Andronicus* —with dramatic quartos which were simply stitched and unbound pamphlets. Crane therefore had to transcribe this missing part from the promptbook, and this confirms the supposition made at page 315 that Crane did not collate the foul papers with the promptbook when he prepared the text.

It is regrettable that Crane for once was not more curious; if he had compared the text of the quarto with the company's book he would surely have found some improvements that were worthy of notice. Such as it is, the folio gives the same text as the Second Quarto with some defects in addition. The truth is that there is no text of *Romeo and Juliet* of which one can say, with Heming and Condell, that it is "cured and perfect of its limbs."

A RETROSPECT

𝒥t is too soon to draw a conclusion. The six plays studied in this volume all belong to the first years of Shakespeare's dramatic career; nothing decisive can be concluded from them. But interesting results have already been obtained; it may be useful to recapitulate them as a starting point for the next volume.

First of all, it is evident that, in a period necessarily of apprenticeship, Shakespeare never was a dramatist in the modern sense of the word. He did not sit at his desk, ready to write a play on a subject of his choice, carefully mapped out in all its details; and with that facility which was to become proverbial, he did not unfold his plan continuously from the first scene to the last. His aim was more limited. When he joined the company of actors to which he was to devote most of his intellectual life, he found a repertory composed of plays some of which had already had a prolonged existence. These were not bad; the one in which "brave Talbot" had drawn "the teares of ten thousand spectators at least (at several times)," or that tragedy on Romeo and Juliet which Arthur Brooke had seen performed and despaired of equaling when he wrote his poem on the same subject, had even achieved memorable success. Their authors certainly possessed the technique of the stage; they knew the kind of incidents that were sure to move or to please an audience, and they could combine these incidents in a way that made them produce the greatest effect. But these incidents were the whole play, the sole source of interest. The characters, psychologically, were little more than what the events in which they were involved required them to be, and one or two epithets were sufficient to determine the limits of their individuality. The dialogue was a facile imitation of the everyday language; its narrowest approach to literary distinction consisted in a few comparisons with the habits of animals or the properties of plants, oratorically used for their probative value as prescribed by the handbooks of rhetoric, and with extremely rare

329

exceptions (that of Marlowe, for instance) it entirely lacked the sublimation obtained by the means of poetry.

Now the qualities absent from those old plays constituted the very essence of Shakespeare's genius. He was a born poet; not simply a writer capable of expressing ideas in rhythmical form but a man whose sensibility was so acute that he reacted to the most inconsequential facts of life in the wonderful universe which surrounded him and incorporated them, transformed into unforgettable memories. He had been especially interested by that strange and complicated creature called man, whose soul he had so deeply probed that, given any situation, he knew what a human being would feel, think, do, and say. Here was a splendid opportunity to utilize these gifts. The plays of the company were still usable if only rejuvenated and improved according to the custom of the time: he felt that he could do this sort of work. And so it happened that Shakespeare set himself the task of recasting the repertoire of his company.

There was no premeditated method in the way these revisions were made. One thing was pretty constant: Shakespeare kept the action much as it had been organized by his predecessors. Only once, in *Richard II*, did he materially alter the subject by suppressing incidents in order to find room for the development of the principal character. In a few cases he added some short, picturesque bit of scene such as the garrulous watch of the soldiers who guarded King Edward or the bustling preparations of the hall for the feast at the Capulets'. But this is very little compared to the changes made in the characters or in the dialogue, which were extensive and varied, depending entirely upon the kind of play to be revised or its weaknesses. In *Richard III*, a tragedy of the Marlovian type, Shakespeare gave his attention mainly to the flexibility of the dialogue. In *Titus Andronicus*, a play of revenge, he emphasized the sorrows of Titus, giving a justification of the transformation of that disciplined soldier into an insurgent and bloodthirsty avenger of his wrongs. In the two parts of *Henry VI* he sought chiefly to humanize the characters in order to counterbalance their political roles. In *Romeo and Juliet* it was less the characters of the two lovers than the exaltation of their love that he brought into prominence. As to the poetical element with which he sprinkled all the plays, its importance increased or decreased according to the attractiveness the subject had for his imagination: it could be overflowingly luxuriant in *Richard II*, rare and scattered in *Richard III*, or moderate in *Henry VI*.

Most of the revisions were made under the pressure of haste. Shakespeare's "mind and hand went together" but the hand slower than the mind. The quartos, when they were printed from his foul papers, have preserved lapses of the pen, double redactions, contradictions between the un-Shakespearean fragments and the Shakespearean additions, showing that Shakespeare had no time to read over the plays when he had revised them.

For the needs of the company were paramount and imperative. A change of playhouse might render it necessary to adapt certain scenes to different equipment of the stage; in periods of stress a play bringing in good receipts became indispensable, which probably explains why a first revision of *Romeo and Juliet* had to be interrupted: if an invitation was received to perform at Court or if governmental opposition had to be overcome it was wise to modify historical characters who were ancestors of the reigning queen, such as Henry VI or Bolingbroke, in order to present them in a more favorable light. In such cases Shakespeare must be ready to meet the urgent need rapidly.

Hence there are different strata in the plays, which an analysis of the versification has brought out clearly. We cannot say "Such a play was revised in such a year." There was a first revision and a last revision and often between the two an intermediary adaptation.

The ghosts of three authors whom I have called A, B, and C have throughout haunted the analysis of the plays. Author C was the oldest of the three; he belonged to the period when it was usual to write plays in rhymed verse, extensive fragments of which are to be found in *Richard II* and in *Romeo and Juliet*. Author A, who succeeded author C, wrote in blank verse; he seems to have had in Lord Strange's company the position of principal purveyor of plays and sometimes that of reviser. The third author, B, was an imitator of Marlowe's hyperbolic style and was casually called in to bring some Marlovian flavor wherever it could be introduced. Author C and author A have a versification and a style so characteristic that if some of their other plays have been published under their names it should be easy to identify them. Author B imitated Marlowe so felicitously that I imagine it will be difficult to discover who he was.

On the other hand, the comparison of quarto texts with the corresponding folio texts has enabled me to give the name of the editor of the First Folio. Ralph Crane had already been suspected by several critics to have had a hand in the publication of this folio but only in his capacity of scribe. A critical examination of some variants makes it indisputable that this editor undertook too freely his task of improving Shakespeare's work; and as a consequence the First Folio has received severe blows from which it is my sincere hope that it may not be able to recover; for the fantastic idea, laid down as an axiom, that plays which in certain cases remained in the hands of the actors for more than thirty years represent the first, unaltered, and therefore the only authentic, form of Shakespeare has led many commentators into blind alleys.

Some of the stage directions have raised a little problem. Where was the theater that had a visible tower, with a staircase, in which some of the plays, possibly all, were first performed in their un-Shakespearean form? There is also a mention of a tower in the first part of *Henry VI*, as was pointed out by Professor Allison Gaw in his study of this play. The attempt to make this tower identical with the superstructure from which a flag was hoisted to announce that a performance was going to begin prevented the idea from being taken seriously. But the example of *The Contention* makes it unquestionable that such a theater existed even before Henslowe made alterations in the Rose in 1591/2. This is a question of minor interest but which deserves to be re-examined, even though I am afraid that our knowledge of theatrical architecture in Elizabethan times may not be sufficient to solve the problem.

INDEX

Wither, George, 10n.
Wolsey, Cardinal Thomas, 25–6, 28
Worcester's, Earl of, company, 1, 5, 9–
   10
Workes of Mercy, both Corporeal and
Spiritual, The (Ralph Crane), 187,
   276–8
Wright, John, 14
Wright, W. A., 280n.
Wyat, Sir Thomas, 60, 92